BEYOND THE NEW ORTHODOXY

To the suffering
masses of Africa
who go without because of bad policy
based on even worse theory

and to my friends
for their forbearance

The Making of Modern Africa

Series Editors: Abebe Zegeye and John Higginson

Beyond the New Orthodoxy

Africa's Debt and Development Crisis in Retrospect

NIKOI KOTE-NIKOI

Avebury

Aldershot · Brookfield USA · Hong Kong · Singapore · Sydney

Published by
Avebury
Ashgate Publishing Ltd
Gower House
Croft Road
Aldershot
Hants GU11 3HR
England

Ashgate Publishing Company
Old Post Road
Brookfield
Vermont 05036
USA

British Library Cataloguing in Publication Data

Kote-Nikoi, Nikoi
    Beyond the new orthodoxy : Africa's debt and development
    crisis in retrospect. - (Making of modern Africa)
    1. Debts, External - Africa 2. Africa - Economic conditions -
    1960-
    I. Title
    336 . 3 ' 435 ' 096

    ISBN 1 85972 484 1

Library of Congress Catalog Card Number: 96-85183

Printed in Great Britain by the Ipswich Book Company, Suffolk

Contents

Tables and Figures

Preface

This project has been long in the gestation. It had its genesis in a desperate need to find, in the literature on the debt and development crises of the "lost decade of development", an analysis in which Africa's experience of the crisis was not deemed tangential, peripheral or an adjunct to Latin America's or Asia's. The bulk of the literature then, of course, was precisely of that bent, with any analysis of Africa's debt-cum-development crisis being only derivative of Latin America's and Asia's. The particularities and structural specificities of the African economies that rendered their crises unique and therefore different from Latin America's and Asia's were thus obscured in these broad analyses of the "Third World debt crisis". Consequently, the solutions proposed for the African crisis were either ineffectual, ultimately, or of questionable validity on epistemic grounds, as they derived not from the reality of the African condition but as a weak reflection of the Asian and Latin American experience. A principal objective of this work is to plug this gap in the literature.

The study is designed to appeal to a broad readership. Students of Africa's economies and African development affairs, generally, will, I hope, find it a useful supplement to the existing literature. Policy makers in Africa who deal with the quotidian demands of "doing development" in an essentially hostile environment should find it accessible and contributive to their thinking about the impact of development policy making. Advanced undergraduate and beginning graduate students in economics and development studies will find it a useful introduction to the political economy of Africa, in general, and the debt crisis that still grips the continent, in particular. And anyone seeking an alternative and uncaricatured analysis of the challenges of development faced by Africa in the past decade-and-a-half should find it of some value.

A passing familiarity with basic neo-classical macro- and microeconomic theoretical concepts will enhance the reader's understanding of some of the technical arguments, but it should not be a major setback not to have exposure to these theories. The juxtaposition of the economic and the political, not as separate analyses but as indispensable and complementary moments of an organic analytical framework, should also help clarify the essential conclusions of the study and, hopefully, make it both more accessible and of greater interest to a wider readership than, say, a strictly economic rendition would have.

Many people have through the years, formally and informally, contributed to my thinking on development issues. Professors Norman Hodges, Stephen Rousseas and Obika Gray of Vassar College gave me my first tastes of critical social theory which have since immensely influenced my thinking about the human prospect in economic development. Professors Carmen Diana Deere and Douglas Vickers of the University of Massachusetts, Amherst, helped deepen my understanding of economics and sharpen my analytical skills. To all of them I owe an intellectual debt of such a magnitude as to be essentially unpayable.

My thanks go also to Professor Frank Holmquist of Hampshire College who read this work in its entirety, and saw it from its very inception through the various stages of its creation. I have also benefited much from numerous conversations we have had on Africa through the years, and for his encouragement and support throughout.

Through the years, my students at the School for International Training have been subjected to various chapters and versions of the manuscript. They have patiently, if not always volitionally, worked through them with due diligence, and have been unstinting with those suggestions and critiques that have made the final product a better work of scholarship than it might otherwise have been. To all of them, my heartfelt 'thank you'. Of course, none of these good people and mentors is responsible for the intellectual inadequacies of the study.

And, finally, I am grateful for the support and understanding of particular friends who have 'been there' through much of this endeavour; for friendships that would ultimately, if not always cheerfully, temporarily take a backseat to allow my intellectual endeavours to flower; for friendships that, in their constancy, would teach me the meaning of friendship; and for friendships that would tolerate my innumerable idiosyncrasies and general hardheadedness at awkward moments. To Dr. Rose Sackey-Milligan, Kango Laré-Lantone, Adrienne Talamas and Dr. Clifford Griffin my most profound gratitude.

Introduction

Financial Crises in Historical Context

International financial crises, because of their potential for rupturing the international system of trade and finance extant, have been described by some, justifiably, as holding a place in inter-country economic relations closely akin to that held by nuclear war in their political relations. The fear of either catastrophe tends to ensure cooperation among nations whose very existences depend on the structure of things as they are. The handling of the "Third World debt crisis" of the 1980s exemplified this characterization in a number of ways. Thus, although the crisis did, at times, strain relations between creditor- and debtor-nations, it never compromised them irrevocably as they, severally and collectively, worked to find acceptable solutions that would keep the structure and dynamics of their trade and finance intact.

In a more important sense, however, the crises of the 1980s succeeded in highlighting, in a way that perhaps no other recent development in international political economy has, the tensions, contradictions and fissiparous tendencies of contemporary global economic relations. And although a significant chunk of these may be attributable to the inequities that inhere in the very structures and conduct of these relations, our search for sound solutions would be incomplete without, *inter alia*, critically and comprehensively interrogating and confronting the theories, policies and institutions undergirding the conduct of international economic and political relations as we know it.

Scholarly analyses of the debt crisis abound. The onset of the crisis is popularly dated to mid-August 1982, when Mexico announced suspension of principal payments on its external obligations. With the benefit of hindsight, however, it is now clear that the crisis had been long in coming, and so recognized by a number of astute analysts and, particularly, banking practitioners who, in the wake of the 1973 oil-price shock and consequent global recession of 1974-75, were much concerned about *when* the crisis would come, not if.[1] In Africa's case in particular, the crisis may have started as far back as 1979, when decades of internal macroeconomic mismanagement combined with adverse global economic developments to push the rate of growth of the continent's external debt substantially beyond that of its income and export earnings. The search for the causes of the crisis, therefore, must of neccessity, precede the Mexican announcement of 1982; for the African case with which we are here concerned, 1970 would be the appropriate, though arguably arbitrary, demarcation for our analysis.

Whatever its chronological point of origin, however, the major institutions charged with the identification and amelioration of such crises were singularly imprescient in their understanding of the impending problem. As late as February 1983, both the World Bank and the International Monetary Fund (IMF) would claim that "there [was] no generalized debt crisis" in the Third World.[2] Similarly the Organization for Economic Cooperation and Development (OECD), perhaps in a bid to attenuate possible adverse systemic reaction would argue, as late as December 1982, four full months after Mexico's *de facto* default, that any debt crisis that existed was temporary and isolated on only three large borrowers: Mexico, Brazil and Argentina.[3] Thus the mechanisms that could, and should, have been put in motion to stem the slide towards a full-blown crisis were either not mobilized at all, or activated so belatedly as to be ineffectual. By year-end 1983, therefore, a debt crisis encompassing nearly all regions of the world, *including the advanced industrial nations* as major creditors and borrowers themselves, was in full bloom. It is, in this regard, particularly important not to identify the debt crisis of the 1980s narrowly as a "Third World debt crisis", as is the popular currency; rather, it should be understood in its proper context of a crisis of the *global* credit system, the effects of which are felt, albeit unevenly, in both the financial and real markets of *all* countries. To limit its scope to its geographic area of incidence is, correspondingly, to limit our appreciation of the import of the crisis for the global economy, and to truncate the search for meaningful solutions in a potentially disastrous manner.

Relevant Historical Perspectives

In the long history of episodic financial disequilibria, the debt crisis of the 1980s stood out, on the supply side, in two particulars. One was the sheer volume of funds involved, some $550 billion at the nominal start of the crisis in 1982; the other was the institutional innovations in international lending and financial markets which made the movement of such sums around the globe not only possible but also immensely profitable and efficient. The crisis was therefore historically acute because it operated on two levels: the degree of exposure of key financial houses in the creditor-North (partially resulting, as we shall see, from the financial market innovations of the 1970s and '80s), and a volume of debt which put debt-service beyond the economic capabilities of the debtor-South for the foreseeable future.

Analysts and policy-makers in the creditor-North were, however, narrowly and myopically occupied (at least until the waning years of the 1980s) with the exposure of the lending institutions, and showed remarkably little concurrent interest, in relative terms, in the plight of the borrowers. The fact that the lenders faced a liquidity or cash-flow crisis brought on by the insolvency of the borrowers seemed quite lost on them, as a frenetic search was launched for solutions to the former's plight but not the latter's. But, it would stand to reason, that if the borrowers' insolvency *did* trigger the lenders' problems, then the debt crisis, properly construed, could not be solved unless both parties' individual crises were addressed. And, to the extent that these sub-crises were functionally linked, they should have been addressed *simultaneously*, not sequentially, if some meaningful degree of success in solving the crisis was to be had.

It is thus remarkable, though not inconsistent with the dominant lines of analyses, that claims are being made with increasing ferocity by some since the late 1980s, that the debt crisis, insofar as it threatens the stability of the exposed financial houses and hence the international system of trade and finance, is actually over.[4] For, as more sober analysts have rightly cautioned, if the term 'debt crisis' refers to the excessive debt acquisition by Southern countries *and* to the threat to the private lenders involved should these borrowers default on their loans then, obviously, the second problem vanishes if the first is solved.   But it hardly follows that the borrowers' crisis will be automatically resolved if the lenders' is, or that the continued presence of the borrowers', once the lenders' is eliminated, will not re-ignite the lenders' anew, in some fashion.[5]

The fact that syndicated international networks of major private lending institutions—one of the innovations of the deregulated financial-capital markets of the 1970s and 1980s—were involved was also a unique feature of the crisis.   But the uniqueness ended with these new forms of institutional mediation of the lending process, and the large sums involved.   The history of international lending holds many parallels to, and lessons for us about, the recent crisis. A quick look at some of the pertinent highlights of this history should reveal the more important lessons and parallels.

In the early 1800s, credit to developing nations came preponderantly from a large number of independent, *individual* investors who bought equity in railroads, mills and other public works in the Americas, Russia, China and Australia.[6]   Because these loans had been organized and underwritten by individual banks, when financial troubles erupted in the borrowing countries leading to a rash of defaults, it was *individual* financial houses that were compromised.   Baring Brothers, arguably the preeminent British merchant bank of the time, could only survive Argentina's defaults of 1890 because of a massive infusion of capital from the Bank of England, acting in its capacity as lender-of-last-resort.[7]   Similarly threatened by international defaults were the Rothschilds and J.P. Morgan.   Ironically, lending to countries in the 'New Worlds' of the Americas and Australia, and to China, had escalated in the last decade or two of the century precisely because Europe—Portugal, Spain, the Balkans, Turkey and Russia, principally—had become uncreditworthy by the last quarter of the century, as many of these countries had defaulted on their international obligations in the period between 1870 and 1895.[8]

Two lessons for the current crisis can already be discerned here. First, unlike the nineteenth century defaults, any mass defaults from the recent crisis could have led to the failure of many of the major banks involved in the international lending business. Thus, ironically, the risk-aversion that led them to pull their resources in a syndicate actually yielded perverse results: it enabled them pull together a volume of moneys so large as to eventually *increase* their risk. Even more importantly, given the institutional linkages among financial centres internationally (but also due to the centrality of money, credit and financial intermediation in the capitalist economic process), failure among these syndicates could have threatened the entire system of production, trade and finance extant.[9] Because those early banking houses were just partnerships, their losses were absorbed entirely by the bankers. Any such losses in the 1980s (and even today) would have had to be absorbed by stockholders (because the banks are joint-stock companies), or even by the government (which is, in actuality, a euphemistic reference to tax payers) if it had chosen, as lender-of-last-resort, to bail out the bank(s) affected.

In the event, however, that the losses were of a singularly monstrous magnitude—as might have happened if, say, Mexico, Brazil and Argentina had defaulted concurrently—the entire system of financial intermediation as it was then, and is currently, organized might have been in jeopardy. By extension, the global system of production and exchange would have been equally gravely impaired. In short, the effects of financial collapse induced by the inability of the principals to comprehensively resolve both the lenders' liquidity and the borrowers' solvency debacle, contrary to the IMF/World Bank and OECD analyses mentioned earlier, would have neither been isolated nor trivial. It is in this more encompassing sense that the crisis should have been understood, and not just narrowly as a 'Third World debt crisis'.

The second lesson can be found in the uncanny parallel that runs between the geographic shift in credit allotment in the nineteenth century and that of the 1970s and early 1980s. One reason why the system's excess liquidity of the 1970s was recycled to developing countries—indeed, one reason for there being functionally an excess, in the first place—was that bankers increasingly came to perceive the stagflated economies of the industrial North as being "inferior soils", literally, for their funds. The booming, newly-industrialized countries of Latin America—Brazil, for one, was growing at 11% annually between 1968 and 1973!—became an attractive alternative lending prospect, their questionable credit history of the recent past notwithstanding.[10]

Do Past Crises Offer Us A Current Solution?

Crises in international finance hardly started in the last century, nor will they end in this one. Indeed, the recent crisis is not even the only one of this century. Charles Kindleberger's work has done much to enhance our understanding of the history and dynamics of these episodes of foreign-lending "mania" inevitably followed by "panics" and, eventually, "revulsions".[11] He concludes at one time that "the problem of developing country debt is rather that [their borrowings]...in the last three-and-a-half years [1978-1981], have been used to finance consumption... [But] the recycling which has postponed default cannot continue indefinitely."[12]

Clearly if the funds borrowed in the 1970s went to finance or subsidize consumption and not investment, then these loans could not be self-liquidating. In other words, they were incapable of generating income with which their servicing costs could have been adequately defrayed. Hence the necessity of seeing policies that would have made the indebted economies not only more consistently productive, but also better export-income performers, as arguably the optimal way out of the 1980s', and the best prevention against a future, debt crisis.

In the absence of such remedial policies, the prospect of default still looms large and real. There is ample precedent for this: as John Makin has argued, the history of international lending is resplendent with debt repudiations brought on by wars, fiat, revolutions, inflation, or failure to implement the requisite remedial policies when needed.[13] Indeed the recorded history of sovereign default stretches as far back as medieval times: in 1329, Edward III defaulted on loans contracted by Edward I from the Peruzzi and Bardi banking families of Florence to finance his wars. The default caused the immediate collapse, not only of those banks, but of Italian banking at large. Similar events were to overtake the Medicis in their dealings with Edward IV a century later.[14]   And the list goes on, even unto modern times: as was intimated earlier, Argentina's default of 1890 nearly bankrupted Baring's of London; other "New World" defaults in the same period engendered "balked disappointment" in financial markets, even as the Portuguese defaults of 1891-92 "incensed financial circles";[15] and the default by some state governments of the U.S. in the 1840s on obligations owed British investors led to the formation of the British Council of Foreign Bondholders in 1868, to seek compensation for losses suffered in the repudiations by Mississippi, Maryland, Pennsylvania and Louisiana.   It is, even today, still trying to collect payment![16]   Thus the possibility of default is very tangible indeed, especially as there is little consistent juridical precedent in international relations governing financial transactions across sovereign frontiers.

Much of the contemporary impetus for default can better be understood by examining the dynamics of the Latin American debt crisis of the 1930s.   The crisis, then, erupted when, beginning in 1928-29, reduced international lending, large domestic budget deficits in Latin America, and a myriad external shocks (including a collapse of commodity prices), presaged the onset of the Great Depression. The debtors' response, starting about 1930, was to cut imports, where possible, and to substitute domestic manufactures for them; to pursue a contractionary internal adjustment; and to default on their bonds, rather than seek a rescheduling/restructuring of their obligations, or refinancing, from their creditor-banks.[17]   As Nafziger has argued, however, it is telling that "those countries that stopped paying their debt service recovered from the Great Depression more quickly than [those] that resisted default, *and had virtually identical access to post-World War II capital markets*."[18] (Emphasis added).

But the cost of the rash of defaults was that it took some twenty years, until the 1950s, for portfolio lending to come up to its historical levels for the region.   This, despite the fact that "both British and American creditors...recovered their principal while receiving interest payments almost as high as those on [their] domestic treasury bonds."[19] It is also worth remembering that nearly all the proposals floated in the 1980s to resolve the crisis at the *global* level were initially devised and proposed in the 1930s.[20]

Diverging Analytics of the Crisis

The analysis of the causes and consequences of the debt crisis that issued from the creditor-North throughout the 1980s was remarkably uniform, and can be summed up thusly: the inability of developing countries to service their debts was threatening the stability of international commerce and payments. The fear inherent in this analysis was one of (what Axel Leijonhufvud describes elsewhere as) a "deviation-amplifying feedback" effect, by which default by a major debtor or group of debtors would initiate a domino effect that could begin with the collapse of their creditor bank or banks, any other banks with which they may have been in syndication, the gradual loss of confidence in the structure and conduct of international finance as we know it, and an eventual systemic contraction of world trade and general economic relations.[21]   The title of Kindleberger's popular study of financial crises—**Manias, Panics, and Crashes**—captures the spirit of this view with admirable accuracy.

Mainstream analysts from the debtor-South were, and still are, largely in acquiescence with this view. But there is an emerging heterodox viewpoint that has it that the crisis should be understood as nothing more than yet another crisis of development as such, one that, in Africa at least, pre-dates 1982 to, perhaps, the first oil-price shock of 1973 and the commodity booms of the mid-1970s. There were, of course, regional variations in its *secondary* causes, but that the crisis itself was an episodic moment in the development process *per se* is, more or less, the preferred interpretation.

Thus, for instance, in Eastern and Central Europe, and in Latin America, the refusal by the banks to refinance existing loans in the early 1980s caused domestic economic retrenchment and, consequently, systemic contraction, which further worsened the countries' ability to service their debts. In sub-Saharan Africa, the economic decline that precipitated the crisis began in the second half of the 1970s, as commodity terms-of-trade worsened for net oil-importers; as natural disasters wreaked havoc with agriculture and forestry; as irredentist and internecine wars raged across the continent; and as the blunders of post-colonial economic policy came home to roost in the stagflated global economy of the time.

For all three regions, however, the high real interest rates induced by the anti-inflationary, tight money policies of 1979-1981 in the industrial-North came at a particularly inauspicious time, and may be seen as having had a more proximate effect than any other single factor in the precipitation of the crisis. Indeed, the majority of the key factors that precipitated the crisis were located outside of the debtor-South.

These divergent readings speak to a gulf between debtor- and creditor-countries as to the appropriate remedial responses to the problem.[22] From the latter have come three sets of solution proposals, each issuing from a specific understanding of the causes of the crisis. The first emerges from a largely conjunctural analysis that links the lending behaviour of banks to their expectations of the policy response of Northern governments to the oil price-shocks of the 1970s. Banks had, apparently, not expected the industrial market economies to embark on as severe and protracted a deflationary adjustment as they did in 1979-80. They had rather expected a reprise of the 1974-76 adjustment, which produced only a brief recession with high inflation, and very low—even negative—real interest rates. In the event, the 1979-80 adjustment was long and deep, creating historically high interest rates, low demand for the South's exports and, consequently, causing a collapse of their revenues and trade terms.

If lenders had guessed wrongly, therefore, and thereby induced the debt crisis by overly bullish lending practices, it stands to reason, the proponents of this view argue, that the crisis would be diffused if macroeconomic policies in the OECD countries were designed to foster growth and drive interest rates down.[23]

The banks, not unexpectedly, were rather partial to this view, for the simple reason that it absolved them of all meaningful culpability (save the innocuous and rather trivial one of less-than-perfect foresight) in the creation of the crisis, and shifted responsibility for its resolution on government policy makers. There was, also not unexpectedly, much discomfiture with this line of reasoning in government circles. The severity of the disinflationary adjustment, policy makers argued, was necessary to induce long-term stability in the economy without which sustained, low-inflation growth would have been impossible.

Banks, they argued, were singularly guilty of imprudent lending practices, and should therefore be apportioned a large measure of the ultimate responsibility.

The second set of solution-proposals shifts responsibility squarely on the economic malfeasances of the debtor-nations. Citing performance differences among different developing countries and regions, the conclusion was arrived at that world economic conditions *per se* could not have accounted for the deterioration in Africa and Latin America while Asia—at least parts of it—appeared to have been doing extraordinarily well. Thus, it was argued, even if OECD growth rates had been adequately and consistently high through the 1970s and early 1980s, it would have benefitted developing countries little if they had persisted in mismanaging their economies and continued in their profligate ways.[24] Thus adequate and proper policy adjustment, preferably under IMF supervision, to rationalize economic practices and structures in these countries, was indispensable to getting out of the debt crisis. The implicit assumption of this analysis was, of course, that there was considerably more slack in the indebted economies than was popularly supposed; the choice between refinancing their debts and adjusting should therefore consistently favour the latter.[25]

For proponents of this view, then, restrictive domestic macropolicies, coupled with rapid trade liberalization, was the key to correcting the debtor-countries' external imbalances. The international financial institutions (IFIs), ably aided by the liberalist dispensation of the Reagan/Bush and Thatcher governments, have been at the forefront of this crusade, preaching trade and policy liberalization with ardent fervour and passionate conviction since 1982. The entire 1987 issue of **World Development Report**, for instance, was devoted to the argument that export-oriented industrialization, free trade, and contractionary domestic consumption was the soundest strategy for correcting these external disequilibria. The premise of all this, of course, was an oft-unspecified assumption of irrational policy making by the debtor-countries in some previous period. But, as Diaz-Alejandro cogently demurs, "blaming victims is an appealing evasion of responsibility, especially when the victims are far from virtuous."[26]

Besides, it has been amply clear from the start that "Africa and other LDCs [were being asked] to adjust to conditions created by external change beyond their control..."[27]

The third set of solutions, while not exclusive of the first two, focusses critically on a financial system that appears prone to excited frenzies of lending and defaulting—a kind of credit-cycle theory in which contagion effects produce alternating periods of credit booms and busts, and in which confidence, as always, is the least predictable variable.[28] Banks, it was argued, tend to suffer from "disaster myopia" when a lending boom is on, strongly confirmed in their belief that the adage "countries do not go bankrupt" is fool-proof protection against repudiation or default. Further, and perhaps more ominously, in the unthinkable event of mass default in the 1980s, there was no clear lender-of-last-resort to stem the resultant instability in the system.[29] For holders of this view, then, systemic integrity and the protection of the *status quo ante* should have been *the* object of any policy aimed at resolving the debt crisis.

This work consciously attempts an analysis of the debt crisis from the debtors', and especially sub-Saharan Africa's, point of view, in a bid to bring a sense of balance to the discourse on the topic. Any solution proposals advanced here are designed to be consistent with Africa's reading of the causes, dynamics and character of the crisis. It is thus a radical departure from, and offers a marked analytical contrast to, the views, understandings, and solutions emanating from the creditor-nations as enunciated above. It highlights, instead, the centrality of the policy dilemma faced by these nations as a result of their indebtedness, namely, how to optimally address the twin but contradictory obligations of servicing very high external debts while simultaneously ensuring internal growth and economic development.

We argue that the debt crisis, from Africa's point of view, turns on these counter-claims on the continent's income. We therefore focus on critically evaluating the appropriateness, usefulness and efficacy of the resurgent liberalism that dominates contemporary African economic policy-making in response, ostensibly, to this policy dilemma. This leads to the proposal of an alternative 'culture of development' *ensconced in the structural peculiarities of Africa's political economy*, on the rationale that the epistemic foundations of the 'new' orthodoxy are not only improper for assessing Africa's debt and related economic problems, but also that policies issuing therefrom actually exacerbate these problems in the long run, even as they impose unnecessarily burdensome costs in the short.

A little over a decade has passed since the official onset of the "Third World debt crisis". This should afford us the requisite distance and analytical sobriety with which to examine Africa's debt crisis afresh. In seeking to do so, this work focusses on the crucial period between 1970 and 1985. It makes the basic argument that Africa's external debt problems in this period have been facilely analyzed as problems of temporary illiquidity susceptible to those traditional remedies that, in effect, only make marginal adjustments to existing economic structures and policies to improve cash-flow. Thus debt restructuring, debt swaps, "structural" adjustment, special international lending programmes, debt refinancing, debt buy-backs, etc., are the preferred policies for short-term debt relief. For the long run, there has emerged a strident advocacy of *laissez-faire* as *the* panacea for external disequilibria.

But while these may work in some debtor-countries, Africa's economies are largely unresponsive to such shocks. Their structural peculiarities render aggregate output elasticities rather low, and the absence of efficient, institutionalized markets makes reliance on market forces for resource allocation, the transmission of reforms, and eventual sustained systemic growth a bit foolhardy. More fundamentally, these neo-liberal policies are 'rational' only if the crisis is seen as a passing liquidity debacle. We argue here, in contradistinction, that the crisis in Africa issues largely from the continent's *systemic* insolvency: i.e. its chronic inability to generate and sustain levels of output and income growth commensurate with the growth rate of its debt and that of its domestic development needs. Thus any temporary cash-flow bottleneck is only a *symptom* of a graver structural malaise; the crisis does not arise from, nor is it analytically reducible to, the symptom.

In other words, Africa's debt crisis of the 1980s did not arise from a short-term problem of illiquidity in essentially sound economies with unarguable structural integrity. It arose from a deeply-entrenched, structural disintegration of the economy itself, on the one hand, and from destabilizing political discourses and practices, on the other. African economies thus lack the structures with which to translate market-based reforms into the sustained income growth without which debt crises are always menacingly imminent. If the existing structures of economy and politics are the root causes of the crisis, then the neo-orthodox remedies can only be intermittently palliative, not consistently curative.

Using the debt crisis thusly conceptualized as nothing more than a powerful metaphor for Africa's structural pathologies, we attempt to demonstrate that the new orthodoxy does not—indeed, cannot— achieve its stated objective of providing "debt relief with growth", and argue, therefore, for an alternative set of analyses and policies that would tackle the crisis at its source.

The book proceeds from critique (of current thinking and policies) through theory to concrete policy proposals, though not always strictly in that order. The first chapter places Africa's debt crisis in its proper economic and historical contexts, and seeks to re-conceptualize and re-define the crisis so as to highlight its uniquenesses and historical specificities. Out of this comes a broad sketch of the main thesis, delineating the salient differences between the structuralist analytical approach to the debt crisis employed here and the essentially marginalist flavour of the 'new' orthodoxy.

The next two chapters examine the causes—internal and external, proximal and distal, economic and political, structural and episodic— of Africa's debt crisis. They focus especially on the peculiar structure of the 'typical' sub-Saharan African economy, and on the impacts (and implications) of formal politics as it is currently practiced on the continent on the structure and size of the debt. We then cursorily examine the Zairean political economy as, perhaps, the best illustration of how all these seemingly disparate forces can converge on African economies to induce severe external disequilibria. A more detailed analysis of the Zairean case, focussing more closely on the policies deployed to deal with its debt crisis, is presented in the fifth chapter.

Chapter Four casts a critical eye on the theories and practices of the resurgent economic orthodoxy of the 1980s in Africa. We attempt to show, both theoretically and by reference to (and inference from) empirical studies, that this new liberalism is on very shaky epistemic ground indeed in the African context, and that the IMF-type structural adjustment policies that it engenders do little—can do little—to provide meaningful relief from the crisis.

We continue this examination in Chapter Five, where we show, through case studies of Zambia and Zaire, that the most frequently deployed "debt relief" strategies, though perfectly well-intended, have been largely ineffectual, since they were in essence attempting to solve deeply-embedded structural problems with marginalist tools. We also cast a critical theoretical look at the economics of the linchpin of the neo-orthodox adjustment, namely, currency devaluation, in seeking to understand the spectacular failure of liberal adjustment policies in the African economy. And, finally, the sixth chapter advances and examines suggestions towards more efficacious theories and policies for analyzing, understanding and solving Africa's debt-cum-development crisis.

Notes

1. See, as examples, Emma Rothschild, Banks: The Coming Crisis, **New York Review of Books** (May 27, 1976), p. 16; and H. van B. Cleveland and W.H.B. Brittain, Are the LDCs In Over Their Heads, **Foreign Affairs** (July 1977), pp. 732-750, both cited by D. Delamaide, **Debt Shock**, pp. 14-15.
2. See World Bank, **World Debt Tables**, (Washington, D.C.: Feb. 1983), cited by Delamaide, op. cit., p.7.
3. OECD, **External Debt of Developing Countries** (Geneva, December 1982), as cited by Delamaide, ibid.
4. See, for instance, Jeffery Sachs, The Debt Crisis at A Turning Point, **Challenge** (May-June 1988), pp.17-26.
5. See, for instance, Tim Congdon, **The Debt Threat** (London: Basil Blackwell, 1988), p. 198.
6. See Delamaide, op.cit., ch. 3, on which much of the argument of this section is based.
7. Anthony Sampson, **The Money Lenders: Banks in a Dangerous World** (London: Hodder and Stoughton, 1981), pp. 35-37. See, also, David Felix, **The Baring Crisis of the 1890s and the International Bond Defaults of the 1930s: Delphic Prophecies on the Outcome of the Current Latin American Debt Crises** (mimeo: Washington Univ., St. Louis, Mo: Dept. of Economics, Nov. 1984).
8. See Herbert Feis, Europe, **The World's Banker, 1870-1914** (New Haven: Yale U.P., 1930), as cited by Delamaide, op.cit., p.54.
9. For insightful analyses of the importance and mode of credit allocation and financial intermediation in the capitalist economy, see James Crotty, The Centrality of Money, Credit, and Financial Intermediation in Marx's Crisis Theory: An Interpretation of Marx's Methodology, in Stephen Resnick and Richard Wolff, eds., **Rethinking Marxism: Essays for Harry Magdoff and Paul Sweezy** (N.Y.: Autonomedia, 1985), ch. 5. From a neo- and/or post-Keynesian perspective, Hyman Minsky's **John Maynard Keynes** (N.Y.: Columbia U.P., 1975) and his **Can It Happen Again: Essays on Instability and Crisis** (Armonk, N.Y.: M.E. Sharpe, 1982); Charles Kindleberger's **The World In Depression, 1929-39** (Berkeley: Univ. of Calif. Press, 1973) and his **Manias, Panics and Crashes** (N.Y.: Basic Books, 1978); and Kindleberger and J.P. Laffargue's (eds.) **Financial Crisis: Theory, History and Policy** (Cambridge: Cambridge Univ. Press, 1982) are equally instructive.

10. See John Makin, **The Global Debt Crisis** (N.Y.: Basic Books, 1984), p.5.
11. Ibid.
12. Ibid.
13. Makin, op.cit., ch. 2. See, also, Carlos Diaz-Alejandro, Stories of the 1930s for the 1980s, in Pedro Armella et.al., eds., **Financial Policies and the World Capital Markets: The Place of Latin American Countries** (Chicago: Univ. of Chicago Press, 1983), pp.5-35.
14. Ibid.
15. Herbert Feis, op. cit, pp. 20-25 and 240-248, as cited by Delamaide, op. cit., p. 54.
16. Makin, op. cit., p. 41.
17. See Diaz-Alejandro, **Stories of the 1930s for the 1980s**; and E. Wayne Nafziger, **The Debt Crisis in Africa** (Baltimore: The Johns Hopkins Press, 1993), pp. 20-21.
18. Nafziger, op. cit., p. 21.
19. Ibid.
20. Ibid.
21. This thesis is found uniformly across the ideological spectrum. For representative examples, see Kindleberger, **Manias, Panics and Crashes** (N.Y.: Basic Books, 1978), especially pp.201-209, for a neo-classical/Keynesian view; and James Crotty, op. cit., for a Marxian perspective. The phrase quoted from Axel Leijonhufvud is from his **On Keynesian Economics and the Economics of Keynes** (N.Y.: Oxford Univ. Press, 1968), ch. II.
22. This section relies heavily on Miles Kahler, Politics and International Debt: Explaining the Debt Crisis, in Miles Kahler, ed., **The Politics of International Debt** (Ithaca: Cornell Univ. Press, 1986), pp. 11-36.
23. For a representative sample of this literature, see William Cline, International Debt and Stability in the World Economy, **Political Analyses in International Economics**, Vol. 4 (Washington, D.C.: Institute of International Economics, 1983); and C. Diaz-Alejandro, Latin American Debt: I Don't Think We Are in Kansas Anymore, **Brookings Papers on Economic Activity**, Vol. 2 (1984), pp. 335-403.
24. Carlos Diaz-Alejandro has pointed out, however, that in Latin America government policies spanned the entire spectrum of possibilities. But they all seem to have foundered, anyway, suggesting that there was a common **external** factor for their failures. See Diaz-Alejandro, **Latin American Debt**, op.cit., p.336.
25. See IMF, **World Economic Outlook**, (Washington, D.C.: April 1983).

26. Diaz-Alejandro, **Latin-American Debt:...**, op.cit., p. 335.
27. Nafziger, op. cit., p. 24.
28. See Kindleberger, **Manias...**, ch. 10 and ch. 11; and Jon Eaton and Mark Gersovitz, **Poor Country Borrowing in Private Financial Markets and the Repudiation Issue** (Princeton, N.J.: International Finance Section, Princeton Univ., 1981); both as cited by Kahler, op. cit., p. 14.
29. See, for instance, Jack Guttentag and Richard Herring, **The Lender of Last Resort Function in An International Context** (Princeton, N.J.: International Finance Section, Princeton Univ., 1983).

Chapter 1

Africa's Debt Crisis
in the Global Context

1.1 The Economic Context of the Debt:
1970-1985

Sub-Saharan Africa (i.e. Africa south of the Maghreb and north of the Republic of South Africa, and hereafter referred to as SSA) had, at the end of 1985, a total external debt of between $102 billion and $120 billion. In absolute magnitude this represented a paltry 10% of the total outstanding debt of the Third World at the time. But SSA had the dubious honour, as Table 1.1 shows, of having watched its debt grow at an average 20% annually in the preceding decade-and-a-half this work is concerned with.[1] This would mean that, between 1970 and 1985, Africa's debt was growing even more rapidly than Latin America's, even though Latin America was more conspicuously associated with "the debt crisis" than any other region of the developing world. Indeed, the rate of growth of Africa's debt seemed to belie the fact that its exports were, in particular years over the period, enjoying a boom on international markets, even as non-credit development transfers to the continent were expanding very rapidly: by 1983, net overseas development assistance (ODA) had grown by about $7.5 billion over the early 1970s' figure, 68% of which were outright grants while 16% consisted of technical assistance.[2]

This favourable resource transfer notwithstanding, several countries in SSA increased their debt obligation at least ten-fold over the period. For some the debt almost tripled in a mere two or three

TABLE 1.1
Sub-Saharan Africa: Long-Term Public and
Publicly-Guaranteed Debt, Average
Annual Nominal Growth Rates, 1970-1984

	Growth Rates, 1970-84			
	1970-75	1975-80	1980-84	1970-84
Countries with prolonged debt problems [a]	19.6	23.8	9.0	20.8
Other, IDA-eligible countries [b]	21.3	20.2	4.7	16.5
Sub-total, IDA countries (average of a + b)	20.6	21.9	7.0	18.6
Other countries [c]	24.6	32.3	13.3	24.2
TOTAL (a, b + c)	21.7	25.2	9.4	20.4

a = Benin, Gambia, Liberia, Madagascar, Mali, Mauritania, Niger, Somalia, Sudan, Tanzania, Togo, Zambia.
b = Burkina, Burundi, CAR, Chad, Ethiopia, Ghana, Guinea, Guinea-Bissau, Kenya, Lesotho, Malawi, Rwanda, Senegal, Sierra Leone, Uganda, Zaire.
c = Cameroon, Côte d'Ivoire, Nigeria, Zimbabwe, Botswana, Congo, Gabon, Mauritius, Swaziland.

Source: World Bank, *Financing Adjustment With Growth SSA, 1986-1990*, Table A.1, p. 53.

years: Benin, for one, went from a $41 million debt in 1970 to $167 million in 1980, and then to $369 million barely two years later. Similarly, Gambia's debt increased from the 1978 level of $28 million to $140 million in 1981, a 400% increase, while oil-exporting Nigeria went from $480 million to over $4.3 billion between 1970 and 1980, and then to nearly $12 billion by 1984.[3] And even though the overall continental debt growth ameliorated somewhat in 1985, to about 9% annually, IMF purchases and arrears on short- and medium-term debt increased significantly.[4] This reflected not only the preponderance of IMF and other multilateral loans in SSA's debt structure, but also the domination of "structural adjustment programmes" (SAPs) in Africa's debt management strategy, and the numerous loan restructurings/reschedulings that African debtors underwent.[5] Increasingly, also, short-term commercial debt at higher (market) rates and of shorter maturity came to replace the long-term, multi- and bilateral concessional loans of the 1970s.[6] Thus soft loans were rapidly replaced by harder ones, such that Africa increasingly had access to fewer international loan-dollars for which it paid stiffer interest rates over shorter periods of time.

Over the same period, the economies of SSA had to contend with some rather rude economic shocks which virtually eliminated their very ability to sustain themselves, and from whose devastating macroeconomic effects they are, even today, still attempting to escape. First, there was a continual shrinkage of their export revenues from the mid-1970s onward, as the world economy reeled from stagflation, and as structural changes in the industrialized economies led to the advent of new growth industries not particularly absorptive of SSA's traditional raw-material exports.[7] These, together with high tariff barriers selectively erected by some industrialized nations against major African exports, and the increasing substitution of man-made for natural inputs (e.g. plastics and nylons for cotton and sisal) exacerbated the dearth of demand on world markets for Africa's exports.

Secondly, for a period of five-to-seven years beginning in 1975, severe droughts, locust invasions and brush fires destroyed some 25% of arable lands and rain forests in West Africa, and as much as 55% of farmlands in the eastern and central parts of the continent. The production of food and non-food primary products was thus heavily compromised for several planting seasons. Not only did the volume of exports and export-revenue consequently drop, as Tables 4.1-4.3 clearly show, but the rate of external borrowing had to be stepped up to finance the importation of basic needs (food, medicines, etc.) and manufacturing inputs.

Thirdly, the two oil-price shocks of the 1970s resulted, for many African countries in, at least, a quadrupling of their oil-import bill. By 1980, therefore, fossil fuels were accounting for some 25% of the total import bills of the non oil-exporting countries of SSA, up from 6% in 1970.[8]

Next, the contractionary monetary policies pursued in the late 1970s and early 1980s to stem the inflationary tide in the industrial-North led, not only to the exacerbation of the demand problems of Africa's exports, but also to a rate of growth of its external debt (as interest rates subsequently shot up) far in excess of that of its export revenues.

And, lastly, because the external debts were denominated in U.S. dollars, as the dollar rose in value from 1980 to 1985 (see Table 1.2 below) the values of debt and interest payment on the debt rose relative to the debtors' currencies and/or to their earnings in non-dollar currencies.   The result was that debtors could not meet interest payments due on past debts, and were obliged to increase their borrowing to meet their delinquent debt-service obligations.   The conjunctural effect of these two classes of forces—a high rate of debt accumulation and a worsening capacity to optimally carry such debt— and that of, at least, two decades of post-colonial macroeconomic mismanagement, was as manifold as it was grave.   It was this combination of events and their impacts that, it will be argued here, properly constituted the economics of Africa's debt crisis.

TABLE 1.2

Factors Contributing to Sub-Saharan
Africa's External Debt Crisis, 1976-1985

	3-month Euro-dollar interest rate (1)	Annual Crude Oil Price (2)	Terms-of-trade of non-oil LDCs* (1976=100) (3)	Trade-weighted value of U.S. dollar (March '73=100) (4)
1976	6.0	13.01	115.6	93.1
1979	8.8	13.07	108.3	84.2
1980	12.0	18.91	105.9	83.2
1981	14.0	31.39	95.5	84.8
1983	16.8	35.03	90.3	100.8
1985	12.2	34.23	84.6	111.7

*For changes in SSA's terms-of-trade specifically, see Table 1.4.

Sources: Figures derived from
   1.   *Barclays Review*, May 1984, p. 32 for Columns (1) and (2).
   2.   *Economic Report of the President*, 1986, p. 373 for Columns (3) and (4).

The key impacts of this constellation of forces included these: (1) an average annual growth rate of output, as Table 1.3 indicates, of about 2% over the period in question for the vast majority of African countries, with a substantial number of them registering negative GDP growth between 1973 and 1983.[9] The growth rate of the "low-income countries" was only 2.1% over the period, on the average; for the "middle-income oil importers" it was 3.0%, though most of the growth in this sub-group came from only two countries: Botswana, with a 10.2% growth rate, and Lesotho, with 5.5%. Even for the "middle-income oil exporters" growth only averaged 1.6% annually, ranging from the Congo's 8% to Gabon's -2%.[10]

These economy-wide growth rates reflected similar trends in each sector of the economy. Across the continent agricultural output, at an average annual rate of 0.7%, barely grew at all. Indeed its share of GDP dropped from the 1970 figure of 42% to about 28% in 1983. Manufactures, which managed a 1.4% growth, saw its contribution to continental output increase from 20% in 1970 to 29% in 1983, and services from 39% to 42%.

TABLE 1.3
SSA: Selected Economic Indicators, 1971-1983

	1971	1975	1978	1979	1980	1981	1982	1984	1985
Economic Growth Rate (%)	3.3	2.7	1.8	1.5	2.7	1.8	1.9	0.1	0.5
Inflation (%)	8.4	15.8	19.0	22.3	23.3	25.8	26.8	22.3	25.2
Average Interest on Foreign Loan Commitments	4.0	5.0	8.0	9.0	9.5	11.6	14.0	10.0	11.0

Sources: Figures derived from
1. IMF. *World Economic Outlook, 1984, Occasional Paper No. 27*, pp. 11, 16 and 25, for the inflation and interest-rate figures of the 1980s.
2. World Bank. *Financing Adjustment with Growth in Sub-Saharan Africa, 1986-90*, p. 53 for the interest-rate figures of the 1970s; and p. 58 for the economic growth figures.
3. UNCTAD, *Handbook of International Trade and Development Statistics, 1984*, pp. 61 and 64 for the inflation figures of the 1980s.

As a consequence of these massive changes in both the level and structure of output, and the adverse international conditions mentioned earlier, SSA's exports could only manage a -5.0% annual growth rate over the period, on the average, even as imports increased by 3.3%.[11] As a result, (2) Africa's balance on current account got progressively negative, as Figure 1.1 clearly depicts. Ethiopia's, for instance, went from $-32.0 million in 1970 to $-201.0 million by 1984; Mali's, from $-2.0 million to $-125.0 million over the same period; Zaire's, from $-64.0 million to $-310.0 million; and Kenya's, from $-49.0 million to $-190.0 million. Even among the net-oil exporters, only Nigeria and Gabon showed significant improvements in their trade balances; for the three others in that sub-group the situation got decidedly worse.

By 1984, therefore, only a handful of SSAn countries had enough international reserves to cover more than two months' worth of imports. Indeed the sub-continent as a whole could only cover 1.6 months'.[12] At the same time, (3) *scheduled* debt service had grown to absorb, by World Bank statistics, an average of 27% of continental export revenue, though *actual* debt service was as high as 60%, on average. Many individual countries experienced even more burdensome debt-service obligations: for instance, Guinea-Bissau and Somalia each had a debt-service ratio (DSR) of 128% in 1985, Sudan's was 158%, Madagascar's 97%, and the Congo's, 77%.[13]

It is worth noting briefly here that this debt service profile arose from two main developments in the international economy only slightly touched upon thus far. One was the repeated restructuring and rescheduling of Africa's debt. Because restructuring is basically a recapitalization process, and is therefore done at the rates obtaining in the market at the time of restructuring; and because these rates tended to be higher than the rates at which the debts were initially contracted, restructuring actually *increased* both the present-value, and the rate of growth, of the debt, while offering little of the relief that it is presumed to offer.

The other involved Africa's revenue profile, i.e. its foreign exchange-earning capacity. This was heavily compromised by the low rates of output growth in both tradables and non-tradables, as

Figure 1.1
Comparative Current Account Balances, 1974-85

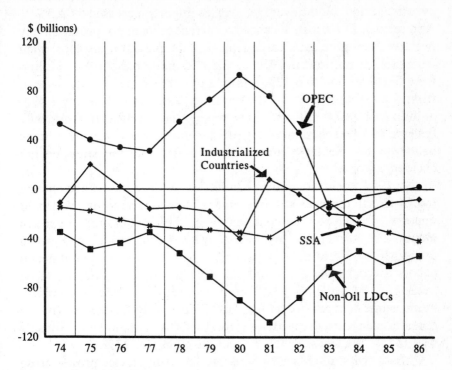

Sources: Data derived from
1.   IMF, *World Economic Outlook, 1984*, pp. 8, 14, 16, 25.
2.   IMF, *International Financial Statistics*, various issues.

alluded to earlier, and the low demand for its exports in a stagflated world economy undergoing fundamental structural change. The dearth of demand led to falling commodity prices, even while prices of manufactured imports from the inflated industrial-North moved ever upward. The resulting decline in the commodity terms of trade, as summarised in Tables 1.4 and 1.5, weakened Africa's foreign-exchange earning performance, which was, in turn, reflected in its DSRs.

TABLE 1.4
The Net Barter Terms-of Trade for SSA, 1970-1984

	Terms-of Trade (1980 = 100)					Annual Growth Rate 1970-1984
	1970	1981	1982	1983	1984	(%)
Ethiopia	156	68	75	86	100	-4.7
Mali	120	110	105	115	116	-1.0
Zaire	197	87	82	90	88	-5.4
Malawi	138	106	107	125	137	-1.6
Tanzania	108	88	88	92	81	-5.2
Uganda	92	75	75	79	98	0.3
Togo	69	91	84	80	88	-
Gambia	143	130	111	113	158	-1.5
Somalia	157	109	114	116	116	-2.6
Benin	177	97	77	88	116	-5.3
Sudan	98	103	87	87	98	-0.9
Ghana	104	69	62	62	70	-1.1
Senegal	101	104	91	87	98	-1.3
Mozambique	112	96	84	90	104	-1.9
Chad	81	105	101	110	108	1.3
Liberia	189	93	93	104	102	-5.3
Zambia	263	81	72	82	74	-8.7
Côte d'Ivoire	97	92	91	98	101	1.3
Mauritius	108	99	94	98	93	-2.7
Rwanda	79	65	64	65	71	-0.4
Nigeria*	19	112	104	93	94	12.3
Cameroon*	96	78	73	74	85	0.1
Congo*	17	118	113	103	104	13.9
Gabon*	17	114	111	102	103	13.9
Angola*	45	110	106	98	102	7.6
CAR	83	97	94	92	99	1.7
B. Faso	134	109	100	110	117	-1.8
Kenya	99	87	88	88	94	-0.9
Madagascar	113	79	80	90	105	-1.8
Niger	170	84	88	92	81	-5.2
Sierra Leone	145	84	85	89	95	-3.3

*Net oil exporters
Source: Derived from World Bank, *Financing Adjustment with Growth in Sub-Saharan Africa, 1986-90*, Table 11, p. 77.

TABLE 1.5
SSA Commodity Prices, 1970-83 (constant 1983 U.S. $)

	1970	'72	'74	'76	'77	'78	'79	'80	'81	'82	'83
COCOA, cents/kg.	195	156	253	286	490	374	326	258	198	168	212
COFFEE, cents/kg.	331	267	235	440	669	395	378	314	269	299	290
SUGAR, cents/kg.	23	39	106	36	23	19	21	58	36	18	19
GROUNDNUT OIL, $/tonne	1091	1032	1743	1036	1102	1187	878	785	994	567	711
COTTON, cents/kg.	182	192	229	237	201	175	167	187	176	155	185
SISAL, $/tonne	438	581	1709	656	664	539	699	699	615	575	565
TOBACCO, $/tonne	2846	2329	2071	1973	2160	1859	2107	2101	2240	2338	2242
BAUXITE, $/tonne	34.6	31.8	37.5	38.0	39.8	37.7	36.2	37.6	38.1	34.9	34.7
IRON ORE, $/tonne	44	31	31	31	28	21	23	24	23	25	24
COPPER, $/1000 tonnes	4.1	2.6	3.3	1.9	1.7	1.5	1.9	2.0	1.7	1.4	1.6
PHOSPHATE, $/tonne	32	28	88	50	40	32	33	43	47	41	36
TEA, cents/kg.	315	254	227	214	347	240	213	203	192	187	233

Source: Kathie Krumm, *The External Debt of Sub-Saharan Africa*, World Bank Staff Working Papers No. 741 (Washington, D.C., 1985), p. 47.

The upshot of all these developments is that (4) SSA has been unable to keep up with its debt obligations since the early 1980s. Indeed, between the years 1980 and 1985, only fifteen (of fourty-four) indebted countries were able to regularly service their debts at all.[14] The debt crisis for Africa, therefore, started not in 1982 but probably in 1979, when the domestic and international economic decline which began nearly a decade earlier fully took root. This decline, to summarize, was manifested externally in the worsening terms of trade and export performance, and internally in the agricultural and ecological devastation wreaked by droughts, locust invasions and desertification; in the internecine and irredentist wars that ravaged the sub-continent; and in the collision of two decades of managerial ineptitude and policy blunders with the stagflated world economy of the time.

But, perhaps, the single most decisive development that drove their external obligations into crisis were the deflationary policies initiated by the U.S. Federal Reserve Bank, and followed in short order by the monetary authorities in the U.K. and (the then) West Germany, from 1979 to 1982. This, undoubtedly, came at a particularly inopportune time, as the resulting increase in interest rates converged with Africa's other problems, domestic and foreign, to precipitate what we now identify as its external debt crisis. A major sub-text of the thesis of this work comes from this particular understanding of this configuration of factors: interest rate shock, and external shocks in general, must be credited with having had a more proximate causal connection to Africa's debt crisis, in that they caused export-revenue growth to lag behind nominal debt growth, even though the underlying conditions that kept reproducing the crisis were of preponderantly domestic origin.[15]

1.2 Redefining Africa's Debt Crisis

Given the small size of Africa's external debt (some 10% of total developing-country debt outstanding at year-end 1985) and its structure (71% of it was owed to official creditors, as summarized in Table 1.6), Africa's debt crisis, until the latter third of the 1980s, did not generate the same level of attention from analysts and policy makers that, say, Latin America's did since the beginning of the decade.

Implicit in this conspicuous passivity, if not outright neglect, was the widely-held belief that Africa's debt was not as serious, in magnitude; that, given its structure, it was not as threatening to global financial stability, in the case of collective default; and that, therefore, African countries should have had little difficulty in bearing this relatively light debt-load. In sum, to the extent that Africa's debt crisis was seen as a genuine crisis at all, it was viewed, like Latin America's, as a mere transfer problem arising from a temporary liquidity crunch.[16] Thus, it was implied, if only African countries would take the necessary steps towards domestic policy adjustment, the liquidity debacle could and would be transcended. In other words, the solutions to Africa's debt crisis lay in tinkering at the margins of their economies (through currency devaluation, general public-sector budgetary austerity, reorientation of spending priorities away from consumption towards "investment", and wholesale privatization of the productive sectors of the economy) in a bid, ostensibly, to generate increased output and, especially, growing net positive export revenues.

TABLE 1.6

SSA's External Debt by Source, Year-End 1984 ($ millions)

	Total Liabilities (including IMF purchases) (1)	Public & Publicly-Guaranteed Long-Term Debt (2)	(2) as % of (1)
Countries with Prolonged Debt Problems[a]	24,822	18,867	76
Other low-income countries[b]	19,803	15,297	77
Other countries[c]	35,642	22,762	64
TOTAL SSA	80,268	56,927	71

a   Includes Benin, Mali, Somalia, Sudan and Tanzania.
b   Includes Chad, Ghana, Kenya, Malawi, Senegal and Zaire.
c   Includes Cameroon, Côte d'Ivoire, Nigeria, Botswana, Zimbabwe and Gabon.
Source: Derived from World Bank, *Financing Adjustment with Growth in Sub-Saharan Africa, 1986-90*, Table A.2, p. 54.

The reasoning behind this set of prescriptions stems from what appears to be a curious (mis)diagnosis of the debt crisis, in terms of both its causes and impacts, but also from a particular ahistoricism that pushes economic orthodoxy towards its false belief in the universal applicability of market remedies for all economic maladies. But, even more curiously, it stems from an analysis which proceeds on the assumption that responsibility for the crisis rests *solely* on some murkily-defined, prior economic malfeasance of the debtor-countries, hence the justification for them bearing the full brunt and costs of any necessary adjustment. This 'domestification' of SSA's external debt problems is, of course, rejected here in favour of the external causes; indeed, this reconceptualization of the crisis, and the prescriptive policies issuing therefrom, constitute the basic thesis of this study.

The arguments in this work are thus informed by the belief that the dilemma faced by African governments in the period under consideration (and even today, arguably) was how best to address the two functionally-related concerns of meeting their external obligations while, simultaneously, ensuring domestic growth and development *without compromising, especially, the latter*. The principal argument is that Africa's external debt crisis was, and remains, wholly unsolvable with the neo-orthodox, liberalist remedies foisted on the indebted nations, because their very analytical premises are fundamentally questionable. The much-touted transfer problems arising from liquidity crunches, it is contended, were/are but phenomenal manifestations of much deeper-set *structural* problems in these economies; that, consequently, the debt problem in Africa was/is anchored more in a solvency than a liquidity crisis, hence it is more long-term and deeply-seated than was popularly supposed; that, indeed, it was/is a problem of *underdevelopment* as such, and should therefore not be seen as distinct and separable from all the other manifestations of this condition (of under-development); that, to fail to so place the debt crisis—in this configurative matrix that uniquely gives it definition and meaning—necessarily leads to remedies which, like those of the neo-orthodox variety, may actually exacerbate, not ameliorate, the crisis in the long run.

It is argued, further, that the optimal solution to *any* debt crisis lies in the ability of the debtor to efficiently marshall and organize, *as an on-going concern*, its productive resources to achieve a level of income growth as great as, but preferably in excess of, the rate of growth of its debt. SSA's debt crisis, in this regard, lay (and still lies) precisely in (1) its inability to attain and sustain a growth rate of income at least equal to the interest on its external debt, and (2) the fact that the growth of that debt, namely the interest plus any currency-translation effects was, and remains, a moving target, particularly difficult to plan for in an era of wildly fluctuating commodity prices, interest rates and dollar-exchange rates.

As encapsulated in (1) and (2), therefore, SSA's debt problems arose not from the sheer quantum of the debt itself, but more from the continent's low domestic production rates; from low commodity prices on international markets resulting in a worsening of trade terms and export performance (SSA's commodity terms-of-trade grew at an annual rate of -2.4% in the period under investigation here, as Table 1.4 shows); and from the unpredictability of its debt growth as variable interest rates came to dominate a debt-service profile increasingly tilted towards non-concessionary obligations.[17] In addition, in an era of quasi-managed but floating exchange rates, the impact of the "currency translation effect" on the debt—i.e. how its value was altered merely by changes in the exchange rate of the U.S. dollar in which it was denominated—is not to be underestimated.[18]

Such remedies as may suffice to eliminate such deep-seated, structural crises must, therefore, come out of a comprehensive analysis of the pertinent structures (including those that mediated the economic causes, structure, growth trends, and domestic and international politics of the debt), against the backdrop of the continent's economic performance and systemic transformations over three decades of post-colonialism. This backdrop must, of necessity, include the manner in, and the extent to, which Africa has been incorporated into, and interacts with, the global system of trade and finance.

The upshot of such an approach is that Africa's debt crisis is, thereby, cast in its proper metaphoric, historical and figurative light. We are forced by this approach to see the debt crisis as just the one of the many manifestations of the "underdeveloped condition" that it really is, nothing more, really, than a metaphor for underdevelopment itself. It requires us to give a place to debt in our '*Weltanschauung*' no more or less important than all the other "symptoms" of underdevelopment. It enables us see cycles of financial and external disequilibria in small, open economies—which occur randomly at various phases of any development experience, and from which no country, including the infant United States, has been immune—as stemming from the same configuration of forces that cause persistent unemployment and low income in the developing economy.

It is thus not particularly surprising that the policies of the resurgent orthodoxy of the 1980s, which came from a different understanding of the dynamics of external indebtedness, have been sporadically successful in *managing* the crisis, but offered no credible, lasting *remedy*. Indeed, empirical studies suggest that they tend to exacerbate both the underdevelopment and the external debt crisis over the long run, and that whatever palliative effects they bring are, at best, intermittent and ambiguous.[19]

If the debt crisis can, therefore, not be separated from the wider and more common problems of underdevelopment—chronically high unemployment rates, low capital formation, low income generation, etc.—then, it would seem that solutions to it would lie in a comprehensive strategy that seeks to tackle underdevelopment as such. In other words, efforts made at tackling the debt problem, narrowly defined (including the neo-orthodox proposal of restructuring entire economies through *laissez-faire* policies), may prove quite inadequate to the task, since they proceed on the assumption that it is a crisis *independent of* (more correctly, separable from) the wider development project. In addition, it is worth remembering that the remedies proposed under the new orthodoxy (debt restructuring and rescheduling, structural adjustment packages, debt-equity swaps, debt buy-backs, policy-induced global economic expansion, etc.) were normally formulated and/or endorsed by the creditors and/or their agents, whose interests lay—still lie—in securing an uninterrupted flow of income from their debt-assets, in the short-run, than in the long-term solution to the structural problems that generated the debt liability for the debtor-nations in the first place. Because of this acute divergence of interests, and because these "remedies" have tended to deepen the cycle of borrowing and sub-optimal domestic economic performance in the medium-run, the debtor-nations of SSA should seek, as a matter of urgent public policy, to redefine the terms of the discourse on the debt. They need to emphasize the argument that *there is no debt crisis outside of the underdevelopment crisis at large, the former being only symptomatic of the latter*. Better yet, that the debt crisis is another crisis of underdevelopment, though underdevelopment is not reducible to debt (or any other) crises, chronic or episodic. Solutions that better reflect their long-term developmental interests and social objectives may then more appropriately be culled from such a discourse, whose moment does not turn on the traditional marginalization of essentially structural economic problems.

Following these lines of thinking, the debt crisis is here more appropriately re-defined as an 'underdevelopmental condition' in which the countries of SSA and elsewhere could not expand their net foreign exchange earning capacities fast enough to meet *both* their external obligations and domestic growth needs, resulting in both a precarious distension of the global system of trade and financial intermediation, and a worsening of the debtors' already-questionable ability to generate rising incomes.[20] This definition locates the crisis where it belonged: within the (under)development project seen in the wider context of the global political economy, historical and contemporary. It also brings to the fore a corollary argument regarding remedial policy: solving the debt crisis, narrowly defined, should not have been, even as it is today in SSA, *the* object of development policy, the sentiment and advise of the creditor-nations to the contrary notwithstanding. The rationale for this lay not in that the debt was relatively small, which it was. Nor in that its servicing was not burdensome, which it was, inordinately. It lay, rather, in that the burdensomeness of Africa's obligations, in terms of the cost in domestic growth and even basic consumption, was (and is) out of all proportion to the size of the debt. Latin America may have been carrying a much larger debt, but Africa's debt—at 100.1% of Gross Continental Product in the best years of the period under study; at better than twice its total export earnings in a good year; and a debt service that absorbed sometimes 60% of some countries' export earnings—was inordinately more burdensome.[21] Latin America may have had the heavier debt, but Africa had, and still has, the heavier debt-load. The "advantage" that Africa is claimed to have had over Latin America by some of the early Northern analysts, in terms of debt size, was thus a dubious one, as adjustments to the crisis in Africa were done not primarily through increased external borrowing (as was the initial response in Latin America) but, as our case studies show, through policy-induced declines in living standards. Thus just as a bankrupt business enterprise liquidates its assets to defray its outstanding liabilities Africa, at the behest of the new classicalists, similarly liquidated its best asset—the material welfare of its peoples—to pay off its creditors. It is still, even today, undergoing this self-liquidation.

Secondly, if indeed the debt crisis was, as we have argued, only one element in a matrix of socio-economic problems which collectively constitute the condition called under-development, then all the elements of that matrix are not independent one of the other. To isolate one and 'solve' it, therefore, will be an exercise which may generate worse problems for the remaining elements of the matrix, and possibly regenerate the debt crisis anew in subsequent periods. The theory of the second best, in other words, may well be operative here.

In addition, an important reason for not concentrating solely or preponderantly on solving the external debt crisis is the long-term potential domestic opportunity cost of doing so. Directing the continent's resources towards the debt throughout the 1980s constrained unduly the domestic growth and development process, the inadequacy of which was at the bottom of the crisis in the first place, and the solution to which is a *sine qua non* for solving the debt crisis itself.[22] Concentrating on the debt as development policy may, therefore, trap SSA in a zero-sum game in which a dollar of debt service may well represent a dollar taken out of potential domestic economic growth, ultimately weakening the continent's ability to generate income in the future, and conceivably pushing it back into a debt crisis once again.

This work thus focusses on two sub-themes in its expostulation: the first is a comprehensive critique of the neo-liberal analyses of, and prescriptions for, Africa's debt crisis. The second is an articulation of an alternative set of solution- proposals based primarily on two issues: the diagnosis that the crisis stemmed from long-term structural problems, of both external and internal origin, which led to the economic insolvency of these countries, and from the identification of the debt crisis as being really a twin-crisis, functionally and analytically inseparable, of debt and underdevelopment.

1.3 *Structural Analyses or a Resurgent Classicalism?*

In the last third of the 1980s, there appeared a slow but reluctant realization in new orthodox circles that Africa's debt crisis may have had more fundamental causes than the popular "liquidity crisis" thesis had intimated. Beginning with World Bank economists, faint echoes of the argument were being heard, often in the same contradictory breath as the usual panoply of selective adjustment policies, for a comprehensive liberalization of all aspects of economic endeavour in Africa.[23] Their analysis, however, was nothing more than a resurgent, pre-Keynesian classicism that argued that unfettered market forces, because they tend to "get the prices right", will inject a measure of efficiency in the allocation of resources that will eventually transform the structures of these economies to put them on a sustained growth path. The only way out of the debt crisis, which simultaneously tackled the underlying causative factors (of underdevelopment), they argued, was a comprehensive *laissez-faire* policy for both the domestic economy and the external sector.

In this spirit, the entire 1987 issue of the World Bank's **World Development Report** was dedicated to the view that trade liberalization and the related foreign-exchange reforms, and privatization and/or liberalization of agriculture and banking were the optimal long-run solutions to Africa's debt-cum-development crises. Specifically, the Report sought to empirically validate the case that outwardly-oriented economies (i.e. those that pursued export-led growth strategies) had better overall performances than those that were inward looking (i.e. practiced import substitution). The former were shown to have achieved higher real GDP and manufactured-exports growth rates with greater production efficiencies (as measured by their lower incremental capital-output ratios), the inference being that efficient resource allocation through unfettered market activity would point the African economies out of their quagmire. Presumably price adjustments, ably aided by a sheepish allegiance to market signals by rationalizing economic agents, will solve all the structural problems of Africa's economies!

We, however, argue later in the work, with the aid of case studies, that even though this is an analytical improvement upon the earlier diagnoses of the neo-liberalists, their remedial proposals, far from curing the malady, may actually deepen and prolong the crisis. On a continent where markets are largely undefined, if at all definable, "getting the prices right" may be quite meaningless or even impossible. Market prices, in these institutional conditions, may actually give the wrong signals to economic agents, leading to decisions and behaviour that may thwart, not enhance, the development process (see Chapter Four). Markets are *social* institutions that function optimally only if they can generate *and* disseminate the relevant information to market participants. Where the information may not be available, reliable or widely disseminable; or where market participation involves only a small segment of economic agents, therefore, the market fails to function as an efficient guide to economic activity.

In much of SSA this is the state-of-affairs: market information may not be readily available, and where available may reveal precious little about real conditions in the economy or market. Structural distortion of market signals appears to be the norm: this is as true of resource (especially labour and capital) markets as it is of product markets, as a later discussion of agricultural production in SSA amply indicates. (The term 'market' is, of course, being used here in the neo-classical economics sense: i.e. an institutional arrangement in which buyers and sellers make buying and selling decisions based on the unconstrained availability of the relevant information, and in which they are driven solely by the 'rationality' of optimizing binary preferences on the assumption that, at a given price, more of a good/service is better than less).

The structural analysis favoured in this study differs from the neo-orthodox view, therefore, in the following particulars: (1) it does not universalize a particular policy recommendation, or even diagnosis, for all sectors and all countries. There is not the implicit belief, for instance, that discretionary intervention in markets (where they functionally exist), or the total absence of free markets, is always and everywhere in Africa the cause of the debt-cum-development crises. (2) It therefore does not prescribe *one* policy (say, structural adjustment) as a cure-all for what are really different nuances of different structural problems with different manifestations in different countries. (3) The *laissez-faire* prescriptions of the new orthodoxy will retain, and even enhance, the existing class structure and political culture of African countries. It is argued here, in Chapters Two and Five, to the contrary, that the class structure itself, and the type of politics it engenders, are major contributors to Africa's crises. Selective, targeted policies that address the pertinent political and economic issues where and how they need addressing are therefore proposed. And, lastly, (4) the *laissez-faire* proposals will enhance the present relationship between Africa and the industrialized economies which, as is expounded in Chapters Two and Three, is itself a not insignificant contributor to the crisis, and for which policies that seek to largely eliminate the "dependent interdependence" nature of the relationship are proposed. In other words, unlike the new liberalists, it is argued here that *less*, not more, of the economic and political relationships between Africa and the international economy is part of the solution. The new liberalist position would indicate a directly contrary belief.

In summary, then, the appropriate policy responses to Africa's debt crisis rested in understanding the crisis as stemming from the particular state of the continent's under-development in the 1980s, generally, and from the nature and dynamics of economic activity between Africa and the industrial nations, in particular. The interaction of these two influences to produce and reproduce Africa's twin crises of external indebtedness and domestic underdevelopment may be schematically sketched as follows: African countries were suffering from an acute debt crisis throughout the 1980s because they borrowed vast sums of money from savings-surplus countries to finance domestic consumption and/or investment activities (in essence, attempting to overcome an income-cum-saving constraint). They resorted to borrowing because, with their endemically capital-deficient economies, they were incapable of generating adequate employment, income and saving (a capital, hence income, constraint). They were unable to service the loans because, achieving only sub-optimal employment and output, they could not generate enough income or savings to satisfy both domestic development requirements and external obligations (effectively, a domestic budgetary constraint, stemming from the two initial constraints). Even if they could, their ability to pay back was constrained by their foreign-exchange earning capability (a transfer constraint), itself constrained by two tenuously-related factors: the domestic output and employment insufficiencies already mentioned and, along trend, unfavourable price fluctuations on their commodity exports, and worsening net barter terms-of-trade, generally. Indeed, their very access to Northern markets was heavily circumscribed by stiff protectionist barriers. Furthermore, they had, and continue to have, rather inflexible production structures based on one or two primary products of a generally "non-strategic" nature, and for which they were/are, by and large, price takers on international markets. This production structure is, itself, a product, or by-product, of centuries of involuntary interaction with Northern economies.

SSA's debt crisis is thus analyzed in this its totality, taking due cognizance of the wider context outside of which the crisis as such would have had no meaning. The analysis therefore necessarily entails a comprehensive reexamination of the demand and supply dimensions of the debt, the external and domestic structures that initiated and reproduced the resulting crisis, the stabilization policies deployed thus far to resolve the crisis, and alternative solutions that could more efficaciously lead to long-term remedy. This latter set of solutions, however, can be appreciated only after a proper understanding of the structural peculiarities of the 'typical' African economy, and how it might respond to the relevant shocks, has been obtained. This is the principal object of the next chapter.

1.4 The Economics of External Imbalances

The orthodox model of the open economy[24] can be simplified and summarized in four principal relationships. The first stems from the Keynesian argument that output is demand-driven, in that the demand for any country's output is determined by local spending on that output plus any foreign spending on it. The country's income, y, then, is the sum of the domestic spending, E, and net exports, X:

$$y = E + X.$$

Domestic demand itself is minimally a function of domestic income and real interest rates, $(r - p)$, where r is the nominal rate of interest and p some expected inflation variable; and net exports depend on domestic income, foreign income, y_f, and the real exchange rate, e. Thus

$$y = E(y, r-p) + X(y, y_f, e).$$

Imports and exports, in this formulation, are assumed to have constant elasticities with respect to domestic and foreign incomes, respectively. The trade variables are seen as lagging exchange rate movements rather significantly, as importers and exporters take time to adjust appropriately to changes in the exchange rate. However, currency depreciation is often seen as being immediately manifested as import-price rises. This would suggest some 'J-curve' effect: an initial perverse response of the trade balance to exchange rate devaluation, in which the volume of imports fall even as its value (in domestic currency terms) rises because of the higher import prices, and in which the initial increases in exports are not large enough to offset the adverse impact on the trade balance.

The second equation of the model is from the monetary sector: an exogenously determined money supply, M, is set to equal the demand for money balances, L, which, of course, depends on income, interest rates and the price level, P:

$$\frac{M}{P} = L\ (y,\ r).$$

The third relation is the exchange-rate determination equation. On the assumption (1) that investors expect returns on their domestic- and foreign-earning assets to be equal; and (2) that the real exchange rate converges gradually on some expected rate, e^*, in the long run, the exchange-rate relation becomes a function of the real interest rate differential between domestically-held and foreign-held assets. Thus the higher Country A's interest rates are in comparison with Country B's, the stronger is its currency relative to B's, as resources will be invested in country A in greater numbers than in B. Thus

$$r - p = r_f - p_f + \lambda\ (e^* - e)$$

which may be rewritten as

$$r = r_f + p - p_f + \lambda\ (e^* - e).$$

Price determination completes the model. The price *level* is assumed known at any given time. The inflation rate is then determined by an expectations-adjusted Phillip's curve in which inflation is a function of output and a core or expected inflation level, p:

$$\left(\frac{\dot{P}}{P}\right) = k(y) + p.$$

Core inflation is, in turn adaptive, in that it adjusts gradually towards actual inflation:

$$p = \theta\left(\frac{\dot{P}}{P} - p\right).$$

The orthodox open-economy model is therefore nothing but a glorified IS-LM model which brings into equilibrium the real and money sectors of the economy. It is also a quasi-dynamic model in three respects: trade elasticities cause lagged adjustments in trade to relative price movements, prices adjust slowly from the Phillip's curve, and inflation expectations are gradual because they are embodied in the notion of the core inflation rate.

Now consider, first, the effects of an expansionary fiscal policy on trade performance and the balance-of-payments. This will raise demand for domestic output which will induce an expansion of production. The demand for money will expand commensurately, pulling interest rates along and, thereby, crowding out private investment. As domestic interest rates rise above foreign rates, the resulting relative appreciation of the currency will dampen net exports at all levels of output. In this model, therefore, excessive government spending leads to an expansion of output domestically, but also causes an overvaluation of the currency which, when left uncorrected, will cause the kinds of trade and balance-of-payments imbalances that can easily degenerate into external debt crises.

Consider, next, the effect on the external balance of an expansionary monetary policy. The immediate effect, by this model, will be to lower domestic interest rates, thereby stimulating investment and production. Lower interest rates will, in turn, cause a depreciation of the currency, as foreign interest rates are now higher than before the monetary expansion. The depreciated currency will induce an expansion of net exports at any output level, thus providing a secondary stimulus to the expansion. The effect of a monetary expansion, therefore, is to stimulate economic expansion but cause a depreciation of the currency, with an unpredictable impact on the trade accounts and balance-of-payments. As we will see next, it is for these reasons of the mutual impact of domestic economic policy on the external balances, and the effect of these external disequilibria in their turn on domestic economic performance, that particular policies came to dominate the adjustment programmes that the debtor countries of Africa were persuaded to implement by the World Bank/IMF in the 1980s.

The Rationale for the Orthodox Adjustment

The level of any of the African debtor-nations' external obligations represents the accumulated stock of net claims by non-Africans on that country as reflected in the annual flows of borrowing included in its balance-of-payments (BOP) accounts. In any given year, therefore, the country's total external debt represents the sum of its BOP deficits (a deficit in the BOP indicating a net inflow of value into the country, hence a debt to outside interests), including interest on any debt outstanding. (The domestic corollary is the national debt, which is the sum of all past budget deficits). To understand how Africa's indebtedness came about over the period in question; how the crisis might have arisen; the choice of adjustment policies by the World Bank and IMF for dealing with the crisis in these countries; or indeed, what alternative remedial policies might have been pursued, Africa's BOP flows over the period must be carefully scrutinized. The theoretical rationale for this is spelled out forthwith, following Seamus O'Cleireacain closely.[25]

The basic accounting identity of the BOP consists of two components each of trade flows—exports (X) and imports (M)—and capital flows—capital inflows (K_{in}) and capital outflows (K_{out}). The sum total of the four determines, in a flexible exchange-rate regime, the country's exchange-rate movements, or its foreign-exchange reserves position if the exchange rate is fixed. Thus

$$BOP: X - M + K_{in} - K_{out} = \dot{R} \qquad ...(1.1)$$

where $\dot{R}$ represents a change in the reserves.

X and K_{in} produce foreign exchange for the country; M and K_{out} consume it. If the sum of these four components is negative, there is a deficit in the BOP. To restore the payments balance, the central bank's foreign-exchange reserve holdings must decline by the amount of the deficit, or the exchange rate of the country's currency vis-a-vis other currencies must fall. Thus a country finances BOP deficits (in effect, its net positive external obligations) by drawing down its reserves, initially, or by borrowing reserves from other countries.

When the country's reserves fall too low, or its creditworthiness drops as a result of excessive borrowing, thereby precluding further borrowing to shore up reserves, the country must start initiating policies to *correct* the BOP imbalance. Such policies are designed to influence each of the four components of the BOP in the appropriate direction. For much of Africa throughout the period under investigation here, these policies, more often than not, employed currency devaluation (and other such market reforms to "get the prices right") as the linchpin of more comprehensive "structural adjustment" packages.

Assuming fixed exchange rates, Equation (1.1) may be re-written as

$$BOP : CA + KA = \dot{R} \qquad ...(1.2)$$

where CA represents the *current account* of the BOP, consisting of the country's net trade in goods and services, *(X - M)*, the *services* component of which often includes income earned on investments and other net factor incomes. Similarly, KA is the balance on the *capital account*, representing the net capital flow component of the BOP, or $(K_{in} - K_{out})$. Clearly, from Equation (1.2), a current-account deficit need not produce an overall BOP deficit if it is offset to the same extent by a capital-account surplus. It is thus important, in seeking to understand the dynamics of SSA's external indebtedness between 1970 and 1985, to examine closely but separately trends in its capital and trade accounts. We begin with a theoretical exposition of the former.

The Capital Account

Let us suppose for the moment that an indebted African country's exchange rate is fixed, and that capital inflows are short- or long-term. *Long-term capital* consists principally of direct private investment (DPI)—i.e. the purchase or creation by foreigners of non-financial, productive real assets, such as mines, factories, plantations and the like—or portfolio investment (PI)—the sale of financial assets (such as bonds, equities and government securities) by citizens, agents or institutions of the country to raise foreign-exchange and, thereby, increase net foreign claims on the country. As financial capital markets in Africa are highly underdeveloped; and as African countries and institutions are not considered 'investment grade' material by the established international financial markets, PI has historically entailed a negligible amount of equity investment, but a significant amount of public-sector borrowing through the sale of government securities, and also direct private-sector borrowing (albeit with public guarantees) from abroad. On the whole, though, the non-borrowing component of PI in Africa's capital inflows has been on a very small scale indeed. That being the case, we may justifiably specify

$$K_{in} = DPI + B \qquad \ldots(1.3)$$

where B is total borrowing by both public and private sectors. When capital outflows are taken into account, we obtain the net capital inflows relation

$$Net\ K_{in} = DPI + net\ B \qquad \ldots(1.4)$$

which, from Equation (1.1), may be re-written as

$$Net\ K_{in} = \dot{R} - (X - M) \qquad \ldots(1.5)$$

From Equation (1.4), we may further re-write this as

$$Net\ B = \dot{R} - (X - M) - net\ DPI \qquad \ldots(1.6).$$

What Equation (1.6) says is that, with a fixed exchange rate, the country uses its external borrowing to shore up its foreign-exchange reserves, R; to finance its current-account or trade deficits, $-(X - M)$; to finance net capital outflows, $-net\ DPI$; or some combination of the three. The level of debt outstanding in any particular year, therefore, represents the cumulative impact of all past reserve replenishments, all previous trade deficits, and all capital outflows. In a simpler interpretation, the relation can be seen as representing the country's financing of its trade deficits, and its acquisition of foreign assets (via R and $-net\ DPI$). These foreign assets may be acquired by both the government (as when the central bank accumulates foreign-exchange reserves and other investments), or the private sector (through legitimate investments and bank accounts, or illegally through capital flight. In comparison with Latin America, though, the extent of capital flight from Africa, albeit difficult to accurately measure, is not that significant, the notoriety of a handful of eggregious cases, like Nigeria and Zaire, notwithstanding)[26].

It is within such a framework of SSA's BOP dynamics that its debt acquisition must be analyzed and understood. Clearly, meaningful solutions to the ensuing crises of debt-and- development cannot be devised without a prior interrogation of the policies that were designed to influence reserves, trade imbalances and capital outflows in, at least, the 1970s. Equally indispensable to this project, it will subsequently be shown, is an appreciation of the political culture and institutional frameworks within which these policies and decisions were/are made—really, the societal matrix (political, ethnic, historical, cultural) which defined the rationality or irrationality of what, on the surface, appeared at the time to be purely economic and public-policy decisions. These and related issues are tackled more comprehensively in Chapter Two.

The Current Account

For the overwhelming majority of SSA's debtor-nations, the accumulation of foreign debt was a direct result of persistent BOP deficits arising from a quarter-century of post-independence development capital inflows (from, mainly, private and multilateral sources) and, more significantly, from persistent current-account deficits. This latter, of course, is neither unusual nor historically unique: all countries, including the United States, in the early infancy of their development, tend to rack up large structural trade deficits, which are then financed with savings from abroad. The extent to which any country can continue to finance these current-account imbalances without significantly altering its exchange-rate and other macroeconomic policies, depends on its success in attracting foreign capital, and on how low it is willing to draw down its foreign-exchange reserves. And it is clear from Equation (1.4) that the borrowing component of net capital inflows can be reduced in direct proportion as the country's success in attracting foreign direct private or equity investment, or in reversing capital flight.

Direct foreign investment in SSA has traditionally meant multinational corporate (MNC) investment. Given the history of multinationals as part of the colonial, and post-colonial, economic and political machinery, many African governments in the 1970s were averse to openly courting them, or indirectly doing so by producing the domestic macroeconomic conditions that would attract their investment. Many MNCs therefore came to view the African economies as being over-regulated; as lacking in workable market structures and other requisite social institutions that enhance profit making; as poorly managed by overly intrusive governments which were politically unpredictable; and as being generally uncreditworthy. DPI therefore was, at best, erratic in the decade beginning in the mid-1970s, and has followed a downward secular trend, generally, to this day.

For the few African countries that actively sought MNC investment, fierce competition amongst them, and between them and all the other countries (including those of the industrialized North) for the same dwindling quantum of investment capital, especially in the aftermath of the Mexican near-default of 1982, has produced a dizzying array of generous tax and other incentives which could only lead, in the long run, to yet more massive outflows of capital from Africa. Clearly, for these countries, the operative principle is that the long-run economic and political costs of MNC investment can only be avoided by accepting the alternative costs of high current indebtedness, and lost employment or income opportunities in the short term. Alas, all through the history of post-independence Africa, it has been just this sort of pragmatism, myopic as it may appear to some, that has helped create an institutionalized propensity to incur external debts. Perhaps this is a reflection or manifestation of the oft-touted political 'softness' of the African state, which we will have occasion to examine extensively in due course.

But even when these imbalances are financed through net capital inflows, there is a limit on the debt component of these inflows. In the course of financing current-account deficits, continuing additions to the existing stock of foreign debt become economically untenable if the annual interest payments on the debt absorb an increasingly large proportion of the foreign-exchange earned by the country through its exports. It is in this sense that a country's *debt-service ratio*—the proportion of export earnings that goes to service the debt—is a critical benchmark for assessing its optimal debt-carrying capacity.

The exact relationship between export earnings, interest payments, debt-service capacity and, therefore, domestic economic solvency and potential, will be detailed in a subsequent section; but there is obviously a close connection between current-account deficits and the efficacy of domestic economic performance. If we view exports as domestic production not consumed domestically, and imports as domestic consumption not produced domestically, we can express this in a Keynesian, aggregate demand 'leakages-injections' equilibrium relation:

$$X + I + G = M + S + T \qquad ...(1.7)$$

where X and M are as previously defined; I represents total domestic investment expenditure; S, gross domestic savings; G, government expenditure; and T, the total tax revenue.

This may be re-written as

$$(X - M) = (S + T) - (G + I) \qquad ...(1.8)$$

or

$$(X - M) = (S - I) + (T - G) \qquad ...(1.9).$$

Equation (1.9) tells us that a trade deficit $(-(X - M))$, in the external sector, may be reflected *domestically* either in a fiscal deficit $(-(T - G))$ and/or as an insufficiency of domestic savings $(-(S - I))$. In other words, a current-account disequilibrium is manifested simultaneously as a disequilibrium in the domestic sector. Further, Equation (1.8) indicates that if external debts are acquired for the purpose of financing current-account deficits $(-(X - M))$, the deficits will persist as long as domestic spending $(I + G)$ exceeds domestic saving $(-(S + T))$, where S is gross domestic voluntary saving and T is, essentially, total 'forced' domestic saving. And if the private sector does generate *net* savings, (i.e. if $S > I$), Equation (1.9) further tells us that the current-account deficits will persist (or occur, if there was not one before) if the public sector deficit $(T - G)$ is larger than the net savings $(S - I)$. If there is a savings gap $(S < I)$, however, the budgetary imbalance can only be financed through external borrowing. Thus "annual domestic savings shortfalls and budget deficits will continue to be mirrored in ongoing current account deficits and, *ceteris paribus*, will produce a continuing need to borrow", thereby incrementally adding to the stock of debt each year in which these conditions obtain.[27] Clearly, from Equation (1.9) a balanced domestic budget is not a prerequisite for a current-account balance. A fiscal deficit can co-exist with a trade balance as long as there is net domestic private savings of the same magnitude as the budget shortfall.

For the overwhelming majority of SSAn countries over the period with which this work is concerned, and perhaps in the entire post-independence era, low domestic savings rates, given low incomes, consistently meant that $S < I$. At the same time, the combination of these low income levels and the absence of substantial private "engines of growth", of both domestic and foreign origin, made the public sector the single most important economic agent by default. Government spending thus consistently outran tax revenues. The resulting annual domestic savings shortfalls and budget deficits, in combination with the massive post-independence import-spending spree for "rapid development", were manifested also as ongoing current-account deficits, necessitating resort to massive and sustained external borowing. And, as the theory would predict, it was these yearly additions to existing debt that caused Africa's debt to grow at some 20% annually, on the average, over the period. We will return to the specifics of the debt dynamics in Chapter Four.

Equation (1.9) also suggests the rationale, at least at the level of theory, for much of the policy prescriptions included in IMF-type structural adjustment packages (SAPs) designed primarily to correct external disequilibria. The clear lesson from the analysis above is that domestic macroeconomic policy *does* influence trade or external-sector performance. Thus, for instance, monetary and fiscal policies, because they by-and-large determine the level of domestic output and therefore national income, indirectly determine the level of imports. But they also affect nominal interest rates and domestic inflation, hence real interest rates. Any differentials between domestic and international real interest rates influence the current account through their impact on domestic savings, investment (and therefore general macroeconomic buoyancy), and the real exchange rate, which latter, of course, largely determines the proportions of domestic consumption expenditure that goes to imports or home-goods.[28]

But much of the IMF adjustment package is a reprise, as O'Cleireacain has argued, of Harry Johnson's 1958 prescription for removing trade deficits, the interminable debates about "conditionality" being no more than arguments over which particular mix of policies would achieve the purpose.[29] Johnson argued that current account deficits will be eliminated if domestic absorption were brought down to the level of domestic production, while the production of tradeables is substituted for that of home goods. Similarly, the consumption of home goods must be substituted for that of imports.[30] And even though these are still, in the main, the objectives of modern SAPs, their near-fanatic fixation with domestic fiscal balances as *the* cure for the external imbalance would appear theoretically unwarranted and even heavy-handed, on the ground. For, as Equation (1.9) shows, *a balanced budget is not necessarily consistent with current-account balances*. And if many of the causative factors of chronic current-account imbalances (e.g. overvalued real-exchange rates caused by high rates of inflation with no commensurate and offsetting devaluation of the currency nor interest rate increases; improvements in real GNP in an economy that runs structural trade deficits; inappropriate levels of real interest rates; etc.) are structural in nature, then to expect a low-income, heavily-indebted country not to run budget deficits, and to meet its domestic investment financing needs out of domestic saving, is politically and economically unrealistic, and potentially punitive in impact. If, on the other hand, these imbalances can be shown definitively to be due to gross mis-pricing in the credit, foreign-exchange and real-goods markets, then the "structural adjustment" package, to the extent that it aims at restoring proper market functioning and sectoral balance generally, may be fully justified on its face. The analytical difficulty is in ascertaining, for any particular indebted nation, and to a credible degree of reliability, whether its external disequilibria stem largely from structural or policy-induced market conditions.

In the SSAn context, the application of these price-driven Johnsonian reform policies to the debtor-nations in the 1980s tended to, in the short run at least, exacerbate the domestic economic crisis even as it improved somewhat the external imbalances.[31] This would suggest, *prima facie*, that the basis of Africa's debt-cum-development crises may be more firmly ensconced in its social *structures*, economic and political, than in dysfunctional markets, though, of course, the latter's influence can hardly be discounted or seriously questioned. It would also suggest, secondly, that ordinary BOP analysis and, more importantly, the adjustment or corrective policies logically issuing from it, may not be adequate to the task of understanding the structural particularities of the African economy that appeared to be driving the external-debt and internal-development crises. Thus, in addition to critically evaluating the logic and policy implications of the orthodox BOP analysis in Africa's debt crisis, we also examine the role of these structural and institutional uniquenesses in producing and reproducing the crisis, and argue, in fact, that they are of greater analytical and policy importance than ordinary market forces in the pursuit of optimal solutions to the crises. At the level of policy, then, long-run institutional and structural economic change is favoured against the current IMF-type orthodoxy that stems from the analysis above, and which essentially has it that disequilibria in the external sector are always and invariably due to domestic excess demand, and therefore correctable with contractionary stabilization policies. In addition, we view the policies of the new orthodoxy that rationalize the functioning of market forces across all sectors of the economy, but especially in the credit, labour and external sectors, as being of equally questionable remedial value for Africa's debt crisis.

Africa's structural uniquenesses suggest to us that improving export performance through better trade terms and output increases; increasing food supplies through measures that will improve supply elasticities in the agriculture sector, in particular, and of aggregate supply, in general; promoting regional economic cooperation; promoting decentralized popular participation in politics as a matter of right; recognizing and exploiting the developmental efficacy of ethnic allegiances and cultural pluralisms; introducing a more equitable and less predatory 'culture of development' in the conduct of inter-country relations; etc. are essential prerequisites for the eventual effectiveness of the price-based reforms that the new orthodoxy advocates. In a sense, then, these structural reforms are logically prior to the market reforms in solving the continent's debt-cum-development crises. Indeed, the latter, in the absence of the former, are only fine-tuning essentially moribund economies *at their margins*. The name "structural adjustment" is thus particularly apt, as the existing structures are kept even more firmly in place by these policies that only "adjust" them on their peripherae but hardly *transforms* them at their core. Yet, it is the manner of structuration of these economies that is, more often than not, at the source of much of the recurrent crises.

Debt-Carrying Capacity

As was mentioned earlier, rising external indebtedness appears to accompany early economic development, even in the presence of sound trade and domestic macroeconomic policies. Indeed, there appears to be identifiable and predictable BOP stages that countries go through in the course of their development. With rising debt, however, comes increasing debt service obligations, and the size of the country's debt is often effectively constrained by its debt-service capacity. Once debt growth surpasses this debt-carrying capacity, a "debt crisis" can be said to have set in. It is thus not the quantum or size of the debt that determines whether a country is experiencing a debt crisis; it is its capacity to carry or service that debt.[32] This does not imply that the size of the debt does not matter when, after all, it may determine carrying capacity; it is only to assert that it is the carrying capacity that, ultimately, counts in determining crisis points.

In the bid to ascertain what its optimal debt-carrying capacity is, Africa's debt crisis has been popularly analyzed as a transfer problem similar to the German transfer problem associated with its post-World War I reparation payments. The transfer burden proper, in this view, consists in the main of the current-account problem of making the payment in foreign currency. The extent of the burden is measured by the debt-service ratio (DSR), the percentage of foreign-exchange earned through exports that goes towards debt service.

But there is an additional, and arguably more insidious, problem with debt service which is logically prior to the transfer problem. It is the domestic *budgetary* problem of collecting in local currency the resources to be transferred in foreign exchange to the creditors. This budget burden is measured as the ratio of debt service to GDP. In essence, it indicates the extent to which the domestic economy has to be squeezed to successfully make the transfer. The impact of both burdens on the African economy is generally deflationary, much as Keynes had argued in 1929 in the case of Germany.[33] But it is the domestic budgetary burden that reveals that, in the case of Africa, the root of the external debt crisis lies in the insolvency of the domestic economy itself; hence the emphasis in this work on looking for lasting solutions in the internal structure of the African economy. Africa's debt crisis of the 1980s, in other words, more so than a mere short-run, temporary and episodic liquidity or transfer debacle, was actually an endemic problem of structural disintegration which manifested itself as long-run economic insolvency. The liquidity or transfer burden is only symptomatic of this deeper problem.

As O'Cleireacain reminds us, it was Avramovic's team, using a modified Harrod-Domar growth model, that seminally showed in a World Bank study that a steady-state solution to a constant debt-to-GDP ratio is a function of the interest rate, the savings rate, the rate of growth of GDP, and the incremental capital-output ratio.[34] This model was later modified by others to show that debt-financed development is really " a race" between debt and income, with both variables growing at compound rates. In the most recent discussions of debt-carrying capacity and the probability of country defaults, William Cline has been consistent in linking countries' debt-service capacities with their debt-service ratios.[35] Reproduced below is a modification of an adaptation of the Cline model of debt dynamics and optimal debt-carrying capacity, the original adaptation being attributed by O'Cleireacain to Simonsen.[36]

Suppose G is the 'resource gap' in a country's BOP (i.e. the non-interest current-account deficit less direct investment inflows plus capital outflows); $G > 0$ indicates a resource gap, and $G < 0$ a surplus on the non-debt components of the BOP. Suppose, also, that D is the level of total foreign debt net of foreign-exchange reserves; r, the nominal interest rate on the debt; X, the value of exports; and x, the growth rate of exports. We may then define the debt-to-export ratio, D/X, as z; and the resource gap as a ratio of annual exports, G/X, as g.

Changes in the debt stock over time may be shown by a differential equation that indicates how changes in the level of indebtedness relate to interest payments on existing debt, or to additional financing requirements for any resource gaps in the BOP. Thus

$$\dot{D} = rD + G \qquad \qquad \text{...(1.10)}$$

where the overdot denotes time derivatives. Clearly, a debtor-country has discretionary influence only over G, since D is the sum of past revenue gaps and r depends largely on the monetary policies of the Northern-creditor countries. The rate of growth of the country's indebtedness is thus

$$\left(\frac{\dot{D}}{D}\right) = r + \left(\frac{G}{D}\right) = r + \left(\frac{g}{z}\right) \quad \text{...(1.11)}$$

The growth rate of the debt-export ratio, $\dot{z}/z$, is $\dot{D}/D - \dot{X}/X$, as $z = D/X$. Substituting Equation (1.11) into this expression, we obtain

$$\left(\frac{\dot{z}}{z}\right) = \left(r + \frac{g}{z}\right) - x.$$

Hence

$$\dot{z} = z\left(r + \frac{g}{z}\right) - xz$$

$$= rz + g - xz$$

$$= (r - x)z + g \qquad \ldots(1.12)$$

Equation (1.12) shows how the "race" between nominal interest rates and export growth rates determines whether a country's debt-to-export ratio falls or rises. Clearly, if $g > 0$ and $r > x$ (i.e. if there is both a resource gap and an export growth that lags behind interest rates), $\dot{z} > 0$ and the debt-export ratio will rise sharply. Technically, a "debt crisis" has begun. Conversely, if $g < 0$ and $r < x$, $\dot{z}$ may decline or hold steady $(\dot{z} \leq 0)$. In other words, "a continual resource gap is consistent with stable or declining debt-export ratios if exports sufficiently outpace interest rates to make z less than or equal to zero."[37] If export growth does not keep up with interest on existing debt (i.e. if $r > x$), a surplus on the non-debt component of the BOP $(g < 0)$ is necessary to prevent the debt-export ratio from rising. Thus, to sustain a resource gap $(g > 0)$ and hold the ratio of debt-to-exports steady $(\dot{z} = 0)$, exports must win the race against interest rates: from Equation (1.12), $\dot{z} = 0$ if, and only if,

$$g = (x - r)z \qquad \ldots(1.13)$$

If export growth lags behind interest rates, there must be a surplus in the BOP $(g < 0)$ to keep the debt-to-exports ratio from rising. A debt crisis is averted, therefore if, and only if, the race between export growth and interest on outstanding debt is not won by the latter (i.e. if $x \geq r$). When exports lag behind interest obligations $(x < r)$, a resource or BOP surplus $(g < 0)$ is necessary to keep debt payments sustainable. Otherwise a debt crisis sets in.

In SSA, the growth rate of exports consistently lagged behind that of the external debt over much of the period of this investigation (see Table 1.7). Hence the crisis cannot be said to be a temporary liquidity bottleneck or a passing transfer debacle. The factors that appear to reproduce these debt dynamics appear to be endemic to the economy. Merely seeking to ease the liquidity/transfer problem may not provide any real relief to these countries when long-term structural insolvency— their inability to produce the requisite level of resources domestically to be transferred to their external creditors—appears to be the culprit here. In short, the very structural underdevelopment of the African economy is what needs to be tackled for the debt crisis to be adequately resolved, since it cannot, in any case, be isolated from the larger, underlying underdevelopment crisis as such. The one determines and fashions the dynamics of the other. They are a crisis-couple, a twin crisis, not analytically separable one from the other.

TABLE 1.7
SSA Debt Dynamics, 1970-1986

	Total External Debt-to-Export Ratio (%)	Growth Rate of Exports (%)	Growth Rate of Debt (%)
1970	60	6.8	6.6
1980	97.2	2.9	21.9
1983	224.2	-14.9	12.4
1984	214.4	9.3	4.5
1985	243.7	1.8	15.7
1986	336.7	-14.6	17.9

Sources: World Bank, *Analysis and Summary Tables, Vol. 1*, 1990 c: pp. 112 and 130; and 1991 b: p. 124.

Notes

1. World Bank, **Financing Adjustment with Growth in Sub-Saharan Africa, 1986-1990** (Washington, D.C.: April 1986), Table A.1, p. 52 and Table A.2, p. 54.
2. World Bank, op.cit., Table 12, p. 78 and Table 19, p. 85; see, also, World Bank, **Price Prospects for Major Primary Commodities, 1984** (Washington, D.C.: 1983), and Kathie Krumm, **The External Debt of Sub-Saharan Africa** (World Bank Staff Working Papers No.741, Washington, D.C., 1985), p. 47.
3. World Bank, **Financing Adjustment...**, Table A.1, p. 53.
4. World Bank, **Financing Adjustment...**, Table A.3, p. 55.
5. For a comprehensive view of the terms of bilateral and commercial bank reschedulings see, in addition, Kathie Krumm, op.cit., Table 10, pp. 54-56.
6. Krumm, op.cit., Table 12, p.58. See, also, W ·ld Bank, **Financing Adjustment...**, Table 17, p. 83.
7. See Tables 4.1, 4.2 and 4.3 in Chapter Four.
8. See World Bank, **Financing Adjustment...**, Table 9, p. 75.
9. World Bank, **Financing Adjustment...**, Table 2, p. 68. See, also, Table 7.
10. Ibid.
11. World Bank, **Financing Adjustment...**, Table 7, p. 73. See, also, Tables 13, 14 and 16.
12. Ibid.
13. World Bank, **Debt Tables, 1988-89** (Washington, D.C.: April 1988) various Tables.
14. Special Report on Banking and Finance, **Africa Economic Digest** (September 1986), p. 2.
15. Cline argues this point convincingly in W.R. Cline, International Debt: Analysis, Experience and Prospects, **Journal of Development Planning**, No. 16 (1985). Extrapolating from his calculations, I have recalculated Africa's debt estimates by causal factor as follows:

    (1) oil-price shocks (1973, 1979): 48%
    (2) world recession (1981-83)   :   24%
    (3) "excess" real interest rates (i.e. real interest rates above their historical average):   8%
    (4) decline in the terms-of-trade :   16%
    (5) decline in trade volume :   4%.

16. See, for instance, Robert Grosse, Resolving Latin America's Transfer Problem, **World Economy**, Vol. 11, No. 3 (Sept. 1988), pp. 417-436; and Seamus O'Cleireacain, **Third World Debt and International Public Policy** (N.Y.: Praeger, 1990), ch. 2.

17. The increasing importance of variable interest rates in Africa's external debt structure also stemmed from the fact that Africa, in the period 1970-1985, did more debt reschedulings than any other region of the Third World. As those restructurings are done at the going rates, usually a mark-up over LIBOR, they introduce a debt-service obligation higher, ultimately, than that which was rescheduled.

18. See World Bank, **Developing Country Debt: Implementing the Concensus** (Washington, D.C.: Feb. 1987), pp. 29-43.

19. See, for instance, Jaime de Pinies, Debt Sustainability and Overadjustment, **World Development**, Vol. 17, No. 1 (1989), pp. 29-43.

20. In arguments relating, perhaps obscurely, to the definition of the term "debt crisis", some notable economists of the North have been arguing since the late 1980s that the debt crisis, insofar as it threatens the stability of the exposed financial houses, is actually over, presumably because they have made adequate provisions through their loan-loss reserves. (See, for instance, Jeffery Sachs, The Debt Crisis at a Turning Point, **Challenge** (May-June, 1988), pp. 17-26). This is a premature celebration, however. The illusion of the death of the crisis stems from the confused usage of a term that has two interdependent, though nominally distinct, arms. As Tim Congdon has argued, 'debt crisis' refers to (1) the problem of excessive debt acquisition by developing countries (and others), and (2) the threat to commercial banks should these borrowers default. Obviously the second problem is automatically solved when the first is. But it hardly follows that the first will disappear if the second is solved; or that the continued presence of the first, once the second is solved, will not reignite the second problem anew, in some fashion. (See Tim Congdon, op. cit., (London: Basil Blackwell, 1988), p.198).

21. See World Bank, **Financing Adjustment...**, Table A.2, p. 54.

22. See Jaime de Piniès, op. cit.

23. See, for instance, World Bank, **Accelerated Development in Sub-Saharan Africa** (Washington, D.C.: 1982), popularly known as the Berg Report; and Bruce Bartlett, The State and the Market in Sub-Saharan Africa, **World Development**, Vol. 12, No. 3 (Sept. 1989), pp. 293-314.

24. We are following Krugman's simple expostulation of the model in P. Krugman, **Has the Adjustment Process Worked**? (Washington, D.C.: Institute for International Economics, 1991), pp. 6-7 and 51-53.

25. See O'Cleireacain, op cit., ch. 2.

26. Given the statistical negligibility of capital flight from Africa, we do not discuss it here to any appreciable extent. The interested reader may wish to see S. O'Cleireacain, op. cit., ch. 2, pp. 26-32 for a focussed discussion of the topic.

27. S. O'Cleireacain, op. cit., p. 21.

28. Ibid.

29. Ibid., citing Harry Johnson, Towards a General Theory of the Balance of Payments, in Harry G. Johnson, **International Trade and Economic Growth** (London: Allen and Unwin, 1958), pp. 153-168.

30. Ibid.

31. See UN Economic Commission for Africa, **African Alternative Framework to Structural Adjustment Programmes for Socio-Economic Recovery and Transformation (AAF-SAP)**, E/ECA/CM.15/6/Rev.3 (Addis Ababa: ECA, April 10, 1989). The following are also of interest in assessing the effectiveness of the neo-liberalist reform policies: Trevor Parfitt, Lies, Damned Lies and Statistics: The World Bank/ECA Structural Adjustment Controversy, **Review of African Political Economy**, No. 47 (Spring 1990), pp. 134-35; Robin King and Michael Robinson, Assessing Structural Adjustment Programs: A Summary of Country Experience, in Weeks, John, ed., **Debt Disaster? Banks, Governments and Multilaterals Confront the Crisis** (N.Y.: NYU Press, 1989), pp. 110-115; many of the pieces in Cornia, G.A., Jolly, R. and Stewart, F., eds., **Adjustment with a Human Face: Protecting the Vulnerable and Promoting Growth, Vol. 1 & 2** (Oxford: Clarendon Press, 1987); and Bonnie Campbell and John Loxley, eds., **Structural Adjustment in Africa** (N.Y.: St. Martin's Press, 1989).

32. Thus, even though the U.S., since the last quarter of 1985, has become the largest debtor-nation in the world, with an external debt, at the end of 1989 of nearly $700 billion or six times Brazil's, it does not—yet—suffer from a debt crisis of the sort we associate with a Brazil.

33. J.M. Keynes, **The Economic Consequences of the Peace** (London: Macmillan, 1919), and his, The German Transfer Problem, **Economic Journal** (March 1929).

34. D. Avramovic et. al., **Economic Growth and External Debt** (Washington, D.C.: World Bank, 1964), as cited by O'Cleireacain, op. cit., p. 44.

35. William Cline, **International Debt: Systemic Risk and Policy Response** (Washington,D.C.: Institute of International Economics, 1983).

36. Mario Simonsen, The Developing-Country Debt Problem, in G. Smith and J. Cuddington, eds., **International Debt and the Developing Countries** (Washington, D.C.: World Bank, 1985), pp. 101-128, as cited by O'Cleireacain, op. cit., p. 44.

37. O'Cleireacain, op. cit., p. 46.

Chapter 2

Distal Causes of
Africa's Debt Crisis

2.1 The Internal Structure

The argument is made in Chapter 1 that Africa's external debt crisis of the 1980s, far from being a passing liquidity or transfer debacle, was actually a much deeper-rooted case of systemic economic insolvency. It could, therefore, not have been cured by marginal adjustments to the economies as they were (and are) structured, but by a complete transformation of the systems of production, distribution and politics informing African policy making and economic behaviour. In essence, nothing short of a *new culture of development* would have sufficed to ameliorate the crisis. This means that the entire corpus of economic development theory as we know it, and especially the practices it has engendered in Africa, need a most radical rethinking; as, indeed, do the remedial policies popularly proposed and implemented by both the debtor- and creditor-nations. This chapter is intended to be a prelude to such a critique.

The first section seeks to formalize the pertinent characteristics of the 'typical' African economy that make it a sub-optimal income producer, and which therefore leave it vulnerable to the vagaries of external developments. The object here is to identify what structural underdevelopment in the African context consists of, and why such an economy can suffer a grave debt crisis even when its debt obligation is relatively small.

An equally important aspect of the internal structure of the African economy, quite indispensable to our understanding of the deeper causes of its crises, is the type of politics practiced formally at the level of the state. The implications of this peculiar brand of politics for external debt accumulation is thus also examined. The argument is made that the structures and practices of both economics and politics in Africa tend to exacerbate the dynamics of the joint crisis of debt and underdevelopment, leaving few, if any, viable institutional checks against policy-induced external indebtedness. In consequence, the call is made for a complete restructuring of African politics to bring about systemic accountability, and to remove, thereby, the forces within the polity that make external debt acquisition a matter of political (and even ethnic) survival for African governments.

As important as the internal structure of politics and economics in shaping the internal dynamics of the crises are forces external to Africa that help shape the course of development policy itself. Foremost among these are the development paradigms emanating from the Euro-American social sciences that have provided the theoretical bases for development practice since the second world war. These paradigms are critically examined in the third section of the chapter, not merely to establish their culpability in making Africa debt-prone but, more importantly, in order to argue for a new theoretical basis for development practice in Africa. The objective of this chapter is, in short, to show how deeply entrenched the major causes of Africa's debt-cum-development crises are; where they may originate (from within or outside the continent); and hence the need for a different culture of development if we are to achieve an efficacious resolution of the crisis *at its source*.

2.2   A Model of the Structural Peculiarities of the African Economy

The model presented here is a descriptive model highlighting the structural uniquenesses of the representative African economy. It follows closely Kaushik Basu's (1984) adaptation of J.M. Flemming's original (1955) model, both of which are erected on some of the key concepts seminally developed in the classic literature of traditional economic development theory by the likes of Nurkse, Leibenstein, Harrod and Scitovsky.[1] One major conclusion to be drawn from this model is that the typical SSAn economy is characterised by a "poverty trap under Nurksian equilibrium", in which resource unemployment, and therefore sub-optimal national income generation, are more often than less the norm; and which tends to reproduce the existing state of economic affairs despite the many, and oftentimes quite drastic, shocks that it receives from within and/or without.

Thus the African economy, in its chronic state of poverty and resource unemployment, appears to contain within it forces that are capable of restoring the existing macroeconomic conditions following a small disturbance. Or, to paraphrase Nurkse, there is "a circular constellation of forces tending to act and react upon one another in such a way as to keep a poor country in a state of poverty."[2] This consistent reproduction of sub-optimal resource employment and income generation inexorably results in a debt crisis whenever the external debt grows at a nominally higher rate than income does. In its turn the debt crisis, thusly initiated, exacerbates the viciousness of the poverty cycle.

The policies of the new orthodoxy that were deployed in the early 1980s to stem the resultant debt-cum-development crises appeared incapable of doing it, mainly because they were, as argued previously, *marginal* solutions being asked to resolve essentially *structural* problems. Recent empirical studies suggest that the three principal prongs of this new orthodoxy—currency devaluation, general budgetary austerity and economic liberalization—tended to exacerbate the poverty that underlay the crisis, thus potentially reproducing the crisis in a more virulent strain than before. Specifically, these policies are shown to have resulted in, for instance, "over-adjustment" in Africa's economies; i.e. they led to unwarranted curbs in imports of crucial consumption and investment goods which induced further reductions in production and employment. These cuts, in turn, resulted in further decreases in income as employment, private spending and public spending all fell simultaneously.[3]

Clearly, as production and employment, and therefore income, all fell, a country's ability to service its debt—the key rationale behind the neo-orthodox stabilization—was threatened anew, ironically by the very results of the remedial strategy. Even where austerity succeeded in boosting public saving, domestic production was still compromised as the savings were used to satisfy external obligations, not to boost local investment.

It would thus seem that the neo-orthodox debt-relief strategy, contrary to its stated objectives, actually deepens, at least in the medium term, the structural constraints that lead to the poor economic performance that is behind the crisis in the first place. In other words, it exacerbates the underdevelopment crisis, which aggravates the debt crisis, which in turn deepens the underdevelopment crisis, then the debt crisis,...in a vicious and ever-widening circle of low-income generation and unmeetable debt-service obligations.

A second conclusion of the model is that these structural impediments to sustained growth can be overcome with "balanced growth" policies of the sort Nurkse argued forcefully for in 1953, policies that ensure complementarity between indigenous resources, domestic production and domestic consumption. The model suggests that an economy whose growth is synchronised across many, if not all, sectors may be less prone to repeated *systemic* failure, and may therefore offer the best long-term check against phenomena like external debt crises of the sort this work is concerned with. This is spelt out more fully in the sixth chapter.

A Theory of Chronic Poverty and Systemic Stagnation

The phenomenon of poverty/underdevelopment appears to have a tendency to reproduce itself with little apparent difficulty on the African continent. There are easily identifiable indicators of this phenomenon, though they acquire different manifestations of form in different countries, and even eras and historical conjunctures. Persistently high resource un- or under-employment, with all it implies about the economy's income-generating capabilities, is the most common of these. And whereas in the industrialized market economies the chronicity of extremely high unemployment and poverty are attenuated somewhat by counter-cyclical macroeconomic (and other social) policies judiciously and discretionarily applied, stagnation appears to have settled in for the count in SSA. An understanding of why this is so is an important prerequisite to the eradication of the forces that precipitate the crises that the sub-continent goes through with some regularity, and it should be the proper focus not only of any analysis towards solving the debt crisis, but of any economic analysis of Africa in general.

The study of economic structures that breed recurring poverty has a long and varied pedigree, none of which has had Africa *per se* as its subject (as contrasted to its object) of inquiry. Any application of these analyses to Africa's problems have thus largely been coincidental, a side-effect of studies done on other economies exhibiting at some time in their history characteristics similar to those found in contemporary Africa. It is perhaps for these and such reasons that the traditional economic development policies have had such an unenviable performance record on the African continent.

The established canon of neo-classical economic development theory began with Rosenstein-Rodan's 1943 research into the causes of stagnation in southern and eastern Europe.[4] In the decade or so following this work, a rich plethora of seminal works were published, virtually establishing (while stylizing) the field of development economics. Key among these were the works of Singer, Scitovsky, Nurkse, Lewis, Domar and Flemming, from which emerged such concepts as "vicious circle of poverty", "big push" and "balanced growth", among others, which came to constitute the syntactic underpinnings of the development economist's language, and the bases of endless debate and contention among theorists and practitioners alike.[5]

For the purposes of the task here at hand, one of the more pertinent conceptual gems from this literature is Nurkse's observation that if an economy persists in its state of underdevelopment despite the many (and sometimes quite drastic) shocks that it receives, it may not be unreasonable to hypothesize that that state of underdevelopment may reflect a state of equilibrium for that economy. This by no means implies that the economy is stuck in this position in some long-term sense, but that there appears to be forces within it, or in interaction with it from without, which are capable of restoring the previous state-of-affairs following a small disturbance, or making it difficult for the economy to move forward from its new position attendant upon such disturbance. Thus a "vicious circle", made up of Nurkse's "circular constellation of forces", seems to be at play here, helping to consistently reproduce a level of poverty and sub-optimal resource employment aptly described elsewhere as a "low-level equilibrium trap."[6]

The characterization of African economies as being in a state of equilibrium has generated much consternation among development practitioners and theorists on/of the continent, ostensibly owing to what the term 'equilibrium' implies about the hopefulness of transcending the seemingly intractable poverty that has gripped the

continent.[7] But the equation of 'equilibrium' with 'stasis' that
undergirds the criticism is not fully warranted, the soundness of its
general thrust notwithstanding. First, it is an equilibrium only insofar
as the economy tends to largely remain put once there. Secondly,
and this is a reflection of the first, small shocks, even when applied
persistently, seem to have a marginal impact on the existing state-of-
affairs or, if the impact is significant, it tends to be of short duration,
and therefore yields little systemic transformation. But, thirdly, the
description of this equilibrium as a poverty trap does suggest, in the
manner of all traps, that it is conceivable to escape and transform the
situation. And therein lies the usefulness and appropriateness of the
concept of "low-level equilibrium trap" in the description of SSA's
economic structures.

Some of the more salient features of the low-level equilibrium
economy is best illustrated with an example. Consider a simplified
version of the Ricardian (and classical, generally) doctrine of
subsistence wages.[8] It is based on a theory of endogenous population
growth erected on two propositions: that in economies of low per
capita income (1) the growth of per capita income above subsistence
leads inexorably to population growth; conversely, (2) its fall puts
downward pressure on population. The reasons for (1) include
declining mortality rates through better diets, health care, etc., but
also volitional increases in fertility. These two propositions, taken
together, illustrate the poverty trap admirably.

Suppose an initial equilibrium at subsistence income. By our
definition, any small disturbance will generate counteractive forces
that move the economy back to subsistence. Clearly, even as per
capita income remains unchanged after the shock, *national* income
and population may well change between the initial and new
equilibrium. In other words, the equilibrium underlying the poverty
trap is unstable. Leibenstein describes it as a "quasi-stable
equilibrium", by which he means an equilibrium at which, after a
shock, some elements return to their original states even as others
move to new positions and levels.[9] Following Leibenstein, an
economy in a poverty trap is described here as an economy in quasi-
stable equilibrium, with (its low) per capita income as one of its
more stable variables.

It is important to note that this quasi-stability is a local, not global,
phenomenon, in that the two initial propositions would cease to hold

if per capita income were to rise above a certain critical level. In other words, a thrust sufficiently large to push the economy out of its poverty trap does exist, but would require a "critical minimum effort" to achieve it, as long as that effort serves to push per capita income above that critical level that initiates and reproduces the sub-optimal performance cycle. Thus, even though it is low per capita income that initiates the forces that keep per capita income low—via propositions (1) and (2) above—in the vicious circle of poverty theory, the 'trap' is not, as is often assumed, unassailable. The last chapter of this work looks at possible ways out of this trap of economic stagnation for Africa.

Balanced Growth and the Theory of Stagnation

There is a supply-side corollary to the 'vicious circle' theory discussed above. It basically has it that capital deficiency tends to yield low income in developing economies, which in turn yields low savings, leading back again to limited investment and capital formation. Nurkse examines the low-level equilibrium trap from this vantage point of capital formation. He sees capital as, as it were, the mediating factor between secular stagnation on the demand side, and production. The supply of capital, he argues, governed as it is by the propensity to save, is inevitably constrained by the low levels of income in developing countries. Low income is, itself, a reflection of low productivity which, in turn, results from inadequate capital formation. Thus closes the circle on a sub-optimal income generation/capital formation economic system.

The demand for capital, he posits further, is governed by inducements to invest. But such incentives may be lacking due to the shallowness of the market—a reflection of the low levels of income consistent with the low productivity of the highly labour-intensive production structures of the economy. The low levels of capital formation and utilization, then, may itself be, at least partially, caused by the low inducement to invest. This closes the second circle: note that the two circles have one common characteristic, low productivity. (See diagram on next page).

Next, Nurkse points to the seeming paradox of his assertion that there is low demand for capital in these obviously capital-deficient economies. His attempt to unravel this takes the line that since these economies can ill-afford, if at all, the requisite capital stock, it has to be provided by external sources which have surplus capital to dispose of. As the bulk of these are private sources, there must be inducements for them to invest in these economies. The commonest inducement is the (Keynesian) expectation of sales of output, hence of profit generation. It is precisely at this juncture that there appears to be deficiencies in the demand for capital: the limited size of the local market, due to low per capita purchasing potential, is a disincentive to investment. But, more importantly, it is the inability of these low-income, low-productivity economies to generate the necessary complementarity in their production and consumption structures *across the economy* that provides the heaviest constraint on investment and, in turn, on sustained income generation and market deepening. Thus closes the third (and much widened) circle on the poverty trap. Note that the deficiency in demand is not a monetary but a real phenomenon. "If it were merely a deficiency of monetary demand, it could easily be remedied through monetary expansion; but the trouble lies deeper."[10]

Nurkse's Vicious Circle of Poverty

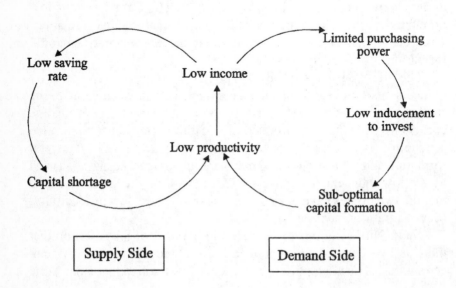

To illustrate the argument, consider a factory that wishes to expand output. Its purchases of additional inputs, including labour, will increase total income in the economy, including profits. Suppose the factory produced shirts. Given that consumers spend less than the total increase in their income on new shirts, clearly the increase in demand falls short of the increase in shirt production. Hence, all things being equal, the price of shirts must fall or, if the price is exogenously fixed, there will be an excess supply of shirts on the market. It is thus entirely plausible that the producer will find the expansion not economically rewarding, personally, causing some dampening of the expected system-wide multiplier effect. It is in this sense that limited market size (and depth) constrains investment expansion and income generation *for a given producer*.

Consider, in contrast, an expansion in the production of *all* commodities, without changing existing demand proportionalities. The expansion in each commodity will generate demand for other goods, hence a market for all goods. Thus the shallow market notwithstanding, the demand deficiency experienced by a single isolated producer vanishes if all producers synchronize their output expansion.[11] This is the concept of balanced growth: the necessity for market/sectoral complementarity in breaking the chronicity of stagnation in the developing economy. Note that this is nothing more than a restatement of the classical Law of Markets, whose bastardized offspring is the better-known Say's Law,[12] and which John Stuart Mill amply captures in these words:

> Every increase of production, if distributed without miscalculation among all types of produce in the proportion in which private interest will dictate, creates, or rather constitutes, its own demand.[13]

This is the manner in which balanced growth, in its many variants, has emerged from the vicious circle of poverty analysis, the implication for policy being that developing countries can only break the poverty deadlock if investment and production expansion are fairly (if not equally) distributed across all sectors.[14]

Balanced Growth and Walrasian Equilibrium

Nurkse's balanced growth theory may be summarized as follows: under some circumstances, there may be no gains to an individual producer from expanding output, owing to market shallowness, though all producers expanding output in tandem could deepen the market enough to expand both their gains and system-wide growth. For Nurkse this seeming paradox is what springs the trap that reproduces underdevelopment in Africa and elsewhere. Many of the key debates in the development literature, from the "big push" to "balanced/ unbalanced growth", have been in reaction to, and criticisms of, this seminal proposition of Nurkse's. It thus behooves us to examine the theoretical soundness of his argument against the claims that the structural problems that undergird Africa's debt crisis can be eliminated with policies that promote balanced growth and sectoral complementarity in the economy.

The critiques levelled at Nurkse appear to stem from the fact that his theory is read through Walrasian lenses, i.e. from the point of view of general equilibrium analytics.[15] The problem lies in juxtaposing Nurkse's proposition with the traditional welfare argument that, in a Walrasian world, every competitive equilibrium is Pareto-optimal.[16] Clearly if, in developing countries, an individual producer cannot profit from increasing output individually, but can if it is done collectively and system-wide, then the kind of equilibria possible are really sub-optimal—which, indeed was Scitovsky's conclusion in his 1954 Walrasian rendition of Nurkse.[17] In Nurkse's model, as was shown earlier, an individual producer contemplating output expansion immediately comes up against market limitations which, in an economy with flexible prices, could actually lead to a decline in the price of his/her product. In Walras' world prices are parametric, hence each individual producer need not worry about problems of insufficient demand. Nurkse's equilibrium, therefore, can be differentiated from Walras' in the assumption it makes about the options faced by each agent. Walras' world has been analyzed extensively. We attempt here to model Nurkse's.

Consider an economy with only two producers, each producing either an amount x_1 of good 1 or x_2 of good 2, and using labour as the only input. If the prices of the two goods are p_1 and p_2 respectively, then total income in the economy is

$$p_1 x_1 + p_2 x_2.$$

Let the marginal propensity to consume be the same across the economy, at c_1 and c_2 for goods 1 and 2 respectively, and let

$$c_1 + c_2 = 1.$$

The proportion of income spent on the ith good is

$$c_i(p_1 x_1 + p_2 x_2),$$

and the corresponding demand is

$$\frac{c_i(p_1 x_1 + p_2 x_2)}{p_i}.$$

The equilibrium condition for each good, equality between its supply and demand, therefore, is

$$\frac{c_1(p_1 x_1 + p_2 x_2)}{p_1} = x_1 \qquad ...(2.1)$$

$$\frac{c_2(p_1 x_1 + p_2 x_2)}{p_2} = x_2 \qquad ...(2.2).$$

Since prices are flexible, any quantity vector $X = (x_1, x_2)$ will give us the price vector $P = (p_1, p_2)$ from Equations (2.1) and (2.2). Since $c_2 = 1 - c_1$, whenever one equation is satisfied, so is the other. In similar fashion, it can be shown that if P satisfies Equation (2.1), any scalar multiple of P will also. In other words, Equation (2.1) only yields relative prices.

If, for convenience, the price vector is normalized such that

$$p_1 + p_2 = 1 \qquad ...(2.3)$$

then, from (2.1) and (2.3) we obtain

$$p_1 = p_1(X) = \frac{c_1 x_2}{(c_2 x_1 + c_1 x_2)}$$

and　　　　　　　　　　　　　　　　　　　　　　　　　　　　...(2.4)

$$p_2 = p_2(X) = \frac{c_2 x_1}{(c_2 x_1 + c_1 x_2)}.$$

This means that given a vector X, $p_1(X)$ and $p_2(X)$ are the prices that ensure that X is the amount of output demanded. Hence the vector

$$\{x_1, x_2, p_1(X), p_2(X)\}$$

will represent an equilibrium if x_1 and x_2 are the outputs of the two producers. The actual amounts they will supply, however, depends on the options open to them. This is precisely where Nurkse's differs from the standard Walrasian model.

If there existed an output vector $X^* = (x_1^*, x_2^*)$,

$$\{x_1^*, x_2^*, p_1(X^*), p_2(X^*)\}$$

will be a Walrasian equilibrium if producers were to treat prices as given at $p_1(X^*)$ and $p_2(X^*)$, and chose to optimally produce x_1 and x_2 quantities of the goods. If

$$(x_1, x_2) = (x_1^*, x_2^*),$$

then we have a Walras competitive equilibrium.[18]

　　Nurkse assumed that, starting at X^*, if more of a good is produced its price will fall (by just enough to clear the market), and that this informs the producer's decision to expand or not to expand production. On the other hand, if production falls, no significant price adjustment is expected. Thus the producer of, say good 2, supposes the price of good 2 depends on its output level in the following manner:

$$p_2 = f_2(x_2) = \begin{cases} p_2(X^*) & \text{if } x_2 \leq x_2{}^* \\[2em] \dfrac{c_2 x_1{}^*}{(c_2 x_1{}^* + c_1 x_2)} & \text{if } x_2 \geq x_2{}^* \end{cases} \qquad \dots(2.5)$$

which may be graphed as

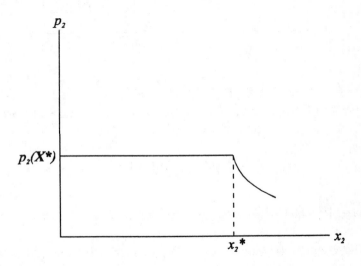

Similarly, for good 1,

$$p_1 = f_1(x_1) = \begin{cases} p_1(X^*) & \text{if } x_1 \leq x_1{}^* \\[2em] \dfrac{c_1 x_2{}^*}{(c_2 x_1 + c_1 x_2{}^*)} & \text{if } x_1 \geq x_1{}^* \end{cases} \qquad \dots(2.6)$$

which may also be graphed as

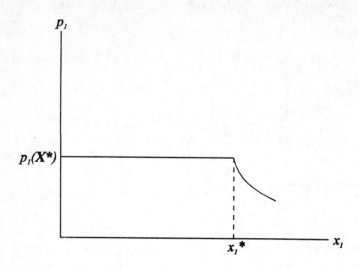

If, based on Equation (2.5), the ith producer still chooses to produce x_i^*, then

$$\{x_1^*, x_2^*, p_1(X^*), p_2(X^*)\}$$

represents a Nurkse equilibrium.

The quantity supplied by the ith producer will be determined by the conditions in the factor (in this case, labour) market. Suppose s/he faces a labour market in which a total of L units of labour are available, and where workers are indifferent between working and not working at subsistence wage, w. The labour-supply curve will look something like:

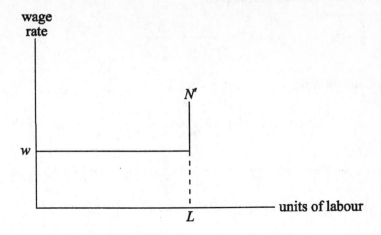

Let l_i be the amount of labour needed to produce one unit of good i. Assume also that at X^* there is no excess demand for labour; i.e.

$$l_1 x_1^* + l_2 x_2^* \le L \qquad ...(2.7)$$

At X^*, the producer of, say, good 1 will be reluctant to expand output if the marginal revenue from such expansion (i.e. for all $x_1 \ge x_1^*$) does not exceed labour costs, wl_1. If $x_2 = x_2^*$, the total revenue of producer 1 is

$$x_1 f_1(x_1).$$

His/her marginal revenue, for increasing outputs of x_1 beyond x_1^* (i.e. for all $x_1 > x_1^*$) is obtained by differentiating the total revenue function with respect to x_1:

$$\frac{d[x_1 f_1(x_1)]}{dx_1}$$

where $f_1(x_1) = \dfrac{c_1 x_2^*}{(c_2 x_1 + c_1 x_2^*)}$ as in Equation (2.6). Thus his/her marginal revenue (MR) equals

$$p_1(X^*) - \frac{c_2 c_1 x_1 x_2^*}{(c_2 x_1^* + c_1 x_2^*)^2},$$

and substituting $x_1 = x_1^*$, we obtain

$$MR_1 = p_1(X^*) - \frac{c_2 c_1 x_1^* x_2^*}{(c_2 x_1^* + c_1 x_2^*)^2}.$$

Producer 1 will thus not expand production of good 1 beyond x_1^* if

$$MR_1 \leq wl_1;$$

i.e. if $\qquad p_1(X^*) - \dfrac{c_2 c_1 x_1^* x_2^*}{(c_2 x_1^* + c_1 x_2^*)} \leq wl_1.$

But $\qquad\qquad\qquad\qquad p_1 = 1 - p_2,$

and from Equation (2.4),

$$p_1 = p_1(X^*) = \frac{c_1 x_2^*}{(c_2 x_1^* + c_1 x_2^*)}.$$

Hence the output-expansion criterion for producer 1 may be rewritten as

$$[p_1(X^*)]^2 \leq wl_1 \qquad \qquad ...(2.8)$$

And, at X^*, s/he will not wish to produce less if

$$p_1(X^*) \geq wl_1 \qquad \qquad ...(2.9)$$

From his/her point of view, therefore, if (2.8) and (2.9) hold, then x_1^* is his/her optimal output.

We may therefore define a Nurkse equilibrium thusly: the vector $[x_1^*, x_2^*, p_1^*, p_2^*]$ may be called a Nurkse equilibrium if, and only if:

Distal Causes of Africa's Debt Crisis

1. $p_i = p_i(X^*)$ $\qquad\qquad\qquad\qquad$ $i = 1,2.$

2. $[p_i(X^*)]^2 \leq wl_i \leq p_i(X^*)$ $\qquad\qquad$ $i = 1,2.$

3. $l_1 x_1^* + l_2 x_2^* \leq L.$

A Nurkse equilibrium at which there is an excess demand for labour at X^* (i.e. where $l_1 x_1^* + l_2 x_2^* < L$) may be referred to as a "poverty trap" or a "low-level equilibrium". A poverty trap thus represents an economy at equilibrium with unemployment, and its self-reproducing dynamic is what makes it a vicious circle.

A simple illustration shows how a Nurkse equilibrium can exist with unemployment. Assume an economy yielding the following data:

$$l_1 = l_2 = 1$$
$$w = \frac{1}{3}$$
$$L = 5$$
$$\text{and} \quad c_1 = c_2 = \frac{1}{2}$$

It can then be computed that

$$x_1 = x_2 = 1$$
$$p_1 = p_2 = \frac{1}{2}$$

is a Nurkse equilibrium, in that all the properties enumerated above are satisfied:

$$\text{if } p_1(X) = \frac{1}{2} \text{, then } [p_1(X)]^2 = \frac{1}{4} \text{ ;}$$
$$\text{and } [p_1(X)]^2 < wl_1 \ (=\frac{1}{3}) < p_1(X).$$

Also, as total employment is $l_1 x_1 + l_2 x_2 = 2$, with three of the five members of the work force unemployed, this must be a poverty trap. The corresponding graphical depiction of this economy—noting that the general conditions (2) and (3) of the Nurkse equilibrium can be specified as

$$\left[\frac{x_j}{(x_i + x_j)}\right]^2 \le \frac{1}{3} \le \left[\frac{x_j}{(x_i + x_j)}\right], \qquad i = 1,2 \ (i \ne j),$$

and $\quad x_1 + x_2 \le 5$

—is as below. It must also be remembered that expanding production of either good will lead to losses for the firm involved, though expansion of both outputs—say, along the ray (λ, λ) up to the point where $\lambda + \lambda = 5$—would benefit both sectors.

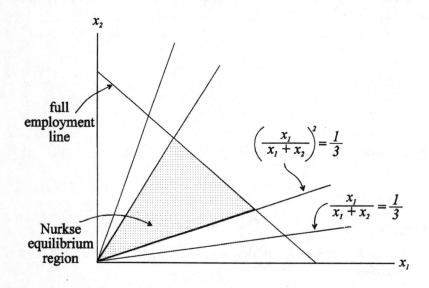

The shaded region represents output vectors where the economy is experiencing a Nurksian equilibrium, i.e. equilibrium with concomittant stagnation.

We have seen that, by definition, at a Nurksian equilibrium, no individual producer acting singly can increase his/her profits by expanding output. An important characteristic of this equilibrium, though, is that if

$$\{x_1^*, x_2^*, p_1^*, p_2^*\}$$

is a Nurkse equilibrium, then any multiple, λ , of this—

$$\{\lambda x_1{}^*, \ \lambda x_2{}^*, \ p_1{}^*, \ p_2{}^*\}$$

—is also a Nurkse equilibrium, where λ is a scalar such that

$$\lambda \, l_1 x_1{}^* + \ \lambda \, l_2 x_2{}^* \le L.$$

This is easily proved: if

$$\{x_1{}^*, x_2{}^*, p_1{}^*, p_2{}^*\}$$

is a Nurkse equilibrium, then it satisfies conditions (1), (2) and (3) above. From Equation (2.4), it is obvious that

$$p_i(X^*) = p_i(\lambda \, X^*)$$

for all $\lambda \ne 0$. Hence

$$\{ \lambda \, x_1{}^*, \ \lambda \, x_2{}^*, p_1{}^*, p_2{}^*\}$$

must satisfy conditions (1) and (2). If λ is restricted so that

$$\lambda \, l_1 x_1{}^* + \lambda \, l_2 x_2{}^* \le L$$

condition (3) is also met. This implies that if the equilibrium

$$\{x_1{}^*, x_2{}^*, \ p_1{}^*, p_2{}^*\}$$

is a poverty trap (i.e. a Nurkse equilibrium with $l_1 x_1{}^* + l_2 x_2{}^* < L$), it is possible to move the economy to full employment by expanding production in all sectors *at the same rate*. Note that such balanced expansion is only a possibility; it is a sufficient, though not necessary, criterion for moving towards full employment. This is the substance of the 'balanced growth' theory.

It is worth noting, also, that along the balanced-growth path, the proportionality of the two goods are maintained. In other words,

$$\frac{p_1{}^* \Delta x_1}{p_2{}^* \Delta x_2} = \frac{c_1}{c_2}$$

where Δx_i is the change in x_i along the balanced growth path. This bears out Nurkse's argument that "an increase in the production of [shirts] alone does not create its own demand. An increase in production over a wide range of consummables, so proportioned as to correspond with the pattern of consumers' preferences, does create its own demand."[19]

It is easy to extend the analysis to include non-labour inputs, such as capital. One can justifiably deduce, by direct analogy, that no single producer will independently increase his/her capital commitments while in the poverty trap, though capital investments appropriately and fairly distributed across all sectors may be economically rewarding, individually and collectively. But, unlike with labour, issues of indivisibility and increasing returns to scale complicate the analysis with capital. This would suggest not only that a sectorally-balanced increase in capital investment (in purely quantitative terms) is possible, but that the deployment of more efficient capital (in purely *qualitative* terms) is equally viable.

As was argued earlier, a poverty trap does not imply a perpetual and intractable, and therefore hopeless, state of underdevelopment. Indeed, implicit within the poverty trap analysis is the possibility of transcending the trap through some minimum amount, or critical mass, of input. This proposition is the basis of the "big push" theories of economic development, or what Leibenstein referred to as the "critical minimum effort" hypothesis.[20]

The gist of the critical minimum effort hypothesis as it relates to Nurkse's model and arguments is that there exists a certain minimum amount of investment necessary to initiate self-reproducing growth in an economy, and that any level of investment smaller than this minimum would not suffice to induce such growth. This would imply that to move the economy out of the poverty trap, a certain minimum injection of inputs is required to stimulate output increases in all sectors. Specifically, that a certain minimum effort is required if there are any fixed costs associated with the expansion. Thus, if starting at X^* with an excess supply of labour, Sector 1 can increase employment only if it is of the magnitude ΔN^{21}, then, to increase output, a minimum

of $\Delta N\left(1 + \dfrac{p_1{}^*}{p_2{}^*} \cdot \dfrac{l_2}{l_1} \cdot \dfrac{c_2}{c_1}\right)$ labour employment has to occur simultaneously.[22] This would be the big push that the economy would need.

What lessons does the Nurksian analysis offer the African debtors? Firstly, this "big push" may be quite indispensable to the proper, lasting resolution of the external debt crisis. Subsequent chapters make the point that the solution to the crisis requires a more sophisticated strategy than structural adjustment; and that the big push necessarily entails a multi-faceted, multi-layered, multi-sectoral strategy, *in both the economic and non-economic spheres*. It may require, for instance that, first, individual economies should be internally sectorally integrated, as a prelude to the integration of these economies into regional entities. This latter might have to occur with a simultaneous de-emphasizing of economic relations with countries not members of the regional union with a bid, very importantly, to curb the net outflow of financial resources from the sub-continent. This would be directly contrary to the liberalist thrust of the new orthodox remedies. Secondly, if a country is caught in a low-level equilibrium trap, the role of government intervention in pointing the way out of the trap is amply demonstrated by Nurkse's model. When private engines of growth are effectively non-existent, or functionally ineffective where they exist, as is indeed the case in much of SSA, and where no producer will individually expand output because it is not personally economically rewarding, government is, by fiat, the next best, and arguably the only viable, alternative for initial economic expansion. This, also, is directly contrary to what the resurgent orthodoxy would have Africa do.

In sum, then, there are four main conclusions about the structure of African economies that can be drawn from Nurkse's model and analysis. The first is that African economies are characterized, by and large, by a "poverty trap under Nurksian equilibrium". Secondly, this state of underdevelopment can be transcended if investment and growth are synchronised across many, if not all sectors of the economy. Thirdly, given their severe sectoral disarticulation and their general outward economic orientation, ensuring their internal structural integration by making them sectorally complementary—i.e. ensuring, to the extent possible, that local consumption is satisfied by local production utilizing local inputs—can be one important way of ensuring balanced growth. Subsequent integration of these internally integrated economies over whole regions, if done right, only ensures the continued reproduction of this growth. And, lastly, a certain critical minimum amount of investment and effort, ideally initiated by the private sector but more likely to be done by the public, given the absence of viable private engines of growth, are necessary to induce that self-reproducing growth that will get the economy out of the poverty trap. A key prerequisite for achieving this level of investment is the reversal of the net outflow of capital from Africa that began in the mid-1980s.

2.3 The Domestic Politics of the Debt Crisis

Much has been made, rightly, of the contribution to Africa's debt-and-development crises of the structure and practice of formal politics on the continent.[23] Indeed the equation of "ruling elites" with "external disequilibria" has been a very popular analytical game played across the pages of many scholarly journals and books on the African debt crisis. Ostensibly, inter- and intra-class (and other) divisions among the wide range of actors who constitute the African ruling class created the atmosphere for irrational economic policy making that ineluctably led to the crises.[24] It is therefore important, to understand the linkages between class structure, governance and the debt crisis, to closely examine the structure and practice of politics on the continent.

Politics in post-colonial Africa, in general, has been described in these analyses, often disparagingly, as an overtly personalized affair. It has also been described, not unrelatedly, and in a paraphrase of Max Weber, as a neo-patrimonial domination of the citizenry by strong leaders (and/or central parties) presiding over essentially weak states.[25] The modalities of this type of politics include an overtly personalized competition for political office but, more importantly, for access to the revenues that are necessary to maintain the tenuous efficacy of the corporatist state. In Africa, where resources of all sorts are in acute short supply, the state has become a resource in itself, it is argued, perhaps *the* most important single economic resource. The ruling authority uses state control of public resources to ensure the loyalty and fealty of a diverse array of client-groups to it, as a way of guaranteeing its reproduction as *the* political authority. Government thus relies largely on a process of preferment and differentiated treatment of various factions of the populace, rather than commitment to a transcendent ideology, belief, development programme, institution, or popular consent, to ensure its survival.[26] Political legitimacy is thus very fragile indeed, and development goals and economic policies are necessarily subjugated to the imperatives of government survival.

The main principle governing political behaviour is thus the successful reproduction of the state, and the preferred (indeed, the most efficient) method of achieving this is centralized control through the discretionary and selective disbursement of the resources under state control. Arising from this is a political culture in which corruption in public office, patronage, clientelism, nepotism, and the distribution of the "spoils of power" have become institutionalized forms of consolidating and guaranteeing political support. Political legitimacy and loyalty in Africa are thus, in a real sense, bought and sold, not earned. They are given in direct proportion as the giver's access to the largesse of government, not out of conviction, nor some primordial attachment to particular principles or ideals. Systemic abuse and unaccountability, therefore, have no checks in this type of neo-patrimonial polity. The developmental pathologies of Zaire, Malawi, Côte d'Ivoire, and others arise directly from this type of politics.

Examples of the developmental priorities and policies engendered by such politics are easy to find across the continent. First, there is a skewing of development programmes in favour of urban centres where the educated elite, whose pluralistic ethnic and class configuration makes their loyalty often more difficult to coerce and retain, live and work. Rural areas are, by and large, used as sources of agricultural surpluses to subsidize urban development and living. Secondly, development resources are more likely to go to members of ethnic or other such ascriptive group(s) most strongly represented in, or most closely affiliated with, government. Thus resource distribution is done not according to need, nor impartially according to a plan for balanced systemic growth, nor indeed according to market conditions, but according to the instinctual African response of taking care of kin, family and clan first. The most recent illustration of this was when, in the late 1970s, at the dawn of what would become arguably the most trying economic times for the Ivory Coast in its entire post-colonial history, President Houphouet-Boigny unilaterally decided to build a new capital-city from scratch in the little backwater of Yamossoukro, his home village which, by all accounts, is not quite suited locationally for the nation's capital. The case of Zaire under Mobutu, which we will have occasion to examine in due course, is equally instructive.

Thirdly, a host of economic policies—tax policy; exchange-rate and foreign-exchange allocation policies; fiscal policy; interest-rate and monetary policies; and agricultural-pricing policy, principally— are often designed to afford a measure of economic rents to those well-placed to enjoy such advantages, namely, the economic and political elites. As these policies are often at variance with what the underlying fundamentals of the economy, or the stabilization needs of the country would dictate, severe distortions are consequently created in the most important sectors of the economy—the foreign-exchange, domestic credit and labour markets—which, in time, are transmitted to the products markets. Systemic disequilibria, internal and external, follow in short order, creating eventually the external debt-cum-internal economic crises of the sort that surfaced in the 1980s.

There were numerous examples of such policies throughout the Africa of the 1970s and 1980s: inappropriate domestic responses to the oil-price shocks of 1973 and '79 that kept living standards and consumption patterns artificially high, necessitating resort to expanded external borrowing; deliberate government maintenance of comparatively low risk-adjusted real rates-of-return on capital, making capital-flight from the capital-scarce economies a rational reaction by wealth-holders, its presumed illegality or anti-socialness notwithstanding; inflationary domestic monetary and fiscal policies, with no corresponding adjustments in the nominal rate-of-exchange, which also led to massive capital outflows; and agricultural pricing policies that turned the domestic terms-of-trade against agriculture, are but a few of the more common examples.[27]

And lastly, as a result of this logic of resource allocation, political differentiation and formal oppositional politics at the level of the state were (still are, in most instances, even in country's that ostensibly are opening the formal political space to a plurality of views and parties) effectively muted, as dissenting voices dared not jeopardize their access to scarce development resources. Equally muted, for much the same reasons were, especially, the voices of rural dwellers and the urban poor, the intermittent ruptures from their ranks notwithstanding. Thus, in a real sense, power at the micro-level—

i.e. effective control over individuals' and sub-national groups' decision-making processes and economic well-being—was centralized in the person of the head-of-state and/or the ruling party, and revolved around an urban and ethnic axis. Economic and political resources, and whatever development there was, thus issued from, and were distributed within, the confines of this axis. African governments allocated economic and political resources in accordance with such considerations as "ethnic arithmetic" and geographical sojourn, rather than economic efficiency or the imperatives of development as such. Modern African governance, in this regard, is thus no more than a functional, albeit modified, extension of the traditional chieftaincy.

There is a rationality to this type of politics, however, and it lies in two factors: (1) in the structure, ideology and dynamics of cultural pluralism and ethnicity in Africa; and (2) in the legacy of the colonial political economy. With regard to the politics of cultural and ethnic pluralism, it must be appreciated that the "lineage-type discourses" motivating formal African politics are hegemonic devices employed by the state to maintain control over subordinate classes and ethnic groups.[28] Unlike in the industrial capitalist nations, the African state cannot rely on the hegemony of capitalist socio-economic relations because capitalist-commodity production is not dominant or even widespread. In the industrialized countries, the predominance of capitalist commodity relations tends to disguise, as Marx argued in the **Grundrisse** and in **Capital Vol. 1**, the exploitation of, say, wage-labour as a transaction among equals, with wages and profits being determined ostensibly by the impartial and impersonal forces of the market. The state can then legitimize itself as a Hobbesian state: impersonal, neutral and above the fray, and instead occupy itself with purveying an ideology of popular nationalism, which helps to coopt the non-hegemonic classes, and keeps substantive social dissent to a minimum.

In contrast, capitalist commodity relations are far from dominant in SSA; indeed, a large proportion of production still takes place within domestic or lineage relations. Even in the so-called 'modern' sector, production is often organized largely around personal relations of direct dependence and fealty between employee and employer— which, incidentally, reflects the same type of social interaction one observes between, say, peasants and their local chiefs, subordinate bureaucrats and ministers-of-state, merchants and their clients, etc.—

rather than impersonally through the market. Therefore state hegemony, to work, must also be based on the deployment of lineage and clientelist relations. But while it appears to ensure compliance by the subordinate groups, it also leads to patronage, ethnic tension, skewed resource distribution and, therefore, economic inefficiency, and skewed development. This suggests that patrimonialism is, on the one hand, an effective means of social control and, on the other, antithetical to systemic development and balanced growth.

It is for these reasons that the argument was made earlier that the practice of formal politics in Africa shored up, and created the necessary institutional conditions for the reproduction of the economic structures that kept, and still keep, SSA in the Nurksian poverty trap that underlay the debt crisis of the 1980s. But it also suggests, as we will demonstrate in due course, that a new political culture, in which power is necessarily decentralized, and in which the authority of the state to control the minutiae of economic and political policy is instrumentally and purposively devolved into the hands of peasants, workers and community groups, should be seen as one important dimension of the long-term solution to the debt crisis.

It must be noted by way of caveat, however, that the type of politics described above is not necessarily intrinsically African. It is partly a legacy of colonialism, and partly a convenient, if opportunistic, fusion of colonial intrigue and indigenous African political structures and social practices.[29] Between the formal onset of colonialism and the advent of political independence (roughly between 1884 and 1957), the broad parameters of political practice and African political participation were determined by the all-powerful colonial state. Colonial economies were structurally linked to, and made to depend upon, metropolitan economies, with the colonial state playing the role of intermediary and facilitator between the colonial economy and metropolitan bourgeois interests. Africa provided labour and primary goods which were routed to the state for onward transmission to the metropole. The subsequent externalization of the African economy, and the dominance of State Marketing Boards in the distribution of goods, are two of the enduring legacies of this relationship, as indeed are the distortions they tend to bring, in the normal course of their functioning, into the economy.

Hegemony over the African peoples was achieved through outright military pacification, and by the systematic cooptation of selected segments of the population (including entire ethnic groups) into cooperation with the colonial authorities.[30] Even local chiefs began to play the role of intermediaries between their African subjects and the colonial state. There thus emerged a hierarchy of politics within African countries, and between Africa and the rest of the world: from the local level to the metropoles through the colonial state via the African chiefs. The chiefs, in looking out narrowly for the particular interests of their subjects, had unwittingly become part of the larger colonial machine, and effectively no longer represented the unadulterated interests of their subjects. This established the pattern for post-colonial African political discourses, in which purposive but selective incorporation of various social groups into the machinery of the state has been the backbone of the corporatist/neo-patrimonial reality.

Contemporary politics in SSA thus carried a heavy baggage from the pre-independence era. The most conspicuous and enduring aspect of this baggage is political instability, some of the reasons for which must be obvious from the preceding analysis. But the origins of the fissions in the polity are more fundamental than that. First, before the balkanization of Africa by the European imperialist powers at the Congress of Berlin in 1884, most of Africa's peoples lived in small, decentralized nation-states occupying a few hundred square miles of territory, at most. (There had been the great empires of Mali, Ghana and Songhai, which fluorished on vast territories in the medieval era, of course, but these, exceptions even in their time, had already vanished from the scene. Later on, in the sixteenth and seventeenth centuries, magnificent empires with more centralized state-apparatuses, and occupying many thousands of square miles at their zenith, emerged and thrived in the forest belt of West Africa (Asante, Benin, Dahomey); in the Central African plains (Kongo, Barotse); and on the southern coast (the Mwenomutapa in present-day Mozambique and Zimbabwe)). By the advent of the European, the majority of the African peoples lived in organized segmentary societies with no clear leadership structures (e.g. the Kikuyu and the Igbo), but with definite *voluntary* and long-established patterns of interaction amongst themselves, and between them and their often more structurated neighbours.

With the arbitrary establishment of the colonial boundaries at Berlin, these flows and interactions were effectively disrupted.

Hundreds of otherwise distinct peoples and societies found themselves
forcefully blended together, often with people they had nothing in
common with, except the colour of their skin, and with whom they
may have been at odds for centuries. In addition, the arbitrariness of
the boundaries meant that ethnically and culturally homogeneous
nations were split between two or more countries, often with different
colonial rulers. Thus the Ewe were split between Ghana and Togo,
the one English, the other French; the Luo between Tanzania and
Kenya; the Fulani between Nigeria, Mali, Niger and Chad; the Somali
between Ethiopia, Somalia amd Kenya; the Maasai between Kenya,
Tanzania and Uganda; the Ndebele between Zimbabwe, South Africa
and Botswana; the Hutu and Tutsi between Rwanda and Burundi; etc.
There was thus a dissolution and reconstitution of peoples in a manner
that was rife with tension and irredentist sentiment. At independence,
therefore, the African state was socially amorphous and systemically
unstable; it had the veneer of the monolithic colonial state structure,
but the complex social and cultural pluralisms of indigenous Africa
that underlay the superstructure were always bubbling menacingly
and fissiparously to the surface.[31] The spate of civil wars and ethnic
conflict that have plagued all corners of the continent since
independence is one manifestation of this inherent structural
instability.[32] The rise of corporatist/clientelist/ neo-patrimonial/ethnic
politics, with its seemingly irrational, ultimately anti-developmental
economic policies and rationality, is another: it stems from a need to
strike a balance between peripheral push (the irredentist pressures)
and central pull (state control).[33]

Thus the contemporary existence of outward-looking, stagnant
economies in non-viable and politically unstable nation-states—as
important in understanding the origins and potential remedies of the
1980s' debt crisis as the external factors—is not a volitional construct
of Africans themselves. Nor is the peculiar character of the second
aspect of the political legacy of colonialism: the question of
governance, political authority, leadership and class rule.

As the colonial rulers were leaving at the dawn of independence,
they transferred power to an emerging elite who would not, and did
not, challenge the historical links between Africa and the metropoles.
Constitutional conferences were held in London and Paris to ensure
that the nascent political order would not threaten the structure of the
interaction between colony and metropole.

As it turned out, the emerging elites did not represent the interests of the population at large. By handing over power to them, therefore, the colonial state was sowing the seeds of discord between the new rulers and their subjects. Kenya provides a good illustration of this: in response to the Mau Mau uprising, the British came up, in 1950, with the Swynnerton Plan, the purpose of which was to ensure that the causes of the uprising (land shortage, land alienation) would not plague the new regime. A land redistribution scheme was devised that had the consequence of creating an inordinately wealthy and politically powerful, land-owning class among the minority Kikuyu, who had been the backbone of Mau Mau. The subsequent discord between the Kikuyu, who assumed power under Jomo Kenyatta upon independence, and other major ethnic groups in Kenya can, in large measure, be traced back to the Swynnerton Plan.[34] And, in the recidivist manner in which these things occur and recur in Africa, the Kalenjin, under current-President arap-Moi, Kenyatta's long-time Vice President and eventual successor, in unspoken alliance with other anti-Kikuyu ethnic groups, are today doing their level best to catch up with the Kikuyu in wealth and political dominance. Recent calls for political opening and "multi-party democracy" in Kenya, led prominently by the Kikuyu and other groups, should thus be seen as a bid by a marginalized ex-hegemon to reclaim its economic and political influence, and not as the flowering of liberal democratic values *per se* on Kenyan soil.

To summarize, then, there are seven identifiable effects on the internal structure of African economies and the conduct of its economic policy, and on the structure and conduct of its politics, from the legacy of the colonial enterprise. The first is the arbitrariness, and therefore artificiality, of the present geopolitical boundaries. This makes the African state itself "a product of external logic, and...[not a reflection of] the geographical or social realities of the African continent."

Secondly, disparate peoples and cultures have been forcefully but unsuccessfully fused into political entities that they do not wholly or primarily identify with. Weak states and governments, and nations often on the brink of implosion, have been the results, as have the type of ethnicity-based clientelist politics and economics that have made Africa so crisis-prone. Thirdly, independent Africa inherited weak and structurally disarticulated economies, economies which had been externalized by colonial policy to serve metropolitan interests, and which therefore had lost their erstwhile capability of relative self-sufficiency. Related to this is the fourth impact, which is that the economies were not only left exposed to the vagaries of external shocks, but were also made structurally and functionally dependent on outside economies and policies. As part of this external exposure, a small contingent of Western-educated elites, separated from the rest of the population not just by the fact of their education but by their differential access to information, the outside world, jobs and high incomes, became the symbol, at one and the same time, of what was possible yet unattainable for the overwhelming bulk of the population. And it is this same elite, a buffer between metropolitan and African identity and interests, that had effective political power to make policy decisions that affected the rest of the population, though not always or necessarily in their interest.

The sixth legacy of colonialism was the extreme fragility of state institutions and other apparati of government. Because the state itself, as created by the colonialists, was essentially alien to the constituent African populations; and because the African populations did not share a common political culture, the fragility of the institutions of governance made public administration in the independent nations extremely problematic and potentially ineffective at the very outset. That the state was unable or unwilling, in the 1970s and '80s, to take the requisite measures to protect domestic economic viability in light of global economic developments; and that, when and where it did, the results were paltry, at best, attests to the tenuous efficacy of government and its institutions.

And, finally, the psychological impact of colonialism—the collective memory of humiliation; of political, economic and cultural dispossession; and of the on-going perception of marginalization and political powerlessness in a world still dominated by one's ex-conquerors—has, perhaps more than any other inheritance from that era, had the most debilitating impact on African society and conduct.[35]

It is hardly surprising, given this legacy, that the post-colonial African state has lurched from crisis to crisis; has devised unrepresentative, and even oppressive, ways of maintaining a chimeral sense of nationhood; and reproduced unremittingly its state of poverty and underdevelopment for nearly thirty-five years. It would appear, then, that it is precisely this structure of politics that has to be dismantled to give other policies a fighting chance to eliminate the crisis-ridden bent of Africa's economies. We return to this proposition in the final chapter.

2.4 The External Environment

While preceding sections of this chapter examined the internal structures that helped (re)produce Africa's debt-and-underdevelopment crises in the 1980s we will, in this section, examine the complementary external factors that did the same. There is, in this study, an implicit indictment of forces external to SSA as the more determinate causes of the debt crisis. The more obvious manifestations of these forces were identified in the first chapter. But of equal concern must be the theories informing the conduct of inter-country trade and finance as we know it, and those that have undergirded the practice of economic development in SSA since the second world war. Indeed the economics of the balance-of-payments, and the analyses of the factors that determine a country's debt-service capacity, as detailed earlier, suggest the need for just such a critical review of these theories, traditions, institutions and practices.

This section of the chapter attempts to do this. The primary objective here is to show the functional linkages between the post-war economic development theories and practices and the strucutral problems of the African economies that led to the debt crisis. Related to that, of course, is an analysis of how the conduct of international exchange in goods and finance, and the very institutional structures within which the exchange takes place, fosters the emergence of such a crisis. Thus the very mode of interaction between Africa and the industrialized nations we see as latently (debt) crisis-ridden. The objective, then, is to examine those external influences which, when they converge on Africa's domestic structural particularities, create and reproduce the underdevelopment crisis out of which the debt crisis arose, and without which it might not have become thusly manifest.

Development Paradigms and Debt Creation

Much of post-war economic development theory has been under a much-deserved attack for some time now. It is under attack, first and foremost, for much the same reasons that the entire corpus of the neo-classical paradigm is under attack, namely, for being excessively abstract, often simple (relative to the 'real world' it seeks to explain) if not simplistic, and largely unrealistic in its arcane formalisms and religious preoccupation with technique at the expense of content.[36] In short, the issue of 'relevance' has been pushed to the fore.

For many Third World economists, the issue of relevance of theory to Third World realities is of particular concern. Our main concern in this section, however, is not with the particular criticisms to which the neo-classical development economics theory has been subjected by Third World economists, but the *results* of the application of these theories to Africa's development effort. Thus the 'goodness and usefulness' of these theories *qua* theory is not of as much interest here as the narrow subject of what they have wrought in their wake by way of development policy. It will be argued, broadly, that the poor performance of these theories in the realm of application is an indication of their epistemic inadequacy in, if not outright irrelevance to, the African context.

The necessity to critically review these theories stems from the fact that they have, at one time or another over the past half-century, held current and influenced development practices in Africa and elsewhere in the South. Indeed, not an insignificant proportion of the propensity to seek external financial resources to, ostensibly, supplement inadequate domestic savings can, and should, be partly attributed to the popular models of the 1950s and 1960s, from Rostow's linear stage-growth theory to the two-gap models, and their logical offspring of more recent vintage. In similar fashion can some of the distortions created by undue emphasis by policy makers on one or another sector of the economy at the expense of all others be traced to the dualism and unbalanced growth models of the period. That these meshed neatly with the imperatives of Africa's neo-patrimonial politics cannot be gainsaid, but the ultimate effect of this convenient marriage was the establishment of a tradition, a significant 'culture', of development, which contributed in no small way not only to the structural distortions of Africa's economies, but also to their propensity to incur external debts over and beyond their optimal debt-carrying capacities.

Secondly, many of these theories have undergone various modifications in response to the rather dismal development experiences of the countries in which their policy recommendations were implemented. It should thus be particularly instructive to assess whether or not these changes are more basic than ephemeral, and whether or not, as a consequence, future development practices based on these modified models will yield more successful results than their older agnates.

There are two broad categories of development theory that have influenced economic development practice in SSA since the 1950s. The first two may be identified under the rubric of 'linear stage-growth' and 'neo-classical structural change' models, both of which come out of the modernization paradigms of the Euro-American social sciences.[37] The third, which will not be reviewed extensively here, consists of an eclectic grab-bag of neo-Marxian ideas loosely affiliated with the world-systems model, and which may be called the 'inter-country dependence' model.

Linear Stage-Growth Theories

A product of the East-West cold war of the 1950s and 1960s, the linear stage-growth model argued primarily that the right quality and mix of saving, investment and foreign aid (including loans) are all that a developing country needs to proceed jauntily along a contiguous series of developmental stages through which all nations, including the currently industrialized ones, must pass on their way to the "take-off" into "self-sustaining growth".[38] As the Northern economists who propounded this theory truly had no real basis on which to analyze prospects for economic growth and structural transformation in these largely agrarian economies emerging from a unique experience of colonial disorientation and structural distortion, the empirical/historical basis of the model were the development experiences of the industrialized countries.

There were two lessons for economic transformation to be learned from these experiences, it was reasoned. One was that no society could effect a 'take-off' in the absence of a critical, minimum amount of savings—of domestic origins, preferably, but to be supplemented with foreign savings, if need be—to generate growth-inducing investment. The second was that the path of structural transformation would mirror that of the industrialized nations. These two propositions would become the two 'sacred cows' of development practice from the 1950s onward.

It will be argued here that these propositions, in concert with the structural distortions bequeathed by the colonial experience, led to the continued externalization of the production structures of Africa's economies, as African countries endeavoured to continually expand their exports in order to secure the all-important quantum of savings (in foreign exchange), without which, presumably, investment and economic growth could not be achieved. And where and when they were unsuccessful in attaining that critical mass, which was nearly always, there was little hesitation about resorting to foreign borrowing to supplement the take, following the theory implicitly. The crucial question of whether or not structural transformation, in particular, and economic processes, in general, are ergodic, especially across historical time and geographical space, was hardly seriously raised or allowed to affect the head-long chase of the take-off.

The effects of this, as have been observed since the latter half of the 1960s, is a structure of production in Africa that is geared not towards satisfying domestic demand, but servicing foreign markets; a distortion of development priorities away from productive, self-liquidating projects with substantial multiplier effects through the economy towards 'white elephant', prestige projects that generate little income, but compare favourably with similar "modern" projects in the industrialized North[39]; a tendency to favour the foreign exchange-earning sectors at the expense of all others, creating sectoral imbalances in the economy and distortions in different markets; a high propensity to borrow from abroad, ostensibly to supplement the insufficient export earnings but also to finance the costly clientelist politics of the state often hidden in the fiscal deficit; and a singular inability to sustain these loans (given inadequate income performance) *and* satisfy the society's basic development needs simultaneously. But perhaps the most insidious impact of this model is that it provided the intellectual context for the application of other, though not unrelated, theories to the development effort. One of the more influential of these, which is examined next, is the neo-classical growth model.

Economic-Growth Theory

The importance of ascertaining the factors that generate, maintain or enhance economic growth in an economy, especially a low-income one, should be self-evident. The implicit thrust of the Rostowian linear stage-growth model is that developing countries can be differentiated from industrialized ones by their inability to generate system-wide growth (the "take-off"), and to sustain it (the "stage of high mass consumption") once generated. But economic growth *qua* growth is important in and of itself for any society whose population, and therefore potential demand, is continually expanding. Growth, which may be achieved by improving productivity in the economy, given inputs; or by expanding the input base, with fixed technologies, is thus a *sine qua non* for, at least, maintaining a society's customary level of subsistence. It is in light of this reality that economic theorizing about development has, more often than not, revolved around one or another theory of economic growth, at times under the mistaken notion of equating growth with development as such. Because it is defined as the long-term change in the real output of the economy, growth is often measured in terms of changes in per capita, not total, output, as total output may indicate economic expansion even as per capita output declines. Yet as growth in per capita output is not always coterminous with improved economic welfare, the equation of growth with development can be particularly misleading.

In this specific regard, some of the very early economic thinkers, particularly the French mercantilists and the English classical political economists, were more sophisticated theorists than present-day neo-classicals. For they postulated that the capacity output of an economy, at any given time, depends not only on the quality and quantity of factors and technology available, but also on the institutional structure extant. By 'institutional structure' they meant the amalgam of social relations that govern the daily conduct of economic life: governmental/political structures; economic structure; psychological and cultural attitudes towards work, change, spending and saving; and the juridical system, among others. Because growth is a thusly multi-layered and multi-determined process, with many of its essential determinants neither economic in character nor easily quantifiable in practice, the economy, they argued, rarely realizes a level of output commensurate with its full-capacity potential. Rather, its *actual* output (as contrasted to its capacity output), though dependent on the forces that determine capacity output, also depend, importantly, on the forces that determine the *extent* to which capacity is realized. In modern, Keynesian language, current output is a function of the factors that determine capacity output, and also of those that determine aggregate demand. Since growth represents changes in output over time, and it is also a complex economic *and* non-economic phenomenon, the study of it must necessarily include the systematic study of input flows, technology, the "social structures of accumulation", and aggregate demand. Neo-classical economics focusses "only on the very narrow part of this process of growth which can be analyzed within the framework of orthodox theory", but "any satisfactory understanding of the process... will require a more comprehensive framework than a single social science can provide."[40]   It is in this sense of a comprehensive analytical framework that the problems of growth and economic development in SSA is discussed here.

The initial impetus in this century for the study of economic growth did not come from concern about, or with, developing countries. The early theorists were concerned to explore the conditions for stable, long-term growth, initially in southern Europe, then in the industrialized countries, generally.[41]   Specifically, they sought to know the factors that determined the height and slope of the potential growth path of the economy; i.e. to understand how, along trend, the *actual* rate of growth could be brought up to the economy's *potential* rate. The two key relationships that emerged from these analyses, and which subsequently heavily influenced economic development policy in Africa, were that (1) the *slope* of the long-run growth path, i.e. the rate of growth of potential output, is determined principally by the rates of growth of the country's labour force, and that of productivity; and (2) the *height* of the growth path, i.e. the absolute level of output at a particular time, is determined by the capital-worker ratio, and the saving rate.   Since the slope of the growth path indicates the economy's growth rate, measures to influence productivity in Africa's economies, in the presence of an assumed elastic supply of labour, became *the* object of development policy.   The thrust of economic policy all through the 1960s, therefore, was to increase the capital-worker ratio—itself a reflection of the second finding that related the absolute level of output to this ratio and the saving rate.

It is quite clear that this conceptual linkage of the saving rate and the capital-labour ratio to productivity and growth—which runs, implicitly or otherwise, through the entire spectrum of neo-classical development economics, from the stage-growth and two-gap models through the atavistic structuralisms of W. Arthur Lewis to the resurgent liberalism of the 1980s—was instrumental in pushing African policy makers towards excessive foreign borrowing, as a supplement to low domestic saving and/or export earning, for domestic capital formation. Reserve replenishment, and the financing of capital outflows and current-account deficits having been taken care of, much of the residual demand for the foreign loans that led to Africa's debt crisis of the 1980s was thusly policy-induced, said policies stemming directly from the neo-classical development paradigm that equated economic growth as such with structural development.

That this type of capital-intensive production skewed Africa's development proirities towards the industrial and extractive, and therefore urban, sectors at the expense of agriculture and food production, and therefore rural areas; that it proved spectacularly unabsorptive of labour, chronically generating high unemployment; and that it resulted in the institutionalization of the export orientation of the economy that had begun under colonialism establishes, *prima facie*, the culpability of the received neo-classical wisdom in sustaining Africa's underdevelopment. As the 1980s debt crisis was linked to the underdevelopment crisis at large, the neo-classical economic growth and related theories must be seen as significant contributors to the crises. It follows, then, that the crisis will not be solved without addressing this its theoretical and epistemic foundation.

Two-gap Models

A discussion of two-gap models would appear to follow logically from the general discussion of growth models above. It will be most useful to discuss them in the context of the external relations of the African countries, particularly as regards international trade, transfers in aid, and the preponderant importance of foreign-exchange to both the development project and the external debt crisis. However, the emphasis here will be a narrower one, namely, an analysis of the economics as such of the model, in order to draw particular analytical conclusions germane to the object of this work.

The basic premise of the two-gap model is that most developing economies do not generate enough domestic savings to match investment opportunities, hence there is a gap between the supply of, and demand for, investable funds; or they do not earn enough foreign exchange to maintain a sufficient level of imports of capital and intermediate goods, hence the foreign-exchange gap. An implicit, though no less important, assumption is that real domestic resources (i.e. local savings) and foreign exchange are not perfect substitutes, and therefore any gaps they manifest may have different qualitative impacts on the economy even if their magnitudes are the same. In other words, there may be a 'quality gap' between foreign exchange and local savings[42] also at work here.

It should follow from these premises, then, that at any given time, only one of these gaps will be dominant or binding on an economy. A dominant savings gap will imply an economy operating at full employment with no foreign-exchange shortages. Such a country should then, theoretically, be perfectly capable of importing say, more capital from abroad. But its factor markets are so tight that it will not be able to expand investment without severely distorting resource allocation and/or generating inflation. Such a country is then said to be experiencing a dearth of productive resources, which is only another way of saying that it has a shortage of domestic saving.[43] The implication of all this is that a 'savings gap' country needs no foreign aid or borrowing.

But this is more the special case than less. Nearly all African countries are bound by the foreign-exchange constraint. They have an excess of non-capital inputs, mainly labour, and are already using all their foreign-exchange holdings for imports, or to satisfy their external obligations. A 'foreign-exchange gap' country is thus a country whose ability and power to purchase imports—conferred by the sale of exports plus any net capital inflows—may not suffice to support the level of growth permitted by the import-purchasing potential of the economy and the level of other inputs. Thus it can expand investment locally only if it secures more capital from abroad. Foreign aid, then, as transfers or credit can, it is implied, be crucial to raising economic growth by helping close the foreign-exchange gap. It is clear here that development policies based on this model necessarily foster external borrowing.

An interesting result emerges from this model upon further analysis. As it is normally expostulated, two-gap models create the impression that foreign-exchange and savings gaps are endogenous, a result of the economy's innate inability to generate enough export revenue and/or local saving. It can be shown, as Colman and Nixson have argued, however, that this need not be the case[44]; that, indeed, the very structure of economic interaction between developing countries and the industrialized ones can determine which constraint, if any, is actually binding on growth.

Suppose F represents net capital inflows. On the assumption that such inflows enhance domestically-available investable resources, the savings constraint may be written as

$$I < F + sY \qquad ...(2.10)$$

where I is the level of investment needed to maintain full employment, and s and Y are, respectively, the saving rate and gross income. Conversely, on the assumption that, for a typical African country, domestic investment has a marginal import share of m_1, and a marginal propensity to import out of income, m_2, the foreign-exchange gap may be written as

$$m_1 I + m_2 Y - X \leq F \qquad ...(2.11)$$

where X is the level of export earnings, and the F term is the critical analytical factor in both constraints. If F, X and Y are all assigned an exogenous current value at the outset, only one of the two inequalities will, in fact, be binding: investment, hence growth, will be constrained to a lower level by one of the two inequalities. Hence a country will be suffering from one or the other malaise, not both, as we have already asserted.

But the interesting result that comes out of the analysis is that, dollar-for-dollar, capital inflows will have a much greater impact on a country with a foreign-exchange gap than one with a savings gap. Two-gap models have thus been used mechanistically to predict a country's need for, and ability to efficiently absorb, foreign aid. But the predictive power of the model is itself constrained by the necessity to fix import parameters (m_1 and m_2) and assign values for X and F. In the case of exports, this is particularly constricting since, as is argued later in Chapter 4, a relaxation of the extensive tariff barriers against African exports to the industrialized countries will, arguably, do more to relieve foreign-exchange shortages than foreign-aid transfers.[45]

Secondly, the substitutability of X and F in Equation (2.11) notwithstanding, they can, in reality, have quite different effects on the economy, especially where F represents or includes significant amounts of interest-bearing loans that must be repaid. Thus, the alteration of both export and import parameters by both African and industrialized-country governmental action *can* determine which constraint is actually binding on growth, or even if either is. Hence the assertion earlier in the chapter that the very nature of the economic relationship between Africa and its Northern trading partners shapes both its internal economic structure and performance, and the character of its debt crisis. The dynamics of trade relations, financial relations, intellectual relations, and even non-credit foreign assistance, would all amply attest to this.[46]

Summary

The neo-classical theories of growth and development which have dominated economic policy and development practice in SSA for decades contributed, in substantive though not immediately obvious ways, to the sub-continent's debt-and-development crises of the 1980s. Their epistemic bases being found in the Euro-American experience, they proved to be particularly unreflective of the structural realities of the African economy, domestically, and quite uncognizant of the character of its external relations, economic and non-economic. They thus tended to exacerbate, not ameliorate, the systemic pathologies found internally, while preserving those found within the global system, both of which have intermittently combined, since the second world war, to plunge Africa into one economic crisis or another.

But the strength of their negative impact comes more from the fact that these theories complement very well the internal structures of Africa's economies and politics. From the Nurksian model examined earlier in the chapter, there is a sense in which it can fairly be said that the policies issuing from these theories have been primarily, though often partially, responsible for the perpetuation of the pathologies and rigidities found in the economic system. And where there were no institutionalized checks against them from the national political dispensation, chances for a comprehensive crisis of underdevelopment (given the poverty trap) and external indebtedness (given the outward orientation of the economy and its inability to respond appropriately to external shocks), were that much more enhanced. It is in this sense that the internal economic and political peculiarities of Africa, and its external relations, of which the neo-classical development paradigm is a part, constitute the distal causes of its twin-crisis of debt and underdevelopment.

If these theories, social structures and policies, which collectively constitute the existing 'culture of development', are the deeper causes of the crises, then they can hardly be relied on to resolve it. We argue in later chapters, therefore, for a new culture of development, premised on a different set of understandings of SSA's development goals; on a clarification of the uniquenesses of its economic and political structures; and on an appreciation of the nature of its participation in the global political economy. This new development culture takes due cognizance of Africans' own understanding of how their relationship of "dependent interdependence" with the outside world shapes and guides their development goals and the social structures within which these goals are defined and pursued[47]. It thus attempts to foster a different theoretical or paradigmatic basis for development practice, aiming more at effecting those structural changes in African economies and polities that would make them more sectorally complementary, more consistently internally integrated and, thereby, more self-sufficient; and, most importantly, that would make them more open to the efficacy of balanced growth in achieving these objectives. It was through such purposive de-emphasizing of the traditional externalization of the economy, it is argued, that Africa's debt and related crises of the 1980s could have been satisfactorily addressed.

Notes

1. See Kaushik Basu, **The Less Developed Economy: A Critique of Contemporary Theory** (Oxford: Basil Blackwell, 1984), ch. 2; and J.M. Flemming, External Economies and the Doctrine of Balanced Growth, **Economic Journal**, Vol. 65 (1955).
2. Ragnar Nurkse, **Problems of Capital Formation in Underdeveloped Countries** (N.Y.: Oxford Univ. Press, 1962), p. 4.
3. See Jaime de Piniés, op. cit.
4. P.N. Rosenstein-Rodan, Problems of Industrialization in Eastern and South-Eastern Europe, Economic Journal, Vol. 53 (June-Sept. 1943), as reprinted in Gerald Meier, ed., **Leading Issues in Economic Development** (London: Oxford Univ. Press, 1970), pp. 45-68.
5. See H. Singer, Economic Progress in Underdeveloped Countries, **Social Research**, Vol. 16 (1949), pp. 18-35; Ragnar Nurkse, op. cit.; Tibor Scitovsky, Two Concepts of External Economies, **Journal of Political Economy**, Vol. 17 (1954), pp. 60-72; W. Arthur Lewis, Economic Development with Unlimited Supplies of Labour, **The Manchester School**, Vol. 22 (1954), pp. 16-33.
6. R.R. Nelson, A Theory of the Low-Level Equilibrium Trap in Underdeveloped Economies, **American Economic Review**, Vol. 46 (1956), pp. 412-422.
7. Some of the main criticisms in this vein have come from the Marxian literature. See, for instance, Paul Baran, **The Political Economy of Growth** (N.Y.: Monthly Review Press, 1968); Samir Amin, **Accumulation on a World Scale** (N.Y.: Monthly Review Press, 1974) and his **Unequal Development** (N.Y.: Monthly Review Press, 1976); F.H. Cardoso, Dependence and Development in Latin America, **New Left Review** (July-Aug. 1972), pp. 83-95; and Clive Thomas, **Dependence and Transformation** (N.Y.: Monthly Review Press, 1974).
8. David Ricardo, **Principles of Political Economy and Taxation** (London: John Murray, 1917), pp. 52-63 of the Dent (1973) edition. See, also, E.K. Hunt, **History of Economic Thought: A Critical Perspective** (California: Wadsworth Publishing, 1979), pp. 80-85.
9. H. Leibenstein, **Economic Backwardness and Economic Growth** (N.Y.: John Wiley, 1957).
10. Nurkse, op. cit., p. 6.
11. Clearly, the feasibility of an increase in demand upon balanced expansion is contingent upon price elasticities: if factor prices are low and demand-inelastic, then expansion is feasible.
12. See Harry Landreth, **History of Economic Theory: Scope, Method and Content** (Boston: Houghton Mifflin, 1976) p. 106 ff.

13. J.S. Mill, **Essays on Some Unsettled Questions on Political Economy** (London: LSE, 1948) as quoted by Nurkse, op. cit., pp. 11-12.

14. See A. Mathur, Balanced vs. Unbalanced Growth—A Reconciliatory View, **Oxford Economic Papers**, Vol. 18 (1966) for a review of the seminal 'balanced growth' literature.

15. Scitovsky attempted just such a (Walrasian) rendition of Nurkse in his Two Concepts of External Economies, **Journal of Political Economy**, Vol. 17 (1954), pp. 60-72.

16. See G. Debreu, **Theory of Value** (N.Y.: John Wiley, 1959), ch. 6.

17. See footnote No. 15.

18. Note that the competitive (horizontal) demand curve each agent faces is not necessarily his/her *actual* demand curve. It may well be the agent's notional or "conjectural" demand curve, i.e. what s/he believes to be the effect on prices of his/her output expansion. This conjectured demand curve is the operative demand curve in defining the equilibrium. For an elaboration of the operative characteristic of the conjectural demand curve, see Nicholas Kaldor, Mrs. Robinson's Economics of Imperfect Competition, **Economica**, Vol. 1 (1934), p.40 ff.

19. Nurkse, op. cit., p. 12.

20. See H. Leibenstein, **Economic Backwardness and Economic Growth** (London: John Wiley, 1957).

21. This is a simple way of depicting the idea of fixed costs.

22. If employment in Sector 1 increases by ΔL_1, a balanced expansion would require that

$$\Delta L_2 = \left[\frac{l_2 c_2 p_1{}^*}{l_1 c_1 p_2{}^*} \right] \Delta L_1.$$

Since the minimum feasible ΔL_1 is ΔN, a balanced expansion would entail a minimum of

$$\Delta N = \left[1 + \left(\frac{p_1{}^* l_2 c_2}{p_2{}^* l_1 c_1} \right) \right]$$

of new employment.

23. The discussion of the modalities of African politics in this section draws heavily on T.W. Parfitt and S.P. Riley, **The African Debt Crisis** (London: Routledge, 1989), especially pp. 37-39 and pp. 79-83. For more particularized discussion of the general topic see, also, Kenneth Good, Debt and the One-Party State in Zambia, **Journal of Modern African Studies**, Vol. 27, No. 2 (1989), pp. 297-313; R.M. Price, Neo-Colonialism and Ghana's Economic Decline: A Critical Assessment, **Canadian Journal of African Studies**, Vol. 18, No. 1 (1984), pp. 160-176; C. Young and T. Turner, **The Rise and Decline of the Zairean State** (Madison: Univ. of Wisconsin Press, 1985); and J.E. Nyang'oro

and T.S. Shaw, eds., **Corporatism in Africa: Comparative Analytics and Practice** (Boulder: Westview Press, 1989).

24. See, for instance, N. Chazan, R. Mortimer, J. Ravenhill and D. Rothchild, **Politics and Society in Contemporary Africa** (Boulder: Lynne Rienner, 1992), ch. 2; and E. Wayne Nafziger, op. cit., ch. 3.

25. See R. Sandbrook, **The Politics of Africa's Economic Stagnation** (Cambridge: Cambridge Univ. Press, 1985).

26. See M. Szeftel, **Conflict, Spoils and Class Formation in Zambia**, Unpublished Ph.D. dissertation, Univ. of Manchester 1978, as cited by Parfitt and Riley, op. cit.; also J.F. Medard, The Underdeveloped State in Africa: Political Clientelism or Neo-Patrimonialism?, in C. Clapham, ed., **Private Patronage and Public Power** (London: Pinter Printers, 1982).

27. See, for further elaboration of some of these policies and their particular import for Africa's debt crisis, World Bank, **Accelerated Development in Sub-Saharan Africa (the Berg Report)**, (Washington, D.C.: World Bank, 1982); E. Wayne Nafziger, op. cit., ch. 3; and S. O'Cleireacain, op. cit., pp. 22-32.

28. See C. Charney, Political Power in the Neo-Colonial African States, **Review of African Political Economy**, Vol. 38 (April 1987), as discussed by Parfitt and Riley, op. cit., p. 37.

29. The arguments of this section rely heavily on Nyang'oro's excellent study of the genesis of clientelist politics in Africa. See J.E. Nyang'oro, The State of Politics in Africa: The Corporatist Factor, **Studies in Comparative International Development**, Vol. 24, No. 1 (Spring 1989), pp. 5-19.

30. The Maji Maji revolt in Tanzania; the Mau Mau uprising in Kenya; a half-century of Anglo-Ashanti wars in Ghana; etc. are some of the military campaigns by which recalcitrant African groups were subdued.

31. See Chazan, Mortimer, Ravenhill and Rothchild, op. cit., pp. 25-29.

32. In the Sudan, the Nilo-Hamitic Africans of the south have been fighting the Arabic northerners since 1966; the Ibos fought the Hausas and the Yorubas (mainly) for an independent Biafran Republic in Nigeria from 1966 to 1970; Uganda's ethnic troubles led to the ouster of the King of the Buganda, the Kabaka Mutesa, in 1966; in Rwanda, the Hutus and the Tutsi have been at each other for a decade; in Ethiopia, every major nationality—the Tigre, Eritrea, Wollo, Oromo—is fighting (or just recently concluded a fight with) the dominant Amhara for either independence, relative autonomy, or the control of the Ethiopian state.

33. See D. Rothchild and V. Olorunsola, Managing Competing Ethnic Claims, in Donald Rothchild and Victor Olorunsola, eds., **State vs. Ethnic Claims: African Policy Dilemmas** (Boulder: Westview Press, 1983).

34. See Christopher Leo, **Land and Class in Kenya** (Toronto: Univ. of Toronto Press, 1984) and Colin Leys, **Underdevelopment in Kenya** (Berkeley: Univ. of California Press, 1975).

35. See Chazan, Mortimer, et.al., op. cit., ch 1.

36. For the latest instalment of these critiques, and a wickedly entertaining one at that, see David Colander, **Why Aren't Economists As Important as Garbagemen?**, (Armonk, N.Y.: M.E. Sharpe, 1992).

37. See the various works of Max Weber, especially **Economy and Society**, G. Roth and C. Wittich, tr., (N.Y.: Bedminster Press, 1968), and **The Theory of Social and Economic Organization**, A.M. Henderson and T. Parsons, tr., (N.Y.: Oxford Univ. Press, 1947). See, also, W.E. Moore, **World Modernization: The Limits of Convergence** (N.Y.: Elsevier North-Holland, 1979); and Manning Nash, ed., Essays on Economic Development and Cultural Change in Honor of Bert F. Hoselitz, Supplement to Vol. 25 of **Economic Development and Cultural Change** (Chicago: Univ. of Chicago Press, 1977).

38. See W.W. Rostow, **The Stages of Economic Growth: A Non-Communist Manifesto** (London: Cambridge Univ. Press, 1960).

39. For revealing examples of 'white elephant' development projects, see Parfitt and Riley, op. cit., especially chapters 3, 4 and 7.

40. Harry Landreth, op. cit., p. 475. The entire section of this book on the history of growth theory, particularly pp. 475-497, is very instructive.

41. See Rosenstein-Rodan, op. cit.

42. For an elaboration of the model, see H.B. Chenery and M. Bruno, Development Alternatives in An Open Economy: The Case of Israel, **Economic Journal**, Vol. 72 (1962), pp. 120-132.

43. This argument implies that any foreign exchange, in the absence of any optimal productive uses, will be used in the conspicuous consumption of imported luxuries. While this may be, it is also quite the case that it may be used to import productive resources. For instance, the oil-rich states of the 1970s that, purportedly, were the prime examples of 'savings gap' LDCs, used their surplus petrodollars to hire vast numbers of workers from neighbouring (and distant) non-oil countries. This was very much the case, for example, in Gabon, Nigeria and Cameroon. It was also true of Saudi Arabia, Iraq, Kuwait and other countries in the Gulf.

44. D. Colman and F. Nixson, **Economics of Change in Less Developed Countries** (N.Y.: John Wiley, 1978), ch. 5.

45. See World Bank, **World Development Report, 1987**, ch. 8, for the types and heights of tariff and non-tariff barriers that Africa's exports to the North faced in the 1980s. See, also, C. Mabbs-Zeno and B. Krissoff, **Tropical Beverages in the GATT**, Paper presented at the World Bank/OECD symposium on 'Implications of Agricultural Trade

Liberalization for Developing Economies', Paris, Oct. 1989 (U.S. Dept. of Agriculture, Economic Research Service, Dec. 1989).

46. Colman and Nixson, op. cit., chapters 4 and 5.
47. See S. Corbridge, The Asymmetry of Interdependence: The U.S. and the Geopolitics of International Financial Relations, **Studies in Comparative International Development**, Vol. XXII, No. 1 (Spring 1988), pp. 3-53.

Chapter 3

Proximal Causes of
Africa's Debt Crisis

3.1 'Treaties of Tyrants' and
'Dangerous Loans to Princes'

Whereas the previous chapter dealt with the more distant, structural bases of the crisis, this one seeks to examine its more proximate causes. It is argued here that there was as strong a supply dimension to the creation of Africa's indebtedness as there was the more conspicuous demand side; that one cannot fully appreciate the character of the crisis without examining the articulation of these two facets of the debt; that, indeed, finding workable solutions to the crisis necessitates such an approach; and that failure to do so results in non-remedial policy responses such as those of the new orthodoxy.

A comprehensive OECD survey of the then-emerging Third World debt crisis in 1983 concluded, *inter alia*, that "[d]eveloping-country debt problems [were] not all the same."[1] In a similar vein can it be argued that the African countries' debt problems were not all alike, as differing administrative capabilities and capacities, coherence of political leadership, conditions and structures of production, etc., all contributed in varying degrees to the level, composition and micro-level impact of the debt. Thus, whereas there were clearly identifiable and generalizable continental patterns of indebtedness, the *local* impact of the debt differed quite radically from one country to the next, in accordance with the socio-political and economic environment. The implications of this, and of the analyses in the last third of the previous chapter, is that an efficacious remedy should have addressed the crisis at the 'meta-level' of global political economy, the macro-level of national economic and development policy, and the micro-level of its impact on the household or individual citizen. The preferred neo-orthodox debt-relief strategy, which was based on the argument that unbridled *laissez-faire* was the answer to the problem everywhere and in all instances, is thus very worrisome indeed, as it has been shown not to have the desired remedial effect on the African economy or, at best, to have varying degrees of *sector-specific*, though not systemic, success in any given country.

But what were the immediate origins or proximal causes of Africa's debt crisis? As was indicated in the first chapter, there is some concensus among analysts that the crisis was precipitated by three sets of factors: (1) external shocks, such as the oil-price hikes of of the 1970s and the interest-rate shocks of the early 1980s; (2) the inefficient and/or inappropriate domestic economic policies and political practices of the African nations and, at times, the creditor-nations as well; and (3) incautious lending practices by commercial banks ably aided by the 1970s' innovations in international finance. Of the three, external shocks, particularly oil-price and interest rate hikes, have often taken the brunt of analysts' blame, the argument being that African countries had no recourse but to resort to external borrowing to finance the trade and budgetary deficits that the quadrupling of their oil-import bill in the 1970s engendered. However, as some have noted, for those countries that were preponderantly or heavily obligated to commercial lenders, expansion of bank lending to them "was not coincident with these two periods of increased financing needs."[2] Bank lending to Zaire, Côte d'Ivoire, Gabon, Nigeria and Zambia, among others, was increasing *before* the first oil shock. OPEC, therefore, cannot be said to be the sole, or even *the* major, proximal precipitator of their debt crises.

A second external factor, not given as prominent a place in the analyses as oil and interest rate shocks, stems from the tendency of commodity terms-of-trade to decline in the long term.[3] African political leaders, especially, viewed the decline in commodity prices that started in the late 1970s (see Tables 1.4 and 1.5), the causes of which are explained below, as *the* major cause of the debt crisis.[4] They were particularly fond of citing the 27% decline in non-oil primary commodity prices between 1980 and 1982, the very period in which the crisis was coming into its most virulent manifestation.

Their argument was that such price declines, even as the prices of manufactured imports crept ever upward, was nothing short of " a regular transfer of wealth from the poor countries to the rich...", which further undermined the ability of countries with such high export-commodity concentrations to weather the crisis.[5]

True as it may be that Africa's export performance is hostage to the vagaries of international commodity prices, and to its dependence on a small cluster of commodities for export revenue, commodity price volatility in the 1980-85 period does not explain why the major net oil-exporters—Nigeria, Congo, Cameroon, especially—became some of the largest debtors on the continent by 1985.[6] Nigeria, certainly, with 97% of its export revenues coming from oil by 1982, did not experience declining trade terms after the sharp initial drop between 1981 and 1982, and yet by 1985 it had become the single largest debtor on the continent.[7] Indeed, over the period covered by this work, Nigeria's commodity terms of trade was on a steep incline along trend!

On the domestic front, many have argued that interventionist, statist policies, which resulted in increased deficit spending by bloated state machineries led, not only to policy inefficiencies and resource wastage in many countries, but also to ever-increasing inflationary pressures on Africa's economies.[8] Since domestic inflation was, in this manner, consistently driven above world inflation levels, the currency exchange rates of these countries became heavily over-valued, killing off all incentives to domestic industry by flooding local markets with artificially cheap imports. These policies also led to wasteful, conspicuous consumption by the elite, who squandered scarce foreign-exchange on foreign luxury goods. The result was increasing budget deficits increasingly financed by external borrowing. Matters were, of course, not helped any by the commercial banks, which imprudently supplied some of the financing required by some of these countries that were clearly on questionable economic footing.[9]

Other analysts have focussed narrowly on the contribution of colonial or neo-colonial economic policies to the growth of Africa's indebtedness. They argue, as African leaders did in the 1980s, that many African colonies, because they were turned into mono-crop, primary-export economies, became particularly susceptible to the vagaries of the international market. At independence, power was handed over to the urban and agricultural elites who were the products and principal beneficiaries of this economic structure, and who therefore had little incentive to dismantle it.[10] Their managerial ineptitude, and their preference for trade and consumption to investment and production, led to a lop-sided dependence on foreign economies which, in itself, was "anti-developmental" in the final instance, as it led to a steady net outflow of capital (in terms of profit repatriation, management and consultancy fees, interest payments, etc.) over the long haul. Africa's economies, they conclude, have therefore institutionalized a tendency towards balance-of-payments deficits, which deficits are then financed by further external borrowing.[11]

On the domestic political front, the role of clientelism and the patrimonialistic tendencies of African governance in the creation of the crisis has already been discussed above.[12] To reiterate briefly, political cleavages in Africa tend to develop along ethnic and regional lines, itself a legacy of the colonial balkanization of 1884, with political factions securing support and tenure through patronage. The state, because it is seen as the single most important repository of economic resources, easily becomes the focus of a spoils system in which different ethnic groups or single-interest factions compete for control over the nation's resources, with which they then finance the necessary patronage networks that keep them in power. This style of governance has led to the misuse and misappropriation of the powers, privileges, resources and perquisites of state authority and, because of its high cost, to a tendency to incur external debts to finance the clientelist imperative. The case of Zaire, introduced in this chapter and fleshed out in the next, epitomizes this and some of the other peculiarities of the African polity that affect the debt crisis. It is quite evident from that case that the interaction of these internal factors with particular global developments produced the precipitatory causes of the crisis.

On the international scene it is worth noting that, by the early 1970s the industrial North was already slipping into recession, precipitating a process of deindustrialization that further worsened the economic downturn. Organized labour had, ostensibly, put a squeeze on profits by successfully pushing up industrial wage rates over the preceding fifteen years or so.[13] In addition the U.S. had, from the latter half of the 1950s, been monetizing parts of the Federal deficit to pay for the Korean and Vietnam wars. This not only increased the system's liquidity significantly, thus precipitating a search for profitable outlets for the 'extra' cash, but was also inflationary, ultimately, for the world economy. Thus, by the mid-1970s, the industrialized countries were already faced with a deep contradiction: an increasing supply of financial capital with a declining demand for it in their stagflated economies.

The oil-price shock of 1973 deepened this contradiction in a number of ways. First, the recession in the North was worsened by the higher oil price. Second, OPEC countries were flooded with revenue that their own economies could either not adequately absorb or absorb fast enough.[14] Much of this money was deposited in the same international banking system already awash in excess liquidity. As the money was moved about in the increasingly deregulated international financial markets, even more liquidity was created on paper.[15] Thus, by the second oil-price shock of 1979, there was already an enormous excess liquidity in the system for which banks were desperately seeking a profitable outlet.

The Third World became that outlet because it was perceived as having an almost limitless capacity for further industrialization and economic expansion, which would only be realized, per the two-gap model, by removing its foreign-exchange constraint. In the short term, of course, these countries needed to finance the four-fold increase in their oil-import bill. And, with the Northern economies already saturated and even declining, there were precious few alternative outlets. The fast pace of investment and economic growth induced by these loans would provide the income with which the loans would be paid, it was reasoned. Optimism was high for all concerned, loan-makers and -recipients alike; caution was particularly in short supply, in the circumstances.

On the lenders' side, the optimism came from the potential profitability of the process. That they had no previous experience with *commercial* lending on this scale internationally (most previous Third World financing booms had been, as was intimated earlier, through bond issues) was not, apparently, a deterrent. 'Innovations' in the lending process would be made to reduce lenders' risk. A certain complacency thus crept into the process fed, among other things, by the protection afforded the banks by variable interest rates. Typically, the rates charged was determined by the London Inter-bank Offered Rate (LIBOR) plus a mark-up. The rate therefore varied with LIBOR which, in turn, fluctuated with dollar interest rates. As

LIBOR is an index of the banks' cost of funds, the loans were profitable as long as the margin (or 'spread') exceeded bank administrative and other costs. In the 1970s, 'spread banking' became one of the major innovations of international banking, especially in the unregulated Euro-currency markets. Its principal effect, as Congdon argues, was to shift the macroeconomic risks associated with interest rate variations onto the borrower, while any specific (i.e. non-interest) risk associated with borrowers' unforeseen economic problems fell on the bank.[16] It was the acceptance of this interest-rate risk by the borrowing countries that made them vulnerable to the rate swings of the early 1980s, which then precipitated the debt crisis as we know it.

The complacency was further added to by the fact that lender-risk was supposed to be further reduced by the practice of loan syndication, which spread exposure across several banks instead of just one. In the event, this might actually have increased the risk of, especially, the smaller banks, which joined consortia to finance loans that they may not, independently or in more sober times, have financed, but which they joined in only because they felt participation and *de facto* stamp-of-approval of the larger banks lessened the likelihood of default. This assumption, in retrospect, proved roundly unwarranted, and may even have led to the involvement of many more banks in the crisis than might otherwise have been the case. The potential for systemic financial disruption, in the event of mass default was thereby that much more magnified by this "innovation" of syndication.[17] As John Makin observes of the optimism, imprudence and complacency of the times,

> The big banks, freed of any restrictions on direct lending abroad, and facing in 1974-75 a sharp recession at home, were attracted by the prospect of a new economic order associated with the rapid development of the resource-rich economies in Latin America, Asia and...Africa. When, during 1973-74...OPEC quadrupled oil prices, the machinery was in place to create, almost overnight, an enormous increase in the potential for international lending... If the world's largest commercial banks were to survive, they had to show themselves able to seize their share of the massive "recycling" required by the oil boom. ... Lending continued to rise...unabated...even when the combined surplus of the oil exporters fell to about $35 billion in 1975 [from $68 billion in 1974]. ... [T]his was..."a blip on the radar" that went unheeded...

...Nor is this problem unique to the twentieth century. Writing of the Medicis' heavy losses...to Edward IV...in the fifteenth century, the historian of their bank opines...: "Rather than refuse deposits, the Medicis succumbed to the temptation of seeking an outlet for surplus cash in making dangerous loans to princes."[18]

Also contributing to this complacent mood was the widespread belief in banking circles of the sovereign-risk theory, which held that since a sovereign nation would always own more than it owed, it could technically never go bankrupt. Its debts would eventually all be paid. Or, as a banker involved with Zaire's debt problems put it in 1979, "Zaire is a country with enormous potential, and it will be a country with enormous potential in one hundred years' time."[19] The fact, for instance, that very few of the 1930s' Latin American debts were ever paid back at par was not allowed to interfere with this optimism. As Liepietz describes it, "they [the bankers] laid siege to potential borrowers", increasing "the international exposure of Western banks.., from $280 billion to $900 billion."[20] And, in another telling observation of bankers' mind-set at the time, Makin writes:

[In the late 1970s and early 1980s], banks expanded their loans to developing countries by 25% a year... The new breed of bankers who engineered this revolution in banking were drawn by the sense of a "new economic order" and by some powerful economies of scale in lending hundreds of millions to a single dictator or minister at a stroke, rather than plodding along placing a hundred thousand here and a hundred thousand there to put up shopping centers or industrial parks."[21]

But, perhaps the single most eloquent statement about bank lending practices came from a besieged Dr. Ulloa, the then-new Prime Minister of Peru who, at the September 1980 annual joint IMF-World Bank meeting in Washington, D.C., was reported to have complained: "I can hardly face going back to the hotel; there are six different banks waiting for me."[22]

What attracted this volume of funds to the Third World, besides the stagnation in the North, was the fact that many of these countries, though monocultural primary producers, seemed genuinely attractive investment prospects. A primary commodity boom was on, leading to an expansion of government receipts from such products as sugar, coffee, groundnuts and cocoa (Table 1.5). The newly-industrializing countries of Latin America were even better prospects: Brazil, for one, was growing at 11% annually between 1968 and 1973, more than twice the average growth rate in the West, and closer to three times the growth rate in many countries, including the United States.[23] After years of mediocre growth, the commodity boom of the 1970s brought an expansion of government spending on development projects and imports, with export revenues often being supplemented with foreign loans.

When the commodity boom suddenly went bust in 1979-80, many African governments were unwilling to, or politically unable to, rein in spending. They rather increased their external borrowing to make up the loss in export revenue. Further, many of these latter loans were contracted to finance prestige, 'white elephant' projects that were either unproductive or plainly wasteful. The Gabonese case is instructive and, alas, all too typical: between 1979 and '81, the Omar Bongo government spent $600 million in export credits, and a further $679 million in syndicated loans, on a road linking the presidential palace with the airport, to enlarge the governing party's offices, and on a fleet of jet aircraft for the President and his ministers.[24] But perhaps the most eggregious contemporary example in SSA is the building of a $200 million basilica, larger than St. Peter's of Rome, by the late President Houphouet-Boigny of Côte d'Ivoire, "with [his] own finances, on [his] own ancestral land", as a gift quietly accepted by Pope John Paul II in 1991 on behalf of the Vatican, in a country where only 15% of the population was Catholic, and only 40% nominally Christian[25]. In these and many such cases, lending institutions took little care in ensuring that their moneys would be put to those supposed productive uses out of which an adequate income to service the debt would come.

For some African countries, however, borrowing was a necessity of survival. Producers of metals, particularly copper and iron, experienced a consistent downturn in prices (Table 1.4) throughout the 1970s. Zambia, Zaire (copper producers), Liberia and Mauritania (iron producers) were able to obtain foreign commercial loans to keep up government spending to stabilize living standards, on the expectation that copper and iron prices would soon return to their historical levels.[26] Since the expected recovery never materialized, by 1982-83 these countries were in even direr debt straits than those which had enjoyed the temporary boom in commodity prices.

By the end of the decade, SSA's external debt had grown to nearly $70 billion from the $6 billion figure at the beginning of it, in 1970. An average of 70% of this new debt was owed to multilaterals like the IMF and World Bank, as the majority of African countries were, despite the commodity boom, not considered particularly creditworthy by commercial lenders. Only 25% of the total was owed to private lenders, and these were concentrated in a handful of countries: Gabon, Côte d'Ivoire, Zaire, Cameroon, Nigeria, Zambia and Botswana.[27] Of the new commercial debt, nearly $10 billion, or about 60% of the total, had been contracted on non-concessional terms.

Two further developments beyond Africa's control would exacerbate this already grievous situation. The first was the second oil shock in 1979; the second, the abandonment by the major industrialized countries of thirty-five years of Keynesian macromanagement in favour of an aberrant monetarism called supply-side economics. Unlike 1973, the second oil-price hike was particularly devastating on Africa's oil importers, as there was no primary commodity boom to offset the resulting balance-of-payments difficulties. Indeed, by helping push the Northern economies deeper into recession, it actually helped turn the terms-of-trade against primary producers as demand for their exports contracted even further. This was exacerbated by the decision to use contractionary monetary policies in the U.S. (supply-side economics) and the U.K. ("Thatcherite monetarism") and (the-then) West Germany to combat the inflationary spiral that had beset their economies. The two levers of this policy was an attack on wages in the U.K. and the U.S., and substantial increments in interest rates over an eighteen-month period to curb credit creation in the financial system.[28]

The effect of monetary contraction was two-fold: first, markets contracted even further, choking off demand for Africa's exports (see Table 3.1), and causing a collapse in commodity prices. Secondly, it transformed the low (and even negative) real interest rates of the mid-1970s into positive rates (about 8% in the early 1980s) by wringing inflation out of the world economy. Thus, for the debtor-nations of SSA, the rate of growth of their external debt, as measured by the growth of interest on it, kept moving up ever faster than their foreign-exchange earnings. And "[a]lthough [they]...were successful in reducing their aggregate current account deficit...[by] 1985, global demand was simply insufficient to generate the foreign exchange to meet foreign debt payments *and* contribute to economic growth."[29]

TABLE 3.1
Growth of Exports, 1965-1986 (Comparative Data)

	Average Annual Change in Export Volume (%)						
	1965-7	73-80	1982	1983	1984	1985	1986
Export volume, by commodity							
LDCs	4.9	4.7	0.2	5.1	11.5	1.4	3.6
Manufactures	11.6	13.8	0.0	11.3	20.3	1.1	6.3
Food	2.9	4.3	-2.5	-1.1	4.6	3.5	-2.6
Non-food	2.7	1.2	-2.0	0.9	5.9	4.4	0.1
Metals & Minerals	4.8	7.0	-0.9	-1.0	1.6	6.1	7.9
Fuels	4.0	-0.8	3.1	2.4	5.2	-1.2	2.4
WORLD*	8.8	4.4	-3.2	0.7	9.5	3.5	3.2
Manufactures	10.7	6.1	-2.7	4.2	12.6	5.2	3.2
Food	5.0	6.6	0.1	-5.1	6.8	0.7	-4.1
Non-food	3.1	1.0	-3.0	-0.5	7.3	7.8	0.0
Metals & Minerals	6.8	8.7	-0.6	-1.5	7.7	3.9	2.4
Fuels	8.6	0.0	-7.0	-6.5	1.2	-2.3	10.2
Export volume, by country group							
LDCs	4.9	4.7	0.2	5.1	11.5	1.4	3.6
Manufactures	11.6	13.8	0.0	11.3	20.3	1.1	6.3
Primary Goods	3.7	1.2	0.4	0.8	4.7	1.6	1.2
SUB-SAHARAN AFRICA	15.0	0.1	-11.0	-4.1	10.3	6.9	3.8
Manufactures	7.5	5.6	-1.8	8.4	1.8	8.6	7.1
Primary Goods	15.3	-0.1	-12.0	-5.0	11.0	6.7	3.4
HIGHLY-INDEBTED COUNTRIES	3.1	1.1	-5.6	0.9	10.4	0.4	0.8
Manufactures	13.4	10.2	-10.7	6.8	29.7	-3.3	2.5
Primary Goods	2.4	-0.4	-4.1	-0.7	4.7	1.8	0.0
INDUSTRIAL-MARKET ECONOMIES	9.4	5.4	-1.8	1.9	10.2	5.3	1.7

*Excludes non-market European economies.
Source: World Bank, *World Development Report, 1987*, Table A.8, p. 175.

Between 1980 and 1985, therefore, the majority of SSAn countries had no option but to increase their external borrowing even at the higher rates of interest. By 1985, SSA's debt had risen to $120 billion, a twenty-fold increase from 1970!

In his classic study of the de Medicis of medieval Florence, Raymond de Roover describes the imprudent banking practices of the family that led to the eventual demise of their financial empire as nothing but a greedy and opportunistic search for outlets for the bank's surplus cash which led them to make "dangerous loans to princes".[30] The recycling frenzy of the 1970s was, similarly, an incautious and greedy bid to make "dangerous loans" to all manner of despots, autocrats, knaves and kakistocrats on the African continent. The factors underlying the supply of credit to these regimes are therefore summarized below under the heading of 'Dangerous Loans to Princes'.

On the demand side, a significant proportion of the loans acquired went to finance, as we have seen, consumption and other unproductive activities, such as the governments' clientelist networks. Since the borrowers and ultimate beneficiaries of these loans were the elite, the statement of the French revolutionary government of 1792 in repudiating royalist debts—"The sovereignty of peoples is not bound by the treaties of tyrants"—is particularly applicable to the African case. The causes of the borrowing binge are therefore also summarized below under 'Treaties of Tyrants'.[31]

The Demand for Debt: Treaties of Tyrants

The most important source of long-term external borrowing in SSA was the post-colonial state which, in the decade or so after the attainment of political independence (approximately between 1957 and 1970), found itself in the position of being the only viable economic entity capable of carrying out those capital projects that had been neglected by the colonizers, but which were indispensable to the economic development of the new nation. Thus did the provision of basic infrastructure and other civil engineering projects (dams, bridges, power plants, communications systems, schools, hospitals, etc.) become, in the absence of local private capital, the sole preserve of the public sector. As the departing colonialists had made little provision for the funding of such high-cost projects, and as the level of local saving was, given per capita income, rather low, the state had to resort to external borrowing to finance the projects. In most cases this was done, as was argued in the previous chapter, in accordance with the popular development theories of the time or, in what amounts to the same thing, at the behest of the Western-trained economists and bureaucrats running the appropriate ministries. Thus, in many African countries, the first decade of independence was nothing short of a decade of mass construction and high acquisition of long-term debt, with everything deemed necessary or feasible being constructed in rapid pursuit of the Rostowian take-off.

The bulk of the financing came either in the form of soft loans from the World Bank and other multilaterals, or as export credits granted by Western banks and governments to facilitate the importation of machinery and other inputs from their countries. Commercial loans contracted with private financial houses were relatively small in number, and smaller still in magnitude. Outright grants made up less than 26% of the total, though the majority of the loans were long-term (an average maturity of 15 years), at concessional rates, and with a generous grace period of better than eight years, on the average.

Given the ready availability of low-cost loans, and in those heady early days of post-independence euphoria and optimism, some SSAn countries pursued policies that led, as has been previously indicated, to the construction of massive prestige projects that, they believed, signalled their parity with the industrialized countries. These projects offered little complementarity to the overall development strategy, thus failing to provide the requisite linkages between the countries' demand structures and production capabilities. They tended, instead, to reinforce the production structures established by the colonialists to service the metropolitan markets, as massive export drives were undertaken to enable the acquisition of foreign inputs for capital projects at home. As investment projects, therefore, they proved to be spectacularly non-self liquidating. In other words, they generated little income, directly or indirectly, by which their initial and operating costs may be defrayed.

Secondly, such poor planning necessarily led to massive fraud and wastage in many countries, as managerial ineptitude and bureaucratic unaccountability combined with the simple availability of opportunity (as cheap loans flooded the countries' treasuries) to create top-heavy kleptocracies given to episodic crises. Indeed, it is the legacy of this climate of policy inefficiency, theft, graft and the institutional blurring of the distinction between private and public wealth that contributed, in its own way, to SSA's debt-and-development crisis in the 1980s.

Thirdly, because the sovereign state was thought to be *de facto* immune from bankruptcy, and in their eagerness to enter the newly-emerging markets, private lenders exercised little of the conservatism, caution, prudence and risk-aversion that sound banking principles normally engender. This, in retrospect, was a prelude to the debt crises of the 1980s, and to the institutional changes in world banking that facilitated such practices.[32] Thus very little monitoring of their loans was done, with the result that one possibility of ensuring their productive (i.e. income-generating) usage, was lost. The long-term debt of these nations, then, was itself a crisis waiting to happen.

All through the 1960s and 1970s, therefore, not only were many SSAn countries saddled with massive long-term debts unproductively employed and waiting to be paid, but there was also a steady stream of short-term loans that were contracted to overcome a variety of unexpected shocks. The first set of shocks was of largely domestic origin, stemming primarily from the massive budget overruns resulting from the high public-sector expenditures of the immediate post-independence period. The second was also internal, but it took the form of natural disasters—the droughts, desertifications, etc. discussed in chapter one—that intermittently plagued Africa from the late 1970s through the early 1980s. But the third set of shocks, and perhaps the one that most engendered the debt crisis and its attendant macroeconomic burdens, was of wholly external origin. This is analyzed below as a supply-side precipitator of the crisis.

The Supply of Debt: Dangerous Loans to Princes

Having discussed earlier the details of the debt-creation process in the international economy in the 1970s, its broad outlines are summarized here in order to contrast the lending process with its complementary borrowing process as analyzed in the preceding section. This should also facilitate later the drawing of the requisite analytical linkages between the debt-creation/debt-acquisition process and the specificities of Africa's debt crisis. Other discretionary economic policies of the industrial North that contributed to the creation of the crises are also examined in this section.

The most widely recognized external shock underlying the debt crisis was the quadrupling of crude oil prices in the mid-1970s. As was mentioned in the first chapter, the immediate impact of this on Africa, with the exception of oil-exporting Nigeria, Cameroon, Angola and Gabon was, at least, a quadrupling of the oil-import bill. Fiscally, this aggravated the budgetary imbalances that had existed since the mid-1960s, as African countries began spending as much as 25% of total government outlays on the importation of oil alone, as compared to an average of 4%-6% over the 1960-1969 period.[33] But, more importantly, given their already weak budgetary positions, it meant resorting to further external borrowing to finance the bulk of their imports. This time around, however, a (historically) greater portion of the lending came from private financial houses newly awash in petro-dollars which they were anxious to recycle, even at negative real rates of interest, in virtually any volume. When coupled with the institutional innovations in world banking—the rise of the comparatively unregulated Eurocurrency markets; the transformation of traditional deposit institutions like Citibank into free-wheeling, 'money-centre' banks with an aggressive international outlook; and the renewed vigor of export credit/export promotion programmes in the stagflated industrial economies[34]—most Third World sovereign borrowers were virtually assured of an almost elastic supply of loan-dollars at near-zero real-interest cost. For the fragile African economies reeling under a decade-and-a-half of fiscal imbalances; massive long-term, albeit concessionary, external debt; sub-optimal domestic economic performance and prospects; continually declining trade terms; and convertible currencies (in which their external obligations were denominated) newly taken off the gold standard, this massive recycling project set the stage for the emergence of high interest rates once the world economy stabilized and the demand for credit rose consequently. With no true prospects of their export performance improving commensurately, the potential for a debt crisis, technically defined, was written into the global economy of the 1970s.[35] It was manifested, for SSA, when the internal structural problems that began nearly two decades earlier converged on this international economic environment. Global economic conditions, in general, and the policies pursued by the industrial countries in that decade, in particular, clearly provided the triggers for Africa's debt crisis in the 1980s.

The paramount features of the 1970s' international economy—low growth, high unemployment and high inflation—were, for the industrialized nations, coming hard upon two-and-a-half decades of uncommonly rapid economic and employment growth, and a level of general prosperity partly made possible by Keynesian macromanagement. The turnaround in their economic fortunes in the 1970s, therefore, elicited an urgent search for remedial action. The regime of policies eventually settled on, though, was, as has been suggested, of a peculiarly pre-Keynesian variety, dominated as it was by a zeal for market deregulation and monetary control. Indeed, an aberrant classical economics was resuscitated under various guises, with policy makers all over the world vying to outdo one another in the extent to which they would reintroduce *laissez-faire* into the public domain.

The most conspicuous policy of this new classicism was the severe restriction of credit initiated by Paul Volcker, Chairman of the U.S. Federal Reserve, in 1978-79, and followed immediately by the conservative governments of (West) Germany and the U.K., in a bid to control an inflationary tide that had proved rather intractable for much of that decade. As a macromanagement tool, it did attain its objective, but only after throwing the world economy into a tailspin that culminated, in 1981-83, in the deepest post-war recession yet. For the purposes of this work, it is the other effect of this policy— historically high interest rates—that is of significance. For it had the impact of driving up the growth rate of the debt, a rate that was increased even further when the fiscal and other economic policies of the Reagan and Thatcher governments created public-sector budgetary deficits and unprecedented private sector borrowing that placed an inordinate demand on capital markets. At the same time, the deep recession induced by monetary contraction led to, for SSA, a 24% drop in export demand[36], an 8% surcharge on debt outstanding as real interest rates soared above their historical average, and a 16% contraction in its commodity terms-of-trade.[37] Coupled with the 48% increase in overall import costs (due, mainly, to the rise in prices of oil and manufactures), and with the slump in domestic production discussed in Chapter One, Africa's debt crisis, by year-end 1979, was well under way.

Two other policy changes in the West contributed either to initiating the crisis, or exacerbating it, once initiated. The first is closely related to the response of industry to the low profit margins that the economy of the 1970s was generating. In the U.S., and parts of Western Europe, falling profitability led to the deindustrialization practices mentioned earlier, with the result, as Bluestone and Harrison have argued, that manufacturing within the continental U.S. and Europe was significantly replaced by an array of service industries consisting mainly of low-wage, low-skill, low-overhead and low-input outfits. The impact of this structural shift in the economic base of the industrialized West—from high raw-material input manufactures to low-input services and even, as Clive Thomas has suggested, declining raw-material absorption in manufacturing as such—was a drastic drop in the demand for Africa's traditional exports[38]. As this led to declines in commodity prices and trade terms, there was a further deterioration in the already-precarious income-generating capacities of Africa's economies, rendering their debt servicing that much more problematic.

The second development stemmed from governments' response to the farm crises that gripped both Europe and the U.S. from the middle years of the 1970s onward. To protect the economic efficacy and integrity of the politically powerful rural household, most governments in the West and in Japan heavily subsidized, on an on-going basis, their native agricultural producers, through price supports, market guarantees, concessional credit, and/or output quotas. The effect of these policies was to keep the costs of agricultural production artificially low, thus making some of Africa's primary exports uncompetitive on world markets, with similar disastrous consequences for its export revenues and share of international markets. As a recent study concludes, "[t]he ending of agricultural protectionism will...boost incomes in developing countries by $26 billion, allowing even the poorest to reduce their foreign debt by 5% a year."[39]

All these developments combined with the long-term budgetary and structural problems of the 1960s and 1970s to precipitate SSA's debt crisis of the 1980s. To isolate any one of these factors, therefore, and impose on it a burden of causality that cannot be sustained, will only lead to policy recommendations that cannot provide sufficient respite from the crisis. It would appear that the remedies of the 'new' orthodoxy, which are analyzed more concretely in the next chapter, come from just such a partial analysis. That they should prove ineffective in practice, therefore, should not be unexpected. The case of Zaire, perhaps more than any other, epitomizes the typical African debtor-nation in which all the factors identified in this and previous chapters have played conspicuous roles over an extended period of time in creating and sustaining the country's crises. The following analysis, which anticipates the case studies of the next chapter, is therefore intended to add empirical substance to the broad deductive assertions made thus far in this chapter.

3.2 Tyrants and Princes in Zaire

Zaire is a vast, mineral-laden country in central Africa whose status in 1985 as the fourth poorest nation in the world, with an income of $140 per capita, contrasted remarkably with its potential wealth and economic viability.[40] For the past thirty years, it has been a major world exporter of cobalt, copper, uranium and diamonds. But by year-end 1985 it was the fourth largest debtor in SSA, with a total external debt of $6 billion which had grown by 18% from the previous year.[41] Its debt-to-GNP ratio stood at 137%, up from 74% in 1980 and, unlike other African countries, only two-thirds of its debt was owed to official creditors. The average terms of its commercial, non-concessional debt was also considerably worse than those of thirty other debtors with substantial commercial debt: the average interest on Zairean debt was 6.9%, as opposed to 2.6% for those other countries; with an average maturity of 14.9 years, as compared to 30.7 years for the others; and a 4.4-year average grace period, when the others enjoyed 7.8-year grace periods.[42] Debt service rose from 16.7% to 66% of export earnings between 1980 and 1985, and by the end of 1985, a full 44% of the national bugdet was going into debt service, as compared to 10% three years earlier.[43]

The causes and sources of poverty and indebtedness in Zaire are many. On the one hand, Zaire was a victim of external developments beyond its control, most prominently the steep decline in copper prices (see Table 1.5) throughout the 1970s: from $4.07 per 1000 tonnes in 1970 to $1.59 per 1000 tonnes in 1983, a 61% drop! As the country's single largest foreign-exchange earner, accounting for 43% of all export earnings, the impact of this on government revenue was devastating: for instance, between 1974 and 1975 alone, there was a $600 million drop in export revenue, with comparable losses in every one but three of the years between 1970 and 1985.[44] Equally devastating were the effects of rising oil prices between 1973 and 1979: by 1977, Zaire was spending 20% of its already falling export revenue, some $200 million, on oil imports, as compared to some $45 million in 1970. The Angolan civil war also had a prominent role in the the country's economic woes, as it brought about the closure of the Benguela Railway, the most efficient transport access to the Shaba copperbelt. The irredentist uprisings by the Katanga in Shaba in 1977 and 1978, of course, did not help matters any.[45]

But equally culpable were internal, policy-induced factors which had very little to do with the international events mentioned above. Topping the list was the undue emphasis by the Mobutu government on costly, ultimately unproductive, prestige industrial projects as the cornerstone of its development strategy. Between 1973 and 1975, for instance, Zaire borrowed $2.6 billion to finance the massive Maluku Steel Mill and the Inga-Shaba electric powerline, among other projects. The mill could produce steel only at eight times the cost of imported steel, and it never operated at better than 10% of its 250,000 tonne capacity. By 1980 it was so deeply in debt that it had to cease operations.[46] The Inga-Shaba powerline was also a spectacular development blunder: it added 1750 megawatts to existing capacity, only 350 megawatts of which actually found productive use.[47] To create demand for the excess power supply, the government set up the Zaire Industrial Free Zone (ZOFI) on the River Zaire estuary, to attract foreign investors with promises of electricity at half its market price. By 1984, only a handful of companies had taken advantage of the offer.

Systemic corruption in the Zairean polity was also very influential in the crisis. Mobutu himself was suspected in 1985 of having personal holdings in Swiss and Belgian bank accounts and properties of some $5 billion, about the size of the country's outstanding external debt at the time.[48] But those close to Mobutu also share in the lucrative spoils: e.g. the Shaba Regional Commissioner was reported to have grossed $100,000 a month in 1975, of which only 2% would have been his official salary; and, in the same year, "a prominent general...had a monthly salary of 45,000 zaires plus [other] informal payments, including 8,000 zaires a month...from a special account in the Banque de Kinshasa."[49] Indeed, corruption and subterranean economic activity, ranging from coffee smuggling to illegal diamond mining to rice marketing, blossomed through the top strata of Zairean society, a development that Callaghy attributes to the imperatives of the patrimonial or clientelist state, but which must also reflect the failure of the formal structures and channels of economic activity, for reasons that will be elaborated shortly.[50]

Throughout the 1980s the formal economy of Zaire was largely mired somewhere between unproductivity and dysfunctionality, as state resources were continually diverted by the elites to finance the extensive clientelist networks that ensured the continuance in power, and the accumulation of personal wealth, of a small group of Zaireans close to the President and the sole political party. No single policy highlighted this predatory process more than the "Zaireanization" programme of 1973-75 under which foreign-owned companies were "indigenized". But, rather than being brought under state control, as nationalization would normally require, these companies were distributed among high government and party officials who, for the most part, had neither the management experience nor the desire to operate them as going concerns. These *acquéreurs* (acquirers) simply liquidated the more desirable assets of these otherwise functional and profitable enterprises, quickly depleting Zaire of its better commercial and manufacturing infrastructure and causing shortages of basic goods as a result. The inflationary spiral which it gave impetus to spurred hoarding and smuggling activities which, in their turn, fed the inflationary pressures in the economy even more. In addition, many *acquéreurs* would neither pay their taxes nor honour the legitimate debts of the businesses they took over. It was soon clear that Zaireanization was not a nationalist development policy as it had initially been proclaimed, but another manifestation of the clientelist state in action. To prevent further erosion of the economy's commercial/industrial base, the government was forced to rescind the programme in 1978, and return the companies to their previous owners.[51]

There are other, equally telling examples of how the greed of the Zairean aristocracy, systemic corruption and clientelist activity led to economic dysfunction in the country. For a long time the parastatal responsible for marketing cobalt and copper on the government's behalf, SOZACOM, was a major source of illicit hard currency for the elite. A small group of ministers and party functionaries were reported to have, between 1973 and 1978, misappropriated $1 billion of the company's earnings to set themselves up in the lucrative, though nominally illicit, currency market. The theft, which was eventually made up with foreign loans, and which was only uncovered when the IMF virtually took over the country's finances in 1982, was suspected to have gone as high as the presidential palace.[52]

The President, of course, had long been known to keep the choicest assets for himself and his immediate family. A plantation of 16,000 hectares, some of the best land for growing cocoa, coffee, rubber and palm nuts in Zaire, was taken over by Mobutu and his wife after "nationalization" in 1973.[53] These, and such activities, did enormous damage to the economy; it is estimated, for instance, that as much as 20% of the national budget was often lost through acts of official corruption.[54] In December 1980, a group of thirteen parliamentarians who wrote an advisory to the President, noting that if even a quarter of the elites' illicit wealth was returned from abroad the country could pay off its foreign debt, found themselves behind bars.[55]

It is easy to see how external and internal circumstances, and especially the peculiar conduct of politics in Africa, earned Zaire the status of one of the continent's most indebted and crisis-ridden economies. Perhaps in no other place in Africa did all the factors identified in this study—structural or long-term; episodic or short-term; domestic or external—as underlying the continent's joint-crisis of debt and underdevelopment converge as clearly as in Zaire. How it dealt with these issues, therefore, is instructive for the search for solutions to the crises. We will therefore pay considerable attention to adjustment in Zaire in the next chapter.

Summary and Conclusion

The events that precipitated SSA's debt crisis in the 1980s are of both domestic and external origin, though the external factors appear to have often preponderated. Internal economic and political policies, by failing to provide those institutional checks with which their more serious debilitating effects could be blunted, only served to magnify the impact of these forces on Africa's debt and development performance.

The emphasis in the literature through the first half of the 1990s was on those internal policy malfeasances of the debtor nations that might have deepened the crisis. The culpability of lenders in greedily, imprudently and bullishly supplying the debt, even in the face of unencouraging macroeconomic data and performance forecasts, was only peripherally addressed. This led to mistaken notions being entertained, even by the World Bank and the IMF, that the causes of the crises lay more *within* the indebted economies, than in their particular mode of interaction *per se* with the system of international trade and finance extant. Thus corrective measures, almost all free market-based policies inspired by the 'new' orthodoxy, were vigorously pursued, thusly placing the cost of adjustment, human and financial, almost exclusively on the indebted countries. The lenders' only cost, if that it was, was the periodic tardiness of debt service payments, the writing down of some problem loans, and the (continually receding) prospects of default. And even if default had occured, governments and central banks were poised to bail out the banks in order to forestall any systemic disruptions. Thus the 'free market' was not going to be allowed, as one would expect in an era of resurgent *laissez-faire*, to discipline lenders for not being sufficiently risk-averse. The 'euthanasia of the rentier' which Keynes, and Ricardo before him, had identified as, at times, a necessary disciplinary force for the continued health of a market economy, was not going to be allowed to take place. Ultimately, then, the culpability of the banks in the creation of the crisis was being heavily discounted by the international system, while that of the debtors was used to exact 'adjustment punishment' on them. This is one of the more telling contradictions of the new orthodoxy—advocating market determinations as the most efficient means to economic development in the borrower-countries, even as the market is partially constrained from taking economic matters to their logical, 'market' conclusion in the lender-countries.

In the next two chapters, we examine what *is* being done in SSA, by way of remedial policy, to tackle the debt crisis, and the effects, successes and/or failures of these policies. An attempt is made to show, using case studies where necessary, how and why some of the structures of economy and politics analyzed in this work help or hinder these policies in providing the required remedy. This is followed, in the final chapter, by a discussion of what *ought* to be done.

Notes

1. OECD, **External Debt of Developing Countries: 1983 Survey** (Geneva: OECD, 1984), pp. 48-49.
2. See, for instance, K. Halberg, International Debt in 1985: Origins and Issues for the Future, in M.P. Clandon, ed., **World Debt Crisis: International Lending on Trial** (Cambridge, MA.: Ballinger Publishing, 1986), p. 9.
3. See Colman and Nixson, op. cit., pp. 90-106; P. Bairoch, The **Economic Development of the Third World since 1900** (London: Methuen, 1975), ch. 6; and P. Shapouri and S. Rosen, **Export Performance in Africa** (Washington, D.C.: U.S. Dept. of Agriculture Economic Research Service, May 1989).
4. See, as an example, Julius Nyerere, An Address, **Development and Change**, Vol. 17, No. 3 (July 1986), p. 387-397; and Ernest Harsch, After Adjustment, **Africa Report**, Vol. 34 (May/June 1989), pp. 47-50.
5. Nyerere, op. cit., p. 389. Some of the statistics on Africa's undiversified export structure, which makes it vulnerable to commodity-price fluctuations, are very revealing indeed. For instance, Nafziger shows that some 80% of Africa's export earnings by 1978 came from its three principal exports, as compared to 61% in 1961. In 1985, six commodities accounted for 70% of continental export revenue. By 1982, Nigeria was obtaining 97% of its export revenue from oil alone; Uganda, 96% from coffee alone; Somalia, 94% from livestock; Burundi, 90% from coffee; Zambia, 89% from copper; Rwanda, 68% from coffee; Ethiopia, 65% from coffee; Ghana, 59% from cocoa; Madagascar, 47% from coffee; Zaire, 43% from copper; Burkina Faso, 40% from cotton; and Sudan, 39% from cotton. In the same year, the so-called tropical beverages—coffee, cocoa and tea—accounted for 24% of continental export revenue. And, on the average, many African countries have export-commodity concentration ratios (i.e. the percentage of their export earnings accounted for by their four leading exports) of around 60%. See Nafziger, op. cit., p.66.
6. At year-end 1985, Nigeria had the largest external debt, some $20 billion, on the continent. Cameroon and Congo each had about $3 billion, and ranked No. 8 and No. 10, respectively, on the African debt charts. See Nafziger, op. cit., p.14.
7. Nafziger, op. cit., Table 4.1, p. 69.
8. See, for instance, World Bank, **Accelerated Development in Sub-Saharan Africa** (Washington, D.C.: 1982), and IMF, **World Economic Outlook** (Washington, D.C.: 1986).

content

9. See P. Nunnenkamp, **The International Debt Crisis of the Third World: Causes and Consequences for the World Economy**, (Sussex: Wheatsheaf Books, 1986), ch. 7.
10. See the case of Kenya as discussed in Chapter 2.
11. For an example of this argument, see P. Korner, G. Maass, T. Siebold and R. Tetzlaff, **The IMF and the Debt Crisis: A Guide to the Third World's Dilemmas** (London: Zed Books, 1986), ch. 1.
12. For a more comprehensive analysis of this phenomenon, see R.H. Jackson and C.G. Rosberg, **Personal Rule in Black Africa: Prince, Aristocrat, Prophet, Tyrant** (Los Angeles: Univ. of California Press, 1982); and R. Sandbrook and J. Barker, **The Politics of Africa's Economic Stagnation** (Cambridge: Cambridge Univ. Press, 1985).
13. For the U.K., see Bob Sutcliffe, **Hard Times** (London: Pluto Press, 1983); and for the U.S., B. Bluestone and B. Harris, **The Deindustrialization of America** (N.Y.: Basic Books, 1982).
14. Between 1973 and 1974 alone, the oil-exporting countries' current account surpluses increased from $7 billion to $68 billion. See H. Lever and C. Huhne, **Debt and Danger: The World Financial Crisis** (Hammondsworth: Penguin, 1985), ch. 2.
15. The industrialized countries had no reserve requirements on offshore lending, even though they kept about a 10% reserve ratio for domestic banking. Thus a single dollar on deposit in, say, New York, may serve as the base for ten, or even a hundred, dollars in loans internationally. There are estimates to the effect that the aggregate amount of offshore direct deposits between 1973 and 1976 was over $300 billion, with banks expanding this many times over through international lending. See R.P. DeWitt and J.F. Petras, Political Economy of International Debt: The Dynamics of Financial Capital, in J.D. Aronson, ed., **Debt and the Less Developed Countries** (Boulder: Westview Press, 1979), p. 20.
16. Tim Congdon, op. cit., ch. 4-7.
17. See Nunnenkamp, op. cit., p. 96.
18. Makin, op. cit., p. 28, citing Raymond de Roover, **The Medici Bank** (N.Y.: NYU Press, 1948).
19. Delamaide, op. cit., p. 57, quoting Meynel from his article 'Erwin Blumenthal', in **Euromoney**, Feb. 1979, p. 14.
20. Alain Liepietz, How Monetarism Has Choked Third World Industrialization, **New Left Review**, No. 145 (May-June, 19840, p. 77.
21. Makin, op. cit., p. 4. For a colourful and delightfully quotable observation of the competitiveness and aggression in private lending at the time, see Anthony Sampson, **The Money Lenders** (N.Y.: Penguin Books, 1981), pp. 18-19.
22. Anthony Sampson, op. cit., p. 19.

23. Makin, op. cit., p. 5.
24. See Lever and Huhne, op. cit., p. 59.
25. As local wags would irreverently have it, perhaps, at 87, 'Le Vieux' was then much less concerned with the politics of development than he was with the politics of entering heaven. See Ofeibea Quist-Arcton, So Old, So Wise?, **BBC's Focus on Africa**, Vol. 4, No. 3 (July-Sept., 1993), pp. 10-11.
26. Krumm, op. cit., p. 8. See also the case study of Zambia in Chapter 5; and Kenneth Good, op. cit., pp. 297-313.
27. Krumm, op. cit., Table 1, p. 45.
28. See Liepietz, op. cit., p. 81.
29. Economist Intelligence Unit, **Multinational Business Quarterly**, Vol. 4 (1986), pp. 17-19.
30. See Makin, op. cit., ch. 1.
31. Makin, op. cit., ch. 2.
32. For further elaborations of banks' changing attitudes and lending practices in the 1970s, see Tim Congdon, op. cit., ch. 4-7, and Richard Lombardi, **Debt Trap: Rethinking the Logic of Development** (N.Y.: Praeger, 1985), chs. 9 and 10.
33. World Bank, **Financing Adjustment...**, Table 9, p. 75.
34. See Lombardi, op. cit., ch. 5.
35. See the analysis in Chapter 1.
36. Shapouri and Rosen, op. cit., Tables 1, 2, 3 and 17.
37. See William Cline, International Debt: Analysis, Experience and Prospects, **Journal of Development Planning**, No. 16 (1985), from which these figures were extrapolated.
38. See Clive Thomas, **The Poor and the Powerless: Economic Policy and Change in the Caribbean** (N.Y.: Monthly Review Press, 1988), ch. 14-15.
39. A. Stoeckel, D. Vincent and S. Cuthbertson, eds., **Macroeconomic Consequences of Farm Support Policies** (Durham: Duke Univ. Press, 1989), p. 35.
40. This section relies heavily on Parfitt and Riley, op. cit., ch. 4; Andrew Schoenholtz, The IMF in Africa: Unnecessary and Undesirable Western Restraints on Development, **Journal of Modern African Studies**, Vol. 25, No. 3 (1987), pp. 403-433; and the various studies of Zaire by T. Callaghy cited below.
41. Trevor and Parfitt, op. cit., Table 4.1, p. 77. See also Nafziger, op. cit., Table 1.8, p. 14.
42. A. Wood, The Funding of the Permanent Crisis: A Study of IMF Intervention in Zaire, in J. Caballero, G. Nott, A. Wood and M. Lajo, **IMF Policies in the Third World; Case Studies of Turkey, Zaire and Peru** (Univ. of East Anglia Development Studies Occasional Paper,

1985), p. 2, as cited by Parfitt and Riley, op. cit., p. 76.

43. World Bank, **World Debt Tables: External Debt of Developing Countries, 1987** (Washington, D.C.: Feb. 1987), p. 195; **African Business** (May 1986), p. 29, as cited by Parfitt and Riley, op. cit., p. 76.

44. See Delamaide, op. cit., p. 60.

45. See C. Young and T. Turner, **The Rise and Decline of the Zairean State** (Madison: Univ. of Wisconsin Press, 1985), p. 280.

46. See Young and Turner, op. cit., pp. 296-298.

47. Economist Intelligence Unit, **Quarterly Economic Review of Zaire, Rwanda and Burundi**, Vol. 3 (London: The Economist, 1984), p 14, as cited by Parfitt and Riley, op. cit., p. 79.

48. See Delamaide, op. cit., p. 60.

49. T. Callaghy, External Actrors and the Relative Autonomy of the Political Aristocracy in Zaire, **Journal of Commonwealth and Comparative Politics**, Vol. 21, No. 3 (1983), p. 69.

50. Ibid. See also Callaghy, **The State-Society Struggle: Zaire in Comparative Perspective** (N.Y.: Columbia Univ. Press, 1984), especially ch. 4.

51. See Young and Turner, op. cit., ch. 11, especially pp. 326-362.

52. **African Business** (Sept. 1984), p. 47, as cited by Parfitt and Riley, op. cit., p. 81.

53. Schoenholtz, op. cit., p. 424.

54. Korner, Maass, et. al., op. cit., p. 100-101, as cited by Parfitt and Riley, op. cit., p. 81.

55. Ibid.

Chapter 4

The Neo-Orthodox Middle Ground

The analysis so far would lead us to the proposition that any remedy prescribed for the debt crisis that was not designed to help overcome the structural bottlenecks of the African economy identified in the second chapter, and that did not, therefore, aim, in the long term, at giving a boost to balanced domestic economic expansion, could not provide a credible solution to the crisis. As Africa's debt crisis was nothing more than a phenomenon of its (under)development crisis writ large, there could not have been any solution to it outside of the (set of) solutions to the underdevelopment crisis as such. To that end, remedies for the debt must necessarily be long-term, curative and strategic, not merely short-term, tactical and palliative. It is on this premise that the arguments and analyses of this and subsequent chapters unfold.

It is argued in these chapters that the solutions popularly pursued from 1980 onward, at the heart of which was systemic liberalization to "let the market work" to induce structural change were, in fact, roundly incapable of achieving a lasting solution, and might well have, as the evaluative studies at the end of this chapter suggest, exacerbated and prolonged the crisis. In this chapter, we will narrowly be concerned with the detail of the economics and politics of these 'new' orthodox policies that the multilateral organizations and Western creditor-nations foisted on the African debtors, and the domestic and international economic and political conditions that should have obtained for the policies to have achieved their stated objectives. The next chapter, following upon the arguments of this one will examine, through case studies of the adjustment process in Zambia and Zaire, the specific institutional and structural conditions that determine the success or failure of IMF-type adjustment processes in the African context. This will then set the stage for the consideration, in Chapter Six, of alternative frameworks for the supercession of the structural pathologies that were shown earlier on (Chapter Two) to underlie the continent's debt and other economic crises. It is out of this detailed consideration of all these factors that, it is hoped, a more comprehensive alternative solution for the debt-underdevelopment crisis, better attuned to the nuances of the African setting, will be forthcoming in the final chapter.

A careful examination of the various weapons in the traditional debt-relief arsenal of the 1980s would suggest that the new orthodoxy was, in fact, recommending what was largely an unviable, indeed a functionally non-existent, middle ground between comprehensive debt forgiveness (by the creditors) and unilateral debt repudiation (by the debtors) as *the* crucial first step towards a meaningful resolution of the debt-underdevelopment crisis. The exclusion of these two strategems—forgiveness and repudiation—was, itself, a reflection of the partial scope of the traditional analysis and understanding of what the African debt crisis truly entailed.

If, indeed, as the orthodox analysis has it, the crisis was no more than a transfer problem arising from a passing liquidity debacle, the logical remedial policy would be one that sought to ease that liquidity bottleneck. This, of course, could be achieved by adjusting the indebted economy at its margins, as IMF/World Bank-sponsored 'structural' adjustment, in fact, does. The necessity of "extreme" measures like repudiation or forgiveness would, therefore, be realistically precluded.

If, on the other hand, SSA's debt crisis was, as is being argued here, ensconced in a long-term *solvency* problem arising from the continent's state of structural economic disarticulation, *and* from the prevailing order of global exchange and finance, these neo-orthodox strategies could prove rather harmful to both debtor and creditor. The attractiveness, rationality and economic viability of repudiation and/or forgiveness then become that much more obvious. In this chapter, a critical theoretical review and empirical assessment of the most frequently deployed neo-orthodox debt solutions in Africa are offered at the outset. These are to serve as a prelude to the case studies of Zambia and Zaire in the following chapter, which cases are used to offer an assessment of the effectiveness of these 'solutions' in meeting the desired reform objectives of the 'typical' indebted African economy.

The principal ingredient of the neo-orthodox remedy is market liberalization. The various tools of that policy are designed to target particular sectors and/or promote particular economic ends in those sectors, but their overall thrust is to achieve a measure of market-mediated resource allocation not advocated with such stridency since the inter-war years. *Laissez-faire* in this context, or, more correctly, the internationalization of supply-side, monetarist economics, is thus the organizing principle of this approach. By it *all* debtors, regardless of debt structure or economic orientation, are assumed to exhibit problems singularly susceptible to the magic of the market-place. Thus "getting the prices right" has become *the* panacea for all economic ills, intermittent or structural.

The debt relief policies that debtors are "encouraged" by creditors and/or their agents to pursue—rescheduling and restructuring, structural adjustment under IMF conditionality, the substitution of equity for debt, debt buy-backs, etc.—are but phenomenal manifestations of the underlying philosophy of universalizing market determination of economic outcomes, *with the concomittant minimization of government's influence on these outcomes*. The long-term goal ("letting the market work") and the short-term means (domestic policy reform) should therefore be seen as one continuum in the neo-orthodox strategy.

It will be argued here that in Africa's case, where the main target of this atavistic celebration of the market has been the agricultural and external sectors, the economies' structural peculiarities have thwarted, and will continue to thwart, the efficacy of naked market forces. Liberalization in Africa, therefore, has tended to worsen, not improve income performance over the medium term, and has therefore served to entrench, not alleviate (the forces that induced) the debt crisis in the first place. Like all the remedies in the popular debt-relief 'menu', therefore, the strategy of economic liberalization betrays a singular lack of understanding of the particularities of the African economy.

4.1 Africa in the Neo-Liberal Ideology[1]

It is something of an irony that many of the policies for which African governments were, in the 1980s, so virulently excoriated "were advocated and financed by some of [these] most confident [of today's] critics."[2] These same critics have become the inflexible purveyors of *laissez-faire* to Africa, their new rationale being that a retreat from government activism is the only means of improving economic performance. As then-U.S. Secretary of State, George Schultz put it, "this [*laissez-faire*] is central to the solution of a lot of problems we see around the world", "the right step at the right time to finally liberate developing countries from slow growth and stagnation."[3]

The strategy of the new orthodoxy, of which the traditional debt-relief policies are a short-term, problem-specific variant is, in fact, a comprehensive strategy revolving around three main policy objectives: unfettered markets, the profit incentive, and the promotion of the private sector at the expense of the public. Free-market pricing, it is argued, is crucial not only for the production of goods (in Africa's case, agricultural goods in particular) but in factor markets as well. Thus wages should be "allowed to find their own level", as determined by supply and demand in the labour market; as should exchange rates, since policy-induced currency over-valuation is seen as particularly damaging to trade performance. Tariff and non-tariff hindrances to the free flow of goods in and out of the country must also be eliminated, as countries come to replace their inward-looking, import substitution strategies of the 1960s and '70s with outward-looking, export oriented ones in the 1980s and '90s.

Concomittant with this line of thinking is the argument that government economic activism—through state-owned enterprises, regulation of business, welfarist attempts at improving income distribution, etc.—even when well-intentioned, and regardless of government's bureaucratic capability is, in the long run, the major (though remediable) cause of poor economic performance in SSA. As U.S.A.I.D. saw it, Cameroon's relatively strong economic performance in the 1970s and early 1980s was attributable to its *laissez-faire* policies.[4] Similarly, "the most striking factor" in Malawi's strong economy was its "significant reliance on market performance." Whatever weaknesses these economies exhibited were summarily explained as stemming from deviations from this general approach to economic policy. Thus, in both countries, "improvements in social indicators [which]...was much smaller than could have been possible", and the neglect of "health, social services, and considerations of personal income distribution" were attributed to deviation from *laissez-faire* policies: "the country did diverge from its market-oriented approach to development and the [negative] consequences were far-reaching."[5]

The chief proselytizers of economic liberalization as the cure-all for Africa's ills in the 1980s, in addition to the conservative governments of the U.S., U.K. and Germany, were the World Bank and International Monetary Fund. These institutions and governments gave *laissez-faire* the respectability of mainstream doctrine in the 1980s, and have since made resource transfers from the North contingent upon a country's adoption of these "economic reforms". In the words of the director of the Africa Bureau of U.S.A.I.D., "if a country is moving in that direction [i.e. towards free-market policies], it would affect their funding levels. Conversely, if a country is moving away from that direction, it would also affect their funding levels."[6]

Given the widespread currency that this strategy has attained, in the North *and* South, a detailed examination of four major characteristics of the African case directly pertinent to the issue of liberalization will be conducted in this chapter. These are: (1) the social, political and logistical requirements for the implementation of liberal reforms in Africa; (2) the indispensability of government for the success of liberal reform; (3) the need for non-governmental "engines of growth" for liberal reform to work; and (4) the inadequacy of market institutions or mechanisms in key sectors of African economies.

Challenges of Implementation

In an era of declining commodity prices, of increased expatriation of capital from Africa, of historically high real interest rates on external obligations, and of declining growth in output and employment all over the continent, implementing *laissez-faire* reforms in Africa in the 1980s necessitated, first and foremost, enhanced net inflows of resources from the outside world—the so-called 'adjustment

financing'—and a strong ability to maintain social and political stability
in the face of the opposition that such reforms inevitably engendered.[7]
Since 1983, however, there has been, on net, a stagnation of resource
flows to Africa, and even negative inflows, in some years.[8] Economic
performance and prospects have been bleak, and general discontent
and social instability, followed inevitably by political repression as
the incumbent governments yielded to the imperative (as they saw it)
of "maintaining law and order", have become commonplace.

The short- and medium-term cost of moving from the extensive
networks of government economic activity extant to a decentralized
economy, no matter how desirable, was the widespread budgetary
austerity and economic contraction found all across the continent.
Some of the specific costs have been: (1) higher prices for, and
curtailed consumption of, foodstuffs—a direct result of the removal
of subsidies and price controls, and an indirect result of the currency
devaluation which was often central to these programmes; (2) higher
prices for, and decreased consumption of, imported goods (including
production inputs), also resulting from devaluation; (3) the curtailment
of domestic production, especially of manufactures, with resultant
declines in (especially urban) employment and national income[9]; (4)
further declines in manufacturing output due to the dismantling of the
protective cover of import-substitution industries; (5) the curtailment
of public services and government expenditures, generally, with the
simultaneous imposition of user fees; (6) a worsening of income
distribution; and (7) general economic slowdown with simultaneous
inflationary pressures caused by the combination of all the factors
above, but especially by the reduction in aggregate demand and
removal of price restraints. Successful liberalization would obviously
have required solutions for all these social costs and hardships the
policy engendered.

Two conditions were key to meeting these costs. The first was a
favourable international economic environment. To mitigate the
insidious effects of these hardships in the short term, increased net
flows of financial resources into Africa was crucial, as even the World
Bank recognized in the mid-1980s: "progress will be achieved only if
the international community provides strong and consistent support
to the reform efforts of the sub-Saharan nations...[through] the
provision of both expertise and concessional funding."[10] However,
for various (domestic budgetary and/or foreign policy) reasons,

governments and financial institutions in the North *curtailed*, all through the 1980s, the flow of resources into Africa, even as they were demanding the stringent, and therefore costly, adjustment of these economies. Net resource transfer to SSA between the years 1981 and 1986 (inclusive), were $5.6, $6.2, $3.5, $0, $-1.4, and $1.5 billion, respectively. There was thus a 73% drop in resource inflows to Africa, on the average, in the very period when *increased* flows were called for.[11] And the likelihood of increased concessionary financial assistance from the donor community in the 1990s to ease the short-term costs of adjustment, with the increased demand on a still-shrinking aid base in the aftermath of the collapse of the socialist bloc, is not much brighter than it was in the 1980s.

There were a number of other international conditions that pointed to the need for such assistance. As was argued in Chapter 1, debt servicing was inordinately burdensome on Africa, despite the small size of its obligations. While real interest rates declined somewhat in the mid-1980s, they remained *historically* high: by year-end 1985, they were as much as five times the level at which some of the debts were initially contracted a decade or so earlier.[12] The steep appreciation of the U.S. dollar between 1981 and 1985 raised the real cost to debtors of dollar-denominated interest and principal payments. The later preponderance of short-term debt in Africa's debt structure also tended to enlarge annual payments, raising the average continental debt-service ratio significantly in the latter half of the 1980s.[13]

Exports, and therefore international economic conditions, were of particular importance in this regard. In 1979 the World Bank had estimated that if GNP in the industrialized North were to grow by 3.5%, exports from Africa would show two-thirds as much expansion as if Northern growth were 4.9%.[14] In the event, economic growth in the industrialized countries between 1980 and 1985 averaged only 2.3%. Hence, by the World Bank's scenario, African exports should have expanded only by about 40% of the rate they would have if growth in the OECD had been about twice as much as it actually was.[15] In the event, exports *dropped* by 31%.[16]

Much of the drop could be attributed to slow economic expansion in the OECD countries; but, rhetoric to the contrary, protectionism and other restrictions of access to Northern markets were so stringent as to further impede export expansion from the Third World.[17] As Tables 4.1 and 4.2 indicate, for much of Africa export performance generally declined over much of the period between 1980 and '86. The slack growth in the North also meant worsening trade terms for all of Africa's non-oil exports, exacerbating debt payment problems as national incomes fell. This deterioration should not be reversed anytime soon, as Northern growth has continued to be unusually sluggish ten years into the "Reagan recovery".

Along with slow export and export-earnings growth, the instability of export earnings had been a drag on economic growth, generally, and a hindrance to planning for debt servicing, in particular. Export instability tended both to destabilize import capacity and hinder further export growth.[18]

TABLE 4.1
Index of Export Volume, Selected Countries (1980=100)

	Kenya	Nigeria	Togo	Zambia
1970	84	58	94	154
1972	96	90	91	161
1974	107	115	66	153
1976	103	105	53	168
1978	99	98	102	137
1979	97	116	74	162
1980	100	100	100	100
1981	94	64	62	92
1982	92	53	53	83
1983	88	50	48	80
1984	87	57	69	77
1985	91	65	57	75

EXPORT SHARE OF GDP

	Kenya	Nigeria	Togo	Zambia
1970	31	18	20	49
1985	27	14	33	46

Source: Sahla Shapouri and Stacey Rosen, *Export Performance in Africa* (U.S. Dept. of Agric. Econ. Res. Service, Washington, D.C., May 1989), p. 4 and p. 9.

TABLE 4.2

Index of Unit Value of Exports,
Selected Countries(U.S. $) (1980=100)

	Kenya	Nigeria	Togo	Côte d'Ivoire
1970	28.5	5.3	26.9	n.a.
1980	100.0	100.0	100.0	100.0
1981	89.9	108.4	82.0	70.2
1982	81.9	99.4	70.7	61.4
1983	80.6	84.6	69.5	60.9
1984	89.3	83.3	83.6	69.1
1985	77.3	n.a.	n.a.	74.5

Source: Sahla Shapouri and Stacey Rosen, *Export Performance in Africa*
(U.S. Dept. of Agric. Econ. Res. Service, Washington, D.C., May 1989), p.
5.

Because, as was shown earlier, SSA exports a small cluster of
primary goods, its export earnings in the 1980s became especially
susceptible to international market instability, particularly to
fluctuating world commodity prices and changes in the domestic output
levels of each traded commodity. In addition, because agricultural
production in Africa tends to be particularly subject to unusually
unpredictable weather and other natural conditions,[19] Africa's
extensive 1970s' droughts and locust invasions did not help the already
unstable earnings picture. Clearly, commodity diversification would
have improved export stability, as a decline in the price and/or exported
volume of one commodity would have had a smaller negative effect
on a country's overall receipts.

Table 4.3 gives some indication of the magnitude of Africa's export
instability. The 'coefficient of variation in export earnings' is defined
here as the difference in the actual observations in export earnings
along trend divided by the mean export earning. By measuring
instability around the trend, growth during the entire period can be
separated from annual variations in the growth path, which is what
instability is.[20]

Clearly, these external circumstances were not propitious for the mitigation of the costs of adjustment in Africa. And in the absence of adequate concessionary transfers; of a reversal in commodity prices and trade terms; and of decreasing interest rates on the external debt, the implementation of liberal reform in the African economy was a recipe, as the evaluative studies will indicate, for economic and political disaster. Certainly, the 'reformed' economies stagnated in short order. But the political opposition to increased food prices, public-sector worker redundancies, stagnating wages and decreased social services was almost always fierce, especially from the urban poor who were often disproportionately affected. Political resistance was often virulent enough to prevent the adoption (or cause the reversal, to varying degrees) of these policies by government, even when and where they made good economic sense. Indeed very few governments in Africa have ever escaped unscathed the disruptive social consequences of the adoption of liberalization policies and their attendant austerity. It has led, for instance, to military take overs in Ghana (1972), Nigeria (1983),[21] Liberia (1980) and Sudan (1986); and to quick policy reversals in Senegal, Zambia and Burkina Faso between 1980 and 1987.[22]

When and where such drastic political outcomes did not follow upon liberalization, workers have sought to win wage increases large enough to, at least, restore their customary standard of living[23] , and producers not favourably affected by devaluation have often had enough market power to pursue compensatory pricing policies, essentially raising prices to make up for any losses in revenue or purchasing potential. As Berg, writing for the World Bank, rightly observed, relative prices probably change very little in Africa after liberalization: "most of the exchange rate adjustments made in Africa over the past several years have been ineffective because domestic prices increased by more than the currency was devalued... It is the same with changes in agricultural prices paid to producers. In many, probably most, cases, the impact on farmer income and incentives has been lost because prices of the things farmers buy have risen by as much or more."[24] Thus it would seem that Africa amply bears Kaldor out when he argues that

> the main objection to this approach is that it assumes that devaluation
> is capable of changing critical price and wage relationships that are
> the outcome of complex political forces and that could not be changed
> by domestic fiscal and monetary policies.[25]

TABLE 4.3

Coefficients of Variation of Export Earnings,
Selected Countries

| Country | 1966-80 | | Real | |
	Nominal	Real	1966-80	1980-86
Kenya	23	31	14	20
Nigeria	53	71	38	40
Togo	40	37	29	24
Zambia	25	31	28	22
Iv. Coast	28	31	15	19
Sudan	23	9	20	2
Tanzania	23	21	14	45
Mali	23	33	31	30
Ethiopia	14	26	21	12
Madagascar	22	40	10	31
Zaire	21	37	28	35
Zimbabwe	18	37	20	13
Average:	26	35	21	22

Source: S. Shapouri and S. Rosen, *Export Performance in Africa* (U.S.D.A.
Econ. Res. Service, May 1989), p. 7.

The Paradox of 'Laissez-faire' and More Government

The second major problem with liberalization is that, contrary to widespread belief, market reorientation of Africa's economies would *not* reduce government participation in the economy to the extent often supposed; certainly not in the immediate term. "Getting the prices right" entails, in practice, something considerably more than simply leaving things to the market: it imposes major *new* responsibilities on government. Even the World Bank, circuitously and reluctantly, eventually came to this conclusion. "Policy reform of incentive structures is only likely to be successful if pursued in the context of more comprehensive policy packages,"[26] which packages would include tasks like (1) the development of a more effective input-delivery system to agriculture; (2) reforming marketing structures; (3) improving transport facilities; and (4) other measures that might induce a quick supply response to price incentives. In short, "making the most of investment requires not only appropriate pricing policies, but also *adequate management capacity in government.*"[27]

This statement is a tacit, though murky, acknowledgment of one of the key peculiarities of the African economy that constrains liberalization as a primary strategy for systemic restructuring, growth and development. It is that the market institution, through which price signals may be created and disseminated to guide production and consumption activities, is largely non-existent and, where defined, is largely ineffective as an information-generating and -transmission mechanism. This is true of both factor and product 'markets'; hence the need for government intervention to provide the necessary conditions, the enabling environment, for the very existence of the market as a functioning institution. This, of course, should come as no great surprise: Karl Polanyi has documented the indispensable role of the state in the creation of workable markets during the transition from feudalism to capitalism in England in his classic **The Great Transformation.** His would be a cogent reminder to the modern-day worshippers of *laissez-faire*: "...[T]hose who wished most ardently to free the state from all unnecessary duties, and whose whole philosophy demanded the restriction of state activities, [can] not but entrust the self-same state with the new powers, organs and instruments required for the establishment of *laissez-faire.*"[28] The World Bank and IMF have also done extensive studies, some cited below, on the role played by government in the newly-industrialized and nominally market-driven economies of Singapore, Taiwan, South Korea, Brazil, and even Japan. From these and other studies it would appear, paradoxically, that Africa would need *more* government, in the short run, in order to get *less* government, in the long.

Since a primary target of Africa's economic liberalization has been the agricultural sector, let us examine why and how a free-market pricing strategy in agriculture would require greater governmental intervention, at least in the short- to medium-term. Agriculture is, unarguably, the most important productive sector in the SSAn economy. It employs 71% of the labour force, and accounts for 34% of GDP. For much of SSA, however, *aggregate* agricultural production tends to have only a limited responsiveness to price changes. An increase in the price of a single crop, *ceteris paribus*, often elicits a substantial supply response from farmers, primarily through shifting resources from other crops to the higher-priced crop. Aggregate farm production, however, does not respond strongly to price increases; indeed, as an IMF study of a sample of twenty SSAn countries showed, the median short-run supply elasticity of agriculture was only 0.13. (The median long-run elasticity, measured over several years, was 0.15, with a mean of 0.21).[29] This would mean that, in the 1980s, to increase agricultural output by, say, 5% after one year, agricultural prices would have had to be increased by about 39%! Moreover, this would have had to be an increase *relative to other prices*, since greater increases in the prices of agricultural inputs, for instance would, as Berg intimated, have neutralized any favourable output responses to the increase in crop prices. Therefore if the prices of other goods are rising, it will take still greater increases in the price of agricultural goods to induce a favourable response from farmers. In time this can lead to generalized inflation, as the upward pressure on agricultural prices soon affects domestic wages and prices, even as devaluation of the currency imports inflation from abroad.

Taking these induced, secondary price effects into account, then, it may well have been the case that a 5% rise in output, as a response to price incentives alone, would have required close to a *doubling* of agricultural prices. Moreover, these steep food-price increases would have had to be in place well in advance (perhaps as much as a year) of any observable increases in food production, as there is about a year's lag between sowing, harvesting and marketing. It is also worth noting, parenthetically, that this inelasticity of agricultural production in Africa is a reflection of a broader, economy-wide inelasticity of aggregate supply.[30] The poor response to price incentives on the farm, therefore, may well extend to other sectors of the economy. The import of this for price liberalization as a growth-inducing strategy is obvious.

Thus, for several substantive reasons, free-market pricing, especially in agriculture, requires more, not less, governmental intervention in the African economy. Food price increases alone often have a limited impact on food production, which is often delayed for at least one year, in any case. Moreover, even limited production gains require price increases of a magnitude that will impose severe hardship and provoke massive opposition. Liberalizing agriculture to obtain price incentives for farmers, therefore, ironically works only if extra-market policies to provide transport facilities, rapid access to all sorts of market information, slower increases in input prices, etc. *precede* liberalization proper. It is, perhaps because of this fact of a necessary balance between the benefits of useful public-sector activity, and the costs of inordinate centralization and bureaucratic ineptitude that Hopkins could find no significant statistical relationship "between a growing government sector and poor performance in the [African] food system...".[31]

Reliable Sources of Growth

The third problem stems from the fact that in Africa there are no organized, viable sources of growth outside of the government sector. Liberalization could not, therefore, lead to the desired supply responses when the economic environment is still dominated either by weak indigenous entrepreneurship or undynamic foreign investment that enjoys monopoly powers in a market or market-segment. Indeed the supply inelasticities that plague all sectors of the economy may well be attributable to the weakness and uncompetitiveness of private capital, local and foreign.

There have been numerous micro-level and country studies of the African business environment which concensually point to the formidable shortcomings of, and hindrances to, business enterprise on the continent.[32] Deficiencies in managerial skills; in job-specific training; in the general level of operational efficiency; etc. are present at all levels of economic endeavour. Compounded by the bureaucratic maze entrepreneurs have to negotiate, businesses in Africa face extreme systemic difficulty in overcoming the technological, organizational and marketing obstacles that thwart progress from cottage to small- to medium-sized, not to mention large-scale, industry. Situate these vulnerabilities in the continent's generally adverse and wholly unpredictable economic and political environment, where a myriad cost-raising and demand-limiting constraints that are not normally present in industrialized countries—e.g. problems of securing proper equipment in reasonable time and maintaining it in proper working order; inexperienced or inadequately trained workers, including managerial staff; inadequate infrastructure, especially reliable communications systems; input and product markets that do not send meaningful price and other signals; unpredictable credit availability and costs; etc.—abound, and it becomes clear why indigenous enterprises have not been successful, despite decades of genuine effort, in providing much development thrust in modern Africa.[33] Even in Nigeria, Côte d'Ivoire, Cameroon and Zimbabwe, where the qualities of entrepreneurship and intermittently propitious macroeconomic and political conditions are reported in good supply, the contribution of the indigenous private sector to growth has been consistently marginal.

Foreign investment has been an equally feeble engine of growth. It is impeded, first and foremost, by a general economic environment similar to, though different in key aspects from, that faced by indigenous enterprise. But they also stunt their potential economic contribution by repatriating rather than reinvesting their profits in their operations. Thirdly, they have often escaped the discipline of the marketplace by securing a broad range of favourable governmental interventions which have made them inefficient and operationally complacent, though still highly profitable, rent-seeking monopolies or oligopolies. They can thus be a drain on scarce government resources, and a warp on development priorities, as some of the interventions they have won include protection against international competition, concessional credit allotment by government, a variety of renewable, long-term tax incentives, and the provision by government of non-financial capital (land, transport facilities, piped-water systems, etc.) at sub-market prices. Despite this, in the aggregate, foreign investment has generated only marginal contributions to, and at times substantial reductions in, economic growth in SSA.

The argument that economic liberalization would bring substantial increases in private non-agricultural, indigenous and foreign, investment, and hence growth, is thus not borne out by the structural realities on the ground. The contribution of private investors in industry and commerce to growth has been so small, despite considerable government intervention in their favour, that nothing short of a revamping of the entire mode of economic and political conduct in modern Africa will induce the favourable supply responses to liberalization that will bring economic growth. Certainly more, if different, governance is needed to provide the institutional framework for the requisite output responses to price and other incentives.

Market Dysfunction

As was intimated earlier, while the unfettered market may, under some circumstances, be part of the solution to Africa's debt-and-underdevelopment quagmire, it is often part of the problem. It frequently gives misleading and socially dysfunctional signals, particularly in the poorer and more sectorally-disarticulated economies on the continent.

Market signals are economically and socially meaningful, as some neo-classical welfare theorists have argued, when revenues from production reflect the *full* (i.e. monetary and non-monetary, including any externalities) social benefits of that production, and when its money costs reflect the full cost of the production to society. Only then do monetary benefits and net social benefits coincide. Under such conditions, when money receipts exceed money costs, the society's benefits from a production activity may be seen as exceeding its costs. The production is then both monetarily profitable and socially beneficial. The example of agricultural production in Africa, of domestically-consumed foodstuffs versus exportable cash-crops, illustrates the argument well.

To keep food prices low, African governments have continuously and forcefully intervened in agriculture markets. That such interventions have had harmful effects on the supply of farm goods cannot be seriously debated.[34] What is often not understood is that such intervention, rather than being injudicious and irrational, is in actuality quite rational in purely economic and social-utility terms. The fundamental reason why governments resort to intervention is that the market-mediated food-supply process functions, not only imperfectly, but often socially harmfully. Foodstuffs are purchased predominantly by low-income Africans while demand for export crops comes from higher-income foreigners. It appears, then, that when the buyers are poor, as in the case of domestic food crops, demand and prices are low; when the buyers are more affluent, as with export crops, demand and prices tend to be comparatively higher. In other words foodstuffs, which are of high *direct* social benefit or "human utility" in Africa, command low prices, while export crops, of considerably lower direct human utility for the exporting country as a whole, command higher prices. The natural, free-market response by farmers is to shift productive resources into export-crop farming, thus constricting the supply of the low-priced but high-utility domestically-consumed foodstuffs, while expanding that of the high-priced but low-utility export crops. African farmers thus supply foreign consumers with huge quantities of agricultural goods of low, direct social benefit to the majority of ordinary Africans, while local consumers face increasing shortages of high social-benefit foodstuffs. There is thus a secular, in-built tendency for food prices to rise in Africa as a result of the chronic supply shortages. This is what necessitates government intervention to hold food prices down.

Of course, these interventions are often made, not directly on such economic grounds as have been argued here, but as an act of political expediency and preservation of political tenure. Rising food prices, especially in urban centres, and in countries where two-thirds of all children suffer a measure of malnutrition[35], evoke passionate opposition and social turmoil which, when not dealt with properly, have been known to lead to the untimely demise of many a government.

In the light of all this, it is hardly surprising that successful implementation of economic liberalism in Africa "is proving to be extremely slow and difficult for administrative, technical and political reasons",[36] or that, even where and when African governments have been willing to consider such reforms, "actual progress in reform and...performance has been ...limited."[37]

Until a favourable international economic climate exists; until an effective system for providing the necessary agricultural inputs, improved transport, a reformed marketing system, and other such measures that will imnprove producer response to price movements have been established; until powerful sources of economic growth have developed and markets that send the requisite signals have been set up, progress in economic reform and performance via the liberalization route will continue to prove elusive. Indeed, the history of the emerging 'successful', market-driven developing economies attests to the indispensability of sustained government intervention in securing these preconditions. A 1985 World Bank study of these "pacesetters" is particularly instructive, in this regard. It argues, for instance, that "[South] Korea's successful economic development...[involved] extensive government planning... [utilizing] the entire register of policy instruments in pursuit of industrial, export and growth objectives"; that its rapid growth since 1970 "has principally arisen from capital accumulation...[enabled by] investment during the important initial phase of...industrialization [which] was often only distantly related to market forces."[38] It is, consequently, particularly difficult, the study continues, to even attempt to construct a reliable index of degrees of market orientation of developing economies: "we cannot...make a convincing case that Korea is more or less a price-guided economy than Mexico or India or any other [developing] country."[39]

Thus even the capitalist success stories were countries in which market liberalization required massive government intervention by way of subsidies, protection from established foreign competitors, guaranteed markets, preferential credit and resource allotment, and other forms of price distortion to create a substantial supply of viable investment opportunities. SSA would also require such government presence, selectively targetted, but even more intensely, and for a longer period of time.

As was indicated earlier liberalization, as advocated by the World Bank and IMF entails, as a corollary policy, privatization of economic activity with the simultaneous curtailment of government spending. The rationale offered for this is that the private sector is, dollar-for-dollar, more efficient than the public; that increased public spending undermines the efficiency of the market, in addition to being inflationary; and, finally, that government deficit spending exacerbates the country's external imbalances through its effects on inflation, real interest rates, and the real exchange rate. But a recent study by Eduardo Borenzstein shows that the effect of expansionary fiscal policy on the foreign debt is not at all unambiguous.[40] He argues, in the context of a two-sector economy producing tradable goods and non-tradables, that expansionary fiscal policy can lead to *either* an increase or a decrease in the level of a country's foreign debt, depending on a long list of domestic economic conditions. For instance, in the long-run ("across steady states"), the effect of a fiscal expansion depends on the relative capital intensity of the two sectors, in addition to the composition of private and public spending. If government expenditures are made preponderantly on non-tradables, "a necessary condition for the reduction in foreign indebtedness is that net (of investment replacement costs) labor productivity be higher in the traded- goods industry."[41] The reverse is true if spending is skewed toward traded goods.

The *short-run* effect of a transitory fiscal expansion depends critically on the extent to which investment reacts to current and prospective profits. Using numerical simulations, Borenzstein shows that the current account will improve "if the drop of investment in the traded-goods sector is large enough to overcome the decline in production and the increase in consumption of that type of goods."[42] This will occur particularly if the response of investment is immediate and sharp, i.e. "if there are low costs of adjustment to investment."[43] In sum, government spending to institutionalize market forces, or to ameliorate the social costs of adjustment, will not necessarily cause a deterioration, contrary to the neo-orthodox claim, in foreign indebtedness, and may actually be quite beneficial to domestic production of both tradables and locally-consumed goods, contingent on such factors as the composition of the expenditure.

Liberalization of Agriculture and Trade: The Case of Tropical Beverages

The claim that liberalization of agricultural and trade policies leads ineluctably to better export performance of the agricultural sector is also challenged by a recent U.S. Department of Agriculture study.[44] One of the key conclusions of this study is that, in the case of tropical beverage inputs (coffee, tea, cocoa)—which happen to be a major trio of exports for many African countries—liberalization would yield higher export earnings only if *both* the producer- and importing-countries liberalize their policies towards agricultural goods, the former by lowering taxes on farm products and paying higher producer prices, and the latter by removing the escalating tariff structure that taxes processed agricultural products from Africa at a higher rate than it does the raw material. In other words, liberalization of agriculture will increase the foreign-exchange earning potential of that sector when African agricultural goods face a tariff structure that does not discourage the processing of those goods prior to export. It, however, decreases earnings if the bulk of exports remains unprocessed, and if protectionism on processed goods is high and rampant (see Tables 4.4-4.6).

TABLE 4.4

Effects of Trade Liberalization on Coffee Exports, by Country or Region

COUNTRY/ REGION	Net Export Volume (1000 tons)			Net Export Value ($ millions)		
	1984-86 levels	non-African policies removed	African policies removed	1984-86 levels	non-African policies removed	African policies removed
Ivory Coast:						
Green	219	221	296	624	634	550
Roast	0	0	1	0	1	2
Soluble	13	13	13	52	54	49
Uganda:						
Green	142	143	335	405	411	659
Roast	0	0	1	0	0	3
Soluble	0	0	0	0	0	1
Kenya:						
Green	109	109	104	311	314	193
Roast	0	0	0	0	0	1
Soluble	0	0	0	0	0	0
Zaire:						
Green	91	92	171	259	264	317
Roast	0	1	2	0	0	6
Soluble	0	0	0	0	0	0
Cameroon:						
Green	81	82	102	231	234	190
Roast	1	1	1	3	3	3
Soluble	0	0	0	0	0	0
Rest of the World:						
Green	384	376	144	1094	1078	268
Roast	-8	18	-30	-24	59	-72
Soluble	1	1	1	4	5	5
Total*:						
Green	3548	3328	3887	10112	10166	7215
Roast	5	71	55	15	222	132
Soluble	156	172	175	668	695	634

*All major LDC producers
Source: C. Mabbs-Zeno and B. Krissoff, *Tropical Beverages in the GATT*, Paper prepared for the OECD/World Bank Symposium on "Agricultural Trade Liberalization: Implications for Developing Countries," Paris (Oct. 1989), pp. 17-18.

TABLE 4.5

Effects of Trade Liberalization on Cocoa Exports, by Country or Region

COUNTRY/ REGION	Net Export Volume (1000 tons)			Net Export Value ($millions)		
	1986 levels	non-African policies removed	African policies removed	1986 levels	non-Africa policies removed	African policies removed
Ivory Coast:						
Bean	465	462	494	995	993	594
Liquor	24	24	24	63	67	44
Cake	35	37	38	38	49	26
Butter	25	26	28	117	125	88
Ghana:						
Bean	198	198	318	424	425	382
Liquor	4	4	4	11	11	8
Cake	0	0	1	0	0	1
Butter	8	8	9	37	39	28
Cameroon:						
Bean	90	89	94	193	192	113
Liquor	4	4	4	11	11	7
Cake	8	8	9	9	11	6
Butter	4	4	5	10	21	15
Nigeria:						
Bean	60	58	78	128	125	94
Liquor	1	1	3	3	3	5
Cake	5	6	9	5	8	6
Butter	10	11	13	47	51	41
Rest of the World:						
Bean	230	227	150	492	486	181
Liquor	-7	-7	-7	-18	-19	-12
Cake	10	12	13	11	16	9
Butter	16	17	19	75	83	61
Total*:						
Bean	1321	1302	1569	2827	2797	1887
Liquor	109	111	118	289	308	216
Cake	107	118	128	116	158	87
Butter	120	127	140	552	609	446

*All major LDC producers
Source: C. Mabbs-Zeno and B. Krissoff, *Tropical Beverages in the GATT*, Paper prepared for the OECD/World Bank Symposium on "Agricultural Trade Liberalization: Implications for Developing Countries," Paris (Oct. 1989), p. 16.

TABLE 4.6
Effects of Trade Liberalization on Tea Exports

COUNTRY/ REGION	Net Export Volume (1000 tons)			Net Export Value ($ millions)		
	1986 levels	non-African policies removed	African policies removed	1986 levels	non-African policies removed	African policies removed
Kenya	116	117	90	179	179	100
Malawi	40	38	105	58	58	117
Total*:	811	810	985	1238	1242	1096

*Includes all LDC net-exporters: Sri Lanka, India, China, Indonesia, Argentina, Bangladesh.
Source: C. Mabbs-Zeno and B. Krissoff, *Tropical Beverages in the GATT*, Paper prepared for the OECD/World Bank Symposium on "Agricultural Trade Liberalization: Implications for Developing Countries," Paris (Oct. 1989), p. 18

Commenting further on the ambiguities of liberalization, the study states

...removal of policies in developed countries [result in] an increase in revenue to producer nations. Liberalizing the policies of producer nations, in contrast, would result in a decline in value of trade of 26%. Simultaneous liberalization of policies in all countries is approximately equal to the sum of these two [effects], that is, a 25% [overall] reduction in trade value. [See Table 4.7]. This loss in trade revenue for producers of tropical products resulting from global trade liberalization is $4 billion. The trade revenue loss results from the export demand elasticities facing the major exporters as a group. These are -0.7, -0.3 and -0.6 for cocoa beans, green coffee, and tea, respectively. They imply that changes in trade revenue have the same sign as changes in international prices following global liberalization.[45]

TABLE 4.7

Effects of Trade Liberalization on
Export Revenue of Supplier Nations

COMMODITY	Export Revenue ($ millions)			Prices ($ per ton)		
	Base levels	non-African policies removed	African policies removed	Base levels	non-African policies removed	African policies removed
COCOA:						
Bean	2827	2797	1887	2139	2145	1202
Liquor	289	308	216	2636	2783	1826
Cake	116	158	87	1075	1332	666
Butter	552	609	446	4672	4763	3197
Sub-total:	3784	3872	2636			
COFFEE:						
Green	10112	10116	7215	2850	2869	1857
Roast	15	222	132	2950	3082	2378
Soluble	668	695	634	4022	4175	3611
Sub-total:	10795	11083	7981			
TEA:	1238	1242	1096	1529	1531	1112
Total:	15817	16197	11713			
Primary*	12939	12963	9102			
Processed*	1640	1992	1515			

*Excluding Tea.
Source: C. Mabbs-Zeno and B. Krissoff, *Tropical Beverages in the GATT*, Paper
prepared for the OECD/World Bank Symposium on "Agricultural Trade
Liberalization: Implications for Developing Countries," Paris (Oct. 1989), p. 15.

On the other hand, exporters' revenue from even processed
agricultural goods remains pretty stable after liberalization:

Removal of developed country policies raised trade revenues from
partially processed forms of cocoa and coffee by 21% to $2 billion.
Removal of LDC policies reduced trade value by 18% to $1.5 billion.
Global liberalization would raise trade value in processed tropical
beverages only slightly.[46]

4.2 Debt Rescheduling and Restructuring

No other debt 'solution' more clearly exemplifies the analytical incompleteness of the new orthodoxy, at least as far as Africa goes, than debt rescheduling and restructuring. The stated objective of this strategy is to alter the debtor-nations' debt-service payments while stretching the outstanding obligation over a longer maturity. SSA, with a mid-1980s debt structure preponderantly tilted toward multi- and bilateral; and public and publicly guaranteed long-term obligations (see Table 4.8), has had to renegotiate its debt payments with the Paris Club, though London Club reschedulings became quite important as the 1980s wore on. Indeed, four out of every five reschedulings done by Third World debtors with either Club, between 1970 and 1985, were with African countries. In the final five years of this period alone, there were no fewer than thirty-one Paris Club reschedulings for thirteen countries in Africa.[47]

TABLE 4.8

Share of Public Debt in SSA's Total External Debt,
Year-End 1984 ($ millions)

	Total Liabilities (including IMF purchases) (1)	Public and Publicly-Guaranteed Long-Term Debt (2)	(2) as % of (1)
Countries with Prolonged Debt Problems[a]	24,822	18,867	76
Other low-income countries[b]	19,803	15,297	77
Other Countries[c]	35,642	22,762	64
TOTAL SSA	80,268	56,927	71

a   Includes Benin, Mali, Somalia, Sudan and Tanzania.
b   Includes Chad, Ghana, Kenya, Malawi, Senegal and Zaire.
c   Includes Cameroon, Ivory Coast, Nigeria, Botswana, Zimbabwe and Gabon.
Sources: World Bank, *Financing Adjustment with Growth in sub-Saharan Africa*, 1986-90, Table1.2, p. 54.

But repeated restructurings may actually have worsened the debt problems of many countries, as the conventions set up by the Clubs for rescheduling tend to offer very little real relief.[48] The most important of these conventions is that a large proportion of the debt is considered ineligible for rescheduling. This includes "obligations to preferred creditors", interest payments to private creditors, and previously rescheduled payments. ('Preferred creditors' refers to multilateral institutions, like the World Bank and IMF). This has meant, first, that many African countries, under the strict interpretation of the convention, did not "qualify" for reschedulings in the early 1980s when they most needed relief.

Secondly, even when countries do qualify, repeated reschedulings would tend to increase the present-value of debt outstanding, as the debt is recapitalized at the prevailing interest rates which, whether they are market or concessionary, are considerably higher than those at which the debts were originally contracted. Besides, renegotiation and other processing fees add considerably to the principal, often between 2% and 5% of the face value of the renegotiated obligation. Thus the 'relief' that comes from lower periodic remittances, once a debt is rescheduled, may prove quite illusory in the long-run.

Thirdly, another Paris Club convention obligates the debtor to simultaneously negotiate a stand-by agreement with the IMF. What this really entails, in terms of conditional adjustment requirements, has been lightly touched upon in earlier chapters, but a more detailed analysis of it is offered later in this chapter, and also in the context of the Zairean and Zambian case studies.

Lastly, the overall Paris Club framework for debt renegotiation involves rescheduling payments coming due on official and officially-guaranteed debt in a limited consolidation period (usually twelve to eighteen months), plus arrears in certain areas, but with a typically brief repayment schedule. Typically, then, 90% of principal and interest is formally rescheduled for a seven- to ten-year maturity, with a three- to five-year grace period. The 10% of the original debt remaining stays on the original payment schedule, and all arrearages are rescheduled with shorter (than the original) maturities, with no grace period.[49] It must be stated, though, that the Paris Club just provides the framework; actual rescheduling is done in bilateral agreements based on this framework.

What debt rescheduling on these terms meant for Africa in the period 1980-1985 is, first and foremost, an increase of $7 billion in the debt outstanding. In other words, the costs associated with successful renegotiation, plus the cost of recapitalization at the new rates, have cost an additional $7 billion. Secondly, since Paris Club convention normally excludes from rescheduling debts owed to multilateral institutions (which hold three-quarters of Africa's debt); debts previously rescheduled; most interest arrears; and arrearages on short-term debt associated with new reschedulings; and, furthermore, since only 90% of the (unexcluded) amortization falling due in the following eighteen months is subject to rescheduling, SSA obtained very minor relief indeed, relative to its debt-service obligations, from debt restructuring and rescheduling. In the long-term, the costs of defraying the higher costs of the rescheduled loans may actually exceed the short-term gains from the rescheduling. As a British banker colourfully but aptly put it,

> ...[B]y itself, rescheduling is not an answer. As long as interest is being added to old debts at a faster rate than national output or exports are growing, the underlying situation is unsatisfactory and becoming even more so as the years go by. Rescheduling bears comparison with the anaesthetic applied at an operation to treat a terminal condition. It may take away the pain and, for a period, put the patient in a better frame of mind for surgery. But it certainly is not a substitute for surgery, and its effects wear away in due course. The debtor nations, just like a patient returning to his senses to discover that nothing has been done, will find to their dismay that—when they are eventually obliged to consider repayment— their external obligations are larger than ever.[50]

4.3 IMF-type Structural Adjustment Programmes (SAPs) in the African Context

In 1979, the World Bank, in a move that further blurred the distinction between its mandate and that of its sister-organization, the International Monetary Fund (IMF), began making structural and sectoral adjustment loans (SALs) not specifically geared to particular development projects, but designed solely for balance-of-payments support. These were long-term loans, of fifteen-to-twenty year maturity, with a five-year grace period, and at terms just 0.5% above the lender's costs; and were made available to a country contingent on a number of key performance conditions that the Bank monitored closely.[51]

The purposes for which the SALs were intended were: to reduce the external deficit as a prelude to the resumption of internal economic growth, and to effect changes in the functioning or structures of the economy that will reduce the likelihood of recurrence of external and/or internal imbalances.

Thus SAPs have both macro- and microeconomic policy objectives. The primary macroeconomic task was to improve the external *and* the internal fiscal balance; i.e. to eliminate any deficits in the BOP and in the government's budget position. At the micro-level, SAPs were designed to institutionalize efficiencies in resource allocation through resort to market pricing. This was done through the removal of governmental and other interventions in the market that were considered price-distortionary; in other words, through deregulation and the promotion of private-sector competition.

The Bank supported the sequencing of these tasks, often advocating macroeconomic restructuring as a prequel to detailed sectoral reforms, on the belief that "appropriate macro-policies [were] essential to [improving] incentives for tradable-goods production, the choice of production techniques, and assessment of relative profitability."[52] The Bank specifically encouraged improving efficiencies in institutions and policies as a major component of adjustment to external disequilibria, and saw any adjustment financing it (and others) provided as only helping prevent a "hard landing" of the economy—i.e. as providing the cushion for the economy to properly adjust from its imbalances without a debilitating economic contraction induced by the often-drastic reductions in consumption and/or investment— and not a substitute for adjustment.[53]

The Bank's role in the adjustment exercises of the 1980s thus came to closely parallel, if not mirror, the IMF's. The Fund's role had always been to provide credit to member-countries with BOP problems, the initial amount of credit to which they were entitled equalling their 'reserve tranche' (i.e. their original contribution of gold or foreign-exchange reserves, or 25% of their initial quotas). A country which wished to borrow over and above this amount agreed to subject itself to certain performance requirements imposed by the Fund, the object of which was to ensure balance in its international payments and stability in its internal prices, over the long haul. This "stand-by arrangement" enabled the member to borrow foreign-exchange in excess of its reserve tranche up to a given amount in a given period of time in the course of adjustment.

The theoretical underpinning of this infamous 'Fund conditionality' has already been dealt with in Chapter One; the policy implications were dealt with earlier in this chapter. Just as a reiteration, therefore, the requirements the adjusting country is subjected to as a prerequisite for expanded borrowing from the Fund include: reducing the government's fiscal deficits through tax increases, cuts in discretionary spending, and improving the probity of tax collection; limiting credit expansion and financial repression; liberalizing trade; devaluing the currency to a level commensurate with the country's economic fundamentals, and allowing the market to thenceforth determine effective real exchange rates; and abolishing price controls by allowing markets to independently allocate goods and services.

The Fund attempts to monitor short term performance targets for most of these policies, and has been known to hold countries rather closely to the agreed benchmarks. It has thus often been accused of callously and single-mindedly pursuing domestic demand reduction policies to attain the adjustment targets in the external sector regardless of the human and development cost on the domestic front. In the 1980s, perhaps in response to these criticisms, the Fund expanded its mission from the traditional short-term adjustment lending to correct external disequilibria to encompass longer-term, growth-oriented lending. It would appear, therefore, that both the Bank and the Fund abandoned their erstwhile strict interpretations of their missions that had distinguished their roles in the international economy, and moved ever more closely to each other functionally, in the 1980s.

In the last three years of the 1980s, the Bank released a series of assessments of some ten years of its structural adjustment programmes in the South.[54] That they engendered no end of controversy, with the Economic Commission for Africa (ECA) releasing an acrimonious rebuttal in 1989 to the African segment of these studies, attests to the extreme ambivalence, if not outright hostility, with which World Bank/IMF SAPs are regarded in Africa and elsewhere in the developing world.[55] The ECA's criticism was not the usual theoretical one about the uncritical application of IMF conditionality in every instance of chronic external disequilibria. Rather, it was an empirical and procedural critique sparked by the Bank's claim that GDP growth during specific periods of adjustment between 1980 and 1987 was stronger in African states that had undergone, and sustained, "strong" SAPs than those which had not. Since anecdotal and emerging statistical evidence suggested the contrary the ECA, using the same World Bank data and country classification, reanalyzed the economic performances of all countries covered in the Bank's studies, with decidedly different results.

The ECA's findings, encapsulated in Figures 4.1 and 4.2, may be summarized as follows: between 1980 and 1987, GDP growth for "strongly adjusting countries" averaged -0.53% annually, as against 2% for "weak" adjustors. Even for the sub-period 1985-1987, the primary focus of the Bank's study of the African adjustors, countries with deep adjustment programmes still recorded the lowest growth rates, except for those countries that enjoyed significant net financial inflows to support their adjustment. Indeed, the strongly-adjusting countries on the whole netted an average annual increase of 18.1% in foreign aid, while those not adjusting experienced a 4.7% decline over the period suggesting, as the ECA implicitly argued, that any gains made by these countries may have resulted more from increased resource inflows than the success or failure as such of SAPs.

Further, argued the ECA, since each country- classification group contained economies with both positive and negative growth rates, growth performance should be seen as depending on a multiplicity of factors, and that "any attempt to establish a one-to-one relationship between growth trends and [the adoption or non-adoption of] structural adjustment programmes is prone to over-simplification and falacies." What the data unambiguously indicated, however, was that countries undergoing SAPs were more able to sustain their debt servicing, and improve their current account balances. All other indicators of domestic economic sustainability, from investment ratios to per capita consumption, were consistently worsened by SAPs (Figure 4.1). The tenor of the World Bank analysis, concluded the ECA, would suggest that the Bank had engaged in "a stark manipulation of data to prove a predetermined position."[56] The report, therefore, could be particularly deceptive as to the efficacy and desirability of Bank/IMF-type SAPs.

In light of this controversy, it will be instructive to examine how structural adjustment under IMF tutelage fared in Zambia and Zaire in the first half of the 1980s. These two countries are, arguably, as

FIGURE 4.1

*Indicators of the Sustainability of Adjustment for SSAn
Countries Implementing IMF-Sponsored SAPs, 1980-85*

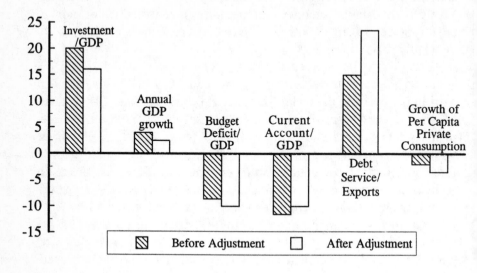

Source: UN-ECA, *The African Alternative Framework to Structural Adjustment
Programmes...*, (April 10, 1989).

FIGURE 4.2

Growth of GDP in SSA by Strength of Adjustment, 1980-87

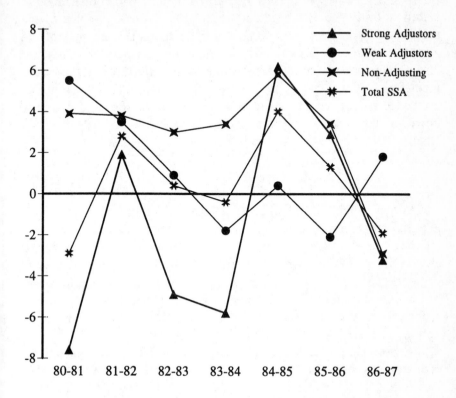

Source: UN-ECA, *The African Alternative Framework to Structural Adjustment Programmes...*, (April 10, 1989).

representative of SSAn countries as any other in terms of economic structure, political culture, external economic relations and, especially, their relationship with the Bank and/or IMF in periods of economic stabilization in the 1980s. In addition, they underwent some of the earliest SAPs in SSA, and so should offer tangible outcomes of the adjustment process easily susceptible to rigorous analysis. They are also perhaps the two best examples of countries in which all the forces identified so far as being the causes of SSA's debt-and- development crises converge very conspicuously. Prior to the case studies, however, the discussion of the theoretical rationale of SAPs begun in Chapter One must be concluded.

*****

As we argued in Chapter One, the magnitude of a country's external indebtedness is a summation of the accumulated stock of net claims by outsiders on that country. These claims are reflected in the annual flows of borrowing recorded in the country's balance-of-payments (BOP) accounts. Thus the total external debt is an indication of the country's past BOP deficits, and the country is said to be in a 'debt crisis' when the sum of these external obligations is growing nominally faster than the country's ability to service it.

It was also established algebraically, in Chapter One, through an ordinary Keynesian macro-equilibrium analysis that $(X - M) = (S + T) - (G + I)$, which was rewritten as $(X - M) = (S - I) + (T - G)$. The first relation was labelled Equation (1.8) and the second (1.9). Equation (1.9) was interpreted as showing that an external disequilibrium (such as a current-account deficit) may be reflected internally as a fiscal deficit and/or an insufficiency of domestic savings; and that, even if external resources are borrowed to finance the current-account imbalance, the imbalance will still persist if public-sector deficits $(T - G)$ exceeded private sector savings $(S - I)$, and if $S > I$.

The policy implications of this analysis are quite clear: to eliminate current-account deficits (and, by extension, BOP deficits or the external debt), the African debtor-nations should ensure that (1) domestic spending is, at most, equal to domestic savings—i.e. $(I + G) \leq (S + T)$; and/or that (2) government spending is, at most, equal to its tax revenues while, simultaneously, domestic savings are, at least, equal to private investment spending—i.e. $G \leq T$ *and* $S \geq I$; and/or

that export revenues are, at least, equal to expenditures on imports—
i.e. $X \geq M$.

In practical terms, this is what the analysis means for African
governments and peoples on the ground: government outlays would
have to be cut even as taxes are raised and user-fees imposed to
eliminate the fiscal deficit and/or improve public-sector savings;
private savings should be boosted, through the appropriate tax and
interest-rate policies, to provide investable funds for private investment
activity; and export production should be boosted, even as import
consumption is lowered in favour of home goods, preferably through
the appropriate exchange-rate and other pricing policies. A debtor-
nation wishing World Bank/IMF stabilization and/or adjustment
funding must implement these reform policies (the so-called IMF
'conditionality') in order to obtain additional resources from *either*
the private commercial banking sector or the multilateral financial
institutions.

To obtain the necessary cuts in government spending to eliminate
budget deficits and increase savings, adjusting African governments,
between 1980 and 1985, reduced or completely eliminated (or caused
the reduction and/or elimination of) the following specific areas of
social policy: subsidies for food, education, health and transportation;
investment in existing, let alone new, infrastructure; public-sector
employment; and wage levels in both private and public sectors.
Significantly, military expenditures did not suffer commensurate
reductions.

The effects of these particular 'reforms' have been horrendous:
every social indicator of welfare has seen significant declines
throughout the continent. In the first place, the share of government
spending in GDP decreased, between 1980 and 1985, for the
overwhelming majority of African countries. A 1987 UNICEF study
of eighteen adjusting SSAn countries showed that, over the period
1980-85, rising debt was accompanied by falling per capita government
spending in 60% of the sample countries, and by a fall in the share of
government outlays for health and education in 47% of them. The
study showed also that very often it was the urban poor, women and
children—the principal consumers of social programmes—on whom
the cuts fell disproportionately, and who therefore experienced
inordinately burdensome decreases in access to health care and
schooling, and alarming rises in child malnutrition, infant mortality

and reduced household caloric intake.[57]   In Ghana, for instance, between 1980 and 1984, the first five years of a SAP, the percentage of preschool children suffering some degree of malnourishment increased from 35% of the preschool population to 54%! Infant mortality also went up significantly, from about 93 to 107 per thousand.[58]   In Uganda, where an IMF-type SAP started in 1982, food-subsidy removals, retrenchment in the public sector, price decontrols and wage-rate declines resulted in "maizemeal prices [rising] 180 times and wages only 11 times...so that nutritional levels deteriorated among the poor..."[59]   And as the case study of Zambia will show, the 62% decline in real terms of food subsidies following the 1983 reforms had a similar skewed distributional and social-welfare impact on the poor. For SSA as a whole there was no improvement, on net, in social indicators from 1980 to 1985. For instance, even though life expectancy at birth increased from 46 to 48 years, the infant mortality rate was largely unaltered, at 126 per thousand. Average daily caloric intake, however, declined by some 10% across the continent. In Ghana, per capita caloric consumption as a percentage of daily requirements declined from 79% to 72% by 1985; from 96% to 92% in Zambia; and from 108% to 105% in Malawi.[60]

Thus the decline in public health was accompanied by a redistribution of resources away from the poorer sectors of the population. Overall output also declined for a myriad reasons, though the decrease in government expenditure, to the extent that it accelerated the decay of infrastructure and increased the rate of unemployment, probably held *the* major responsibility for the fall in aggregate demand that precipitated the losses in production. Wage levels dropped significantly, albeit differentially, for various segments of the labour force, further exacerbating the dearth of demand as household and individual consumption levels, and therefore standards of living, were commensurately adjusted downward. Using 1980 as a benchmark, real non-agricultural wages had dropped by 40% in Tanzania by 1983; by 33% in Zambia by 1984; by 22% in Kenya by 1985; by 24% in Malawi by 1984; and by 10% in Mauritius by 1983.[61]

To achieve the desired increases in gross domestic savings and, it was hoped, new capital formation, interest rates were increased, through restrictive monetary and credit policies, as an incentive to savers. A second, though no less important, motive for the freeing of interest rates was the rationalisation of the process of capital allocation, which process had often been severely distorted by governments' policies of financial repression.[62]   In addition, the decrease in government spending and increases in taxes; the imposition of user-fees and better tax collection systems; and the suppression of wages to increase profitability were also designed to effect an increase in private- and public-sector revenues and savings.

The effect of these initiatives was predictable: investment activity actually declined in most adjusting countries in the period 1981-85 as the cost of funds soared, and as people shifted from higher-risk, long-term *capital formation* to low-risk *commercial activities* with a quicker turn-over. The decline in real net capital formation exacerbated the unemployment problems that started with the public-sector redundancies, further eroding the standard-of-living of the labouring classes. And the decline in wages relative to profits, together with the cuts in social spending, helped aggravate substantially this distribution of income from labour to capital.

There was, however, a deeper, structural reason for the collapse of investment. Most of the adjusting countries suffered from a debt overhang. In other words, their debts were so large in relation to their incomes that, with no net resource inflows, and with little short-term prospects of otherwise reducing the debt significantly, potential investors came to form rather low expectations of the economies' prospects.   This collapse in expectations became an effective disincentive for resource commitment. People came to expect that significant proportions of any growth that might be achieved would be transferred abroad to meet the external obligation. The debt thus became, functionally, a tax on investment, in the sense that portions of any future returns on investment were expected to be transferred to creditors abroad. Countries with such debt overhang often have a tendency to, in this manner, attain only sub-optimal investment levels, with greater portions of income going to consumption or to capital flight[63]. Most of the African adjustors fit this profile neatly: consumption levels, in the aftermath of all the shocks enumerated in Chapter One, were already very low in the period 1980-85. The domestic budgetary task of gathering resources locally to be transferred abroad in foreign currency to meet the debt obligation thus manifested itself as discretionary reductions in investment. By 1985, therefore, gross domestic investment's share of GDP had fallen to 12% from the 23% figure of 1980; and domestic saving's share of GDP had fallen from 20% to 15%.

Because much of the African debt was the result of the structural trade deficits ran almost continuously since independence, stabilization and adjustment in the 1980s often focused on the external sector. The objective was to make the value of exports at least equal that of imports; and so the task was to increase export earnings, while lowering spending on imports by switching consumption to home goods. Expenditure switching, as part of a general strategy of demand restraint and the promotion of traded-goods' production, therefore, were some of the desired outcomes of adjustment. And the preferred method of achieving this, according to the IMF, was devaluation of local currencies vis-à-vis hard currencies and, subsequently, the decontrol of foreign-exchange markets. In other words, a free functioning market in foreign exchange and, as argued immediately above, domestic capital markets.

The results of steep currency devaluation—Ghana's *cedi*, for instance, went from C1.75:$1 to C90:$1 between 1980 and 1986—included, almost always, short-run inflation, as the prices of imports and those of goods with a high import-content went up. There was also, as argued earlier, often a shift in production to export crops from local foodstuffs, though export revenues from these did not appreciate much, and even fell in many instances. Environmental degradation, as export crop cultivation tends to be more intensive and chemical-dependent than that of home goods, increasingly became a problem. Finally, there was a redistribution of income towards export-producing farmers and exporters in general, creating disparities where they did not exist previously in the rural sector, and in urban areas and occupations as well.[64] Indeed, recent evaluations of adjustment results indicate that commercial farmers, particularly those engaged in export-crop and import-replacement production; their farm and other employees; and traders dealing in the export of these goods were the primary beneficiaries, in terms of increased incomes, of exchange-rate and related adjustments. Producers of locally-consumed foodstuffs, public-sector workers, and those in the informal sector were decidedly worse off after adjustment.[65]

These outcomes of the devaluation exercise merit closer examination. Between 1977 and 1983, Third World agricultural exports increased by 21%; but as agricultural trade terms fell by 30%, the purchasing power of the increased exports actually fell by 15% (i.e. 1.21 volume x 0.7 terms-of-trade = 0.85). Thus to improve trade performance through currency devaluation, it was not sufficient to seek improvements in export *volume* alone. The terms at which the commodities were traded should also have beeen taken into account.

But even seeking increases in the quantum of exported commodities is, itself, not unproblematic, as our earlier analysis of African agriculture indicated. The low short-run supply elasticities make it unlikely that farm-price decontrol *alone* will suffice to induce immediate output increases. And even though long-run supply elasticites are a little more favourable, output responses along trend are also constrained by infrastructure problems, foreign-exchange shortages, dysfunctional markets, and other such structural bottlenecks.

Secondly, much of the analysis suffers from a fallacy of composition. A single exporter of agricultural commodities is often a price taker whose export volumes can be expanded almost infinitely at a given price, since it faces an elastic demand curve. However, what holds for one country does not hold for the dozens of countries all expanding commodity exports simultaneously under IMF-type adjustment programmes. As most of these adjusting African debtors all substantially expanded their exports of the same basket of commodities, relative prices fell steeply. This subsequently reduced their terms-of-trade and decreased their export-purchasing power between 1980 and 1985. Things were not helped much by the escalating tariff structure the OECD countries maintained against many incoming African commodities. Thus it would appear that the export trap—largely determined by export-crop demand and supply elasticities—was as culpable in the failure of currency devaluations to increase Africa's export-earnings and thereby reduce its trade deficits as any government anti-agriculture policies.[66]

But, here again, Africa's structural peculiarities make reliance on devaluation for improving trade performance a risky proposition, at best. For devaluation to improve the trade balance, the sum of the export and import demand elasticities must be, at least, unity. But in Africa these elasticities are, in the short run, considerably smaller, and therefore do not meet the sufficient conditions for trade improvement. Given the perversity of short-run elasticities, African policy makers have little faith in the ability of currency devaluation to achieve the desired balances in the external accounts. Thus many African countries were more apt to rely on falling real incomes (as their economies stagnated) to suppress import demand as a quick way of correcting BOP deficits in the early 1980s, than on exchange-rate adjustments and expenditure switching. We will have occasion, in the next chapter, to more closely examine the economics of currency devaluation as the linchpin of structural adjustment, and also the reasons why lower incomes were more likely than devaluation to be used to curb import demand.

And, lastly, in keeping with the objective of providing institutional incentives to boost the private sector at the expense of the public, and towards which objective much of the "getting the prices right" initiatives enunciated above were implicitly geared, private investors were afforded a series of privileges under the SAP. These included generous investment tax breaks, infrastructural support for capital projects, and the unrestricted movement of goods in/out of the country, including profits. The impact of this was to skew development objectives in favour of multinational corporations (MNCs) and, therefore, the external sector—the very structural orientation of the economy that needed changing in the first palce. It also unevenly distributed development resources across the country and/or sectors of the economy, while leaving the regulation of economic activity largely to the vagaries of the market. And, because the same elite groups which had got the economy into the crises were the local partners and/or agents of the MNCs, the policy solidified the very class structures, alliances and policies that begged undermining if true remedy for the crises was to be had.

The economic impact of these adjustment activities for the overwhelming majority of African debtors was, therefore, decidedly mixed. The Bank and Fund often proclaimed the general effectiveness of adjustment, even though their own empirical assessments did not *unambiguously* point to success, and even as independent studies showed a larger degree of failure than success. As Nafziger has concluded, "taken as a whole, [these evaluative studies] show[ed] that the record of growth, external balance, and social indicators of sub-Saharan countries with strong Bank/Fund adjustment programs *was no better than those with weak or no adjustment programs.*"[67] (Emphasis added). Worse yet, Bank/Fund-type adjustment reduced investment and social spending, potentially jeopardizing countries' recovery and future growth prospects. For this and such reasons, "many African leaders see no evidence that national planners do any worse than the Bretton Woods twins, [for] at least national adjustment plans provide indigenous people with experience and learning benefits."[68] Following is a sampling of some of the empirical assessments of the 1980s' economic adjustment processes in SSA, drawn from both independent researchers and official Bank/Fund sources. We, in turn, are drawing heavily from Nafziger's contextualization of them in his latest work.[69]

The Bank's own evaluation of adjustment results from fifty-four developing countries showed that better than half of them were successful in improving their current account performances, through faster export growth and import decline, than did their non-adjusting counterparts. But this result was attenuated somewhat by the fact that many of the adjustors suffered worse foreign-exchange shortages than the non-adjustors and, on the average, had somewhat the same economic growth rates as non-adjustors over the long run, despite their better short-run growth performance. In addition, adjustors' social indicators as a whole were higher, on the average, though their household caloric intake was worse, than those of non-adjustors. And, as indicated earlier, for much of SSA, social welfare indices were all decidedly down after adjustment.[70]

For SSA, in particular, the Bank's evaluation indicated that current account balances and debt-service ratios (DSRs) improved more for low-income adjustors than their non-adjusting counterparts, but their growth and inflation performances were worse; and middle-income adjustors experienced higher growth, though worse inflation, rates than non-adjustors. For both income-classes of countries, however, adjustment appeared to have been at the expense of investment, and therefore the long-term growth outlook did not look very promising.

The Fund's studies suggested that the contractionary effects of monetary and fiscal restraint that accompany adjustment are often short term and temporary, soon overtaken by the higher growth and trade performance induced by interest-rate, exchange-rate, and market reforms. It is the long lag between reform and results that, ostensibly, creates the impression of policy failure. However, UNCTAD found that the performance of a sample of a dozen least-developed economies that underwent structural adjustment in the 1980s was not distinguishable from that of other least-developed countries which did no adjusting.[71] Similarly, a larger study of ninety-three adjusting developing countries found "no evidence of a statistically better (or worse) performance for Bank/Fund loan recipient countries."[72]   And the ECA's 1989 critique of the World Bank's assessment of the African adjustment suggested that, except in two areas—current account as a ratio of GDP, and private per capita consumption—SSA experienced declines in all the key target indices after adjustment, from DSRs to investment levels to budget deficits (see Figure 4.1).   And the improvements in those two indices were very marginal indeed.

Following in the same vein, a study by Frances Stewart found that, in the period 1980-87, African countries undergoing strong IMF-sanctioned adjustment had growth performances comparable to those of countries pursuing only weak adjustments. For all the adjustors, however, only imports seemed to have moved in the requisite (i.e. downward) direction; export revenue and real investment worsened, the current account imbalance and the domestic fiscal deficit persisted, real income declined, more people moved below the poverty datum line than before adjustment, and the extent of physical deterioration of infrastructure was palpable. It would appear then that "Bank/Fund [adjustment] policies did not meet [even] their short-run objectives and were undermining [long-run] growth potential."[73]

Carefully selecting adjusting and non-adjusting countries with similar preadjustment characteristics (to minimize the possibility of biasing their evaluation or using an unrepresentative sample)[74], Mosley, Harrigan and Toye found that both adjusting and non-adjusting countries had worse growth rates in the early 1980s than in the late 1970s, but the adjustors had a decidedly worse overall growth performance. Indeed those adjustors who adhered most strictly to the Fund's policy conditionality were the worst performers, having experienced the largest fall in real domestic investment though the greater improvement in the current accounts. (They had smaller declines in export growth and greater reductions in the growth of imports than the non-adjustors). And even though the standard deviations on their regression estimates were large, all the differences between adjustors and non-adjustors were significant at the 5% level.

But, even more tellingly, when growth was regressed against financial flows, compliance with conditionality, and exogenous variables such as terms-of-trade and weather conditions, Mosley et.al. found that, between 1980 and '86, Bank/Fund adjustment-support financing correlated negatively with growth, though compliance with policy conditionalities had a positive correlation with it. This suggests that the overall effect of Bank/Fund adjustment-support programmes on an adjusting economy—from loans to the Policy Framework Program (PFPs) to performance conditions—is, at best, neutral. More probably, though, it is negative, "since the negative money effect is immediate, while the positive compliance effect, from price-based and other reforms, is lagged at least a year and [may not even] materialize."[75] Further regression analyses revealed that, in the very short run, Bank financial flows correlated strongly negatively, and policy compliance strongly positively, with improved export performance; but one-to-two years after adjustment begins, the relationships are reversed, suggesting that "the net effect of Bank programs on export growth is negative [up to a year after adjustment begins] but positive two years hence."[76] Similarly, IMF stand-by credit was negatively correlated with growth in SSA, while improved weather conditions and trade terms were, not unexpectedly, positively correlated with it. In explaining the unexpected negative effect of financial inflows on growth, Mosley et.al. hypothesize that such money flows tend to have a perverse effect on policy reform by reducing the pressure on government, while also causing an effective devaluation of the local currency vis-à-vis hard currencies.

It is with these evaluations of IMF-type adjustment programmes in the backdrop that we turn to look at the specificities of the adjustment process as it unfolded in Zambia and Zaire. We first assess the roles of the countries' economic and political institutions, and their social structures, in mediating the larger reform process. Secondly, we consider the normative question of whether or not structural adjustment of the stock IMF/Bank variety should, in all cases, and regardless of historical and structural uniquenesses, be the vehicle for the stabilization of an unbalanced open economy, and for sectoral policy reform in general. We examine the economics of currency devaluation, arguably *the* key component of the neo-liberal adjustment, for the purpose.

Notes

1. This section borrows extensively from S. Schatz, Laissez-faireism for Africa?, **Journal of Modern African Studies**, Vol. 25, No. 1 (1987), pp. 129-138.
2. M. Faber and R. Green, Sub-Saharan Africa's Economic Malaise: Some Questions and Answers, in Rose Tore, ed., **Crisis and Recovery in Sub-Saharan Africa** (Paris: OECD, 1985), p. 25.
3. George P. Schultz, U.S. Secretary of State, speaking at an international conference on privatization organized by U.S.A.I.D., as reported in the **New York Times** (Feb. 20, 1986).
4. S. Schiavo-Campo et.al., **The Tortoise Walk: Public Policy and Private Activity in the Economic Development of Cameroon** (Washington, D.C.: A.I.D. Evaluation Special Study No. 10, 1983), p. 51.
5. Jerome Wolgin et. al., **The Private Sector and the Economic Development of Malawi** (Washington, D.C.: A.I.D. Evaluation Special Study No. 11, 1983), pp. 45-46.
6. **New York Times** (Feb. 20, 1986).
7. See World Bank, **Sub-Saharan Africa: Progress Report on Development Prospects and Programs** (Washington, D.C.: 1983), pp. 7-10.
8. See Nafziger, op. cit., pp. 33-34.
9. Thus, for instance, in Nigeria, capacity utilization in the manufacturing sector declined to 23% in 1983 from 83% the previous year due to a 40% devaluation of the 'naira' in 1981. See S. Schatz, Pirate Capitalism and the Inert Economy of Nigeria, **Journal of Modern African Studies**, Vol. 22, No. 1 (March 1985), pp. 32-50.
10. World Bank, **Toward Sustained Development in Sub-Saharan Africa** (Washington, D.C.: 1983), p. v.
11. See Nafziger, op. cit., Table 2.2, p. 29.
12. S. Schatz, **Laissez-faireism for Africa?**, p. 134.
13. See Faber and Green, op. cit., p. 20.
14. World Bank, **World Development Report 1979** (Washington, D.C.: 1979), p. 17.
15. World Bank, **World Development Report 1985** (Washington, D.C.: 1985) p. 138.
16. Nafziger, op. cit., Table 1.4, p. 7, citing World Bank data.
17. See World Bank, **World Development Report 1985** for the types and heights of tariffs erected by the industrialized countries against Third World exports.
18. See Shapouri and Rosen, op. cit., pp. 2-8.

19. For the role of climate on Africa's development crises of the 1980s', see D.R.F. Taylor, Development from Within and Survival in Rural Africa: A Synthesis of Theory and Practice, in D.R.F. Taylor and F. Mackenzie, eds., **Development From Within: Survival in Rural Africa** (London: Routledge, 1992), ch. 10, especially pp. 217-221.

20. See B. Massell, Export Instability and Economic Structure, **American Economic Review**, Vol. LX, No. 4 (1970), pp. 618-630.

21. See D. Rothchild and E. Gyimah-Boadi, Ghana's Economic Decline and Development Strategies, in J. Ravenhill, ed., **Africa in Economic Crisis** (Boulder: Westview, 1988), p. 353.

22. See Raymond Hopkins, **Overburdened Government and Underfed Populace: The Role of Food Subsidies in Africa's Economic Crisis**, Paper presented at the conference on 'The Crisis and Challenge of African Development', Philadelphia, Sept. 1985.

23. Examples abound in Africa of post-adjustment efforts to roll back some of the more severe costs of economic reform on the poor. Ghana's Programme of Adjustment to Mitigate the Social Costs of Adjustment (PAMSCAD) of 1986 was the first of its kind sanctioned by the World Bank on the continent.

24. Elliot Berg, The World Bank's Strategy, in J. Ravenhill, ed., **Africa in Economic Crisis**, p. 69. See, also, World Bank, **Sub-Saharan Africa: Progress Report...**, p. 8.

25. N. Kaldor, Devaluation and Adjustment in Developing Countries, **Finance and Development** (Washington, D.C.: June 1983), p. 35.

26. World Bank, **Sub-Saharan Africa: Progress Report...**, p. 10.

27. World Bank, **Toward Sustained Development...**, p. 1.

28. Karl Polanyi, **The Great Transformation: The Politics and Economics of Our Times** (Boston: Beacon Press, 1944), pp. 140-1.

29. Marian E. Bond, **Agricultural Response to Prices in Sub-Saharan African Countries**, IMF Staff Papers, Vol. 30, No. 4 (Washington, D.C.: 1983), pp. 716-725. See, also, World Bank, **Accelerated Development...**, p. 55.

30. See, for instance, S. Schatz, **Pirate Capitalism...**, p. 47.

31. R. Hopkins, **Overburdened Government...**, p. 17.

32. For a study of both positive and negative attributes of Nigerian entrepreneurship, for example, see S. Schatz, **Nigerian Capitalism** (Los Angeles: Univ. of California Press, 1977), ch. 5 and ch. 6.

33. Ibid.

34. See Alec Nove, **The Economics of Feasible Socialism** (London: G. Allen and Unwin, 1983), pp. 193-194.

35. See Alan Berg, **The Nutrition Factor: Its Role in National Development** (Washington, D.C.: World Bank, 1983), p. 5.

36. World Bank, **Sub-Saharan Africa: Progress Report...**, p. 7.

37. World Bank, **Toward Sustained Development...**, pp. 39-40.
38. S. Yusuf and R. Kyle Peters, **Capital Accumulation and Economic Growth: The Korean Paradigm** (Washington, D.C.: World Bank Staff Working Papers No. 712, 1985), p.1 and pp. 19-28.
39. Yusuf and Peters, op. cit., p. 47.
40. E. Borenzstein, Fiscal Policy and Foreign Debt, **Journal of International Economics**, Vol. 26 (1989), pp. 53-75.
41. Borenzstein, op. cit., p. 73.
42. Ibid.
43. Borenzstein, op. cit., p. 63.
44. Mabbs-Zeno and Krissoff, op. cit.
45. Mabbs-Zeno and Krissoff, op. cit., p. 12.
46. Ibid.
47. See Krumm, op. cit., Table 9, p. 53.
48. See 'A Tale of Two Clubs', **West Africa** (Feb. 29, 1988), pp. 1348-1350.
49. See Krumm, op. cit., pp. 16-17. Also, Schoenholtz, op. cit., pp. 415-420.
50. Tim Congdon, op. cit., p. 150.
51. See Nafziger, op. cit., p. 100
52. Ibid.
53. For a detailing of the "hard landing" scenario for economies adjusting to external disequilibria, see S. Marris, Deficits and the Dollar: The World Economy at Risk, in Institute for International Economics, **Policy Analyses in International Economics**, Vol. 14 (Washington, D.C.: 1987).
54. World Bank, **Africa's Adjustment and Growth in the 1990s** (Washington, D.C.: 1989); World Bank, **Adjustment Lending: An Evaluation of Ten Years of Experience** (Washington, D.C.: 1988); World Bank, **Sub-Saharan Africa: From Crisis to Sustainable Growth: A Long-Term Perspective Study** (Washington, D.C.: 1989).
55. See U.N. Economic Commission for Africa (ECA), **African Alternative Framework to Structural Adjustment Programmes for Socio-Economic Recovery and Transformation**, E/ECA/CM. 15/6/Rev.3 (Addis Ababa, April 10, 1989).
56. See 'Rift Over Economic Policy', **Africa News**, Vol. 31, No. 1 (May 1, 1989), pp. 5-8.
57. See P. Pinstrup-Andersen, M. Jaramillo and F. Stewart, The Impact on Government Expenditure, in Cornia, G., Jolly, R. and Stewart, F., eds., **Adjustment with A Human Face: Protecting the Vulnerable and Promoting Growth Vol. 1** (Oxford: Clarendon Press, 1987), pp. 74-78.
58. See Nafziger, op. cit., Table 7.1, p. 158.

59. See Nafziger, op. cit., p. 157.
60. See Nafziger, op. cit., o. 159, quoting FAO estimates.
61. Nafziger, op. cit., p. 158.
62. See Nafziger, op. cit., pp. 150-154.
63. Nafziger, op. cit., p. 160, citing S. Claessens and I. Diwan, Liquidity, Debt Relief, and Conditionality, in Husain, I. and Diwan, I., eds., **Dealing with the Debt Crisis** (World Bank: Washington, D.C., 1989), pp. 213-215.
64. See S. Commander, Prices, Market and Rigidities, in Commander, S., ed., **Structural Adjustment and Agriculture: Theory and Practice in Africa and Latin America** (London: Overseas Development Institute, 1989), p. 239.
65. Commander, op. cit., p. 239.
66. See Nafziger, op. cit., p. 112.
67. Nafziger, op. cit., p. 173-4.
68. Ibid.
69. Nafziger, op. cit., pp. 168-174.
70. Nafziger, op. cit., p. 171, citing various studies in Cornia, Jolly and Stewart, op. cit.; and World Bank, **Adjustment Lending:...**, pp. 2-4.
71. See UNCTAD, **Trade and Development Report**, 1991 (New York: United Nations, 1991).
72. Nafziger, op. cit., p. 170, citing Faini, R., de Melo, J., Senhadji, A., and Stanton, J., in **World Development**, Vol. 19 (August, 1991), pp. 957-67.
73. Nafziger, op. cit., p. 171, citing F. Stewart, **Are Adjustment Policies in Africa Consistent with Long-run Development Needs?**, Paper presented at the American Economic Association Annual Meeting (Washington, D.C., Dec. 30, 1990), pp. 33-34.
74. For instance, Kenya was contrasted to Tanzania, Sierra Leone to Senegal, Côte d'Ivoire to Cameroon, Zimbabwe to Malawi, etc.
75. Nafziger, op. cit., p.172. Also, Mosley, P., Harrigan, J., and Toye, J., **Aid and Power: The World Bank and Policy-based Lending, Vol. 1** (London: Routledge, 1991), pp. 181-232.
76. Ibid.

Chapter 5

The IMF/World Bank and Structural Adjustment in Zambia and Zaire

In July of 1944, at the Bretton Woods conference that established the IMF under its mandate of stabilizing international flows in trade and payments in the post-World War II era, John Maynard Keynes had argued for a world-system in which the burden of economic adjustment would be borne preponderantly by nations running balance-of-payments surpluses. He had, specifically, proposed mandating expansionary policies, including perhaps an appreciation of their currencies relative to other countries', for those running external surpluses, in order to spare the deficit countries the necessity of a debilitating and (humanly) costly contractionary adjustment.

The U.S. representative there present, a high Treasury Department official named Harry Dexter White, anticipating the impending global economic hegemony of the U.S. after the war, firmly opposed Keynes, and succeeded in getting adopted the policy that stands to this day: that the onus for removing external disequilibria be placed on deficit countries.

Had Keynes prevailed, the surplus-running industrialized countries of the 1980s would have had to bear the burden of international adjustment, which they could afford more readily than could the indebted South. But, even more importantly, the South was being "required to adjust to conditions created by external change beyond their control", conditions that included structural changes in the post-WW II economy, symbolized by the declining hegemonic presence of the United Stattes; unpredictably wild gyrations in commodity prices; an anemic global economy in which job creation no longer accompanied economic growth; and historically high real interest rates.

At the same, "the global economic system lack[ed] a mechanism for encouraging...adjustment [by the industrialized countries]."[1] The upshot of this was that, in the world economy of the 1980s, the requirement that the poorer, deficit-nations bore the costs of adjustment was tantamount to a redistribution of income from the poor to the rich."[2] The Zambian and Zairean experiences, among others in Africa and the developing world in general, were exemplars of this dynamic of adjustment.

5.1 Structural Adjustment in the Zambian Experience

In the nearly three decades of political independence Zambia, like Zaire, has managed to institutionalize the high degree of external economic dependency that it inherited from the British colonialists like no other south-central African country has. Imported inputs, for instance, have come to account for some 35% of all manufacturing and mining costs over the period. Minerals (copper, zinc, cobalt) contribute more than 92% of export revenue, with copper being the single most lucrative source of foreign-exchange, bringing in some 87% of the total. Coffee and a few other primary products make up the remainder. Nonetheless, for the latter two-thirds of the period with which this work is concerned (1975-1985), external borrowing came to provide the principal source of financing for government programmes and budget deficits.[3]

Given the specific degree of export concentration and import intensity, and the general extent of openness of the economy, Zambia is particularly susceptible to economic and political developments outside of it. When, for instance, the terms-of-trade for copper fell by some 50% in 1975, merchandise imports fell by about a quarter, undermining production and employment in the manufacturing, mining and construction sectors.[4] The slide in its export prices had, of course, started three years earlier with the collapse of zinc and cobalt prices. Taking the commodity terms-of-trade for 1970 as 100, Zambia's trade terms fell to 46 in 1975 and 29 in 1985; and its export-purchasing power to 41 in 1975 and 15 in 1985, again in relation to a 1970 index figure of 100. By 1985, therefore, the economy had all but stagnated, with living standards for the majority of the population having fallen sharply as an immediate result of the near-30% drop in real wages, and as a cumulative result of the -1.3% annual growth of per capita GNP between 1965 and 1983.[5]

The impact of the economic crisis was very unevenly distributed across the population, in that the downturn was accompanied by a widening of the gap between income groups, in a country that already had the worst case of income inequality in SSA in the 1970s.[6] Thus, even as the level of national income was dropping from the late 1970s through the 1980s, the share of that income going to the richest 5% was increasing, substantially expanding the number of families on or below the poverty datum line. The import of these distributive dynamics for the subsequent adjustment of the 1980s, as far as the general living standard and the very efficacy of the adjustment policies went, was as grave as it was instructive.

Like many other SSAn countries, Zambia had emphasized industrialization after independence in 1964, with a modicum of success: it, at least, saw manufacturing share of GDP increase steadily into the mid-1970s. It invested heavily in those aspects of the economy deemed complementary to rapid industrialization, such as infrastructure and education, but thoroughly neglected agriculture. In addition, it instituted a wide array of controls on the economy and established a high propensity to import, which came to deepen its structural openness and economic vulnerability to external forces. The apartheid regime in South Africa did not help matters any, with its concerted economic and military siege of the 'front-line' states that were providing economic, political and logistical support to the African National Congress and other anti-apartheid groups. Landlocked Zambia, the nominal headquarters in exile of the ANC, bore the full brunt of the destabilization; indeed, the UN Economic Commission for Africa estimates that the nations of the region lost a full quarter of their GDP, some $60 billion, between 1980 and 1988 as a result of South Africa's direct attacks and covert sabotage.[7] The shocks that came with the collapse of commodity prices and the quadrupling of oil prices in the 1970s thus fed into an-already precariously structured and externally vulnerable economy, an economy already listing dangerously toward the financial abyss.

By 1980, therefore, Zambia was facing the prospect of making deep policy adjustments in the most adverse internal, and the most inauspicious international, economic circumstances: commodity prices and export-earnings were headed downward, the external debt was expanding (as, indeed, was the internal debt), financial inflows from the increasingly credit-tight system were dwindling, and the IMF/ World Bank had started bargaining rather stiffly on performance requirements and policy options for increased adjustment or stabilization borrowing.

The sub-text of the IMF's analysis of the country's debt and development problems may be summarized as follows: the government persisted in pursuing a policy of fiscal expansion for the ten years leading up to 1980. But when commodity prices collapsed, first in 1975 but also in 1980, spending was not commensurately curtailed. Instead, government resorted to a series of external borrowings and internal monetary and credit expansions to finance the budget deficit. The former, in conjunction with the trade-related balance-of-payments deficits consequent upon the commodity-price collapse, led to a quantum increase in the external debt, while the latter fed inflationary pressures already present in the economy. These would eventually result in the over-valuation of the *kwacha*.

The overvalued currency had two major effects. First, it exacerbated the trade deficit by overpricing Zambian exports abroad while artificially underpricing imports, with the resulting trade deficits being financed with even more foreign borrowing and some expansion of domestic credit. Secondly, it led to the blossoming of the parallel market in foreign-exchange, with the gap between the official rate and the parallel market rate widening with time. And the situation was hardly helped by the way the country's exports were marketed. The main export goods, copper and coffee, were bought in-country and sold abroad exclusively by the monopolistic government marketing boards. Because they paid sub-market prices to producers, they stifled all incentive for expanded *legal* production in those key industries. As it became immensely more profitable for producers to market their goods in parallel markets, smuggling and subterranean economic activity became the order of the day, with parallel markets fluorishing in many sectors of the economy besides coffee and minerals. This served to undermine the 'formal' economy, with government revenues (from both exports and taxes) falling in short order.

In addition, the indirect expansion of domestic credit to finance the fiscal deficit (through policies of financial repression of the banking sector which created an oligopolistic and highly controlled sector obliged to hold government debt at near-zero interest cost to government[8]) had the effect of driving interest rates and, subsequently, the saving rate, down. By 1982, therefore, Zambia was facing growing external debts with dwindling domestic savings and export revenues. By 1984, long- and medium-term debt stood at $4.5 billion, 20% of which was owed to foreign commercial banks, and the remainder to sovereign lenders and the multilateral financial institutions. Debt service, which was absorbing nearly one-half of export revenue in 1982, could only be accomodated by cutting imports of both consumer goods and manufacturing inputs to about a third of their 1970 level, and even more steeply between 1982 and 1985.[9]

To ameliorate the impact of input cuts on manufacturing and mining (which are highly import-dependent because of their relative capital intensity), and therefore on employment, the government, starting in late 1981, began relying more heavily on IMF credits to repay old debts and to maintain imports of essentials. By 1984 it owed the Fund $600 million, having been persuaded by same to modify or abandon, as a precondition for the loans, its commitment to egalitarian social and economic policies, as they were deemed too fiscally expansionary. Key among these reforms were the abolishing of price controls on all goods; the spinning-off of parastatal companies either to private ownership or, at worst, as autonomous entities facing hard budget constraints; the relaxation of foreign-exchange controls, credit controls and related measures that suppressed the financial sector; and, of course, deep cuts in overall social spending.

If done right the result, claimed the Fund, would be increased production efficiencies in the economy, a reallocation of scarce resources from consumption to investment, and an amelioration of the country's balance-of-payments difficulties. The costs of the adjustment were said to be only a short-term, and therefore temporary, problem, and so no provision was made to mitigate their disproportionate incidence on the poor, even though the government conceded that "the poor would bear the brunt of the adjustment."[10] Thus even as domestic consumption and (public) investment were allowed to lapse, the government faithfully maintained its regular debt servicing so as to keep adjustment financing flowing in. This, more than anything else, prompted the "bread riots" in Lusaka in 1986, which forced the temporary rescindment of the more welfare-damaging aspects of the adjustment programme.

The IMF in the Zambian Adjustment

The 1984 stabilization package revealed clearly the IMF's operative core understanding of Zambia's economic problems. In a real sense the Fund's analysis came largely unmodified from Harry Johnson's famous 1958 argument that the most efficient way to remove current account deficits is to bring domestic consumption down to the level of domestic production, to reorient production away from non-tradables towards exports, and to switch consumption expenditure from the consumption of imports to the consumption of home goods.[11] Indeed, as O'Clearaicain has argued, the substance of the contemporary debates about IMF conditionality is really about which of these policies, and in what combinations, would best be suited for a given situation of external disequilibrium.[12]

The Zambian adjustment package, following the theory implicitly, called for (1) a 10%-15% decline in real wages, mainly through increases in the price of corn-meal and fertilizer, and the general decontrol of the prices of other staples; (2) nominal government control, if at all, of parastatals; (3) a 50% cumulative devaluation of the *kwacha*, to occur simultaneously with a reduction in the relevant taxes so that exporters could retain greater shares of their foreign-exchange earnings; (4) the imposition of a ceiling on credit expansion, with interest rates being determined solely by credit-market forces; (5) stringent limits on the budget deficit and on foreign borrowing; and (6) accelerating remittances for suppliers, investors, expatriate employees and foreign creditors.

As is its wont, the policy target of the Fund's stabilization programme was the BOP deficit. The detail of the package suggested that the Fund saw Zambia's BOP problems as arising principally from excessive government intervention in setting prices (including wages) in the economy, and in directly allocating resources (including foreign exchange), which then effectively (though artificially) boosted consumption spending at the expense of investment. The resulting growth in aggregate demand pushed Zambian inflation above world inflation levels which, coupled with the overvaluation of the *kwacha* resulting partly from foreign-exchange controls, undermined the country's ability to expand its exports, service its debts comfortably, and produce import substitutes.

In a fuller statement of this basic view, the Fund argued that state intervention—in the form of deficit spending, price and foreign-exchange controls, and parastatal ownership—had fostered the inefficient use of resources, driven production costs up, and put a squeeze on profitability. The excessive cost of the bloated bureaucracy and social services had fuelled inflation and diverted resources to consumption, not only from the more productive private sector but even from the parastatals. The parastatals, of course, had already been rendered inefficient by excessive government control, and by the removal of the discipline of the profit motive through soft budget constraints. Government control of consumer prices had also, said the Fund, stimulated household spending, decreasing even further the amount of resources available for investment. The overvaluation of the currency resulting from some of these policies had made imports cheaper and exports costlier than would otherwise have been the case, fostering, thereby, increased expenditure on imports at the expense of domestic goods. In addition, government rationing of foreign-exchange kept otherwise non-viable enterprises in business, while potentially efficient and profitable firms operated below capacity. This compromised the dynamism of the market place, in particular, and of Zambian entrepreneurship, generally. And, finally, government-supported high real wages ate into already-low profit margins, stifling, especially, foreign investment.[13] An immediate cut in real wages was therefore necessary to lay down the conditions for the achievement of the long-term goal of higher incomes and sustained development.[14]

A 1984 World Bank **Country Economic Memorandum** on Zambia, though more specific and less doctrinaire than the IMF document did, nonetheless, shore up and elaborate further the basic IMF analysis. It argued that government credit policies discouraged saving, favoured urban over rural development, and inappropriately fostered capital-intensive production, thereby constraining job creation. To get the economy on a sounder development path the Bank, also, advocated reducing the budget deficit, expanding export production, encouraging "genuine import substitution", reducing capital intensity in many sectors, and pursuing those credit-sector reforms that would enhance local saving.

The Bank's preferred tool for achieving these goals, like the Fund's, was the elimination of governmental control over the economy:

> First, functions and responsibilities of certain ministries and parastatals will have to be redefined to steer their activities from direct control and, at present, crisis management, more towards policy analysis and support of the productive sectors. Second, for incentives and market forces to have any effect, it is essential that private individuals—farmers, industrialists and traders alike—be allowed to react to them with private decisions to invest, produce and trade.[15]

In addition, the Bank urged wage restraint "to protect Zambia's international competitive position", to encourage more labour-intensive production, and to "enhance profitability of enterprises" in order "to increase corporate savings for reinvestment."[16]

The general thrust of the World Bank/IMF analysis thus reflects their faithful adherence to Harry Johnson's seminal theoretical position. Theirs is a long-held, institutional axiom that has it that BOP problems in the South result, *invariably and in the final analysis*, from excessive domestic demand. As summarized by a Fund analyst

> Balance-of-payments difficulties reflect imbalances in the economy, typically when a country maintains a level and structure of aggregate demand, as well as an associated set of production and factor prices that are not compatible with its productive capacity.[17]

As, in this view, external disequilibria reflect the domestic excess demand manifested in public-sector deficits; and the excess demand, in turn, results from high consumption levels relative to investment, from unwarranted price controls, and from currency overvaluation, it follows that effective reduction of internal demand will necessitate curbing government spending, allowing markets to determine factor and product prices, reducing real wages, and achieving the *de facto* devaluation of the currency through the decontrol of foreign-exchange allocation. As another IMF official puts it, "...there is [no] alternative to a decline in wages if internal balance is to be restored." But "devaluation provides the best solution, as it is easier and quicker that demand management" in "[increasing] the relative share of wages", thus encouraging investment.[18]

An examination of this conceptualization and understanding of the Zambian economy by the Bank and Fund against the actuality on the ground, however, exposes analytical inadequacies of both a theoretical and 'factual' nature. As most of the underlying assumptions applied only marginally, if at all, to the Zambian economic and historical reality, the adjustment package to which the country was subjected would appear to be of questionable remedial value. Indeed, its inability to secure even the stated short-term and medium-term objectives of stabilization and growth, seven years into the programme, is eloquent testimony to this.

Economic Orthodoxy Meets Economic Reality

The distinguishing characteristic of the Fund/Bank understanding of the Zambian economic crisis was the primacy it placed on the BOP deficits *as the country's central economic problem*. For the overwhelming majority of the population, however, the most immediate concern was, as Makgetla has argued, with low and falling incomes and living standards.[19] And although external imbalances could not, and should not, continue unchecked, seeking a balance in external payments *at any price* was equally politically unfeasible and economically undesirable. Perhaps, it is in recognition of this that the Fund insists that governments not divulge details of stand-by and stabilization agreements: according to Makgetla, this may reasonably be construed as a bid to prevent open, democratic discussion of a country's real economic problems *as experienced by the citizenry*, and the consensual identification of policy options to meet the crisis.[20] But, more cynically, it ensures the implementation of the Fund's shock treatment without the populace's informed consent.

Achieving the macroeconomic and sectoral adjustments required by the Fund without depressing the already-low Zambian living standard was feasible only if the economy generated enough income and other resources to finance the necessary social investments at negligible cost in consumption to the poor majority. If, as the Fund argued, BOP difficulties and low investment spending were due to excessive consumption by the population *as a whole*, clearly no such strategy existed. But if the Fund's analysis was wrong, then a more 'social-welfare' oriented adjustment policy implemented over a longer adjustment horizon should have been viewed as equally desirable and feasible. For this reason, we next critically examine the detail of the

Fund's analysis in light of Zambia's material realities, in order to
assess whether or not the deflationary adjustment mandated by the
Fund was the best possible policy option for Zambia at the time. We
will focus on two main areas: resource availability and resource
utilization patterns.

As in all of SSA, investment spending in Zambia tends to reflect
consumption patterns which, in turn, are determined largely by the
distribution of income in the society. Vast income inequality means
that a few live in relative luxury, as far as their levels and patterns of
consumption go, while the majority hover around subsistence. The
level and distribution of investment spending tend to correlate highly
with this distribution of consumption and income: huge investment
outlays are made to meet the consumption needs of the minority high-
income group, while the production of consumption necessities for
the vast majority attracts relatively smaller investment commitments.
Secondly, a significant share of national income is repatriated abroad—
as profits by foreign investors, as payments on foreign obligations,
or in capital flight.

Thus, in SSA as a whole, national income is not split neatly and
merely between consumption and investment. It is very conspicuously
split between the luxury and non-luxury components of these. Thus
the aggregated Keynesian income-expenditure expression, $Y = C + I$,
hardly captures the full operative extent of income/expenditure
distribution in Africa. To capture this, the relation would have to be
disaggregated: consumption would have one component each of
necessaries and luxuries, as would investment; and net capital outflows
(which includes capital flight) would have to be added. Thus an
expression such as

$$Y = (C_n + C_l) + (I_n + I_l) + K_{out}$$

would be more accurate and instructive. K_{out}, Y and I are as have
been previously defined, and C is consumption expenditure. The
subscripts n and l denote necessities and luxuries, respectively. Note
also that government expenditures and net exports are easily subsumed
under one or another of these spending terms.

Only if a relatively small share of national income is expended on
luxuries and capital exports must government seek to reduce
consumption of necessities to correct internal and external
disequilibria. In practice, IMF-type adjustment policies tend to

indiscriminately curb *total* demand; but, as the empirical evaluations of these policies revealed in the previous chapter, this tends to affect the poor disproportionately, as it is often the C_n and I_n sub-categories that are targetted. Further, removing price controls on essential goods when wages are stagnant or even dropping, as often happens under adjustment, magnifies further the impact on the poor, who have a greater propensity to spend larger proportions of additional income on necessities. Salaried employees, even when their incomes do not keep pace with inflation do, nonetheless, blunt the ravages of price decontrol by winning better fringe benefits and other non-cash subsidies and subventions from employers, including government, the biggest employer of all.

Investment spending in Zambia dropped significantly between 1975 and 1985, from 25% of GDP to about 10%. The data on consumption expenditure, though not always consistent, would suggest that the Fund's implicit argument that increased *general* consumption caused this decline in investment is, at best, fatuous. What the data indicate is that, whereas by 1980 total consumption had risen by 5% in real terms over the 1977-78 level it, thereafter, fluctuated wildly, dropping, by 1984, to its 1977 level (Table 5.1). And with a 3%-a-year growth in population over the period, *per capita* consumption was probably actually falling. And as Table 5.1 further suggests, the fall in investment between 1982 and 1984 may not have been caused by increases in consumption but, rather, by the massive increase in capital outflows.

TABLE 5.1
Zambia: GDP by Type of Expenditure* at 1977 Prices

	Average 1977-78	Average 1979-81	Average 1982-84
GDP	K 1922 million	K 2017 m.	K2023 m.
Consumption share of GDP (%)	78	83	78
Investment share of GDP (%) (gross fixed capital formation)	22	17	12
Trade share (%)	-0.2	-2	9

Source: Central Statistical Office, *Monthly Digest of Statistics* (Lusaka: April-May 1985), p. xxi, Table 53.

Besides, wage and salary movements in the first half of the decade of the 1980s do not support the Fund's crowding-out thesis of consumption spending: government wage policy between 1980 and 1985 tended to reinforce income inequalities that had developed with the 40% plunge in average real wages between 1975 and 1983.[21] Some analysts have suggested that the Fund-mandated price and wage restraints of 1983 and 1984 may have further lowered real wages anywhere between 10% and 15% a year.[22] The government, however, granted the largest wage increases to top civil servants, further widening the already-wide gulf between income classes.[23] Furthermore, a condition for granting the salary increases was the abolishing of government subsidies on essential commodities (flour and cornmeal), which affected the lowest income groups even more adversely than the skewed salary adjustments.[24] Thus, between 1975 and 1984, the share in the national income of the wealthiest 5% of the population rose from 35% to 50%.[25]

With this redistribution of income away from the poor, aggregate consumption actually fell in the period, even though expenditure on luxuries appears to have picked up. (By 'luxuries' we mean that basket of goods the consumption of which is restricted to a small group of people by virtue of their economic and political hegemony, and which is not generally found in the consumption set of the average citizen not a member of this hegemonic group. Additionally, the proportion of income spent on that basket tends to rise with income). And although data on expenditure on luxuries in Zambia in the period are difficult to come by, the little anecdotal evidence that exists is quite suggestive. For example, between 5% to 10% of total government outlays for housing went for office- or home-construction for the small high-income group.[26] Imported construction material for these buildings comprised one-tenth of all imports into the country over the period. And in 1982 alone, an estimated $35 million was taken out of the country on shopping sprees by this same elite group, while the government spent $2.5 million to import Mercedes limousines for a regional summit conference in February of 1983.[27]

The increasing capital outflow of the 1980s is easier to document (see Table 5.2). Between 1974 and 1979, net factor payments abroad averaged 140 million *kwacha*. In the ensuing two years, this figure nearly doubled, and had climbed to K330 million by 1984. In 1982, investment-income repatriated abroad in foreign currency totaled some $190 million, 25% of which went as fees to the IMF and 40% as interest payments on long- and medium-term debt to various foreign creditors. Repatriated profits by multinationals alone came up to about \$35 million.[28]

TABLE 5.2
Zambia: Net Capital Flows, 1970-84 (in kwacha)

	Average 1980-82	Average 1983-84	Average 1980-82	Average 1983-84
Total inflows*	K 45 m	K 115 m	K 295 m	K 130 m
of which:				
Medium- and long-term loans	32%	48%	77%	92%
Factor incomes paid abroad	K 110 m	K 140 m	K 240 m	K 330 m
of which:				
Investment income	64%	66%	81%	89%
Net Capital Flow	-K 61 m	-K 24 m	-K 45 m	-K 200 m

*Private investment, grants, and long- and medium-term borrowing by government.
Source: World Bank, *Zambia: Country Economic Memorandum—Issues and Options for Diversification* (Wash., D.C., April 1984), p. 52.

As Table 5.2 shows, investment-income paid abroad was absorbing a rising share of income generated in the Zambian economy. Even the World Bank could not help but acknowledge that "a net outflow of resources" through the early 1980s "…[constrained] domestic expenditure below GDP and [accounted] for the slow growth in consumption."[29] This capital outflow, which had equalled one-fifth of the nominal value of all investments between 1970 and 1975, came to account for over a quarter of it by the period 1978-1982, and exceeded a full one-half of it during the following two years.[30]

The Fund's rationale for advocating the skewing of resource distribution towards the high-income elites, and for satisfying foreign claims (debt payments or profit repatriation) is a variant of the usual incentive thesis of economic orthodoxy: it, ostensibly, encourages investment by the recipients of these resources. And, indeed, the central bank of the country was in full concordance with this view, as it considered the outflow of funds " a necessary consequence of the increase in foreign investment which the country...[could not] afford to do without."[31] But as the figures in Table 5.1 indicate, gross fixed capital formation dropped continuously between 1977 and 1984: from 22% of GDP to 12% of it. In the event, then, the convergence of world-views between the government's own institutions and policy makers and the Fund blinded them to the possibility of alternative adjustment paths, much to the detriment, as we shall soon see, of the country and, especially, of the poor, who constitute the majority of the population.

Like many African countries Zambia found out that, beginning in the mid-1970s, foreign direct private investment (DPI) remained marginal despite the easing of capital- and profit-repatriation restrictions, and the provision of other investment-inducing incentives. (See the analysis of Africa's engines of growth in the previous chapter). Credit availability improved but only on stiffer terms, which eventually induced an outflow of capital; indeed, despite a series of foreign borrowings between 1975 and 1984, there was only a brief three-year period (1980-82) in which there was a net inflow of capital to Zambia. Government borrowing abroad rose most sharply between 1975 and 1982, but fell equally sharply shortly thereafter, as general Third-World lending was curbed in the aftermath of Mexico's *de facto* default of 1982, and also as a result of the IMF's limiting of Zambia's foreign-borrowing activities. As Table 5.2 indicates, government borrowing made up a countinually rising share of capital inflows, cresting at 92% of the total in 1983. This notwithstanding, the net outflow of funds reached a record K200 million in that same year.

It would appear, therefore that, contrary to the IMF's analysis of Zambia's economic problems, which provided the basis of the adjustment package subsequently designed for the country, Zambia generated an adequate amount of resources internally to expand investment activity *with no necessity to curb consumption*. If the bulk of these resources were used unproductively (i.e. to not generate even more resources), or sub-optimally for luxury consumption, or for capital export or capital flight, then the causes of the country's economic malaise would appear to be located, first, in its domestic income distribution and consumption *patterns* and, secondly, in the character of its relationship with international capital at large. To search for the causes (and therefore solutions) in the aggregate *level* of domestic demand alone, or even preponderantly, misses the mark. To get the full flavour and importance of this observation, we need to examine patterns of resource use in Zambia at the time.

As was indicated earlier, the Fund's analysis had also suggested that excessive and arbitrary intervention by the government in the economy, through regulation of business and various markets, discouraged capital formation. The analytical basis of this suggestion can also be found in the orthodox economic theory, namely, that unfettered competition in a free-market economy can best (i.e. most efficiently) allocate the nation's resources; and that, in the absence of monopoly powers and government intrusion, enterprises will, by and large, be subjected to the laws and discipline of the market. They will endeavour to reduce operating costs to optimize profits, and act otherwise 'rationally'. In a country where there is inefficient resource allocation and use beyond the merely episodic, therefore, government intervention and/or non-competitive economic structures and practices must be held accountable.

For Zambia and much of SSA, accordingly, the Fund's recommendation was for government to cede structural changes and economic adjustment to the market. The state should not set about actively guiding or controlling the direction and content of investment or resource use, for example, since that may be distortionary of the 'natural' inclinations of the marketplace. If the market 'naturally' fostered the production of luxury goods or tradables, the long-run stimulus to growth and welfare would, it was argued, outweigh the short-term loss in production in basic necessities, and/or the domestic sectoral disarticulation that export-led development normally engenders.

But, as we have seen in previous analyses, markets in SSA, if and where defined, can and do give very misleading signals indeed. Besides, the Fund's analysis, coming as it does from the orthodox theory of perfect competition, was based on assumptions of full employment, factor mobility and production efficiency, phenomena rather rare in the African economy, and concepts very difficult to grasp within the context of the particular structures of economy at work in these countries. The Fund, in particular, and economic orthodoxy, in general, thus tend to overestimate the capacity and capability of the unaided market to bring about the *desired and required* patterns of resource use, income distribution and structural change in African economies. Let us elaborate further.

Consider for a moment the notion of efficiency. The orthodox economic theory defines efficiency, for the firm, as the lowest-cost production consistent with profit maximization, and for the market, as equality in supply and demand (i.e. market clearing). But these would only translate into *systemic* efficiency if (1) market demand perfectly reflected social needs, and (2) full employment prevailed. Market demand will represent society's needs only to the extent that income distribution is equal. If income distribution is ignored, then the orthodox definition of market efficiency would imply that whatever income inequalities currently exist in the society under study are optimal for that society. In Zambia's case, and sub-Saharan Africa's, for that matter, where highly unequal income distribution tends to make effective demand unreflective of the needs of the vast majority; where, in other words, measured market demand largely reflects the requirements of foreigners and the small group of local, high-income, mainly urban consumers, this would be analytically unjustifiable. Efficiency, as a macro-analytic notion, therefore, loses much efficacy in the African context, calling into question the entire IMF analysis of the Zambian economic malaise and the prescription for it.

But efficiency has problems even as a micro-analytic concept. Since production costs reflect only employed production inputs, the existence of resource unemployment undermines the orthodox notion of enterprise, or production, efficiency. From the standpoint of a country's economic development, broader employment, even if it means a low average worker productivity, may be seen as efficient if it brings about better income distribution and moderate but sustained growth rates. It is eminently more socially efficient, in other words, to employ more people and other resources at a comparatively lower level of productivity to produce necessities than to have them otherwise unemployed, or partially employed, producing luxuries.

Consider, secondly, the assumptions of perfect factor mobility and full employment underlying the Fund's essentially Walrasian analysis. As structural adjustment is actually practiced, these concepts allow the Fund and government the latitude to avoid detailing, or taking due cognizance of, the impact of adjustment on the ground.

For if, for instance, export prices for a particular tradable were to fall and import costs for another rise, the Fund's analysis would indicate that, in a market-driven economy, firms will react by moving to more profitable sectors to produce alternative tradable goods or import substitutes. The Fund's policy prescriptions, following the path of this market-determined adjustment, would argue that state enterprises should be similarly subjected to the production flexibilities induced by market forces, and not kept going in their inefficient ways by state subsidy. In other words, they either achieve greater efficiency in response to market signals, or the factors they so inefficiently employ should be moved to other lines of production. And the preferred way of introducing them to the discipline of the market is abruptly, 'shocking' them into immediate and rapid *sectoral* conformity with market forces in the short run, as a prelude to the attainment of more comprehensive *systemic* adjustment in the long run.

In the context of Zambia's development realities and social needs, however, this approach to structural change may have been simplistic. First, the adjustment horizon, in terms of when the desired effects were expected to be seen, remained some ill-defined 'long run'. Any immediate cost of adjustment, any negative social consequences, became by definition "short run, temporary difficulties": after all, the Walrasian model 'proves' that long-run equilibria are Pareto-optimal. This 'rationalization of the long run' permitted both government and the Fund to gloss over the short-run sufferings of workers who lost jobs and wages due to retrenchment in the public sector, or of the lower-income majority who bore the brunt of lower social spending and higher prices for consumption goods and essential services.

Secondly, structural adjustment at the original level of employment can be achieved only on the assumption of perfect factor mobility in a closed economy. But, in fact, most workers in Africa cannot easily or costlessly move from one job to another; there are the perpetual constraints of skills, labour-market information, government regulations, family and ethnic issues, etc. to be considered. Moreover, as all too often happens in Africa, capital may move out on short or no notice, especially on termination of their tax holiday, leaving workers otherwise willing and ready to work without their jobs or viable alternative employment. Labour mobility is thus more the exception than the rule.

Consider now the Fund's recommendation of curbing wage growth as a means of curtailing domestic demand, and also to enhance profitability as an inducement to investment. In some indirect way, this is consistent with the programme of rapid adjustment to achieve the stated long-term objectives, in that the immediate adverse impact it has on the populace is seen as a necessary short-term cost for the higher, long-term gain. If the short-term was taken as an equally important policy period, it would become amply obvious that the curbing of wages, even though it may attract investment in the short run, also reduces aggregate demand and worker productivity, which is a decided disincentive to investment, in the long run. Low wages are a disincentive to work; but they may also decrease the productivity of otherwise able workers, as ill-fed workers tire easily, have low morale and tend to be generally not as healthy as better-paid workers. An illustration of Makgetla's from the mid-1980s' Zambia illuminates the point perfectly.

The poverty datum line for a Zambian family of five in 1985 was K300 per month. When, as a result of the adjustment of 1984, prices rose across the board, but particularly steeply for food and transportation, with no offsetting increases in nominal wages, many workers resorted to walking an hour each way to work because they could not afford the new fares. To maintain their customary level of living, many of these workers, and even some professionals and senior bureaucrats, started small retail or farming concerns on the side. They typically spent many hours of normal work-time either promoting these ventures, or diverting resources from their primary employment to provide inputs for them. This, obviously, did not augur well for their employers, including government, nor for worker productivity. But, in addition, it created a whole new, and much more insidious, parallel economy on a scale much larger than that which had existed before adjustment, and which the adjustment was partially intended to eliminate.[32]

Thirdly, to stimulate output, the IMF package called for higher producer prices across the board. In effect, the Fund was predicting high price elasticities of supply *without* any prior country-specific research on Zambian output responses to price changes. But, as we saw in the previous chapter, aggregate output elasticities are extremely low in SSA, especially in the short run. And in Zambia in particular, two key factors tended to limit output responses in small-scale enterprises, including peasant farms. The first was that higher producer prices did not necessarily increase producer *revenues* significantly. This was particularly true where infrastructure was poor or non-existent, or where input prices tended to rise simultaneously (both of which occured, especially in the rural sector, with some consistency from the late 1970s through the mid-1980s). The second was that, even when revenues increased with producer prices, it did not necessarily induce increased output. As was argued earlier in the case of African agriculture in general, inadequate financial and physical infrastructure limits peasant access to inputs rather severely. In the manufacturing sector, the shallow domestic demand is often unable to absorb any supply increases anyway, and so output expansion in response to price incentives are not readily forthcoming—much as Nurkse's theory, detailed in Chapter Two, had predicted. In addition, transport costs, trade barriers and relatively low productivity make the manufactured goods, were they to remain unabsorbed by the domestic market, uncompetitive internationally, effectively closing off exports as a viable alternative outlet.

It was thus hardly surprising that, with the implementation of rapid price increases for maize in Zambia between 1982 and 1985, resulting in a tripling of the price of roller cornmeal (the main staple), there was no appreciable increase in corn production even as late as 1986-1987. And the price increases were implemented despite the availability of micro-level and sectoral data which consistently showed no significant correlation between price and output variations in the maize crop in the ten years preceding 1984.[33]

Given this general inelasticity of supply, raising prices on produced goods (and thence inputs) only causes consumer hardship without the benefit of increased increases in production. Repeated price hikes may "end shortages", but primarily by reducing consumption, and at the cost of generalized inflation. The seeming abundance of goods on the markets of adjusting African nations is thus a chimera obscuring fundamental problems of supply inelasticities, and reflecting, rather, a general decline in consumption levels due to high prices and low wages. It would thus appear to be true for Zambia, as it is for most other SSAn countries, that government intervention to provide infrastructure, improved production techniques and marketing information will prove more effective in raising output than isolated price increases.

5.2 Exchange-Rate Policy
in the Zambian Adjustment

Because Zambia's economy is small, open and externally
dependent, its economic health is preponderantly influenced by the
price of foreign exchange and its allocation among competing projects.
As part of the adjustment, the IMF pushed for a free-market valuation
of the exchange rate, on the argument that "realistic prices" for foreign
currency in terms of local currency would force entrepreneurs to react
rationally to external developments; that it would reduce the corruption
accompanying the bureaucratic allocation of foreign-exchange at the
central bank; and that, finally, it would eliminate the parallel market
in foreign currency then fluorishing in Lusaka. Some government
officials did the Fund one better by arguing that, while floating the
currency would mean its *de facto* devaluation and the consequent
demise of companies that could no longer afford imported inputs,
devaluation would, in time, "enable companies in Zambia to cut back
their dependence on imports, increase [their] use of local raw
materials, and find export markets previously limited by the
unreasonable rate of exchange."[34]

The government commenced the removal of foreign-exchange
controls in 1984, when it allowed the mines to retain 35%, and other
exporters 50%, of their foreign-exchange earnings. This immediately
gave control of 40% of all foreign-exchange earnings to the private
sector and parastatals. In addition, the *kwacha* was eventually pushed
down to K1:(U.S.)$0.45 early in 1985; it had been as high as K1:$1.27
in 1980.   Weekly auctions of foreign-exchange began in 1985,
essentially letting the market set its price and allocation, at the same
time as the system of imports control through the use of import licenses
was abolished in favour of assessing importers an *ad valorem* fee of
5% of the value of their imports.

Imperfect as the auctioning process was as a market-determination
of the *kwacha*'s exchange rate[35], it produced a rapid and substantial
devaluation of the currency: by November 1985, it was trading at
K1:$0.15 and at K1:$0.17 by mid-December. Criticism of the extent
and speed of the devaluation was immediate and extensive, and
focussed largely on the stated rationale for it, namely, the country's
huge external imbalances. Since devaluation aims at curbing imports

and expanding exports, the devaluation of the *kwacha* would imply that Zambia's BOP difficulties stemmed largely from excessive imports and inadequate exports.

Yet, as we argued earlier, debt service and other capital outflows were the major drag on the BOP. Luxuries, and associated inputs, accounted for a large share of imports, which meant that the consumption habits of a small minority was contributing disproportionately to the country's external imbalances. By our definition of luxuries (p.172), a good one-half of all manufactured output in Zambia would have been considered luxury goods. And on the optimistic assumption that these were no more import-intensive than other types of manufactures, 15% of imported inputs, or 10% of all imports, went to the production of luxury goods, while other luxuries were imported directly.

It would seem, then, that a policy-induced shift of production away from luxuries toward more widely-used consummables; and softer terms on the foreign debt would have, arguably, done more to alleviate the country's BOP difficulties than a drastic devaluation of the currency. Thus getting the external account under control *on a more permanent basis* would have required, not less, but more vigorous though selective government intervention to direct foreign-exchange away from the unproductive consumption habits of the minority. As the IMF analysis stood in 1985, devaluation was recommended on the assumption that the structures of manufacturing and agriculture were 'rational' within the context of the country's long-term development objectives, since the effect of devaluation was to calcify the structure of production extant.[36] Yet it was the institutionalized sectoral disarticulation and outward orientation of the existing structures that produced Zambia's economic woes in the first place.

In the event, the Fund did not make the crucial distinction between luxuries and essentials when laying all culpability on imports; nor did government. Nor, indeed, did either reflect on the fact that export demand was neither elastic nor stable. If devaluation evinced greater output and exports, at a time when many of Zambia's competitors were also undergoing currency devaluation to correct external imbalances, Zambia could find itself exporting more goods and getting shrinking revenues for them, as trade terms worsened with the vastly increased quantum of exports. As it happens, both its export volume and earnings fell between 1980 and '86, the former by 6.5% and the latter by 12.5% (see p. 184)

Secondly, the projection that heavy devaluation would eventually lead to economic expansion ignores the (negative) effects of devaluation on investment. Large, sudden shocks—e.g. sudden price rises and unanticipated shifts in resource allocation induced by currency devaluation—tend to destabilize the economy over the medium term. They also foster inflationary pressures and low profit expectations. In Zambia, the prices of both consumer and capital goods rose rapidly after foreign-exchange auctioning started, the most conspicuous of these being the doubling of petroleum prices within three days of the first auction. In the first month of auctioning alone, retailers passed on the entire rise in their costs to consumers, inducing a 30%-100% increase in the prices of consumer items. Hyperinflation crept fast on the economy, even after the *kwacha*'s value had stabilized. This not only served to discourage investment; it also fed the vicious circle by which devaluation led to the importation of inflation through higher-priced imports, the consequent expansion of aggregate demand and domestic inflation, and further devaluations necessitated by the increasing BOP deficit induced by the inflationary spiral, starting the cycle all over again.

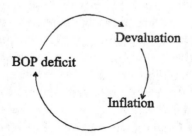

The remedy for this dual spiral, in the Fund's view, was for wages to rise less rapidly than commodity prices. Lower wages would, ostensibly, offset the higher cost of imported inputs and make exports more price-competitive.[37] Otherwise the "inflation-devaluation spiral can be very damaging, not only because it fails to correct the disequilibrium, but also because it undermines the credibility of exchange-rate depreciation as a policy instrument."[38] Following this argument, real wages would have had to have been cut by 52% to compensate for the higher cost of imported inputs—clearly, a politically unfeasible policy option.

In Zambia, the drag on investment and economic expansion consequent upon devaluation was further exacerbated by the way the government chose, with the approval of the Fund, to deal with the inflationary pressures on the economy. The central bank was ordered to tighten credit availability to push up interest rates, in a bid to mop up any excess liquidity in the system. A credit ceiling was imposed, which served to drive up the prime rate to 26% in late 1985, with higher-risk borrowers paying as much as a 35% rate of interest. In effect, to control the inflationary effects of devaluation, the government imposed deflationary measures on the already-stagnating economy. Investment spending consequently dropped sharply, the most adversely affected being small-scale enterprises and farmers. Indeed many farmers "abandoned maize planting because of the high cost of seasonal loans."[39] The Chairman of Barclays Bank in Zambia was reported to have traced the poor investment response of firms to the new opportunities and incentives opened up by the adjustment process to the high interest rates and the uncertainty of the new economic environment.[40] Besides, as interest rates in neighbouring countries (e.g. Zimbabwe) were half as high as in Zambia, Zambian exports to the region became suddenly uncompetitive.

Nor was import substitution a viable alternative growth strategy. Clothing manufacturers, for example, still found it more cost-effective, even after devaluation, to import textiles, as local manufacturers could not extend suppliers' credit at competitive rates.[41] New investment in both agriculture and manufacturing was thusly rendered virtually non-existent in 1986 and 1987.

Foreign investment also slacked off markedly. Even if local conditions yielded high returns in local currency, the steep devaluation meant that the foreign-exchange equivalent of these profits may actually represent a fall in overall profitability for foreign capital. Moreover, the continuing instability in the exchange rate increased the risk to foreign investors of long-term commitments. Many foreign firms consequently pulled out of the country altogether, sometimes relocating in neighbouring states like Zimbabwe, Malawi and Botswana.

Finally, as was mentioned earlier, the effectiveness of devaluation for increased output and exports depends on the elasticities of supply and demand for a country's exports, as well as those for its imports and their substitutes.[42] In effect the Fund and other advocates of devaluation assumed unlimited demand on foreign markets for Zambia's exports, and a high price elasticity of supply for local production. Neither assumption, of course, was justified, as nearly all the countries in the region pursued the same adjustment policies of devaluation and import substitution with much the same set of tradable commodities. Between 1980 and 1986, therefore, Zambia's export volume actually declined by 6.5%,[43] and its export earnings by 12.5%.[44] Export share of GDP declined from 49% to 46% in the same period, as did GDP growth, from an average of 1.8% annually between 1966 and 1980 to 0.1% between 1980 and 1986.[45] And as regards the main export, copper—which accounts for 87% of total exports—the volume exported declined an average 4.2% per year between 1980 and 1985, such that if its 1980 export volume was 100, it was only 86 by 1985.[46]

There were other reasons, than export elasticities, why Zambia's export performance suffered under structural adjustment. One was that, with a heavy reliance on imported inputs, production costs soared after the steep devaluation, partly because the volume of inputs imported into the country dropped by 17% and partly because devaluation just drives up the prices of imports.[47] Secondly, transfer pricing was rampant in the economy. With the unstable exchange-rate regime, companies resorted to invoicing their exports in foreign currency to by-pass the necessity of continuously changing their prices as the *kwacha* depreciated.[48] And, thirdly, transnational corporations refused to export to neighbouring countries where they had subsidiaries, closing off potential outlets for Zambian manufactures. Thus, for instance, the Zambian branch of Lever Brothers would not export to neighbouring Zaire, because the market there was reserved for a sister-company based in South Africa.[49]

To stem the tide of weak export performances, Zambia sought, with IMF and World Bank encouragement, to diversify its exports and their markets. It began cultivating new commodities like garlic and strawberries ("non-traditional exports", so-called) destined for the Middle-Eastern and continental European markets. But strawberries and garlic do not have a market within Zambia. So export diversification built around them is subject to the same criticism as the expansion of traditional exports: they do not help create sectoral articulation of the economy, they do not go to satisfy local demand, and their inputs still come from abroad. In short, diversifying into non-traditional exports still leaves the economy outwardly-oriented and internally-disintegrated, and leaves Zambia as susceptible to external economic forces as it always was.

The World Bank eventually acknowledged that Zambia was experiencing formidable export difficulties, for which it offered three possible explanations: higher input costs, increased competition in the region and, curiously enough, "a lack of past export experience."[50] Yet the Bank still argued that the country's economic future lay in export expansion, and the preferred strategy for achieving this was the continued devaluation of the *kwacha*. Indeed, argued the Bank, the *kwacha* should be continuously devalued until local production costs were low enough to compensate for the increased (imported) input costs, at which juncture exports would, once again, become competitive.[51] Given the trade picture described above, however, this would appear to be an unrealistically optimistic position to take, and it would appear that the Bank, despite acknowledgement of the structural obstacles to increased export performance, was still content to focus on *policy inadequacies* within the country, rather than on the *structural hurdles* on the ground.

The impact of the devaluation on domestic demand was equally problematic. As imported input costs soared, producers had either to raise prices to cover their rising costs, switch to local-input substitutes, or cease operations altogether. Most advocates of devaluation predicted that the second option was the most likely to be taken; in other words, devaluation would create more import substitution and expanded linkages across sectors, for the simple reason that many Zambian firms could not hike prices, even in the short run, without cutting demand too far to cover even prime costs.

But switching to domestic sources of input, and establishing or expanding production units take time, organizational capacity, and a measure of broad macroeconomic stability, all of which were in acute short supply in the aftermath of the adjustment process. There was also the unspoken assumption that local inputs were always, and for all purposes, perfect or near-perfect substitutes for imported ones, which is a questionable supposition, at best. It would thus seem reasonable to concur with Makgetla's argument, in counter to the devaluation-optimists', that only with a less drastic adjustment, which allows time for the research, investment and retooling needed to reshape production and the economy towards greater sectoral complementarity, vertical integration, and self-reliance, can a high level of production be maintained in the aftermath of a devaluation of the magnitude underwent by Zambia.[52]   What that devaluation did was to force market forces to determine the structure of imports. Since prices increased uniformly for all imports, the elasticity of demand for different categories of goods—which reflected, in part, Zambia's severely skewed income distribution—was crucial in determining what was imported.   According to the central bank's data on purchasers' stated intentions, 25% of the foreign-exchange sold at the first ten auctions was bought explicitly to finance the importation of consumer goods (mostly luxuries, by our definition).[53] The bank pronounced this "quite reasonable" (even though the actual proportion is more likely to have been higher, as there was no legal compulsion to use openly purchased foreign-exchange for the stated intent), but argued that it was bound to fall before long, as the rising prices of luxury imports would eventually push demand down.

Given Zambia's highly unequal income distribution, however, the demand for luxuries may be as stable as that for other types of goods, with the possible exception of the most basic necessities.   Thus devaluation had the insidious effect of limiting, in the final analysis, demand on basic necessities (through commodity price increases) while not affecting the demand for luxuries.   All these developments notwithstanding, advocates of devaluation-led structural adjustment stuck tenaciously to their belief in the 'J-curve': that, upon the devaluation of the *kwacha*, Zambia's economic performance, especially its trade balance, will worsen before it improves (see diagram below).   In other words, that those negative consequences are necessarily inevitable short-run costs, and that, eventually, market forces would restore efficient resource use and stable growth.

But local farmers, consumers, trade unions, and the business community were far less optimistic about even these long-term prospects.   As far as most Zambians were concerned, the short-term results did not bode well for the future.   They saw the government and the IMF/World Bank justifications of the adjustment as too abstract, apologetic, and reflective of a lack of knowledge about, or empathy with, the material realities of economic life in contemporary

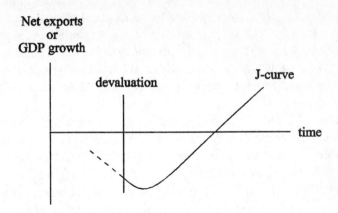

Zambia. The Zambian Federation of Employers, for instance, complained that the government undertook the stabilization and adjustment processes "without prior consultation with other social partners"—a reflection, no doubt, of the secrecy that the Fund demands about its stabilization accords with governments.[54]

It would appear, then, that the experience of IMF-sponsored structural adjustment in Zambia attests to the paradigmatic ahistoricism that leads the 'new' economic orthodoxy to the uncritical espousal of market solutions for the debt-and-development crisis in all countries, regardless of the specific dynamics and structural capabilities of their economies. It is not the case, as we show theoretically below, that in Africa currency devaluation, free-market resource allocation, and less government spending will, inexorably, lead to improved trade performance, greater production efficiencies, and higher growth, even in the long run. As Zambia's experience shows, the structural obstacles on the ground can confound even the most elegant and best-intentioned theories and analyses, and that the chances of success of each adjustment policy or package is enhanced the more reflective it is of these structural nuances. In Africa's case, in particular, the absence of institutionalized market mechanisms of any reliablity makes market-driven economic policy particularly prone to, at best, failure, and at worst, further systemic distortion in the long run, either of which will aggravate economic crises to one degree or another. Severe 'shock' adjustment is also particularly destructive in such an economy, as the negative effects of the shock, amplified by the dysfunctional markets, may prove uncontrollable in the short run, and even undermine whatever long-term potential improvements reform policies may have. A gradualist approach, in which government intervention judiciously but efficiently applied to select areas of economic activity, and in which enough time is allowed for the requisite adjustments to be made by both investors and consumers to the new economic order, will serve to mitigate some of the more painful immediate costs of adjustment, and ensure both the economic and political viability of reform.

Secondly, IMF-type SAPs are based on the assumption that the existing structural configuration of the economy is adequate and desirable. Whatever problems of external imbalance, government budget overruns, and internal programmatic inefficiencies exist can thus be corrected with the proper *policy adjustment*. The issue, however, goes beyond that, as Zambia's case clearly attests to; mere policy reform thus just begs the question. The primary pathology of the African economy, which underlies its underdevelopment, and hence its debt, crisis, is the pervasiveness and intractability of its sectoral disarticulation, and therefore the irrationality of its current structures of production and consumption. Local inputs are rarely used for production to satisfy local demand; hence very little systemic propensity is developed toward generating enough (or sustained) national output sectorally balanced to promote a system-wide multiplier effect. This underscores the perpetual need for external resources, from production inputs and financing to even the very intellectual and cultural models with which to study African society.

Thus the orientation of the economic structures is precisely *not* adequate or desirable. The objective of any corrective policy, therefore, should be to *transform* this structure completely, not merely reform or adjust it. We, in the next chapter, make some suggestions towards a 'new culture of development' that may effect such a transformation. It is our contention that unless this is done, SSA will always be prone to low income performance, to a high propensity for external indebtedness and dependence, and to intermittent but predictable economic crises.

Finally, Zambia's experience reveals the political difficulty that African governments encounter with the skewed distribution of the costs of adjustment. As will become even more clearly evident in the case of Zaire, there tends to be a quick atrophying of political will when the hungry populace demands a rolling back of some of the reforms. And where income maldistribution serves to maldistribute also the costs of adjustment and losses in living standards, IMF-type structural adjustment and market-oriented reform are a veritable recipe for social rupture—a case Karl Polanyi made powerfully some fifty years ago for a different but not unrelated context, but which seems to be lost in the contemporary resurgence of mass blind adulation of the market. That these reforms are often accompanied by political and military repression should thus not be particularly surprising.

At a more basic level, however, the question needs be asked: if, as in the case of Zambia, the two main factors that precipitated the debt-and-development crisis were the deterioration of trade terms and the rise in the cost of debt service, neither of which were within the control of the debtor-nations, why was it that *they* were required to undergo a strong contractionary adjustment when the problem obviously did not arise solely, or even preponderantly, from their conduct of economic policy? Might there not have been an equal need for the restructuring of the *international* political economy to ameliorate the forces that worsened commodity trade terms and/or pushed up interest rates? For, as Killick has argued, "as long as the [industrialized economies] remain characterised by protectionist, anti-trade...and deflationary macroeconomic policies,...the scope for [meaningful] adjustment through the domestic efforts of developing-country governments will remain severely limited."[55] It was also precisely this possibility of a perpetual imbalance in countries' external accounts that Keynes' proposal at Bretton Woods had sought to prevent. In retrospect, his was a very prescient reading of the world economy.

5.3 *Some Theoretical Considerations of Currency Devaluation as Adjustment Policy*

As we have seen with the example of Zambia, currency devaluation is the cornerstone of most stabilization and adjustment programmes. It is also quite evident that steep devaluation has drastic effects on the economy, not all always intended or desired. Devaluation, as concept and policy, also evokes passionate responses from all sectors of society, some informed but many not, while its mode of implementation and efficacy are forever the subject of endless debate and contention among and between policy makers, theorists, and the public at large. It is for these reasons of ambiguity in its economic outcomes, and the political passions it generates, that governments of adjusting countries consistently resist drastic devaluation until so compelled by outside forces. And even though governments have been known to unfairly put responsibility for inevitable devaluations on these 'outside forces', it is the case that the rules of the international monetary and payments system, as encapsulated in the Articles of Agreement of the IMF, require devaluation as a corrective policy when a country's BOP are in "fundamental disequilibrium", whatever the causes of that disequilibrium may be.[56]

Much of the drama surrounding devaluation exercises often stems from the clash between the sharply instinctive, though sometimes exaggerated and ill-informed, responses of various groups in society whose narrow short-term economic interests are threatened by the policy, and the overly optimistic, exaggerated, pompous and theory-driven views of the technical designers and implementors of the policy. The trauma it evokes, especially in the former group, however, is very real, hardly exaggerated, and it stems from the rather limited time horizon in which the policy is implemented and/or is expected to yield results. In sum, they see too many dynamic changes in too many sectors of the economy expected from too few discrete changes in the exchange rate in too short a period of time. This introduces too many uncertainties into their economic lives, making them understandably antipathetic towards exchange-rate reform.

In this section, we consider, at the level of theory, three inter-related issues. One is the various uses to which the foreign-exchange system is put in a typical African economy that might generate the passionate interest in preserving the *status quo ante*, and how that pattern of use differs from that in the industrialized countries from which the theories emanated. The second is how these uses uniquely contextualize the implementation and outcomes of devaluation as an adjustment tool in Africa; and, therefore, thirdly, how the orthodox analysis of the economics of devaluation should be modified to reflect the institutional nuances of the African foreign-exchange system, so as to fully grasp the reasons for the drama, trauma and frequent inefficacy of devaluation as an adjustment policy in Africa. In doing this, we follow closely a set of analyses seminally developed by Richard Cooper in the early 1970s.[57]

Functions of the Foreign-Exchange System

The foreign-exchange system in Africa is often used as a supplement for inadequate or ineffective macroeconomic policymaking capacity in government. It is thus not merely the monetary counterpart to the international exchange of real goods and services, nor simply the medium by which the exchange-rate as an allocator of the stock of foreign-exchange is determined, as might be the case in the industrialized North. Rather the system, in addition, is called upon to perform functions such as altering the terms-of-trade and relative prices, generally; promoting industrialization; increasing government revenue; fostering import-substitution investment; and even changing the distribution of income between classes.

This is all done through multiple exchange-rate policies that, for instance, would favour primary-commodity exporters over consumer-goods importers (the former would face a lower rate of exchange than the latter), but exporters of non-traditional goods over both primary-commodity exporters and net importers. Such a policy would be intended to stimulate, in varying degrees, investment in non-traditional goods, in import-substitution manufacturing, and in primary goods, while discouraging expenditure on imported consumer items. The government, meanwhile, would collect substantial revenue from the gap between the buying price and the selling price of foreign-exchange. On a similar rationale of stimulating manufacturing and employment, imported investment goods would often face lower exchange rates than, say, imported consumer goods, though this has been known to yield the perverse result of encouraging capital- and import-intensive production not particularly absorptive of labour. The redistributive character of such a tiered regime of exchange rates—between and among consumers, various classes of producers and exporters, and government—should be obvious. Equally obvious is the necessity of policing the policy, as it inevitably induces arbitrage.

The primary function of the exchange rate—the allocation of the quantum of foreign-exchange available among competing uses—is often subsumed within these other objectives. When imbalances appear in the external accounts, therefore, governments initially take other (than devaluation) measures to deal with the problem, in order not to upset these other ends for which the system has been employed. They may, for instance, raise some tariffs and make other marginal adjustments, but these have often proved inadequate to the task of correcting the imbalance, even as they compromised some of the broader policy objectives imposed on the system. When, as a final resort, and under pressure from the IMF, the full devaluation is eventually implemented, it provides the political cover for the dismantling of a whole host of policies built into the system that may otherwise prove politically unpopular to eliminate. As Robert Cooper argues, "...an objective achieved indirectly is often socially acceptable when direct action would not be. ... It is much easier for an interest group to mobilize successfully against an export tax than it is to mobilize against an overvalued currency supplemented by high import tariffs and possibly accompanied by some export subsidies, even though the two systems might have precisely the same effects."[58] This would indicate, he continues, that "currency devaluation in many developing countries...[is] a good deal more complex than a simple adjustment of the exchange rate, and the analysis must be modified to take these other adjustments into account."[59]

Cooper identifies four distinct, though not functionally mutually exclusive, types of devaluation for adjusting developing economies with multiple, multi-tasked exchange-rate regimes: straight devaluation involving a discrete lowering of the principal exchange rate; devaluation within the context of a contractionary stabilization package; devaluation as part of a (trade or general) liberalization programme; and devaluation with a unification of exchange rates.[60] Clearly, a single policy of devaluation may well involve unifying and subsequently reducing the value of the currency vis-à-vis foreign currencies as part of a short-term stabilization of the external sector, all within the context of achieving a liberal trade regime for the country in the medium term.

As these devaluations can all be done simultaneously, Cooper's discrete categorisation of them is heuristic, merely for analytical tractability. Clearly, they must all be considered in coming to an adequate understanding of the system-wide and specific economic effects of devaluation in Africa. It is also important to understand at the outset, Cooper suggests, whether devaluation is necessitated by open payments deficits, or by a situation in which "a latent deficit is suppressed by import controls and related measures which are removed upon devaluation." In reality, of course, most devaluing countries tend to be experiencing both of these. Equally important is an understanding of whether the country is pursuing potentially inflationary monetary or fiscal policies, "as opposed to merely having costs that have gotten out of line in the course of past inflation."[61] Here, too, the reality is likely to be a bit of both.

Elasticities

Under the fixed exchange-rate regimes found in many African countries, currency devaluation was the sole province of government. The magnitude of the devaluation necessary to eliminate the BOP deficit (hence eliminate the excess demand for foreign-exchange) is an inverse function of the elasticities of demand and supply of foreign exchange: the larger would be the devaluation required the lower the elasticities. But a complication arises from the fact that these elasticities are not constant: elasticities of demand for exports and imports tend to be smaller in the short run than in the long. One would therefore expect the (positive) trade or BOP effects of devaluation to increase with time (the J-curve effect).

The positive trade effects of devaluation are obtained in the orthodox theory, however, through an unrealistic assumption of the infiniteness of the elasticities of supply of traded goods; i.e. that the prices of exported goods are constant in the exporter's currency. Under this assumption of infinite supply elasticities, for devaluation to improve the trade balance and be expansionary for the domestic economy, it is sufficient, though not necessary, that the absolute value of the sum of the elasticity of demand for exports (E_x) and that of imports (E_m) exceed unity: $E_x + E_m > 1$. This is called the Marshall-Lerner condition. Note that this is not a neccessary condition for devaluation to improve trade performance, because if the supply elasticities are sufficiently low the trade balance will improve, even if they do not exceed one upon summation.

Given this assumption, the elasticities of supply and demand for foreign exchange are determined by the elasticities of demand for imports and exports. A devaluation would cause an increase in the price of imports; at a given level of income, we would expect the quantity of imports (and hence foreign-exchange) demanded, to drop. Indeed, in time, there will be an increasing substitution of domestic equivalents for the costlier imports, indicating that the long-run demand elasticity for imports is greater than its short-run equivalent.

As a result, the effectiveness of devaluation as an adjustment policy, as measured by its effect on trade, hence on the demand for foreign exchange, is likely to be greater in the long-run than in the short. The same devaluation would also cause a decrease in the foreign-currency price of exports, spurring foreign demand for the exported goods at every level of income. Here, too, the longer the adjustment period, the greater the increase in the amount of exports demanded will be and, if the exporting country is successful in meeting the expanded demand, the greater will be its supply of foreign exchange, *ceteris paribus*.

Note, however, that the results of devaluation in Zambia and many other adjusting African economies in the 1980s were not quite in accordance with the theory. Because short-run demand elasticites were low, the balance of trade worsened upon devaluation, as would be expected. But the long-run improvement the theory would have us expect never quite materialized, and many African countries found themselves stuck on the bottom loop of the J-curve. The main reason for the failure of devaluation, it would appear, was the continuing demand inelasticity for Africa's exports even over the medium run, and the decline in trade terms resulting from it and, for certain commodities, from the glut on export markets occasioned by expanded production by all the adjusting countries. For *individual* country-producers of certain commodities (rubber, copper and coffee, for example) for which they have no domestic absorption, however, there was not much output response to the increase in export demand, as it would have required expanding capacity by bringing new fields, mines or farmland under development, a task not easily achievable in the short run. This contrasts sharply with the situation in most Northern economies, where goods produced for the domestic market also have export potential, enabling quick expansion of export supply by either switching from home consumption to foreign consumption, or utilizing existing capacity to expand total output for both markets.[62]

It is, of course, more than likely that demand elasticities for imports would be low for a country importing predominantly production inputs like capital equipment, semi-processed goods and raw materials, as indeed is the case for most African nations. (It even holds for those nations that have largely succeeded with import-substition production because, having already made most of the easy substitutions, "imports [have come to] depend largely on output rather

than income and are not very sensitive to relative price changes."[63])
But it may well be the case that a programme of devaluation with
trade liberalization, such as that undertaken by the African countries,
causes a drop in the prices of those imports that were most tightly
controlled under the old exchange-rate regime. This encourages the
consumption of these imports which, when combined with the potential
worsening or non-improvement of export performance after
devaluation, could actually exacerbate the trade imbalance.

For these and similar reasons related to the character of trade and
output elasticities in the developing world, Cooper cautions against
the unbridled optimism of the advocates of devaluation. For the short
run, at least, such caution is justified though, he argues, in the long
run devaluation almost always helps improve the trade balance.[64]

Macrodynamics

If, because of low elasticities and the expanded use to which the
foreign-exchange system is put in Africa, devaluation does not yield
a net improvement in the trade balance, at least in the short term,
then there is little necessity for a commensurate or compensatory
reduction in aggregate expenditure or increase in gross output. But
as devaluation still has an impact on domestic macroeconomic
outcomes, and on macroeconomic policy-making in the adjustment
process, it is still worth investigating the character of these influences.

Consider the following macro model:

$$Y = E + D \qquad\qquad r = r(Y, p, L)$$
$$E = E(Y, R, e) \qquad L = H + R$$
$$D = D(Y, e) \qquad\qquad R = D + K$$

where Y is the level of output/income in the devaluing country; E is
its gross domestic spending; D, the trade balance; L, the money supply;
H, domestic credit; R, the international reserves; and K, the capital
inflow, all measured in nominal domestic currency units.

The exchange rate, defined as the cost in dollars of a unit of local
currency, is represented by e; r is the interest rate on non-cash financial
assets; and p is the domestic price level. The domestic price of all
production in the economy, both tradables and home goods, is assumed

fixed; so p only varies if a devaluation increases local-currency import prices. And as the foreign price of imports is assumed to be constant, devaluation would imply a worsening of the terms of trade. The interest rate is determined at the point of equality between the demand for real money balances and the supply of it.

As the model is specified, the impact of devaluation on domestic output, Y, will be the combined effects of the individual impacts of same on Y's components, i.e. domestic expenditure (E) and the trade balance (D). But the impact on output will, in turn, affect income, expenditure, imports, etc., through a multiplier process. To understand the quality and dynamics of the impact, and whether or not it is contractionary or expansionary, we need to differentiate the model to obtain:

$$dY = \frac{1}{s - D_Y - E_r r_Y \, [D_e de + E_e de + E_r (r_L dL + r_p dp)]}.$$

The subscripts indicate partial differentiation with respect to the particular variable, and $s = 1 - E_y$. The interpretation of the equation is quite straight forward: the change in income depends on the three terms in the square brackets—on the change in the trade balance induced by the devaluation $(D_e de)$, on the change in expenditure levels resulting from the devaluation $(E_e de)$, and on the changes in expenditure induced by the interest-rate adjustments stemming from the changes in the money-supply and the price level $(E_r (r_L dL + r_p dp))$, all modified by an income multiplier $(1/s - D_Y - E_r r_y)$. To assess whether the devaluation would be deflationary or expansionary for the economy, we need to consider each of these terms in turn.

The trade balance, as we saw above, may actually worsen immediately following a devaluation, especially if it is done within a context of import liberalization, as it will induce an increase in imports even as exports respond only with a lag. Thus the immediate impact on the domestic economy is likely to be deflationary, though exports may well stimulate the economy in the long run. In addition, "any discrepancy between the local-currency value of a dollar's worth of imports and a dollar's worth of exports, for example due to tariffs, means that even a parallel expansion of imports and exports will be deflationary, provided the government does not spend the additional revenue at once."[65]

Thirdly, devaluation will be deflationary to the extent that it effectively substitutes price rationing for the quantity rationing of the old exchange-rate regime. The central bank, as the vendor of foreign exchange, now becomes the collector of scarcity rents, displacing those importers under the pre-devaluation regime who had the priviledge of holding the few import licenses awarded. And, lastly, because demand elasticities for imports are so low, the sharp rise in the domestic-currency price of imports following upon a devaluation will cause a nominal increase in import spending, even if the quantity of imports, or their foreign-currency price, falls. In addition, the fact of net financial and other capital inflows into developing economies tends to ensure that imports exceed exports; thus exports would have to expand astronomically at their pre-devaluation price if the trade balance, in terms of local currency, is to improve after a devaluation. As Cooper describes it, "devaluation, [in this respect], is like an efficient revenue-oriented excise tax, increasing the price far more than it reduces the quantity."[66] He also establishes that the trade-balance effect of devaluation will be deflationary under the following conditions: if B is the trade balance measured in foreign-currency units, then

$$B = eD$$

and

$$dB = e(1+k)dD + kB,$$

in which k, the proportionate devaluation, is negative. For an initial trade deficit, therefore, kB is positive, making dD potentially negative even if the trade balance in foreign currency improves. This will obtain providing the elasticity of demand for imports, E_m, is smaller than one, and if the foreign elasticity of demand for the country's exports, E_x, is low enough (though it may be greater than one).[67] Note that these elasticities fall in-between the Marshall-Lerner sufficient condition, under which devaluation improves the trade picture and is expansionary. Indeed, "many developing countries meet the conditions for falling into the middle region [between the Marshall-Lerner boundaries], with continuing aid-financed trade deficits, low elasticities of demand for imports, and moderate foreign elasticities of demand for their exports, at least in the short run that is relevant for considering the impact effect on income. Therefore, the foreign sector may well exert a deflationary impact on the economy following devaluation, and indeed did so in 14 of 24 devaluations [studied]."[68]

The effect of devaluation on domestic spending, E, is multifaceted and therefore more complicated. Some of the effects arise directly from the change in the exchange rate while others are caused by devaluation-induced changes in the monetary system. Cooper identifies six broad categories of such effects: the speculative, the distributive, debt servicing, credit squeeze, money demand, and resource efficiency effects, each of which will be examined closely here.[69]

Speculative spending arises when, in anticipation of the price rises that devaluation will induce, consumers and producers stock up on goods prior to the devaluation. Since, in this manner, private holdings of goods are rendered larger in the post-devaluation period than it might otherwise be, total spending drops after devaluation while the accumulated stocks are drawn down. It is, however, quite possible that, if the devaluation is expected to lead to generalized inflation or to further devaluations, spending will increase in the immediate aftermath of a devaluation. But empirical evidence points to the former more often overwhelming the possibility of the latter.

The distributive effects of devaluation we have already elaborated at some length in various analyses. To reiterate briefly, devaluation tends to tilt the distribution of income towards exporters, of both primary and manufactured goods, and away from those who produce for local consumption, often small farmers and uncompetitive manufacturers. Thus the rural elite and the urban elite tend to gain, while urban or industrial workers and peasants lose. Because the losers are greater in number, and have a higher marginal propensity to spend than the gainers, this redistribution combines with the induced price increases to curb overall domestic expenditure, on both imports and home-produced goods.[70] Note also that when a reduction in tariffs accompany the devaluation (say, as part of a broader policy of liberalization), government tends to lose revenue; those who are privilegded enough to hold import quotas lose the rents that they could collect through the quotas; when devaluation spurs inflation, those on fixed incomes lose purchasing power: all these losses have a deleterious effect on domestic spending.

Devaluation also increases the debt-servicing costs of the country, as it increases the quantum of domestic resources necessary to pay obligations denominated in foreign currency. Where the bulk of the debt is publicly held, the internal budgetary problem of raising the local-currency equivalent of the funds to be transferred abroad in foreign exchange is sufficiently daunting to make policy makers lukewarm towards devaluation as a major adjustment or stabilization policy. And where the private capitalist sector holds the majority of the external liabilities, devaluation can even lead to bankruptcies, at worst or, at best, a significant curtailing of planned business investment spending. In either scenario, spending must be cut in order to meet the expanded external obligation.

We have established that the trade account in local-currency terms can run deeper into deficit following a devaluation. This can result in a domestic credit squeeze—from, for instance, the fact that importers pay more for foreign-exchange than exporters receive for their exports—if the monetary authorities do not take the requisite steps to enhance credit availability. The scarcity of credit often leads to higher interest rates, with a subsequent reduction in consumer and investment spending. In addition, to the extent that prices rise upon devaluation, the real value of the available money stock will be smaller after devaluation. This will, generally, induce lower domestic spending, especially where export goods are also purchased by local consumers.

But, lastly, in the long run, when all the necessary resource switching and other responses have been completed, there should be a greater efficiency of resource allocation and utilization which should lead to improvements in real income. Devaluation, in the long run, therefore, may help boost expenditures, if the monetary authorities duly support the increased demand for money balances that will accompany the higher efficiency of resource use.

In sum, then, devaluation is likely to have a deflationary effect on the economy in the short run, and may only improve macroeconomic performance when and if the requisite adjustments to the devaluation have been successfully completed. It would therefore appear prudent for devaluing governments to simultaneously conduct an expansionary policy to cushion the economy from the impact of devaluation. However, since devaluation often takes place in the context of excessively expansionary macropolicies, the Fund/World Bank demands contractionary government policies; but implementing contractionary stabilization at the same time as currency devaluation might very well mire the economy in deep recession. This, indeed, was the experience of Zambia and the other adjusting African nations in the 1980s. As Cooper rightly argues in his study, "unless devaluation is very successful in stimulating exports or...investment, the absorption approach to devaluation is of less relevance to devaluation in developing countries except in manifestly inflationary situations. The real problem will often be getting adequate capacity in the export sector, not releasing resources overall."[71]

Thus, contrary to the conventional wisdom fostered by the dominant orthodoxy, a modest *expansionary* policy accompanying a devaluation may be what is needed to soften the deflationary macroeconomic impact of currency devaluation. This, done in moderation, timed properly, and withdrawn or scaled down as the positive effects of devaluation on the trade balance starts becoming manifest, will mitigate against some of the more debilitating social and economic costs of devaluation, thusly helping to mitigate some of the trauma and justified political opposition to the reforms from below.

5.4 *Adjustment and Drama in Zaire*

In the light of Zambia's experiences with external imbalances and IMF/World Bank-mandated economic-policy reform, we take a second, more detailed look at the Zairean case, in order (1) to illustrate the impact of country-specific, structural characteristics on the debt experience; (2) to provide contrast with the Zambian experience; (3) to show how the geo-political importance of a debtor-country in the Cold War affected the dynamics of its economic adjustment; and (4) to show how clientelist politics determine the internal dynamics of Africa's debt-and-development crisis. We therefore focus less on the mechanics of how Zaire got to be one of the most indebted countries in SSA, than on how it dealt with the domestic responses generated by its reform efforts, and on how it accomodated the IMF's conditions and demands. For the detail of Zaire's debt and adjustment experiences we, as before, rely on Parfitt and Riley.[72]

Early Attempts at Economic Adjustment

In the wake of the 1973 oil-price hike, the collapse of copper prices in 1975, the world recession of 1974-75, and the discovery of ubiquitous corruption in the national polity, Zaire's debt problems ran out of control, literally, in 1975. The country stopped payment of principal and interest on its commercial debt, some $700 million a year, in that year. The IMF intervened in March 1976 with its first (of five) stabilization programmes for the country. This involved the usual panoply of adjustment policies, such as those we encountered in the case of Zambia. But Zaire's was centered specifically around (1) differential taxation of the different economic sectors and activities; (2) reductions in state spending; (3) the introduction of market pricing (to, supposedly, eliminate the corruption that appeared endemic to state allocation of resources, to undermine parallel markets, and to ensure efficient resource allocation); and (4) trade liberalization.

The first programme, and its successor, lapsed rather quickly, as Zaire could not meet the Fund's minimum performance criteria. Some have argued that the government *would not* meet the Fund's terms: "Mobutu and his aristocracy had no intention of living up to the agreements, [since]...they do not view international organizations and aid agencies as sources of development assistance but rather as channels for access to more...foreign exchange."[73]

After these initial failures, Zaire's commercial creditors, in desperation, prevailed upon the IMF to instal its own economic and financial management team in the central bank in Kinshasa. Led by a retired Bundesbank official, Erwin Blumenthal, the team, as a first order of business, tightened limits on credit and foreign-exchange facilities. From December 1978, access to credit and foreign-exchange at the central bank was denied to many influential Zaireans, badly undercutting the source of Mobutu's power, the clientelist networks.

The ensuing conflict between the Zairean elite and the IMF team was vicious. The team was subjected to frequent harassment and personnel changes by government officials. On one occasion, a powerful army general, who happened also to be the President's father-in-law, had his soldiers threaten team members with sub-machine guns when he was denied foreign-exchange for an overseas trip. Blumenthal reported that, getting to the end of his one-year assignment, he resorted to sleeping with a shotgun under his bed and maintaining twenty-four hour radio contact with the (then) West German and U.S. embassies. In assessing the situation on the ground at the time, he writes, presciently, that

> [It was] alarmingly clear that the corruptive system in Zaire with all its wicked and ugly manifestations, its mismanagement and fraud, will destroy all endeavours of institutions, of friendly governments, and of the commercial banks towards recovery and rehabilitation of Zaire's economy. Sure, there will be new promises by Mobutu, by members of his government, rescheduling, and rescheduling again of [the] growing external public debt, but no...prospect for Zaire's creditors [of getting] their money back in any foreseeable future.[74]

Subsequent attempts at debt control also foundered. In 1979, Zaire hired a team of prominent investment banking firms—Lehman Brothers, Lazard Frères, Kuhn-Loeb and S.G. Warburg—to handle its negotiations with both its commercial and multilateral creditors. However, all performance conditions agreed upon for rescheduling were roundly violated by Zaire, mainly as a result of the intransigence of the 'aristocracy'. For instance, a 1981 $1.06 billion stand-by agreement with the IMF was suspended due to failure to cut the government's budget deficit. In 1982 the bankers, in frustration, abrogated their contract with Zaire. But, as some have suggested, the government's sole intention may have been to use the bankers to provide international legitimacy for its 'adjustment' effort, so as to continue attracting overseas funds while it continued its usual practices.[75]

By 1983, economic conditions had worsened considerably due to further declines in copper and cobalt prices and, of course, the government's inability to sustain meaningful reforms. The government had little option but to approach the IMF, once again, but this time apparently chastened and transformed for the better, for funding. In December of 1983, after it had actually implemented cuts in spending, tightened controls over the budget, began price and trade liberalization, devalued the *zaire* by 77.5%, and abolished SOZACOM (though not, evidently, before fierce resistance from the elites), a compensatory finance facility of SDR 114.5 million and a 15-month stand-by loan of SDR 228 million were extended by the Fund. The government scrupulously observed successive stabilization agreements in apparent realization that there were few viable alternative plans of action. These included floating the *zaire* after the initial 1983 devaluation, further reductions in public spending, and a policy of privatization.[76]

Macro-Level Results

By 1984, the reforms had been immensely successful, at least on paper. The flotation of the *zaire* seemed to have succeeded in eliminating profitability in the currency black market by reducing the differential between the offical and black-market rates by between 90% and 95% of its pre-flotation value. (The official rate had been as much as five times the parallel market rate). This reduced the incentive for arbitraging in the currency markets, and completely eliminated the incentive to smuggle goods, thereby raising legal export volumes by 20% in 1984 alone. Diamond exports increased by 55%; and, after price decontrol, agricultural output expanded by an estimated 100%-200%, though the bulk of the gain came from cash crops, particularly rice and coffee.[77] In the same year, 1984, the budget deficit fell from 10.5% of GDP to 3.6%, while GDP itself managed a modest 2% growth, and a further 2.5% the following year. Official inflation, according to the government's National Statistical Institute (INS), fell from 101% in 1983 to 14.3% in 1984.[78] Zaire, it seemed, was finally facing its economic realities head-on.

On the strength of these achievements, creditors were, by 1985, willing, once again, to resume lending to the Mobutu regime, and to consider rescheduling the country's outstanding arrearages. But all was not as well as the figures were suggesting. First, government claims that inflation was abating were contradicted by independent studies by the Economic and Social Research Institute (IRES) at the University of Kinshasa which claimed that inflation had, in fact, *risen*, from 42.3% in 1983 to 76.7% in 1984.[79] Anecdotal evidence tended to support IRES: for instance, Callaghy reports that the impact of the December 1983 stabilization "was quickly felt by most of Zaire. The price of oil, other fuels, [and] key food items rose between 200% and 300% over the next three months."[80] Secondly, whilst GNP grew by 2% in 1984, population grew by 3%, suggesting that per capita income probably fell. Thirdly, price liberalization in agriculture was not uniformly successful in inducing production increases. Zaire is a huge country, with a land mass three times that of Texas, but with only ten thousand kilometres of regularly usable roads. Three thousand of these are all-weather roads, but only 15% of these are in the rural areas. This means that, for many farmers, transportation costs are routinely prohibitively high: in fact some estimates have it that nearly 40% of the typical Zairean farmer's yearly revenues goes to cover transportation costs.[81] Thus only those farmers with access to cheap and reliable transportation—like the big commercial, cash-crop farmers—were able to take advantage of the increased producer prices to boost farm output. Food crops, grown almost exclusively by small peasant holders for local consumption, showed no such increases. This, of course, is consistent with our finding earlier that agricultural liberalization in Africa does not have a consistent impact on sectoral output across the board, but rather tends to favour export-crops over food-crops.

Thus local consumers were bearing the greater burden of the stabilization, as they faced higher food prices but fewer quantities of it with frozen or decreasing wages, while foregn consumers—and nearly all cash-crops were exported—reaped the direct benefits, as they got greater quantities of cocoa, coffee, palm kernels, etc. at depressed prices. There was thus an uneven distribution of the costs and benefits of stabilization at the international level and, even more conspicuouly, within the country itself. This, again, accords with both our theoretical and empirical findings of earlier chapters.

As in Zambia, the domestic distributional impact of the stabilization in Zaire fell neatly along class lines. As the government was capping wages while liberalizing (hence raising) consumer prices, senior government officials and prominent businesspeople were known to have made "private arrangements" with the requisite authorities to deflect some of the new costs, such as increased taxes, away from them. This tended to undermine the state's already-weak revenue position, necessitating further increases in business taxes and user-fees—a clear disincentive for private-sector investment. But it also meant that budgetary austerity got even more stringent, with the result that the requisite investment in public and social infrastructure, without which the modest initial gains of adjustment could not be sustained, were not made. Indeed, the government's "investment budget" for 1985, initially set at an already-reduced $65 million, was reduced to $40 million in April of that year, and the depreciation of the zaire further reduced it to $38 million by November. All this, while estimates for the rehabilitation (let alone expansion) of the country's roads, telecommunications, grain silos, and other vital infrastructure were running about $100 million.[82]

Furthermore, as in Zambia, liberalization of the external sector meant that the unconstrained repatriation of the profits of the foreign firms that dominate mining and manufacturing in Zaire enhanced the outflow of much-needed capital, further undermining the sustainability of the improvements in the economy, and especially in the light of World Bank projections at the time that Zaire's debt would keep rising until 1992, after which it would decline very slowly.[83] Coupled with the $1.2 billion of debt service that the Paris Club rescheduling added to the country's debt, payment for which was due between 1985 and 1991, Zaire's adjustment programme actually poised the country for continued resource hemorrhaging. And the post-adjustment figures bear this out: in 1984, the total of debt payments and profit repatriation amounted to $191.5 million more than it received in capital flows. Between 1983 and 1986, there was a net outflow of $800 million, mainly due to debt payments, and between $850 million and a billion dollars in each of those years for "services", as Table 5.3 partially shows. This, while it was estimated that even if the country's debt was rescheduled to bring debt service down to 20% of export earnings between 1985 and 1990, it would require a minimum net annual inflow of $430 million to keep net transfers at zero.[84] Clearly, this was no way out of the country's debt crisis. In fact, it was a recipe for further indebtedness, the increased immiserization of Zaireans, and eventual systemic economic collapse, as events in the 1990s have amply borne out.

Micro-Level Results

The Zairean adjustment had its most severe adverse impact on the same middle- and lower-income groups who have traditionally borne the brunt of the Mobutu kleptocratic and neo-patrimonial rule. As has already been noted, inflationary pressures started mounting within a year of the commencement of the reform programme, triggering price rises of between 200% and 300% in the major food staples even as money wages increased by only 20% over the year.[85] Indeed Parfitt and Riley report that, at year-end 1985, a sack of maize, which fed a family of five for a month, was selling at 700 *zaires*, while a teacher's wages stayed at its 1000 *zaires* monthly level.[86]

TABLE 5.3
Zaire's Balance-of-Payments, 1980-1984 ($ millions)

	1980	1981	1981	1983	1984
Exports (fob)	1988	1475	1454	1523	1787
Imports (fob)	1436	1269	1124	1114	1170
TRADE BALANCE:	552	206	329	409	617
Services (net) [a]	-883	-864	-870	-898	-966
Net transfers (non-debt) [b]	183	240	172	177	120
CURRENT ACCOUNT BALANCE:	-148	-418	-369	-312	-229
Public capital [c]	-22	-166	-156	-226	-187
Private capital (+ errors & omissions)	-80	-145	-128	74	-55
SDR allocation	20	19	-	-	-
OVERALL BALANCE:	-230	-710	-653	-464	-471

a: includes interest and investment income
b: public and private unrequited transfers
c: net medium- and long-term borrowing
Source: Banque du Zaire; quoted in Economist Intelligence Unit, *Zaire to the 1990s: Will the Retrenchment Work?*, Special Report 227 by Gregory Kronsten (London: The Economist, 1986), p. 46.

Austerity meant wage stagnation coupled with massive retrenchment and lay-offs in the public sector. In the first year of adjustment alone, 31.5% of the 260,000 public-sector employees, the bulk of them coming from the lower echelons of the civil service, were made redundant. Conspicuously unaffected by the cuts were highly-placed bureaucrats and party functionaries. Essential services, especially health and education, were roundly decimated, inducing resort to all sorts of nefarious practices by the few lucky survivors to make ends meet: it was reported, for instance, that in some schools headmasters dismissed most of their staff but kept their names on the payroll anyway so as to pocket their salaries. In one Kinshasa secondary school, a teaching staff of forty was, in this manner, reduced to five.[87] Room-and-board for university students, formerly provided at state expense, was also withdrawn, penalizing, especially, lower-income students.

The response by the lower-income groups to this encroachment on their living standards was predictable. As in many other adjusting African countries, survival for Zaireans meant a much more widespread resort to parallel economies and markets. As MacGaffey points out, "people…organized their production and distribution of foodstuffs, systems of export and import, and even the necessary infrastructure to make them (the alternative economy) work."[88] Rural farmers, for example, were likely to send foodstuffs to relatives in the cities in exchange for cloth, kerosene and manufactures not readily available in their villages. Thus key to the survival mechanism was the culture of extended family networks, (the mutual obligations of) kinship, and 'hometown' affiliations.

Social and political unrest also, inevitably, arose amongst those most acutely affected. A bitter strike by dockworkers at the Matadi harbour on the River Zaire in January 1985 brought all commercial traffic on the river—the main mode of conveyance for food and people across much of the country—to a halt. Their sole demand was an immediate 50% increase in wages, in challenge to the 25% IMF-imposed limit then in force. Mobutu had to personally intervene to persuade the workers to accept the 25% raise. On July 19, 1985, twenty-one senior parliamentarians, including the legislature's First Vice-President, asserted in a protest document that even after the massive public-sector retrenchments, many civil servants had not been paid for months, and that the alleged successes of the adjustment programme had not filtered down to the general populace. Resentment of, and opposition to, the reforms were thus widespread and intense, prompting Mobutu himself to acknowlegde to a Western diplomat that "Kinshasa is a powder keg that can blow [at] any minute."[89]

The response of government, whenever cajoling or persuasion failed, was brutal suppression of opposition, often with the tacit support and assistance of the regime's creditors. For example, West Germany provided DM 2.5 million to set up a new Civil Guard of 20,000 men, two of whose specialties were crowd control and domestic counter-insurgency. The U.S. also promised, in 1985, a 50% increase in military aid over the ensuing several years. As one observer noted, "a U.S.-West German axis has been emerging [in Zaire] in which the Americans provide finance and the Germans hardware and know-how."[90] Others speculated that the arrest of seven membes of the opposition Union for Democracy and Social Progress in December 1985 was timed to coincide with talks with the IMF, and to impress the regime's creditors that popular discontent with adjustment would not be permitted to compromise the programme.

Crisis Management after 1985

Although the period after 1985 falls, strictly speaking, outside the purview of our analysis, developments in the Zairean debt/development crisis since 1985 should help us cast further light on the economics and politics of adjustment in the African setting. We therefore take a brief walk through these developments to further illumine the adjustment process as it unfolded throughout the 1980s.

Mid-1986 saw the first signs of recidivism in Zaire's policies and international posture. First, the government pleaded with the IMF and its commercial creditors for more financing for the three-year old adjustment.[91] When the response was not favourable Mobutu, in May 1986, raised public-sector wages by 150%, seemingly in defiance of the creditors, including the Fund, but also partly in response to political pressures from the streets. Next, he lowered the price of potable water by 75%, and nationalised the Bank of Kinshasa "to boost savings."[92] In October, he declared that debt service would, from January 1987 onward, be limited (à la President Alan Garcia of Peru) to 10% of export earnings and 20% of the national budget. He suspended flotation of the *zaire* and restored, by fiat, its parity with SDR. He reduced interest rates, increased the capital budget by 20%, and raised budget outlays for salaries by 20%. In addition, national and regional administrative budgets were increased 35%; internal debt service was limited to 5% of budget, and a priority system for the allocation of foreign-exchange was instituted.

Next, he dismissed his conspicuously pro-IMF Prime Minister and appointed a strong critic of adjustment to the post of finance minister.[93] Noting that the adjustment programme had, even by Zaire's standards, led to an inordinate transfer of capital out of the country at a time when Zaire was being forced to forgo badly-needed social investments, Mobutu declared that

any future programme with the IMF should be seen as a
supplementary aid to national efforts, and concluded with a view to
a real launch of the Zaire economy, and no longer simply as a
programme of austerity and stabilization.[94]

In retrospect, the government was not rebelling against the Fund as
these new policies and declarations might have suggested. Rather, it
was positioning itself to gain advantage in Zaire's imminent re-
negotiations with the Fund, with the help of the Reagan administration,
for whom Mobutu had done not a few clandestine favours on the
African continent.[95]

The U.S. administration duly facilitated the re-negotiations to
favour Zaire, prompting the resignation of a senior official of the
IMF in protest. He said in his resignation letter to the Fund's board
that he was "disgusted" with the undue use of U.S. influence to ease
lending conditionalities for particular favoured client-governments,
notably Zaire's and Egypt's, while other, more deserving countries
like Ghana and Nigeria were summarily refused such concessions.[96]

The full effect of the U.S's intervention was first felt during the
internecine negotiations with the Fund over Zaire's 1987 budget. The
government had projected a spending deficit for the year of Z8 billion,
which it subsequently revised downward to Z3.84 billion. In
negotiation with the Fund, however, the figure of 6 billion *zaires*
was, somehow, mutually agreed upon as being "more realistic", so
the government immediately set forth to boost its outlays for capital-
spending and civil-service remuneration commensurately. As a U.S.
government source describes it, they (the Reagan administration)
succeeded in "persuading the IMF [to meet] Zaire halfway on the
wage-increase issue" by allowing "small increases" in public-sector
pay.[97] In the event, these 'small increases' amounted to a total of
20% as of June 1987, in addition to the 40% of May 1986.[98] The
IMF was also "persuaded" to reinstate the April 1986 stand-by
arrangement that was automatically abrogated when Mobutu
unilaterally placed limits on debt service. The new arrangement was
worth $12.6 million, part of which would be compensation for export-
revenue losses stemming from the falling prices of copper and cobalt.
In exchange, Zaire agreed to continue or reinstate many of the original
stabilization measures, including the flotation of the *zaire*.

In sum, the dynamics of the debt-underdevelopment couple in Zaire encompassed all the variables that we identified as causes or conditions-of-existence of the crisis in the African economy. The top-heavy, clientelist state apparatus meshed conveniently with the economy's skewed structure and with external factors to create a seemingly intractable problem of circularly-connected underdevelopment and external debt crises. The traditional IMF stabilization and adjustment package was found to be both contractionary and the cause of price increases in many consumer items. Price liberalization in agriculture had the effect of stimulating production in that portion of the sector already tied into the global economy, while production of domestic staples showed no appreciable response. Liberalization of the external sector, through direct devaluation or flotation of the currency, had the effect of eliminating the brisk black-market trade in foreign currency, but also facilitated capital outflows that crippled social investment, while inducing further foreign borrowing.

But the real victims of adjustment, in terms of those whose standards-of-living were knowingly compromised, were the lower income strata, who found their real purchasing potential dwindling by the month. Thus whereas the programme succeeded in eliminating some parallel markets (such as in currency), it also enhanced them in foodstuffs and other commodities used by the vast majority of ordinary Zaireans who could no longer participate in 'formal' market activity. And although the patronage system that had prepetuated the financial frauds, economic mismanagement and systemic maldevelopment made a few concessions to the adjustment programme, these were, in the greater scheme of things, rather minor, for they did not jeopardize the basic living standards of the elite to any appreciable extent. At best they sacrificed a few luxury items, but never their very livelihoods. It also became abundantly clear that the solution to the debt crisis preferred by the small but powerful elite, with the support or intrigue of the external creditors or their agents, is the liquidating of the very livelihoods of the poor and powerless. Any strategy that might seriously threaten their priviledges was not seriously entertained.

5.5 Summary: The Orthodox Adjustment and its Impacts

In the light of the Zambian and Zairean experiences, we provide in this section a detailed summary of the eight *specific* instruments of the orthodox adjustment and their *specific* impacts on the African economy and society.[99] These structural *adjustment* policies will, in the final chapter, be contrasted with structural *transformation* policies more closely reflective of Africa's structural uniquenesses, and which, consistent with our thesis, aim at overcoming those structural bottlenecks that logically precede the policy incompetencies the World Bank/IMF adjustment traditionally targets. We focus on the structures primarily because, as has been argued from the start, and in contrast to the Fund/Bank view, we believe that the causes of the twin-crisis of external debt and internal non-development in Africa are to be found in the very character (i.e. structure) of economy and politics extant. Bad governance and policy making are, often, a reflection of these structural inadequacies, not the causes of them. Focussing adjustment on existing policy regimes, therefore, can only bring temporary relief from the sharp teeth of the crisis, but not a cure of any long-term durability.

Instrument 1: Reducing or eliminating the budget-deficit through cuts in social spending on health, education, transport and food subsidies.
Social Impact: Its full effect is seen over the long haul, as it undermines and compromises the enabling social environment for the development of human capital. In the short term, it creates unemployment as it necessitates retrenchment in the public sector.

Instrument 2: Privatization of economic activity.
Social Impact: It undermines growth in the short term, as the necessary systemic adjustments are made to the new economic dispensation; but it also eliminates the redistributive effects that some measure of state control or ownership fosters. Thus it might increase allocative efficiency at the cost of distributive equity.

Instrument 3: Excessive reliance on market forces for "getting the prices right" in structurally-distorted and systemically imperfect market situations.

Social Impact: This creates further distortions in resource allocation and overall social welfare, as the *theory of the second best* becomes operative in these conditions. And, by creating deviations from production and consumption patterns deemed appropriate to a country's social objectives, it distorts the country's development priorities, potentially derailing its desired transformation agenda. It may also generate inflation as it pushes up production costs in many sectors.

Instrument 4: Currency devaluation through open foreign-exchange markets, currency auctions, and the removal of institutional control over foreign-exchange distribution.

Social Impact: The immediate effect is to increase the domestic cost of imported inputs. As most African production is import-intensive, this undermines capacity utilization and induces secondary inflation with simultaneous stagnation. Secondly, it provides both the incentive and the opportunity to direct scarce foreign exchange to speculative activities and to capital flight. To the extent, also, that it lowers the foreign-market cost of exports, it helps entrench the very structures of production and trade that are, ultimately, the causes of the debt-and-development crises. Its distributive effects also tend to favour exporters and producers of cash-crops over producers for the home market. Finally, its inflationary impact means that the living standards of the majority of citizens get compromised, as their cost if living rise even as their money incomes stagnate or even fall.

Instrument 5: The widespread promotion of traditional exports on the assumption of comparative advantage and, as part of the new orthodoxy, of non-traditional exports (NTEs), on the unstated assumption that NTEs are more capable of effecting those structural transformations that traditional exports do not effect.

Social Impact: This undermines a universal development objective of shifting the structure of domestic production to meet domestic demand, compromising thereby goals of national self-sufficiency in, at least, food production. In addition, the extended production of cash crops, because cash-crop production tends to be land-, capital- and chemical-intensive, has led to untold environmental degradation in much of the Sudanic and rain-forest belts, among others. This has increased the incidence, frequency or severity of soil erosion, drought and desertification across the continent. It has also led to imbalances in the output mix, as one or another favoured product experiences periodic excess supply and therefore declines in its price- and/or trade-terms.

Instrument 6: Import liberalization as an adjunct or consequence of currency devaluation.
Social Impact: Like much of the trade-related policy reforms accompanying the orthodox adjustment, this policy serves to entrench external dependence. As it also undermines local industry, it tends to compromise goals of economic self-sufficiency. In addition, if it creates an explosion of demand for imports, it intensifies the country's foreign-exchange constraints.

Instrument 7: High domestic real interest rates.
Social Impact: To the extent that movements in interest rates reflect a rationalization of the credit markets (through, for instance, the elimination of government policies that repress the financial sector), the overall *long-term* developmental impact of the reform should be positive. But if it is the result of an induced, systemic credit contraction then, in the short term, the combination of stagflation and high interest rates discourage investment and production activity, and rather induce a shift of resources towards speculation and trading, which are perceived as having more rapid turnovers and lower risks.

Instrument 8: An across-the-board credit squeeze.
Social Impact: Overall economic activity tends to contract. Manufacturing, especially, is severely adversely affected, as net investment and capacity utilization in the sector drop, and some enterprises fold altogether. This accentuates the usual shortage of consumer and intermediate goods, leading to both inflationary pressures and social unrest.

5.6 *Conclusion*

IMF-type adjustment programmes worsen the debtor's ability to generate rising incomes, and hence its future ability to service its external obligations *and* achieve a comforatble margin of economic growth. As the ECA's study indicated (Figure 4.1) this type of adjustment, in fact, enables a country to do the one (debt servicing) at the expense of the other (domestic growth), because the structural transformation necessary for the simultaneous performance of both are undermined by the policies of the adjustment.

More insidiously, this type of adjustment leads to unplanned shifts in income distribution in countries in which resource maldistribution and material polarities are already pervasive social problems. The policy dilemma identified at the outset as facing African governments, therefore—i.e. not servicing their external debts at the expense of domestic growth—is deepened by a reform programme that, as its name suggests, merely helps the country *adjust* to its disequilibria, as though the structure of the economy is, itself, largely sound and functionally appropriate to the country's development objectives. The Zambian and Zairean experiences, however, would indicate that the basic structures of the economy and of politics are precisely what need transforming.

Two recent sets of comparative empirical studies confirm our basic conclusions on the adjustment programmes of the new orthodoxy. The first is an analysis of the macroeconomic effects of adjustment done by an IMF economist, Jaime de Piniès, in which he shows that, for both Africa and Latin America, the immediate impact of adjustment in the 1980s was one of "overadjustment", which often induced a drag on growth. He means by that that, given the underlying balance-of-payments fundamentals, and given the degree of solvency of these regions (as measured by the ratio of interest rate-to-export growth; by that of import-to-export growth; and by the initial debt-to-export and import-to-export ratios), IMF-type structural adjustment programmes led to "excess retraint" on imports and, subsequently, domestic production, such that the debtor-countries were placed on a *less* solvent path—and therefore, ultimately, a potentially worsened *future* debt crisis—than before the adjustment.[100]

His estimates of the nominal value of foregone imports for SSA, at various interest-to-export growth ratios, are summarized under Table

5.4. What they indicate is that, in 1985 for instance, "Africa could have imported [at least] $5 billion more than it did and [maintained the same level] of solvency. Similarly, when more reasonable rates of import growth are allowed for net energy importers in 1986 (9%) than those that prevailed in 1985 (-7%), the amount of excess import restraint is reduced to a small but still positive amount."[101]

TABLE 5.4
Sub-Saharan Africa's "Overadjustment"[a]
to Structural Adjustment

$\dot{r}/\dot{X}$	1985[b]	1986[c]
	(millions of dollars)	
1.01	6150	200
1.02	6110	160
1.03	6060	110
1.04	5990	40

a: 'Overadjustment' refers to excessive import restraint; (i.e. warranted - actual imports).
b: Import growth was -7%
c: Import growth was 9%.

$\dot{r}/\dot{X}$:   ratio of interest growth to export growth.
Source: Jaime de Piniès, "Debt Sustainability and Over-Adjustment," *World Development*, Vol. 17, No. 1 (1989), p. 34.

Given that Africa's production is import-intensive; and given also that, in much of the period under study, Africa was a net food importer, these figures would translate, in the short term, into significant declines in consumption levels, and a worsening of production, employment and growth possibilities over the medium- to long-run. This adverse impact on output, even in the absence of worsening trade terms, would therefore not bode well for export performance. And to the extent that its export revenues grew more slowly than its external obligations, Africa's debt crisis would be that much further exacerbated.

The other set of studies focusses on the effects of currency devaluation as part of a general programme of adjustment to external disequilibria in small, open economies. These studies conclude, in consonance with our case studies, that devaluation has a contractionary effect on these economies, which is then exacerbated by a redistribution of income from wages to profits. This redistribution, when foreign capital is present, raises the foreign component of domestic income, as the increased profit accrue mainly to the owners of the foreign capital even while the fall in wages is absorbed almost completely by local residents. The net effect is negative growth in both domestic output (GDP) and national income (GNP), as consumption and employment drop.[102]

Further, when the economy has an external deficit, the optimal mix of exchange-rate and fiscal policies that will restore the BOP equilibrium and minimize the decline in output depends on the magnitude of the devaluation. Thus an excessive devaluation, coupled with a contractionary fiscal policy—the main policy mix of the orthodox adjustment—tends to be unnecessarily deflationary in the short run.[103]

Notes

1. See Nafziger, op. cit., p. 24.
2. Ibid.
3. This case-study relies principally on Neva S. Makgetla, Theoretical and Practical Implications of IMF Conditionality in Zambia, **Journal of Modern African Studies**, Vol. 24, No. 3 (1986), pp. 395-422. It also relies substantially on the following works: World Bank, **Zambia: Country Economic Memorandum—Issues and Options for Diversification** (Washington, D.C.: April 1984); Kenneth Good, Debt and the One-Party State in Zambia, **Journal of Modern African Studies**, Vol. 27, No. 2 (1989), pp. 297-313; and Oxford International Associates, **External Debt Management in Zambia** (Oxford: Dec. 1988).
4. See World Bank, **Zambia: Country Economic Memorandum...**, Tables 2.01, 3.06, 3.07 and 9.04.
5. Nafziger, op. cit., p. 123.
6. Nafziger, op. cit., p. 128.
7. UN Economic Commission for Africa, **South African Destabilization: The Economic Cost of Frontline Resistance to Apartheid** (Addis Ababa: ECA, 1989). The countries in question are Angola, Botswana, Lesotho, Malawi, Mozambique, Swaziland, Tanzania, Zambia and Zimbabwe.
8. See Nafziger, op. cit., p. 95, and pp. 150-153.
9. According to the Zambian Minister of Finance, a full one-half of all import cuts were done in the latter period. See L.J. Mwananshiku, Address at Opening Ceremony of the **Workshop on the Economic Problems Facing Zambia**, Univ. of Zambia, Lusaka, Nov. 1985, as cited by Makgetla, op. cit.
10. E. Kaunga, official of the Zambia Industrial and Mining Corporation (ZIMCO), at the Univ. of Zambia Workshop, as cited by Makgetla, op. cit.
11. Harry Johnson, Towards a General Theory of the Balance of Payments, in H.G. Johnson, **International Trade and Economic Growth** (London: G. Allen and Unwin, 1958), pp. 153-168.
12. O'Clearaicain, op. cit., p. 21 and chapter 7.
13. See the IMF-inspired Zambian Government publication **Restructuring in the Midst of Crisis** (Lusaka: 1984).
14. Ibid.
15. World Bank, **Zambia: Country Economic Memorandum** (Washington, D.C.: 1984), pp. 21-23.
16. Ibid., p. 27.

17. Wanda Tseng, The Effects of Adjustment, **Finance and Development** (Washington, D.C.: Dec. 1984), p. 261.
18. K. Nashabishi, Devaluation in the Developing Countries: The Difficult Choices, **Finance and Development** (Washington, D.C.: March 1983), p. 119.
19. See Makgetla, op. cit.
20. Ibid.
21. Central Statistical Office, **Monthly Digest of Statistics** (April-May, 1985), as cited by Makgetla, op. cit. Nominal wages are deflated by the low-income cost-of-living index.
22. Theodore Valentine, Income-Distribution Issues in A Structurally-Dependent Economy: An Analysis of Growing Income Inequality in Zambia, in I.D.R.C., **The Zambian Economy: Problems and Prospects** (Ottawa: 1985), p. 93.
23. Ibid.
24. Government of Zambia, **Report of the Administrative Commission of Inquiry Into the Salaries, Salary Structures and Conditions of Service of the Zambian Public and Teaching Services, the Local Government Service, the Judicial Service, the Zambian Police and the Prisons Service** (Lusaka: 1980), Vol. 1, as cited by Makgetla, op. cit.
25. See Valentine, op. cit., p. 94.
26. N. Makgetla, Investment in the Third World: The Zambian Experience, in I.D.R.C., op. cit., p. 193.
27. See Makgetla, **Investment in the Third World:...**, for details.
28. World Bank, **Zambia: Country Economic Memorandum**, p. 35.
29. Ibid.
30. Government of Zambia, **Monthly Digest of Statistics** (April-May, 1985), Tables 53 and 57, as cited by **Makgetla, Theoretical and Practical Implications...**
31. Bank of Zambia, **Annual Report** (Lusaka: 1982), as cited by Makgetla, **Theoretical and Practical Implications...**
32. See Makgetla, **Theoretical and Practical Implications...**
33. J. Hassan, **Agricultural Development and Pricing Policy**, unpublished M.A. thesis, Univ. of Zambia, Lusaka, 1986, as cited by Makgetla, **Theoretical and Practical Implications...**
34. G. Mbulo of the Bank of Zambia Foreign Exchange Committee at the Univ. of Zambia Workshop, as cited by Makgetla, **Theoretical and Practical Implications...**
35. Nafziger reports that some 100 firms, 99 of whom were foreign-owned, captured 90% of the foreign-exchange market through the auctions, effectively shutting out indigenous capital from access to hard currency. Many factories, including state-owned ones, were thus forced to operate below capacity, as they could not import enough inputs or find acceptable

or adequate local-origin substitutes; others were forced to cease operations altogether. Farms with local ownership also went under, even as more heavily-capitalized foreign-owned farms fluorished and came to dominate commercial agriculture. Thus devaluation, and the manner in which it was done, had three principal effects on the structure of the Zambian economy: it increased the economy's oligopolization rather than promoted competition, in both non-mining primary activities and manufacturing; it increased foreign-ownership of capital at the expense of local ownership; and concretized even more firmly the outward orientation of the economy that makes it so susceptible to external forces. See Nafziger, op. cit., p. 128.

36. See footnote 32.
37. Nashabishi, op. cit., p. 17.
38. Ibid.
39. M.D. Macheleta and P.L. Tembo, **Central Banking and Credit Control in Zambia** (Lusaka, 1985), as cited by Makgetla, **Theoretical and Practical Implications...**
40. Francis Nkhoma, at the Univ. of Zambia Workshop (Lusaka: Nov. 1985), as cited by Makgetla, **Theoretical and Practical Implications...**
41. Ibid.
42. See Stephen Baker, **An Introduction to International Economics** (N.Y.: Harcourt Brace Jovanovich, 1990), ch. 9.
43. Shapouri and Rosen, **Export Performance in Africa**, Table 2, p. 4.
44. Shapouri and Rosen, op. cit., Table 1, p. 2.
45. Shapouri and Rosen, op. cit., Table 6, p. 9.
46. Shapouri and Rosen, op. cit., Table 8, p. 12; and Table 13, p. 20.
47. Shapouri and Rosen, op. cit., Table 6, p. 9.
48. Nkhoma, op. cit.
49. Nkhoma, op. cit.
50. World Bank, **Zambia: Country Economic Memorandum**, p. 2.
51. Ibid.
52. Makgetla, **Theoretical and Practical Implications...**
53. For instance, in Nov. 1985, Zambia Airways spent nearly K2 million to import cars for its executives with foreign-exchange bought at one of the weekly auctions.
54. E.C. Chibwe of the Zambia Federation of Employers at the Univ. of Zambia Workshop, as cited by Makgetla, **Theoretical and Practical Implications...**
55. Debate between Tony Killick and Barhan Nowzad on 'The IMF's Role in Developing Countries', **Finance and Development**, Vol. 21, No. 3 (Sept. 1984), p. 26.

56. See A. Schoenholtz, The IMF in Africa: Unnecessary and Undesirable Western Restraint on Development, **Journal of Modern African Studies,** Vol. 25, No. 3 (1987), pp. 403-433.
57. See Richard N. Cooper, **Economic Policy in an Interdependednt World: Essays in World Economics** (Cambridge, MA.: The MIT Press, 1986), ch. 9.
58. Cooper, op. cit., p. 201.
59. Cooper, op. cit., p.202.
60. Ibid.
61. Cooper, op. cit., p. 203.
62. Ibid.
63. Ibid.
64. Cooper, op. cit., p. 206.
65. Cooper, op. cit., p. 207-8.
66. Ibid.
67. Cooper, op. cit., pp. 208-9. For a more detailed analysis of this condition, see R.N. Cooper, Devaluation and Aggregate Demand in Aid-Receiving Countries, in J.Bhagwati et.al., eds., **Trade, Balance of Payments, and Growth** (Amsterdam: North-Holland, 1971), pp. 335-376.
68. Cooper, op. cit., pp. 209-10.
69. Cooper, op. cit., pp. 210-213.
70. Cooper cites a study by Carlos Diaz-Alejandro of the 1959 Argentine devaluation which, in consequence of the resulting income shift toward the landowning elite, led to a significant decrease in domestic spending and on imports. C. Diaz-Alejendro, **Exchange-Rate Devaluation in a Semi-Industrialized Country** (Cambridge, MA.: The MIT Press, 1965).
71. Cooper, op. cit., p. 213.
72. T. Parfitt and S. Riley, **The African Debt Crisis**, ch. 4
73. T. Callaghy, Africa's Debt Crisis, **Journal of International Affairs,** Vol. 38, No. 1 (1984), p. 67.
74. Quoted in Callaghy, **External Actors...**, p. 75.
75. See Callaghy, **Africa's Debt Crisis**, p. 68.
76. Africa Research Bulletin, **Economic Series** (April 1985), p. 7689.
77. Financial Times, **Survey of Zaire** (London: July 9, 1985), pp. 1-2.
78. Economist Intelligence Unit, **Zaire to the 1990s**, p. 17 and pp. 27-29.
79. Economist Intelligence Unit, **Zaire to the 1990s**, p. 29.
80. Callaghy, **Africa's Debt Crisis**, p. 72.
81. Financial Times, **Survey of Zaire**, p. 8.
82. Economist Intelligence Unit, **Quarterly Economic Review of Zaire**, Vol. 3 (1985), p. 5.
83. Financial Times, **Survey of Zaire**, pp. 1-3.

84. See **Africa Economic Digest** (March 15, 1986), p. 14, and Economist Intelligence Unit, **Zaire to the 1990s**, p. 57.

85. Callaghy, **Africa's Debt Crisis**, p. 72.

86. Parfitt and Riley, op. cit., p. 90.

87. Economist Intelligence Unit, **Quarterly Economic Review of Zaire...**, Vol. 3 (1984), p. 12.

88. Janet MacGaffey, Fending-for-Yourself: The Organization of the Second Economy in Zaire, in Nzongola-Ntalaja, ed., **The Crisis in Zaire: Myths and Realities** (N.J.: Africa World Press, 1986), pp. 144-145.

89. **Africa Confidential**, Vol. 27, No. 19 (Sept. 17, 1986), p. 6.

90. **New African** (May 1985), p. 45.

91. See **Africa Economic Digest** (March 15, 1986), p. 14.

92. **African Business** (Oct. 1986), p. 36.

93. The PM was Kengo wa Dondo; the new finance minister was Mabi Mlumba. For details, see **Africa Research Bulletin** (Nov. 30, 1986), pp. 8440-8442; Economist Intelligence Unit, **Country Report: Zaire...**, Vol. 4 (1986), pp. 11-12; and **West Africa** (Jan. 5, 1987), p. 17.

94. **Africa Research Bulletin** (Nov. 30, 1986), p. 8441.

95. Mobutu has been, throughout the decades of the Cold War, a consistent protector of American, French and German interests in Africa. For instance, at U.S. urging, Mobutu in the early 1980s, threatened to call for an all-Black OAU, in a bid to get Libya expelled from the Organization. In Sept. 1986, he sent a contingent of 350 Zairean and French troops to Togo to help stabilize the embattled Eyadema government, itself a protégé of conservative German politicians. He assisted, again at America's behest, the Chadian army in routing the Libyans at Oudi-Doum in March 1987; but for several months prior to that, he was training 2,000 Chadian commandos at the Kotakoli Military Centre in Zaire, and had provided Zairean air force pilots to the Chadian military. (See **Africa Research Bulletin** of May 15, 1987, pp. 8468-8469). For years, he had also made available the Kamina Air Base as a staging post for the delivery of arms to Jonas Savimbi's 'contras' in Angola. (See **Africa Confidential**, Vol. 28, No. 16 of Aug. 5, 1987, pp. 8451-8452). This, apparently, was his trump card against the Reagan administration, as the operation was top secret, run by the CIA, using aircraft leased from St. Lucia Airways in the Caribbean, and employing African-American military personnel exclusively.

96. The official in question was C. David Finch, head of the Fund's Exchange and Trade Relations department, whose story was recounted in **West Africa** (March 30, 1987), p. 625.

97. **West Africa** (March 30, 1987), p. 624.

98. **West Africa** (March 30, 1987), p. 625.

99. Our summary reflects closely the U.N. Economic Commission for Africa's analysis, which is largely consistent with ours in its broad configuration, of the more severe adverse effects of the World Bank/ IMF-type adjustment on African economies. See ECA, **African Alternative Framework**, ch. 5, pp. 37-38.
100. Jaime de Piniès, **Debt Sustainability...**, p. 34
101. Ibid.
102. L. Barbone and F. Rivera-Batíz, Foreign Capital and the Contractionary Effects of Devaluation, with an Application to Jamaica, **Journal of Development Economics**, Vol. 26 (1987), pp. 1-15.
103. P. Meller and A. Solimano, A Simple Macro Model for a Small Open Economy Facing A Binding External Constraint (Chile), **Journal of Development Economics**, Vol. 26 (1987), pp. 25-35.

Chapter 6

Towards a New Culture
of Development

The major conclusion from the analyses of the last two chapters is that the neo-orthodox option tended to deepen Africa's debt-cum-development crisis over the medium term. Given the (joint) domestic-structural and external dimensions of the crisis, we argue in this chapter that the crisis can only be adequately tackled with policies that seek to address both the domestic and external conditions that keep output and income growth in Africa consistently low. We seek, thus, to pose as an alternative to the new orthodoxy an essentially structuralist analysis and policy regime which, of necessity, aim at effecting the long-term transformation of the very structures of the economy that the marginal adjustments of the resurgent orthodoxy, in essence, preserve.

But there are other features of this approach that contrast sharply with, and mark important points of departure from, the orthodox view. One is that a structuralist analysis precludes us, in our search for viable solutions for a multi-dimensioned crisis, from yielding to the reductionist, and therefore facile, temptation of targetting, say, external imbalances narrowly, as though they were functionally and structurally independent of the built-in inadequacies of the domestic economy. The types of remedial policies consistent with our analysis should be capable of, for instance, performing the following tasks: (1) prevent the intermittent recurrence, over substantial stretches of time, of the net positive outflow of financial and other resources from SSA; (2) stem the vicious cycle that leads from the development crisis to the debt crisis and back; and (3) reorient macroeconomic policy from its current preponderant preoccupation with the external debt *per se* to one that puts the development of the domestic economy first and foremost.

We, in short, seek a whole new culture of development premised upon the integration of production with domestic consumption needs *at both the individual country and regional- economy levels.* This reflects our belief in regional economic systems as being a viable alternative development strategy for Africa in a hostile international economic environment, but also in the proposition that a regionalist policy cannot succeed or acquire efficacy without the prior sectoral integration of the constituent economies.[1]

A key component of this new development culture is the critical confrontation of the instinctive averse reaction that most African governments have to the diffusion of economic decision-making away from the centre, i.e. from the control of the state. Whereas one does not wish to underplay the historical and conjunctural necessity of (economic and political) policy centralization in the immediate post-colonial period, one also has an immense appreciation of the fact that the state in Africa today is, as was abundantly obvious from our case studies, unwieldy, unaccountable, wasteful of preciously scarce resources, and potentially despotic. But, even more disturbingly, it harbours, ultimately, an anti-development rationality deep in its bowels. In the new scheme of things envisaged here, the state will be reduced to (1) providing the usual public goods and services; (2) creating an enabling environment in which the peasantry, community groups, independent entrepreneurs, etc. can increase their efficiency and productivity, as economically productive, socially engaged, and politically particpatory entities, by acquiring genuine control over their own lot; and (3) maintaining and enforcing the 'rules of the game' among all groups and interests in society. This devolved, minimalist state, to the extent that it thereby ceases to be the sole repository of policy-making powers or productive resources, and thus no longer the prized target of the clientelist politics we analyzed in Chapter Two will, in this manner, be made more accountable to the citizenry at large. Such accountability will then constitute, it is hoped, an effective check against those excesses and absolutisms that have made official corruption and managerial ineptitude such important contributors to Africa's debt-and-development crisis.

The decentralization of economic activity and decision-making that will accompany the devolution of the state—a process, by the way, already underway in parts of the continent—will, we believe, enhance the prospects of democratic control over the means of production and the organs of political power. It need not, therefore, nor should it be, interpreted, as some otherwise well-meaning Northern commentators have done, as being synonymous with an uncritical promotion of unbridled capitalism. Indeed, our proposal for effective decentralization is premised on the belief that the people's unconstrained control over their productive capacity, widely construed, and over the products of their efforts, including the surplus, and not merely democratic control over their places of work, is the most effective way of preventing the rise and institutionalization of hegemonic classes and tendencies in African society, be they from the bureaucracy, large capitalist firms, or traditional and cultural elites. In this regard, we are in complete philosophical concordance with Roemer's contention that class-based oppression need not occur, as most 'labour-process' theorists and other Northern neo-Marxists have argued, narrowly at the point of production, but may exist more pervasively, and therefore more insidiously, in the very fact of the uneven distribution and control of the means of production and of political power which, in contemporary Africa, clearly favours the state at the expense of the small producer and peasant.[2]

What is at stake, and that which our proposals seek to restore, is the *long-term* solvency, not temporary liquidity, of the African economy. Solvency, as is used here, refers to both the ability *and* willingness of these countries to pay their external obligations. Ability-to-pay derives from an economy's success in reproducing itself at, at least, its customary level of subsistence, and in its capacity to earn enough externally to cover its foreign obligations without jeopardizing that internal reproduction. In other words, ability-to-pay derives, as we saw in the first chapter, from maintaining an interest-to-income (specifically, foreign-exchange earnings) growth ratio of less than unity.

Willingness-to-pay, while not quantifiable, depends jointly on the debtor's ability-to-pay and the terms under which the creditor seeks to ensure uninterrupted income flows from its debt-asset. Thus payments will be more forthcoming, assuming ability-to-pay, if debtor and creditor can mutually agree on debt service terms that do not compromise either party's independent economic agenda unduly. Any policy, therefore, that seeks to change the structure of the African economy and/or that of the international system of trade and finance, to enable the former achieve the objective of a sustained rate of income growth above its debt growth, falls under the ambit of the new culture of development.

6.1 Restoring Solvency in the Short Run

A range of policies were crafted and implemented in the 1980s to attempt to resolve the liquidity problems of the indebted African countries. That they aimed at restoring liquidity necessarily meant that their objectives were short term and stabilization-oriented, their (as it happens, erroneous popular) identification with "structural adjustment" notwithstanding. An assessment of these policies and/or proposals—interest rate reform, debt buy-backs, debt-equity swaps, debt forgiveness, etc.—will be the object of this section of the chapter. We focus on a theoretical evaluation of their effectiveness and efficacy as debt-relief strategies, especially in the light of the institutional and structural peculiarities of the typical African economy discussed earlier. We then contrast them with our proposals for restoring solvency to these economies. Detailed *empirical* evaluations and discussions of these strategies, however, may be found by the interested reader elsewhere.[3]

Interest Rates, Inflation and Debt Buy-backs

As was argued previously, even though the forces that sustained and deepened Africa's debt crisis in the 1970s and 1980s were structural and long-term, of both internal and external origin, the proximate causes of the crisis were to be found in short-term, external forces quite out of the purview and control of the debtors themselves. Despite often genuine efforts at correcting their external imbalances, the debt-to-exports ratio of many African countries kept rising, as repeated reschedulings and floating dollar exchange-rates came to dominate the continent's debt-relief profile. Thus, with the debt-to-exports ratio at 254% by the last year of the period this work is concerned with (see Table 6.1), even full rescheduling of principal payments due over the ensuing five years would have permitted no growth in imports, even if export earnings were growing at an

TABLE 6.1
Debt Burden Indicators for Sub-Saharan Africa, 1970-85 (in %)

	1970	1975	1980	1982	1985
Ratio of External Debt to Exports of Goods and Services:					
Sub-Saharan Africa	65.4	65.2	94.1	190.9	253.6
15 most debt-distressed Third World countries*	162.5	133.9	169.5	271.9	301.2
Ratio of External Debt to GDP:					
Sub-Saharan Africa	14.1	17.1	27.2	38.7	51.2
15 most debt-distressed Third World countries*	19.6	18.5	33.1	43.0	47.8
Ratio of Debt Service Payments to Exports:					
Sub-Saharan Africa	10.7	27.2	50.9	57.6	62.2
15 most debt-distressed Third World countries*	24.8	27.7	30.0	40.3	46.4

* Average for Argentina, Bolivia, Brazil, Chile, Columbia, Ivory Coast, Ecuador, Mexico, Morocco, Nigeria, Peru, Phillipines, Uruguay, Venezuela, and Yugoslavia.

Sources: J. Greene, *The External Debt Problem of Sub-Saharan Africa*, Table 2, p. 5.

optimistic 3% per year.[4] SSA, therefore was, through the latter half of the 1980s, and as indicated by Table 6.1, becoming more debt-distressed at a much faster rate than the fifteen most debt-distressed Third World countries of the 1970s and 1980s. This led to a drying-up of both domestic savings and net financial inflows, the former from the disruption of the financial system arising from the BOP adjustments made under IMF/World Bank auspices, and the latter from the negative resource flows resulting from the high real interest rates of the 1980s, but also from the fact that Africa was increasingly seen by the international financial system as being generally uncreditworthy. Domestic investment spending and direct private investment from abroad did, as we have already seen, drop off sharply as a result. And, to the extent that the relevant interest rates did not fall commensurately, the adverse impact on future growth of this investment shortfall cannot bode well for the countries' ability-to-pay in the 1990s and beyond.

What this suggests, therefore, is that without a change in the relationship between dollar-interest rates and the rate of increase of commodity prices, Africa's debt problems of the 1980s will continue to be intractable far into the 1990s. From 1981 to 1985, prime rates were, on average, nearly 15% a year higher than the change in U.S. crude material prices (in the official producer price index), and 20% or more a year higher than the change in most commodity price indices.[5] Clearly, Africa could manage its debt better (i.e. acquire the ability and willingness to pay) if there were a comparable five-year period in which the increase in commodity prices was 20% or more a year above its interest obligations.

But, as Congdon has argued, thusly reversing the growth trends in commodity prices and interest rates will necessarily be inflationary, in this sense: suppose nominal interest rates are driven as low as 5%. Then a twenty percentage-point differential between interest rates and the rate of increase of commodity prices will imply commodity inflation of 25% a year. In the present world economy—indeed, since the mid-1980s—most of Africa's commodity-exports have been experiencing price slumps because of excess supply conditions and the sluggishness in the Northern economies; thus their prices will not rise unless there is a considerable above-trend growth in the world economy to absorb the excess. Such a high rate of growth can put pressure on capacity, creating shortages that can, in short order, foment a 20% inflation in commodity prices. Prices of manufactures will, consequently, go up, resulting in a generalized inflation of the world economy.[6]

Thus, in what may be the ultimate ironic turn of events, the debt crisis, which was precipitated by Paul Volcker's anti-inflationary programme of monetary contraction in the early 1980s, may well be resolved only by a return to the same inflationary environment that precipitated the crisis. To expect, however, that there will be a deliberate return to a policy-induced inflationary economy by Northern governments, even in the noble cause of solving a potentially disastrous crisis of the international financial system, would be wishful thinking indeed. On the other hand, commodity producers could themselves initiate commodity price rises by withholding output from the market, as coffee exporters and others attempted, with limited success, in the late 1980s, if they can secure alternative sources of finance in the interim.

Another short-term remedy suggested by our analysis is the substitution of concessionary loans, preferably by the multilateral financial institutions and sovereign lenders, for the existing high-interest portions of Africa's loan-portfolio. A 1988 United Nations study, for instance, recommends refinancing IMF purchases through the Fund's Enhanced Structural Adjustment Facility (ESAF).[7] The IMF has argued, however, that ESAF was set up to increase resource availability to low-income countries pursuing growth-oriented adjustment, and not to replace outstanding debt obligations.

Secondly, a shift to concessionary financing, which could reduce the gap between interest-rate and export growth sufficiently to ease the payments burden on Africa, will prove unattractive to creditor-nations and -institutions, as it bears semblances of debt forgiveness. A related possibility would be the creation of a new international debt-buying facility which would acquire the outstanding debt owed to multilateral organizations, and replace existing debt-service obligations with new, concessional loans—something akin to Corden's 1988 proposal for buying commercial-bank debt.[8] A facility of this sort will have the advantage of providing short-term relief without obliging international organizations and donors to provide new loans to the debt-distressed nations. This is particularly important as multilaterals, as a rule, neither reschedule outstanding debt-service obligations (since they rely mostly on the recycling of existing resources to fund new programmes), nor provide cash assistance or aid aimed specifically at meeting these obligations. The African debtors, with large debts to these organizations have, therefore, little choice but to meet their obligations, or fall into arrears. But falling into arrears is not costless: it typically leads to a cutting-off of funds from the particular organization, and a downward revision of a country's creditworthiness by other institutions or aid programmes, or even commecial banks.

The debt buy-out facility can therefore provide real short-term respite for Africa, which it can then use as a bridge in restoring its liquidity. The prospects of such a facility being funded by the international community, however, are not particularly bright, given the current political dispensation in the North, and the fiscal constraints of the leading donors. Funding such a facility might also mean, in the absence of increased bilateral-donor funding, a reallocation of existing aid resources, not only among programmes but also across countries in favour of those with major debt problems. But as aid is often offered with political undertones, the likelihood of such substitutability may be rather small.

A third method by which liquidity may be restored in the short term is by stabilizing the exchange-rate of the major convertible currencies, especially the U.S. dollar, in which most international debt is denominated, as the value of such debts tend to change with movements in the exchange rate. For instance, according to the World Bank, the depreciation of the dollar in 1985 increased the year-end value of total outstanding Third World debt by 4.5%. For sub-Saharan Africa, specifically, the debt grew by 9.4% in that year. Even when the effect of the depreciation is adjusted for, the (currency-adjusted) growth rate was still a significant 2.6%; in other words, the dollar's depreciation alone accounted for as much as 72% of the nominal growth of Africa's debt in 1985![9]

Of course, movements in the dollar's exchange rate are dependent partly on movements in U.S. interest rates; and both are functionally linked to the U.S.'s colossal internal indebtedness—from consumer debt and state- and federal-government budgetary deficits through trade-related external imbalances to the over-leveraged business sector—which kept real interest rates, for much of the decade of the 1980s, consistently above their historical average. Thus, until these underlying factors are tackled by the U.S. and the other Northern countries in similar economic situations, interest-rate and exchange-rate fluctuations will continue to compromise attempts at controlling the debt crisis for the foreseeable future. Thankfully, with the advent of the Clinton administration, there appears to be a new political disposition towards tackling these problems at their source. How real or adequate these efforts will prove over time, if implemented as envisaged; and how effective they will be in reining in fluctuations in these key rates are, of course, *a priori* indeterminable, contingent as they are on a whole gamut of global forces and domestic political interests.

In sum, given the structural inflexibilities of the African economy, the policies that may provide genuine debt relief by causing debt-growth reduction relative to income growth over the short run, will result largely from the macropolicies and goodwill of the creditor-nations. Adjust as they may, without commensurate action by Northern governments to eliminate imbalances in *their* economies, African governments can do little to bring interest rates down and commodity prices up. The prospects of these adjustments occuring to the degree they need to in the North, however, are not good, for a myriad of country-specific reasons. But were they even to occur, we would argue that whatever relief they will bring, however real, will be short-lived, as the structural substrate on which the crises are manifested will not have been at all addressed.

Debt Forgiveness and Repudiation

Until late in the 1980s, debt forgiveness—the conversion by creditors of a country's external debt retroactively into grants-in-aid—was a much-maligned and underrated strategy for debt relief. Outright debt forgiveness, which would have effectively reduced the growth rate of the debt to zero was, given the size and structure of Africa's debt, economically and politicallly feasible, in that creditors could have forgiven it without significantly compromising the efficacy of international finance as we know it. Creditors, however, for a long time strenuously objected to this course of action, not on the basis of the unsoundness of the economic argument behind forgiveness, but rather on their political objection to what they considered to be its likely precedential effect on international lending in general. If one nation's debt was forgiven, they argued, all other debtors would seek similar treatment; and where the bulk of the debt was held by private commercial houses, such mass cancellation would compromise the viability of the international lending business. There were thus considerations of 'moral hazard' to be contended with in deciding to forgive debt. For these and such reasons, the likelihood of *mass* debt cancellation remains rather low, the broad steps taken tentatively in the late 1980s towards writing off portions of some individual countries' debts notwithstanding.

The extent of these partial cancellations indicate, however, that there is increasing receptivity among the creditors to the inevitability of cancellation as perhaps the single best strategy for providing debt relief for Africa. The number of cancellations increased markedly in the late 1980s, and involved all the 'Group of 7' nations. The (then) Federal Republic of Germany, for one, adopted a comprehensive programme by which DM 6.4 billion owed it by twenty-eight SSAn countries would be forgiven. And even though this was only an 8% cancellation rate (as far as German debt in Africa went), and did not therefore make a giant impact on the continent's debt pressures— Nafziger reports that debt-service cancellations only brought Africa a $5 million saving in 1987[10] —it certainly brought some relief to the *individual* beneficiaries. For instance, Malawi was thusly relieved of the equivalent of $14 million by the German cancellation in 1989[11], while Ghana enjoyed a DM 500 million reprieve.[12] Similarly France, in the same year, took some steps towards cancelling some of its ex-African colonies' arrears on interest payments owed it. It also relieved other African countries of substantial obligations: Ghana, for one, had a $26 million French debt cancelled in December 1989, and obtained a pledge that the grant element in future French aid would be doubled, to 70%. In addition, France softened the terms of future borrowing for Ghana, to a 1.5% rate of interest (down from the 3.75% of the time), with a repayment period of thirty (as compared to the-then fifteen-to-twenty) years.[13]

In 1987 Japan, France, the United States, Canada and Germany also proposed to convert to grants, under Paris Club auspices, some $2 billion of non-concessional loans to SSA by 1990.[14] And in the summer of 1989, the U.S. again floated a proposal to cancel its nearly $1 billion of "development loans" to SSA, which would have eliminated nearly 12% of the region's $8.5 billion debt obligation to the U.S. government. But, here again, even this substantial gesture would have made nary a dent in the nearly $170 billion gross continental external debt of the time. The U.S. has also made significant *bilateral* debt-relief overtures to specific countries: in November 1989, it cancelled an $82 million Nigerian debt, deferring payment on a further $274 million until 1995, "in recognition of Nigeria's economic reforms."[15]

It would appear, then, that the OECD was gradually coming around to implementing the proposal agreed at the September, 1988 annual joint-meeting of the World Bank and IMF, to cancel a third of the bilateral debts of the "least-developed countries" to bring them some relief. Note from Table 6.2, however, that the bulk of the debt of the "severely indebted middle-income" African countries at the time of these proposals— some 90% of it, to be precise—was not from official bilateral loans, though 42% of the "severely indebted low-income countries" debt was. Thus, even though the main beneficiaries of these cancellations were the ones who could most use it, the poorest countries on the continent, the volume of cancellations could hardly have afforded the degree of relief across the continent that only a programme of comprehensive debt forgiveness would have.

TABLE 6.2
SSA's Debt Structure, 1987, By Income and Debt Categories

DEBT CATEGORY	Severely Indebted Low-Income Africa	Severely Indebted Middle-Income Africa
Official direct bilateral		
$ billions	30	44
% of total	42	10
Creditor-guaranteed*		
$ billions	6	34
% of total	9	6
Multilateral		
$ billions	26	83
% of total	36	16
Private (including short-term debt)**		
$ billions	9	357
% of total	13	68

*   Suppliers' credits & fixed-rate commercial bank loans.
** Private loans not publicly-guaranteed & variable rate commercial loans & short-term debt & "nationalization obligations".
Source: C. Humphreys and J. Underwood, The External Debt Difficulties of Low-Income Africa, in I. Husain and Diwan, I., eds., *Dealing with the Debt Crisis* (World Bank: Washington, D.C., 1989), p. 50.

A related strategy to debt forgiveness, in terms of its potential economic impact on the debtor-nations, is unilateral debt repudiation by the debtors themselves. This will effectively stem the resource hemorrhaging of the continent, freeing it up for internal economic restructuring. As Cline, Sachs, and other analysts have argued, a strong economic and political case can be made for repudiating (at least a portion of) the debt as soon as net resource transfers become negative, in the stead of a severe deflationary adjustment.[16] By year-end 1985 many African debtors had, at least, defaulted on, if not *de facto* repudiated, their debts, as only eleven (of a possible forty-four) of them had kept up with debt servicing continuously since 1981. And whereas one cannot credibly attribute this rate of default to Cline's or Sachs' analysis, it was quite clear that most of Africa, by 1985, had neither the ability nor the willingness to pay their debts.[17]

The advantages of debt repudiation lie in two factors. First, in implementation. The act of repudiation, unlike debt forgiveness, lies outside the purview and control of the creditors. In other words, they are uncharacteristically relegated to the position of reacting to the act after the fact. This gives the debtor unusual control over the disposition of the debt. Secondly, the debtor-nation has received whatever benefit it will receive from the resource inflow and, by repudiating, it cuts the costs attached to reversing that flow.

But there are punitive costs attached to repudiation. The most obvious one is the possibility of sanctions by lenders, in terms of exclusion from future borrowing, or seizure or attachment of the debtor's properties and other assets, such as its foreign reserves, within the creditor's government's jurisdiction. Whether the costs of repudiation (sanctions, reduced creditworthiness) are sufficient to deter repudiation in all cases, however, is hardly a settled issue. Indeed, the history of international finance is littered with numerous instances of "busted bonds", for which very little credible sanctions were exacted.[18] Thus, true as it may be that capital markets tend to have a memory, it is also quite true, we would contend, that their memory is necessarily porous and infirm, tempered as it is by the prospect of increased or renewed profit-making in a constantly changing global financial environment. Otherwise it would be difficult to explain how and why the 1930s' Latin-American defaults scarcely deterred lenders, in something like twenty years later, from resuming loan-making to the region, and how and why barely four decades after those defaults, loans of unprecedented magnitudes were finding their way to the region at near-zero real-interest cost.

The decision-making criterion for debt repudiation should therefore be, broadly, not whether the immediate benefits outweigh the costs of sanctions and decreased creditworthiness, but rather whether solvency, as we have defined it in this work, is enhanced or restored in the long-term by repudiation.

But even by this criterion, the chances of outright, public repudiation by African governments of their foreign obligations are, at best, remote, even though they have no such compunctions about repudiating *internal* debts. Africa's policy makers, in league or intrigue with the small but powerful private sector are, as we saw in the cases of Zambia and Zaire, the ones who least suffer the direct ravages of the economic adjustment to external imbalances. At worst, they forgo their customary consumption of a few imported luxury items, as imports in general are initially curtailed to save foreign exchange; but their general standard-of-living is hardly seriously threatened. It is the broad mass of workers and peasants, and especially women and children, who are most directly and debilitatingly affected by the imperatives of the debt burden. Thus, ironically, those nearer subsistence are the ones who, in real economic terms, bear the brunt of the past policy malfeasances of the same elite who are now most unwilling to take the steps necessary to rectify their errors.

Secondly, African elites are mortified by the prospect of disengaging from a world-system from which they derive, however indirectly, their high standard of living, their social hegemony and political power, and even their sense of identity. They thus have little incentive to, and every reason not to, repudiate the debt. As a proven method of restoring liquidity in the short-term, therefore, debt repudiation will not be readily forthcoming from Africa. It is precisely because all the viable (at least in theory) short-run 'solutions' analyzed thus far offer little hope of substantial remedy, even if implemented, that we argue, more importantly, for structural solutions to the debt crisis.

Debt-Equity Swaps

Although debt relief in Africa in the 1980s was often achieved through some combination of the two strategies of rescheduling or restructuring and economic adjustment, the conversion of debt obligations into equity shares was also utilized by, especially, those countries with substantial commercial debt in their debt-portfolios. Nigeria, Côte d'Ivoire, Congo, Cameroon and Gabon have been the primary users of this strategy to date, though other debtors also have expressed increasing interest in, or have begun actively strategizing about, converting their external, hard-currency denominated debt into domestic debt or equity. (The Sudan, Kenya, Zaire and Senegal fall into this latter category). We thus examine next the specificities of this method of debt relief, given the spreading interest it has evoked in Africa. We are especially interested in assessing its *actual* potential for providing relief, not what governments believe it will do for their debt burden, and also what its merits are from the point of view of both the seller and third-party buyer of such debt. We follow closely the seminal work done in this area by Graham Bird.[19]

1. The Theory and Mechanics of Debt Swapping

The rationale for debt swapping is to convert the debtor-country's foreign-currency denominated debt into debt or equity denominated in local currency. Since it is essentially effected through trade there has to be a buyer, hence demand, for such debt, and a seller, hence supply, of it. The buyer purchases the debt from its holder (a commercial bank in the United States, say), thus enabling the holder to realize (i.e. cash-in) a proportion of the face value of its debt-asset. Thus, for instance while, in 1988, U.S. banks were realizing as much as 40%-70% of the face value of their loans to much of Latin America and Eastern Europe in the secondary market for developing-country debt (Table 6.3), they were realizing only between 2% and 24% on their African loans. But as Fig. 6.1 shows, all developing country commercial debt was being heavily and continuously discounted by the market through the latter half of the 1980s.

TABLE 6.3

Secondary Market Prices of U.S. Bank Loans to Selected Developing Countries, 1988. (Face Value = 1)

Latin America		Sub-Saharan Africa	
Argentina	.18	Côte d'Ivoire	.06
Bolivia	.11	Morocco	.44
Brazil	.32	Nigeria	.24
Chile	.64	Sudan	.02
Colombia	.60	Zaire	.19
Costa Rica	.14		
Ecuador	.14		
Mexico	.44		
Peru	.04		
Uruguay	.55		
Venezuela	.54		

Sources: K. Rogoff, Symposium on New Institutions for Developing Country Debt, *Journal of Economic Perspectives*, Vol. 4 (Winter, 1990), p. 4; P. Kenen, Organizing Debt Relief: The Need for A New Institution, *Journal of Economic Perspectives*, Vol. 4 (Winter, 1990), p. 9; and Salomon Bros., *Indicative Prices for Developing Country Debt*, July 1989, as cited by Nafziger, *The Debt Crisis in Africa*, p. 3.

Figure 6.1
Secondary Market Bids on Commercial-Bank
Debt of Developing Countries, 1986-1990

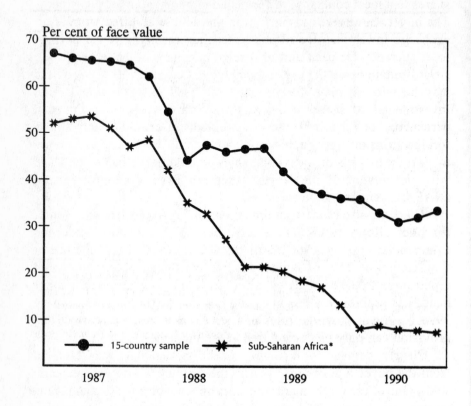

* Excluding Nigeria.
Source: U.N., *World Economic Survey 1990,* (New York), p. 89.

The buyer, who may either be a native/resident of the debtor-nation, or a foreigner, in turn sells the debt back to the government of the issuing country in exchange for real assets, such as equity shares in a local company, or for debt denominated in local currency. The buyer, however, can only swap the debt at an effective rate-of-exchange lower than the official rate, thus receiving fewer units of local currency for each unit of foreign currency. Further, there are strict limitations on the uses to which local currency thusly acquired may be put. It may, for instance, be used only for new capital investments, or shares in an existing company up to a stipulated percentage, or for joint ventures. Mexico, for example, only allows foreign firms or individuals participating in debt conversion schemes to own up to 15% of local companies, though how that will change with the advent of the North American Free Trade Agreement (NAFTA) remains to be seen.

There are also often strict limitations on profit repatriation. Chile, for one, allows foreign investors, but not local ones, under its Compendium of Rules for International Exchange, the remittance of a maximum of 25% of dividends after the fourth year, and capital repatriation to the same extent after ten years. Mexico, on the other hand, has prohibited all capital- and profit-repatriation until January 1998.[20] Again, how the rules of a Free Trade Area will affect this provision can only be conjectured at the moment.

Clearly, demand for a country's debt on secondary markets stem from the buyer's desire to invest in the country whose debt is being sold. One of the more importatnt determinants of this demand is thus buyers' assessments of a country's economic prospects and overall stability. Also important are the size of the discount, the effective rate-of-exchange, and limitations on profit remittances and capital repatriation. The demand function for debt may thus look like this:

$$Q_d = Q_d(I, A, K, D, T, C_d),$$

where I denotes the availability of investment opportunities in the debtor-country; A, the availability of, and return on, alternative investment opportunities; K, limitations on the repatriation of capital and the remittance of profits; D, the discount rate; C_d, the country's creditworthiness as assessed by the potential buyer; and T, the 'conversion charge', since buyers receive fewer domestic-currency units per dollar than at the official exchange rate. We may reasonably expect demand to vary negatively with K, R and T, but positively with I, D and C_d.

Since there is no conceivable need for third-party intermediation, the secondary market for developing-country debt is supplied directly by the holders of that debt, mainly U.S. commercial banks. They can, in principle, directly convert their dollar-denominated claims into local-currency claims; but their willingness to do this will, of course, depend on their currency preferences, which will, in turn, be a function, among others, of expected exchange-rate movements. The supply function may thus look like this:

$$Q_s = Q_s(S, W, C_s, R, D),$$

where S is the size of the debt held; W, the extent to which the debt has already been written down; C_s, the holder's assessment of the debtor-country's creditworthiness; R, the holder's preferences between risk and return, a rising R indicating an increase in risk aversion; and D is as previously defined. Again, we expect the supply of debt to rise as S rises, as C_s and D fall, and as the holder becomes more risk-averse.

The principal advantage to the banks of selling off risky debt is that it reduces their risk. Banks' supply of debt to secondary markets is, however, constrained by two factors. One is the fact that many of the original loans were syndicated, making it difficult for any particular bank to spin off a component of the loan for trade on the secondary market. Indeed, whether or not any one bank or sub-group within the lending syndicate can do this is very much an unanswered legal question. The second is that, as selling off a component of a syndicated loan effectively writes down the value of all the other loans, there is a strong disincentive for each bank to act independently. For these reasons, large money-centre banks might be less willing to sell their syndicated loans unless they can sell all of it (or, at least, the greater proportion of it). Thus only small banks with small and/or highly concentrated debt exposure, or large banks whose loans have already been written down, are likely to supply their debt-holdings to the secondary market. Given the structure of Africa's external debt, and given the fact that its commercial debt was largely syndicated, debt-equity swaps may thus not provide significant *continental* relief, though individual countries may well benefit substantially.[21]

The market's function is to reconcile the different preferences and perceptions of country-creditworthiness on the supply and demand sides, and to establish a market-clearing price. There are, however, two categories of price operational in this exchange, and they must be analytically distinguished one from the other. One is the price of the debt, which would tend to be inversely related to the size of the discount, and the other is the price of debt conversion, which is different for the buyer and the seller involved in the trade. For the seller, the conversion price *is* the discount on the debt, assuming zero transaction costs. For the buyer, however, it is the discount plus any differentials between the official and effective rates of exchange. As that differential nears zero, the demand for convertible debt will rise with the size of the discount, even as its supply varies inversely with it. Thus demand will be negatively related to the price of the debt, and supply positively to it. The expected return to a debt-buyer, π^e, will thus depend on the exchange-rate differential between the official, e, and the effective, e', rates used by the debtor-country to convert any secondary-market debt purchases into local currency or debt, and the discounted price of the debt, p_d. Thus

$$\pi^e = \frac{\frac{e}{e'} \cdot p_d}{p_d}$$

If $e/e' < 1$ and $p_d = e/e'$, the exchange-rate differential neutralizes the discount, driving the return to the buyer, upon conversion, to zero. Return will be positive if $p_d < e/e'$. More accurately, the discount on the debt will have to make up for the exchange rate differential plus any transaction costs associated with the conversion in order to elicit a demand for debt on the secondary market.

An African debtor-country interested in successfully swapping its external debt for local equity appears, therefore, to be constrained to taking those steps that will ensure demand for its debt on the secondary market. First, it would have to keep $\pi^e > 0$ by minimizing the domestic-currency cost of converting dollar-denominated debts. Widening the differential between the official and effective rates of exchange will reduce demand; indeed, the maximum return on converted debt will be attained if the official rate is also the effective rate, i.e. if $e/e' = 1$. Secondly, it must take steps to ensure solid domestic economic performance, as better investor expectations of the economic future does much to improve the demand for debt. Of course, a conspicuously better outlook for the domestic economy might have the effect of decreasing the supply of debt, which will cause its price to rise as the discount on it falls, affecting demand adversely. This may well be offset, however, by the increased country creditworthiness that better expectations will bring. African countries should therefore evaluate these offsetting outcomes carefully before embarking on creating a climate designed to foster demand for their debt by third-party investors. As we show in the ensuing analysis, however, their decision needs to be predicated on other considerations as well.

2. *Economic Impact of Debt Swapping*

There are four principal impacts on the economy of a country that trades its external debts for domestic equity. These are (1) the direct effect on the size of the country's debt; (2) the induced effects on its creditworthiness; (3) the impact on its domestic money supply; and (4) the impact on the exchange rate of its currency.

The paramount objective of debt swaps, from the debtor's point of view, is to replace the external obligation with the more manageable domestic debt. By reducing foreign claims on precious foreign-exchange resources, the country's export revenue can be stewarded towards domestic growth needs. In addition, as the government, at any given moment, has greater discretionary control over the country's currency than it does over its net foreign-exchange position, converting dollar-denominated debt into domestic-currency debt eases the country's debt-service burden, thus ameliorating short-term balance-of-payments pressures. The domestic growth that the freed foreign-exchange can induce will also help the long-term solvency needed to resolve the current, and prevent future, debt-cum-development crises.

The second impact of debt swapping is on the country's creditworthiness, hence its ability to attract more capital from abroad. The reduced external obligation achieved through debt swapping will, all things equal, improve creditworthiness; but the discount on the debt that facilitated the debt swap in the first place is an indicator of the country's low creditworthiness. Thus, ironically, for a heavily-indebted country to achieve *future* improved creditworthiness through debt swapping, it has to accept a lower *current* international credit rating.

But things are not always as clear-cut as all that. Debt conversion may increase domestic money stocks and, therefore, inflationary pressures. If this leads to an overvaluation of the currency, with the government economically unwilling or politically unable to take the requisite actions to correct it, the country's credit rating is bound to suffer. It is only when conversion leads, directly or indirectly, to a perception of greater economic viability that it enhances creditworthiness. The upshot of all this is that the effect of debt conversion on a country's creditworthiness is not unambiguous, and therefore cannot be used as an *a priori* determinant of continued or enhanced capital inflows.

We have already seen how countries with declared conversion schemes impose limits on the types, extent and uses to which converted debt may be put. One of the main rationales for such controls is the uncertain impact that the provision of local currency in exchange for external debt has on the domestic money supply and fiscal balance. The instinctive fear, it seems, is that if large sums are converted the domestic money supply will increase tremendously, creating an expansionary effect on the economy that could generate inflation. This fear is, of course, not without merit, as most developing countries do not have well-developed financial markets through which excess liquidity may be sterilized (say, by bond issues). There is thus some reason to believe that debt swaps may improve external imbalances at the expense of domestic price stability.

Secondly, conversion necessarily means an increase in the government's domestic debt. As revenues will have to be raised to service this debt, inflationary pressures (if the debt is monetized), higher taxes, or even a fresh round of external borrowing cannot be ruled out of the country's fiscal future.

Another reason for the regulation of debt conversion is the concern, hinted at above, over its effects on exchange rates, especially in those countries where a large proportion of the demand for convertible debt may come from the citizens or residents themselves (as happened in Chile in the 1980s). The fear here is that debt conversion will increase the domestic money-supply and the demand for foreign-exchange on the parallel market, thus putting downward pressure on the price of the currency. And if the country's external debt is written down so far as to cause deterioration in confidence, this might weaken the capital account and cause the exchange rate to fall even further.

On the other hand, as argued above, a significant decrease in a country's external debt due to conversion will, conceivably, boost confidence and hence the demand for local currency from foreign investors. The value of the currency will then increase, and the nominal exchange rate will appreciate.

It would seem, therefore, that the short-run effects of debt swapping or conversion on a country's exchange rate depends principally on whether the preponderant demand for its convertible debt comes from within or without; i.e. from foreigners or residents. High internal demand will cause a depreciation in the exchange rate, while high external demand will have the opposite effect.

In general, then, it is difficult to draw firm, unambiguous conclusions about the efficacy of debt-equity swaps in resolving Africa's debt crisis. There are, clearly, economic advantages to both the individual sellers of the debt, the commercial banks, and their ultimate buyers, the indebted countries. But the impact on the debtor-country's overall debt and development crises is rather murky and contextual, conditioned as it is on the country's specific regulations and initial position.

It also bears remembering that only countries with significant commercial debt have used this strategy to date. Many are from Latin America, Central Europe and Asia, but Africa has a skeletal representation in the likes of Nigeria, Côte d'Ivoire, Gabon and Zaire. Since 1985 Nigeria, in particular, has pursued debt conversions purposefully, for the simple reason that the country's external debt has the highest commercial-source content in sub-Saharan Africa. Indeed, by November 1989, Nigeria had converted a total of $11 million of commercial debt to domestic equity, with $234 million still on offer. The main preference of purchasers was manufacturing equity, which accounted for about one-half of the total equity purchased with converted debt. (By contrast, less than 20% of equity purchased was in the agricultural sector). In the first quarter of 1990, another $5.8 billion of commercial debt was to have come on the market, showing that demand for Nigeria's debt firmed up considerably between 1988 and 1990 and, selling at twenty-four cents on a one-dollar face-value, it was the least discounted debt among the sub-Saharan debts.[22]

For the overwhelming majority of African debtors, however, with greater proportions of multi- and bi-lateral debt than commercial ones, debt swaps will afford only marginal relief at best since, on the supply side, the foreign governments and multilateral agencies that hold their debts are unlikely to offer them on the secondary market.   On the demand side, with the exception of a handful of countries, Africa is seen as neither particularly creditworthy nor with particularly good economic prospects.   Very few *new* investors will thus purchase Africa's debt, even at a considerable discount.   Secondly, because very little of the total debt will be offered on the secondary market anyway, the short-term benefit (in terms of reduction in the quantum of debt) will be minimal.   And, thirdly, whatever demand there is is bound to come more from foreigners than from Africans, with the possible exchange-rate consequences as argued above.

But the most worrisome aspect of debt-for-equity swaps is the potential long-term export of capital that foreign investment of this sort ultimately induces, the operative restrictions imposed by the government notwithstanding.   Africa has not been particularly successful at stemming this outflow for three hundred years, and there is little reason to suppose that this record will improve over the next hundred.   The fear of losing more control over Africa's economic future than has already been lost has made many governments rather reluctant to participate in debt conversion schemes of all stripes. Indeed, in some of the more uncompromising government circles, debt-equity swaps are pejoratively referred to as 'imperialism-by-invitation'.[23]

6.2 *Restoring Solvency in the Long Run*

The main conclusion from the preceding analyses is that the policies most frequently employed to restore short-term liquidity are often inadequate to the task.   The liquidity bottlenecks are seldom substantially breached; hence the underlying structural crisis, which the liquidity problem only symptomizes, are even farther away from the touch of any corrective policies.   It is for this reason that we are compelled to argue in favour of policies that, in the bid to rein in the external imbalances, tackle the insolvency of the African economy at its source.   In other words, we advocate policies that seek to overcome those domestic and external *structural* bottlenecks with which we have been concerned throughout this work, structures that, as we have attempted to show, initiated and then helped reproduce the cycle that began with Africa's economic underdevelopment and led, through its external imbalances, back to exacerbate the same internal distortions that started the cycle in the first place. Thus, more so than the structural *adjustment* that the neo-orthodox school espouses, and out of which much of the policy options analyzed thus far comes, we argue for structural *transcending* or *transformation* policies, for the individual African economy, and also on a regional basis.

What distinguishes our proposals from those of the new orthodoxy is that ours aim not primarily at solving the debt crisis *per se*, but at tackling those forces endemic to the economy that make it prone to crises of all sorts, including external disequilibria. Thus, for instance, we advocate policies that will integrate production with domestic consumption needs, in the first instance; and, thence, a regional system of production and trade that will enable the downgrading of the primacy of the existing system of international trade and finance in Africa's economic endeavours. This, of course, is in consonance with our core contention that the global political economy, in its current configuration, generated those forces principally responsible for the onset of the crisis. We seek, in sum, as a more durable solution for the debt-and-development crisis that has gripped Africa since the late 1970s, to functionally link the continent's resource base with its production capabilities and consumption needs, on both the regional and local levels, and in the context of the continent's social and political particularities and needs, *without rendering African economic activity necessarily autarchic*.

Domestic Structural Integration

Regional economic integration has, in the second half of this century come to assume, perhaps in the wake of the unfolding success of the European Union, a place of prominence on the menu of economic development options of many countries and governments. There is not a region in the world that has not, at the very least, paid lip service to the idea of some sort of economic confederation with its neighbours: the Andean Pact, the Carribean Community and Common Market (CARICOM), the Economic Community of West African States (ECOWAS), the *Union Monétaire Ouest Afrique*, the Southeast Asia Co-prosperity Sphere, the Enterprise for the Americas...all represent intended or realized degrees of formalized economic cooperation among neighbouring countries. Of course, the consolidation of European integration in the fitful moves towards a full monetary and economic union after 1992, and the contentious outlines of the nascent North American Free Trade Agreement (NAFTA) are but the most recent, and arguably the best known, attempts at regionalism involving major world economies.

We would argue, however, that the *internal* integration, structurally, of the constituent economies of any regional economic grouping is logically prior to the integration of the individual economies across the region. This is particularly indispensable in those parts of the world where the individual economies are not sufficiently organic in their own right. Thus, in Africa, where structural *dis*integration is, as we have seen, more the rule than the exception, any attempts at formal inter-country economic linkage across regions are apt to be condemned to failure as long as the constituent economies remain sectorally uncomplementary within themselves. It is this sectoral complementarity—the 'forward and backward linkages' between resource endowment, production techniques and final demand—that will provide the structural transcendence necessary for sustained income growth and, thence, the alleviation of the debt-and-development crisis. We argue, accordingly, for four sets of economic policies, much of which has already been spelt out in fine detail by the U.N. Economic Commission for Africa, and which policies are designed to achieve the long-term internal restructuring objectives that we are calling for here, while also enabling the economies to adjust to their present disequilibria. Because the ECA analysis agrees, in essence, with ours, and in order to prevent a reinventing of an already manufactured wheel, we reproduce here the substantive element of the ECA agenda, the four cornerstones of which embrace policies that would seek to (1) diversify while strengthening Africa's production capacity; (2) improve both the level and distribution of income on the continent; (3) reorient budget priorities towards the satisfaction of basic needs; and (4) create institutional support for the transformative process.[24]

The specific policy measures undergirding this transformative process collectively constitute one component of what we have labelled 'the new culture of development' for Africa. They, and their desired transformative effects, are summarized below. The contrast with the adjustment policies of the new orthodoxy, which policies have, heretofore, dominated the theory and practice of debt resolution in the field, and which we have detailed elsewhere in this work, should be obvious.

OBJECTIVE ONE:
To Strengthen Production Capacity and Change the Output Mix

Specific Policy Measure	Desired Transformative Effect
1. Land reform to provide greater access and legal entitlement to, especially, women.	Increased food production and rural employment. A narrowing of rural-urban and male-female income differentials.
2. Making agriculture the single greatest recipient of public investment outlays.	Strengthening rural infrastructure and institutions while increasing rural productivity and employment.
3. Shifting a country's import profile towards agricultural inputs, and basing manufacturing on agricultural output and the extractive industries.	Expanding both agricultural and industrial employment. Increased domestic provision of basic food and manufacturing needs, thus avoiding import strangulation when foreign exchange availability falls. Enhanced complementarity between agriculture, mining and manufacturing.
4. Credit allocation to favour agriculture and the manufacturing of basic foods.	Enhanced capacity of the economy to satisfy basic needs while increasing employment.

5. Instituting a range of interest rates that make loans
for speculative activity relatively costlier than those
for productive activity.

Provide a better enabling
environment for local en-
trepreneurship. Mobilizing
meagre domestic savings for
productive investment.

6. Strengthening rural financial
institutions.

Mobilization of rural saving. Improved rural financial intermediation.

7. Using the existence of multiple exchange rates to enhance
capital inflows and discourage
its outflow, and to control the
import mix.

Ensure the repatriation of
capital from, especially,
nationals living abroad.
Curb capital flight. Imp-
rove the BOP while limiting
the importation of non-
essential or luxury items.

8. Differential export subsidies,
removal of trade barriers and
the increased utilization of
counter-trade to boost intra-
African commerce.

Reduction in external de-
pendence. Provides a bet-
ter product mix for consumers. Promotes economic
integration across the continent. Improvement of
countries' BOP and national
incomes.

OBJECTIVE TWO:
Improving Income Performance and Distribution

Specific Policy Measure	Desired Transformative Effect
1. Increasing the efficiency and probity of the tax collection system.	A fairer distribution of the tax burden and increasing government revenues.
2. Reduction of government spending on the non-productive public sector, such as the military.	Improve resource allocation and the BOP position.

3. Removal of subventions to insolvent, especially non-strategic, parastatals.

    Encourage fiscal prudence and efficiency of state owned enterprises. Reduction of budget deficit.

4. Reprioritizing government's spending to favour productive and infrastructural investments with little or no import content.

    Improvement of the BOP. Sustaining growth through strategically funded production units.

5. Establishing a price floor for food crops to be managed through strategic food reserves.

    Encourage food production. Improve rural-urban income differentials. Control of inflation. Reversal or curtailment of rural-urban migration.

OBJECTIVE THREE:
Provision of Basic Needs

Specific Policy Measure	Desired Transformative Effect
1. Increasing social spending to about 30% of total government expenditures, to be subsequently kept at a 'maintenance rate' determined by inflation and the growth rate of the population. Education, health and women's programmes should be the primary targets.	Providing the minimal social needs of all to improve the human-capital base. Raise the living standards of the majority.
2. Selective pricing policies to increase the supply of essential commodities necessary for the maintenance of a socially-stable atmosphere for development.	Increase the affordability, hence distribution, of consumer goods and crucial intermediate inputs. Control of inflation, and provision of the social stability necessary for long-term productive investment.

3. A multi-layered trade policy which can allow for the outright banning of particular luxuries. High import taxes on conspicuous consumption and factor inputs that have domestic substitutes. Mass education to foster the use of locally-produced goods.

Changes in consumption patterns to raise the market share of locally-produced goods. Production to be turned inward, both to satisfy local demand and to use local inputs.

4. Strengthening intra-African monetary and financial cooperation, as well as payments and clearing arrangements.

Increased regional self-reliance, and production for a wider market. Enhancing prospects for regional structural integration. Improving individual countries' BOP.

5. Limitation of debt service ratios, preferably with the consent of creditors, to levels consistent with each country's growth and development needs.

Freeing of scarce resources for domestic investment. Improving countries' BOP.

6. Export incentives for select products, especially agro-based manufactures.

Promotion of export diversification, hence the provision of a cushion against the vicissitudes of international primary-goods markets. Making export earning more predictable, while promoting manufacturing and export growth.

OBJECTIVE FOUR:
Creating Institutional Support for the Transformation Process

Specific Policy Measure	Desired Transformative Effect
1. Strengthening agricultural research and extension services.	Acceleration of the drive toward food self-sufficiency, especially in grains and cereals. Provision of a solid base for manufacturing.
2. Creating rural institutions to support cottage industry with credit, marketing information, etc. based on indigenous technologies and the participation of women.	Promotion of 'integrated rural development', and enhancement of the attractiveness of rural areas as residential and vocational areas. Promoting the development of rural technologies and boosting rural employment.
3. Legislation of a framework of ownership that will provide the incentive for different groups to participate in the development process.	Enable popular participation in production, marketing, and the development process in general. Undermining the usual heavy-handedness of central authority that stifles initiative. Making traditionally marginalized groups, like women, those in the informal sector, and ethnic minorities more viable contributors to the development process.

4. Active promotion by government of community-based development institutions and self-help organizations and programmes.	Ensure democratic (i.e. community-based) control of the development process. Mobilization of human resources by ensuring ownership of, hence better commitment to, development initiatives. Shift of power over people's lives away from central government to their own communities. This, in culturally pluralistic countries, is indispensable to the development project.

The sucessful implementation of policies such as these will be the prelude to, and form the basis of, the process of regional integration, the theory and mechanics of which are critically discussed in the following section. Our alternative view of regionalism in Africa, as a strategy for restoring long-term solvency and preventing the recurrence of external debt crises, is modelled in the conclusion of that discussion.

Regional Economic Systems

The call for a regionalist development strategy for Africa is an old one. The early, post-independence nationalist leaders—Nkrumah of Ghana, Keita of Mali, Toure of Guinea, Nyerere of Tanzania, Ahidjo of Cameroon, Balewa of Nigeria, Nasser of Egypt, Kaunda of Zambia, among others—were all of a mind to create a 'United States of Africa' as a bulwark against Western imperialism. The formation of the Organization of African Unity (OAU) in 1963 was the culmination of their efforts towards this essentially *political* agenda.

The emergence of the consciousness to protect the African economy as well from the post-colonial encroachments of the ex-colonial masters came much later. Thus the theory and rationale for regional, or even continental, integration has been more finely developed in the area of politics. The *economic* theory for same has been more a reflection of the theories of regionalism seminally developed by European economists for the post-war European economic integration agenda. As such, the institutional specificities of the African political economy are not reflected in Africans' own theoretical understanding of *their* economic integration. The economic integrationist experiments of the past two decades or so have therefore been pursued more on faith than on solid, contextually germane, economic reasoning. That they have proved miserable failures, therefore, could hardly be surprising.

Yet there are sound theoretical reasons, wholly reflective of Africa's structural realities, why integration should be pursued as public policy, and why it should succeed in providing the self-sufficient economic development that rightly motivated the initial fascination with the concept. These reasons and theories emerge most readily from a thorough critique of the neo-classical theory of integration, and from an understanding of the institutions of global political economy that African economies operate under. It also helps to understand the process of integration itself as the *end-product* of an organic process that starts from within the individual countries that wish to integrate their economies, as discussed above. In other words, workable integration begins with the sectoral integration of the constituent economies, and only then proceeds to the regional integration of these internally-integrated economies. The one fails in the absence of the other, and each acquires practical efficacy only if implemented as a complementary policy of the other.

African integration experiments of the past failed to take due cognizance of this logical priorness of internal, complementary, sectoral linkages. Whatever regional system was erected, therefore, stood on very wobbly foundations indeed, as disintegrated *national* economies cannot provide an adequate basis for an integrated *regional* economy. It is against this backdrop that we propose regional economic integration as, arguably, *the* key element of the new culture of development. We commence, then, as a prelude to a theory of African economic integration, "at the commencement": with a critique of the neo-classical theory of integration.

Whereas regional economic integration amongst industrialized nations seeks to join, at the margin, the already-developed production and distribution structures of the constituent economies, among African countries integration should, more appropriately, aim at developing those very structures that will enhance production activity. African countries should seek, through integration, to push out the region's production possibilities frontier to ensure economic self-reliance, and to increase its political bargaining power against all others. Thus the Vinerian criteria of 'trade creation' and 'trade diversion' on which the economic efficacy of regional integration is traditionally evaluated[25] are, for reasons that will soon be obvious, precisely the wrong criteria on which African integration should be judged, since the objective here is to expand and transform the structures of production, not merely to create or divert trade through selective tariff policy.[26]

But even with this objective, trade *does* get expanded among members of the union, whether or not they are the lowest-cost producers in the world, and de-emphasized with non-union countries, whether or not *they* are the lowest-cost producers. Trade diversion, in the pure Vinerian sense, is thus bound to preponderate over its creation, at least in the short run, given the current external orientation of Africa's economies, and given also the differences in production costs between Africa and its traditional trading partners.

The neo-classical theory would therefore advise, as it intermittently has, against African integration.[27] But net trade diversion, in our view, *is* the desired objective of integration in Africa; its occurence, therefore, is an indication of the success, not failure, of regionalism. For most of these countries, net trade diversion is the desirable long-term economic and political objective of their overall development strategy, even though it may come at the cost of a net decrease in welfare in the short run. In other words, for them, short-term gains in welfare made through net trade creation should be seen as less important than the achievement of absolute increases in output, even at less-than-optimal production efficiencies, in the long run. In addition, it is envisaged that over the long haul, the region's production structures and relationships can be transformed, through integration, to complement its demand structures, not contradict them, as free trade with the larger world has traditionally done.[28]

This, indeed, explains why there has been a greater number of integration schemes among developing countries since 1945, the advise of Western development 'experts' to the contrary notwithstanding, than among the industrialized ones.[29] The emphasis in the neo-classical customs union theory on trade and its 'static' effects as the evaluative criteria for regional integration thus affords very little understanding of the process, or its long-run objectives, in the African context.[30]

It would appear, therefore, that long-term, *dynamic* considerations probably provide a better rationale for regional economic integration in SSA. For while there may be little economic justification within the confines of the static, neo-classical theories of integration—as exemplified by the Vinerian theory of customs unions—for regionalism, the contrary would be true on long-term, dynamic grounds.[31] Viner's conclusions, it appears, are rightly constrained to industrial Europe, where integration seeks to maintain production and distribution facilities, and a sustained level of growth, that essentially already exist. In Africa, where the objective is to create those very structures to attain a pattern of development that would engender self-sufficiency, those conclusions would have to be taken with a healthy dose of skepticism.

Clearly, what is called for, and what we will attempt to provide here, is an alternative theory of integration that will reflect the integral relationship between regionalism and the wider quest for development and long-term structural change in Africa, which change we see as indispensable to the resolution of the current debt crisis. The theory should reflect, also, the proposition that the effects of integration, given this objective, must be evaluated by their contribution to the development process as such, and not necessarily to short-term gains in allocative efficiency. It should reflect, in short, the strategy of "developmental regionalism for collective betterment."[32]

We will thus attempt here to extend the critique of the neo-classical theory of integration through a reformulation of (1) the *concept* of economic integration, and (2) how it relates to structural transformation and sustained economic growth in the small, open (i.e. structurally-dependent and outwardly oriented) non-industrialized economies of sub-Saharan Africa.

1. The Neo-Classical Theory of Regional Economic Integration

The term 'regional economic integration' has been used variously, and according to the agenda of the times, to denote any purposive arrangement or process that entails less-hindered trade or monetary relations and/or capital and labour movements among sovereign nations. We here, however, employ the term in the broader sense in which it was initially popularized by the likes of Bela Balassa, namely, a state of affairs, collective strategy, or joint endeavour to join formally and structurally the otherwise self-contained economies of more-or-less geographically contiguous independent nations.[33]

In the context of the neo-classical theory, regional integration is basically concerned with the promotion of efficiency in resource allocation and utilization and, as such, the following criteria constitute two of the key 'necessary conditions' for a successful process of integration: (1) the unrestricted movement, across national boundaries, of produced goods and factors, which therefore necessitates (2) the elimination of systematic discrimination through the repeal of tariffs and other barriers to trade. This process by which trade is liberalized through the elimination of discriminatory policies is termed, after Tinbergen, 'negative integration'.[34]

In addition, the neo-classical theory sees, as an adjunct to the process of trade-led integration, policies that would enhance the market's position as the prime allocator of resources. Institutions should therefore be eliminated, or created, to ensure that the market "provides the right signals", and "to give effect to the integrating force of the market." This is called 'positive integration'.[35]

The neo-classical theory of integration, therefore, covers "that branch of tariff theory which deals with the effects of geographically discriminatory changes in tariff barriers", the expectation being that the removal of protectionist barriers will enhance the economic welfare of all concerned.[36]

The actual process of integration takes different forms among different sets of countries. The neo-classical theory covers four basic types, each distinguished from the next at the margin to reflect different degrees of integration. These are Free Trade Areas (FTA), Customs Unions (CU), Common Markets (CM) and Economic Unions (EU). FTAs and CUs both involve the unrestricted, tariff-free movement of goods within an integrated area. They are distinguished one from the other by the fact that, with FTAs, each country promulgates its own tariffs against all other countries (i.e. all countries not members of the FTA). With a CU, however, there is a common tariff policy by the regional group—a common external tariff, or CET—against the rest of the world. In a CM, not only is there a CU, hence the unrestricted movement of goods within the integrated region, but also the unrestricted movement of labour and other productive inputs, so that both product and factor markets are effectively integrated across national borders. An EU involves, in addition to the integration of product and factor markets, the harmonization of fiscal and, especially, monetary policy. One may, in addition, justifiably consider a fifth and even higher level of integration, in which there is not a mere harmonization of policy but a complete unification of policy and policy-making. This may be called Economic Integration proper, or EI.

As can be surmised from Table 6.4, higher degrees of integration increase the extent of interdependence among members of the union. At the lowest level of integration, FTAs link, through trade, the demand for goods and services of a country with the supply of them from a neighbouring country. At the next level, CMs increase the dependence of the neighbours' factor and product markets on one another, such that the assumption of policies regarding those markets by one affects all others in the Market. This clearly necessitates some degree of consultation on, if not coordination of, policies among members, which is the *de facto* elevation of the union to the level of an EU. This, in turn, will call for deeper levels still of policy coordination, eventually resulting in an EI.

It follows, then, that "there are only two truly stable forms of [regional economic integration]: free trade areas and complete economic integration. All other forms...simply constitute intermediate and temporary stages in the process of the voluntary integration of national states by piecemeal methods. These transitional forms...for economic, political and other reasons are inherently unstable."[37] This by no means implies that CUs (or any other type of low-level integration) will inexorably lead to higher forms of regional integration. Clearly the willingness of sovereign authorities to cede increasing control over portions of their sovereignty to some supranational entity will always be a formidable obstacle to the intrinsic evolutionism of regionalized economic systems.

It should be obvious from this that whatever form the union eventually assumes—i.e. whatever the degree of formal integration—there are three characteristics that inhere in economic integration. The first is the elimination of discriminatory practices in trade among members of the union. The second is the maintenance of discriminatory barriers against all non-members; and the third entails the circumscription of each member-country's ability to make economic policy independently.

TABLE 6.4
Types and Characteristics of Regional Economic Systems

TYPES	Tariff-free movement of goods & services	Common External Tariff	Free movement of productive inputs	Harmonization of fiscal and monetary policies	Unification of all economic policies
1. Free-trade Area (FTA)	*				
2. Customs Union (CU)	*	*			
3. Common Market (CM)	*	*	*		
4. Economic Union (EU)	*	*	*	*	
5. Economic Integration (EI)	*	*	*	*	*

Source: T. Hitiris, *European Community Economics*, (N.Y.: St. Martin's Press, 1991), p. 2.

Clearly, then, even though much of the literature focusses on Customs Unions, the neo-classical theory of regional economic integration goes well beyond ordinary CU theory, in that whereas the latter is, in principle, just a branch of tariff and pure trade theory, the former concerns itself also with inter-country factor movements, the harmonization of trade policies within the union, and the coordination of instruments of economic policy. But since the type of integration that has occured in SSA thus far has been consistently of the CU variety, with the expressed but never realized intent of eventually elevating it to EU status, we here limit our discussion and critique to the theory of Customs Unions.

2. *The Neo-Classical Theory of Customs Unions*

The basic theory is concerned with the effects of a CU on resource allocation, specialization in production, and welfare gains for both individual members of the CU and the regionalized economy as a whole. For a CU to have any positive allocational effects—i.e. to generate the trade effects unattainable without a CU—it is necessary that the prospective members' tariffs should differ substantively for at least some products. It is the subsequent coordination and harmonization of tariffs that generates the allocational effects of the CU.

In CU theory, the effectiveness of the integration process is measured through the concepts of trade creation and diversion mentioned earlier. 'Trade creation' is defined as the shift in supply sources from a high-cost producer outside of the integrated region to a low-cost one within it. Alternatively, if the good is domestically produced but at high cost, the trade-creating shift is from this high-cost local supply source to a lower-cost producer in a partner country within the union.

The volume of trade created is expected to be greater (1) the higher the level of pre-integration tariff and other trade barriers; (2) the greater the volume of exports; (3) the more efficiently and extensively the lower tariffs are translated into lower domestic prices after integration; (4) the higher the price elasticity of demand for imports; and (5) the higher the elasticity of supply of exports. Consequently, the magnitude of any trade created depends on both the structure and character of pre-integration trade flows, and on such features of the integrated region as the extent of reduction of the relevant tariff and non-tariff barriers.

Trade creation, when it occurs, has two principal effects. The first is a production effect: it eliminates the production of a particular good in the importing country and increases the demand in same for the partner's output of the good, while also saving the importer the high cost of producing that good locally. The second is a consumption effect, in that consumers can now obtain the good at a lower price, thereby gaining 'consumer surplus' in the substitution of low-cost imports for higher-cost ones, while increasing consumption of the partner's product. It is the combined impact of the production and consumption effects that technically constitutes the trade creation effect of the CU.

By 'trade diversion' is meant the union-induced shift from low-cost supply sources outside of the union to a higher-cost source within it. Trade diversion is also a function of the first three factors identified above as determining the extent of the trade creation effect. But, in addition, it also depends on (4) the elasticity of substitution between a trading partner's products and those of a non-member country, and (5) the volume of imports from the rest of the world. Trade diversion, when *it* occurs, generates two separate effects opposite to those emerging from, and constituting, trade creation, namely, an increase in the cost of goods, and the consequent loss of consumer surplus.

The merits of a particular CU, then, are decided solely by the criterion of the relative magnitudes of trade created and diverted. If, on balance, more trade is created than is diverted, the union is deemed beneficial to global economic welfare. If more is diverted than is created, the union is deemed detrimental to welfare, and hence has no economic basis for existence. It is on the basis of just this criterion that a recent World Bank conference study asserts that South-South integration in Africa, Latin America, Asia and the Middle East are "a mistake not worth repeating".[38]

The theory also recognizes at least two other possible outcomes of the creation of a functioning customs union. One is the often-unintended effect of increasing the union's terms-of-trade against the rest of the world. The other is the exploitation of scale economies enabled by the expansion of the market upon integration, which then allows cost reduction in the production of goods and services. We will examine the role played by scale economies in the entire integration process in due course. The terms-of-trade effect is of less relevance to our argument, though the interested reader can find it amply treated elsewhere.[39]

3. A Critique of Customs Union Theory

In the light of the theoretical framework outlined above; given, also, (1) the external orientation of the typical African economy; (2) that, on average, industrialized nations produce at a lower unit cost than do African countries; (3) that the primary motivation for African integration is the political objective of breaking Africa's dependence on the industrialized countries; then, for any given tariff, elasticities of demand and supply for a good or service, and relative costs, when an African country shifts its imports from an industrialized country-source to a neighbour with which it is in union, it is bound to divert more trade than create it. It would seem, therefore, that regional economic integration in SSA is not economically justifiable, as indeed Lipsey and Viner implicitly argued, and as the recent World Bank publication mentioned above appears to have definitively concluded.

But the overwhelming majority of post-World War II formal integration experiments have taken place in Africa and elsewhere in the developing world. This would suggest, on purely empirical grounds, that from the perspective of these countries, and the neo-classical theory notwithstanding, regional integration in whatever form is more beneficial than less. It would appear, then, that the objectives of integration in the developing world are markedly different from those in the industrialized areas, which differences result from, and are amplified by, the structural constraints and historical realities these small economies face in an inhospitable world political economy. A theory of integration that seeks to explain the process in, say, Europe, therefore, can hardly be uncritically applied to parallel phenomena in Africa. Besides, the key assumptions on which the Vinerian postulates underlying the theory hold—full employment, constant returns to scale, perfect factor mobility, equality between private and social production costs, etc.—can no more be ascribed to industrialized economies than to developing ones, perhaps even less so to the latter.

What, then, are the *differentia specifica* of economic integration in Africa? The major difference is, of course, historical. European integration seeks to remove any constraints on trade, in order to improve allocation efficiencies in economies with highly developed (i.e. internally integrated) production and distribution structures, and with consistently positive growth rates along trend, in a more-or-less stable socio-political environment. Among African nations, on the other hand, the prime objective is the more basic one of attaining a level of growth commensurate with a minimal level of social welfare, and then to, at least, sustain it. The desire is primarily to expand the integrated region's (hence the constituent economies') production possibilities, with only secondary regard, if any, to economic efficiency in the abstract. If, in the pursuit of the main objective, some measure of efficiency is also attained, this will be regarded as largely coincidental, a by-product at best, albeit a welcome one.

In Africa, then, regional integration has, as its objective, long-term, dynamic and fundamental structural transformation, not merely the static, marginal and reallocational one that, we are arguing here, the industrialized countries have. To judge African integration by the same static criterion of net trade creation, therefore, can be misleading, and certainly not terribly revealing of any insights into how integration may be used to solve the debt-cum-development crisis.

Another shortcoming of the traditional CU theory as applied to Africa emerges, again, from its emphasis on trade and trade-related issues. Not only does this orientation make the theory not particularly different from static tariff theory[40], but it lends itself neither to analyzing dynamic gains from integration nor non-trade issues pertaining thereto. Thus, for instance, the issue of whether or not regional integration can succeed without a prior integration of, say, the primary and secondary sectors of each member-economy, cannot be addressed within the framework of the theory. Yet the result of integrating otherwise disarticulated economies may well be systemic *dis*integration in the long run, and hence the non-attainment of the objectives desired with the integration experiment: this much we learned from the economic history of the British Empire. For a more contemporary illustration, one could argue that the desire to bring developing countries more systematically into the world economy that led to the massive transfer of financial capital to them in the 1970s foundered on much the same grounds: those economies were not structurally competent to absorb and/or efficiently utilize that capital. The result was the debt crisis of the 1980s and the greater marginalization of most of these countries in, not their better integration into, the world economy.

There is, in fairness, increasingly greater agreement among (especially Third World) economists that although rigorous analytical results can be obtained from the static criteria of trade creation and diversion, those criteria may not be entirely relevant to the understanding of integration among, especially developing, nations, for two principal reasons. First, trade diversion need not lead to a loss in efficiency (or welfare), because even though the new supplier may be less efficient than the old, the duty-free price it or the consumer faces as a result of integration may well be lower than the pre-integration price. Secondly, there is extensive empirical evidence that suggests that 'static' costs and benefits, on the whole, tend to be rather modest.[41]

For these and such reasons, we contend here that the theoretical basis on which regional economic integration in Africa is appraised is woefully inadequate; that integration offers a viable avenue for overcoming the long-term structural bottlenecks of the African economy that underlie its debt crisis; that successful integration presents opportunities for redefining the economic and political relationship between Africa and the industrialized North along less dependent lines, and in such a way as to neutralize those forces that make that relationship latently crisis-ridden; that comparisons of the performance of, say, the EU and ECOWAS, on the basis of the neo-classical static CU theory, can hardly be instructive, and may even be obscuring of pertinent historical and conjunctural issues that may explain the difference; that the defining characteristics of African integration are not now, and cannot generally be, addressed within the neo-classical theory as expostulated above; and that, therefore, an alternative theory of integration more germane to the historical realities, structural particularities and developmental objectives of Africa, is very much needed. We suggest here a possible line of attack toward such a theory.

4. *Towards a Theory of Integration for Africa*

The argument on which our critique turns is that static gains from integration, as measured by net trade creation, may be less significant for developing countries, in the long term, than dynamic considerations.[42] Even at the lowest levels of formal regional economic integration, an FTA or CU could increase economic growth among the trading partners as a result of (1) the exploitation of the internal economies-of-scale made possible by the expanded market that integration produces; (2) the external economies realized as whole industries expand in response to the expansion of the market upon integration, and the cost reductions that both it and internal scale economies afford; (3) the regional or country polarization effects that may result from the adjustment costs of trade creation in one region (or country) and/or the skewing of investment toward one region or country; and (4) the efficiency and smoothness of investment and trade activities enabled by the removal of trade and other barriers, but also by the general buoyancy (potential or realized) of the macroeconomic environment.[43]

It is not necessarily the case, however, that all member-economies of the union will enjoy similar economic gains from factors (1)-(4), or even enjoy them at the same time, should they materialize across the board. We can reasonably expect, for instance, the effects of (1), (2) and (4) to be nil, or slightly positive, for all the partners. But the effects of polarization is bound, by definition, to be unevenly distributed, with the least-developed economies incurring the heaviest adjustment costs. But even this can be ameliorated by the transitional arrangements negotiated by the partners. For instance, investment could be initially preponderantly targetted at the poorer economies to ease their adjustment burden, in addition to staggering the reduction of tariffs over a period of time, with the wealthier and healthier economies reducing theirs the earliest and the fastest. Our analysis is predicated on these and related observations.

We assume, for analytical tractability that, first, systemic growth in a typical African country is initiated by either the agricultural or industrial sector. Second, that systemic stagnation may be attributable to the small size of the economy (i.e. its lack of market depth), and/or to production inefficiencies. When such a country enters into some kind of integrative arrangement with its neighbours, there will immediately result a quantum increase in its effective market size that will enable the exploitation of scale economies in production. This will result in increases in industrial and/or agricultural output and income, leading to an increase in nominal purchasing potential, a 'deepening' of the market, and a consequent rise in output to satisfy the growing demand. Our hypothesis, therefore, is that a CU will lift the economy from its state of secular low growth towards a self-sustaining path of higher growth, even though this is not to affirm that a CU is a necessary or sufficient condition for growth stimulation.

The task, then, is to analyze the conditions under which a small, stagnated economy, not previously formally linked to any other, may be brought to sustained growth through regional integration of the CU variety. Further, we seek to refute the claim of the orthodox CU theory that developing countries are not structurally conducive to welfare gains through regional integration.

Our model thus hopes to capture the argument that sustained gains from integration emerge from, and are constituted in the main by, an acceleration in the rate of growth of income of member-countries made possible by the exploitation of scale economies in production, which, in turn, is made possible by the extension or deepening of the market through regional integration. To keep the analysis simple, the model examines one country, it presumably being representative of all others in the union, and pays particular attention to the effects of scale economies and increased market size on economic growth. The focus is on the industrial sector, since the bulk of Africa's imports that are regulated in a CU are manufactures or their inputs. But the model can easily be adapted to place the focus on agriculture.

Suppose, then, that an economy in a CU in Africa has two sectors, an industrial sector and an agricultural one. If I and A stand for the value of industrial and agricultural output, respectively, the value of total output or income is given by the identity

$$Y = I + A \qquad \ldots (6.1)$$

There exist potential scale economies in the industrial sector, which can only be realized if the size of the market exceeds a critical minimum amount, Z^*. In other words, for market size at most equal to Z^*, no economies of scale can be reaped. We may write this as:

$$E = \begin{cases} 1 & Z \leq Z^* \\ h(Z) > 1 & Z > Z^* \end{cases} \qquad \ldots (6.2)$$

where E is an index of output gains from exploiting scale economies. Since units are chosen such that $E = 1$ represents the absence of scale economies, we may sketch Equation (6.2) as follows:

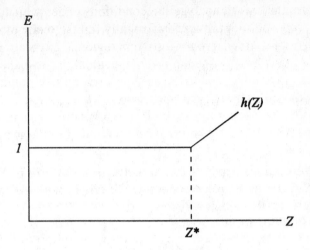

We may further choose a convenient form of the function, h, say

$$h(Z) = aZ^\alpha, \; h(Z) > 1 \text{ for all } Z > Z^*; \text{ and } a, \; \alpha > 0 \dots(6.3)$$

such that for all $Z > Z^*$,

$$E = aZ^\alpha \qquad \dots(6.4)$$

$$\text{and} \left(\frac{\dot{E}}{E}\right) = \alpha \left(\frac{\dot{Z}}{Z}\right) \qquad \dots(6.5)$$

where $\dot{E}/E \equiv g_E$, the (percentage) growth rate of the economies-of-scale parameter, and $\dot{Z}/Z \equiv g_Z$, the growth rate of market size.

We can simplify Equation (6.5) as follows:

$$g_E = \Psi(g_Z); \; \Psi(0), \; \Psi' > (0) \qquad \dots(6.6)$$

Equation (6.6) positively relates percentage increases in market size (beyond Z^*) to percentage increases in the economies-of- scale parameter. In other words, increases in market size will call forth increased gains from economies of scale.

Suppose no scale economies are realizable in the industrial sector. If I_w represents output without scale economies, we can assume that

$$I_w = F(K,L) \qquad \dots(6.7)$$

where F is linear homogeneous, and F_K, $F_L > 0$. In other words, output depends on capital and labour inputs, and the production function is characterized by constant returns to scale. (K and L represent capital stock and labour, respectively, employed in the industrial sector).

If I represents industrial output *with* scale economies, we may specify

$$I = E.I_w, \quad E \geq 1 \qquad ...(6.8)$$

where E, of course, depends on market size according to Equation (6.2). If $E = 1$, there are no economies of large scale production; if $E > 1$, there exist scale economies.

Given (6.8), it follows that

$$\left(\frac{\dot{I}}{I}\right) = \left(\frac{\dot{E}}{E}\right) + \left(\frac{\dot{I_w}}{I_w}\right) \qquad ...(6.9)$$

But, from (6.7),

$$\left(\frac{\dot{I_w}}{I_w}\right) = w_k\left(\frac{\dot{K}}{K}\right) + w_L\left(\frac{\dot{L}}{L}\right) \qquad ...(6.10)$$

where $w_K = F_K.K/I_w$, or the relative share of capital in output, and $w_L = F_L.L/I_w$, the relative share of labour in output. Combining Equations (6.9) and (6.10), we obtain

$$g_I = f(g_E, g_K, g_L), \quad f_i > 0 \text{ for all } i \quad ...(6.11)$$

where

$$f(g_E, g_K, g_L) = g_E + w_K g_K + w_L g_L \quad ...(6.12)$$

The f_i's are partial derivatives; $g_I \equiv \dot{I}/I$, the (percentage) growth rate of industrial output; $g_K \equiv \dot{K}/K$, the (percentage) growth rate of the industrial capital stock; and $g_L \equiv \dot{L}/L$, the growth rate of the industrial labour force.

For a given g_K and g_L, Equation (6.11) reduces to

$$g_I = \emptyset(g_E); \quad \emptyset' > 0, \quad \emptyset(0) \geq 0 \quad ...(6.13)$$

Thus, for given g_K and g_L, the rate of growth of industrial output depends only on the rate of increase of the economies-of-scale index, in that the higher g_E is, the higher g_I will be. If the values of g_I and g_L are positive, $\emptyset(0) > 0$; but if capital and labour are stagnant, then $\emptyset(0) = 0$.

It follows from income identity (6.1) that

$$g_Y = \lambda g_I + (1 - \lambda)g_A, \quad 0 < \lambda < 1 \quad ...(6.14)$$

where λ is the share of industrial output in total income, or I/Y; $(1 - \lambda)$ the share of agriculture in income, or A/Y; and $g_A \equiv \dot{A}/A$ is the (percentage) growth rate of agricultural output. If $y = Y/P$, i.e. income per capita, then

$$g_y = g_Y - g_P \quad\quad ...(6.15)$$

where $g_Y \equiv \dot{Y}/Y$ is the (percentage) growth of national income; g_y, the growth rate of income per head; and $g_P \equiv \dot{P}/P$, the growth rate of population. Thus the growth rate of income per head is equal to the growth rate of income less that of population.

Combining (6.14) and (6.15), we obtain

$$g_y = H(g_I, g_A, g_P) \quad\quad 0 < \lambda < 1 \quad ...(6.16)$$
$$H_1, H_2 > 0$$
$$H_3 < 0$$

where

$$H(g_I, g_A, g_P) = \lambda g_I + (1 - \lambda)g_A - g_P \quad ...(6.17)$$

For any given g_A and g_P, g_y depends only on g_I; i.e.

$$g_y = \theta(g_I); \quad \theta' > 0, \; \theta(0) \leq 0 \quad ...(6.18)$$

which says that the growth rate of income per head is positively related to the growth rate of industrial output. If we assume that, even under the worst circumstances, the growth rate of population in a representative African country just about equals the growth rate of agricultural output, $\theta(0)$ will, at most, be zero.

Market size is a function of the level of demand, and the key determinant of the demand for industrial goods can be assumed to be income per capita. Before integration, market demand is clearly related to per capita income in the particular country. After a CU is formed, demand should be related to the per capita income of the Union. For simplicity, however, we assume that individual member-countries' per capita incomes grow at the same rate as Union per capita income. Hence

$$Z = D(y), \quad D' > 0 \qquad \ldots(6.19)$$

If we adopt a simple form of D, say

$$Z = by^\beta, \quad b, \ \beta > 0 \qquad \ldots(6.20)$$

differentiating and dividing by Z yields

$$g_z = \beta g_y \qquad \ldots(6.21)$$

or, more generally,

$$g_z = \Omega(g_y); \quad \Omega' > 0, \ \Omega(0) = 0 \ \ldots(6.22)$$

Equation (6.22) thus says that the growth rate of market size depends directly on the growth rate of income per head, and that if per capita income is stagnant, so is market size.

We have now obtained the four basic relations needed for our discussion: (1) the demand relation, Equation (6.22); (2) the income growth equation, Equation (6.18); (3) the industrial production relation, Equation (6.13); and the scale-market size relation, Equation (6.6). We argue, using these relations, that with a CU, a normally stationary (i.e. stagnated) African economy can be pushed towards a dynamic growth path of industrial and general economic development.

What are the characteristic features of the stationary economy which are of particular interest for regional integration? First, because of the small size of the market—i.e. $Z < Z^*$—production tends to be below capacity and otherwise inefficient. Producers are, consequently, unable to reap gains from scale economies. Industrial output thus grows sluggishly, if at all. This low growth rate is insufficient to offset the high growth rate of the population, making output per head, at best, stagnate. Since per capita output is not rising, neither do demand and market size. Scale economies are thus not reaped, and industrial output does not grow rapidly, and so on and so forth.[44] Thus, a lack of increase in income per head implies a stationary demand, which offers little incentive for industrial expansion, which means, in turn, no increase in income per head. This, in fact, is essentially the same argument underlying the characterization, in the second chapter, of the African economy as one of a poverty trap under Nurksian equilibrium, in which low income per head leads to low investment which, in turn, leads to low growth, resulting yet again in low income per head; etc. Thus the typical African economy is caught in this vicious circle which has often and aptly been described as a 'low level equilibrium trap'.

Suppose now that an exogenous event occurs that increases market size beyond Z^*. According to Equation (6.6), any increases in market size beyond Z^* generates benefits from scale economies, i.e. $g_E > 0$. Even if g_L and $g_K = 0$, a positive g_E is still associated with a positive g_I; hence gains from scale economies result in a substantial rise in the growth rate of industrial output via Equation (6.13). Equation (6.18) indicates that this will lead to an increase in income per head, which then increases demand and market size (Equation (6.22)). The increase in market size now leads to a rise in the gains from scale economies during the next period, which results in an increase in output, which leads to a rise in per capita income, and so on.[45] Figure 6.1 captures this dynamic diagramatically.

FIGURE 6.2
A Dynamic Growth Process in a Regionally-Integrated African Economy

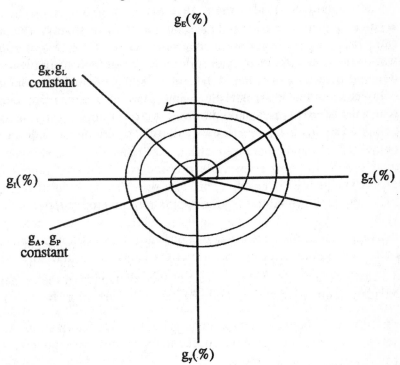

This is the dynamic economic process that we seek. It is propelled, among other things, by a circular positive feedback effect—a counter to the deviation-amplifying feedback loop of Chapter Two that causes the poverty trap under Nurksian equilibrium. In short growth, once thusly initiated, feeds upon itself; and even though the rate may ameliorate in time (for instance, as the economy reaches the limits of its production possibilities), by then the necessary structural transformations would have taken place to ensure self-sustaining economic development.

The unspecified 'exogenous event' that initiated this chain of development could very well be a CU. To appreciate the potential catalytic function of the CU, it is worth bearing in mind that the formation of a CU causes a quantum increase in market size (beyond Z^*, by assumption) which sets in motion the forces that increase both demand and production, the one responding to the growth in the other in a circular dynamic. Clearly, the larger the CU, the larger the initial increase in market size, hence the larger the induced increases in external economies, output growth rates, per capita income and demand, etc. Thus a larger feedback process requires the formation of a CU with as many members as is geographically, economically and politically feasible.

We would conclude, then, that contrary to the neo-classical argument, there are strong indications, at least in theory, that SSA can pursue regional economic integration as a strategy for structural transformation, and to provide a long-term solution to its debt and development crises. But this, to be sustainable, must have a complementary political structure that gives all classes of citizens a real stake in the economy and the development project. This corollary political restructuring for this new culture of development is discussed next.

6.3 The New Politics of the New Culture

Much of our analysis of Africa's debt-and-development crisis hinges on (1) the structure and dynamics of Africa's interaction with the rest of the world; (2) the structure and dynamics of the domestic African economy proper; and (3) the structure and dynamics of governance and political participation in Africa. The new culture of development envisaged here thus focusses on these three dimensions of the problem.

It is important, in this regard, to detail those aspects of the crisis that are within the jurisdiction and control, by and large, of the African countries, and specify lines of policy that they can independently pursue to make the necessary adjustments. We began with the domestic, regional and international economic space; we move now to the political.

As we saw in Chapter Two, formal political practice in post-colonial Africa takes place within the same overly centralized structures of governance bequeathed by the colonialists. It has taken on some variation of form, if not content, across the continent, reflecting more historical and personality differences than ideological or regional ones. But the state, usually headed by a strong personality, dominates political practice across the continent, defining nearly completely the extent of formal participation by the broader populace in policy debates and decision-making. This is true for both civilian and military governments, as it is for the synchretic part-military/part-civil administrations that now dot the continent. It is equally true for the nominally capitalist as well as the 'socialist' regimes.

Many non-African students of African politics have tended, on account of this, to confuse the *overt* forms of political structuration with the *totality* of political practice and, especially, of political participation by the populace. Thus one dominant theme of Western studies of post-colonial African politics is that it is characterized by the singular absence of mass-participatory structures[46]; that, by implication, African populations are a passive, politically unsophisticated, uninvolved peoples, on whom politics—such as it is—is practiced, often by an unelected government, and for whom real discourses about society and economy are either functionally non-existent, or heavily circumscribed, where allowed.[47]

The second dominant theme, elaborated somewhat in Chapter Two, is that, given the multiplicity of ethnic and other claims on the central polity, African states are 'soft' or weak states, particularly susceptible to the centrifugal forces tugging at them from both within and without, and in which the necessary practice of clientelist or patrimonial politics to hold the fissiparous elements together preempts participatory politics of any meaningful sort.[48]

We would argue, however, that whereas these may be true on the level of *formal* political discourse, the heavy demands made on African populations by developments in the international economy since the mid-1970s has induced a resurgence of non-formal and decentralized, but particularly effective, politics that strongly belies these beliefs. As in the realm of economics, there are two forms of political participation in contemporary Africa, the one formal, narrowly participatory and state-centred, the other informal (though not necessarily unstructured), broad-based and community-oriented. The bulk of political activity and popular participation takes place in this latter sphere, in much the same way that the bulk of national and personal income in SSA is generated in the informal economic sector. Thus what may be seen as "political non-participation" or "disengagement" really reflects the bankruptcy of *centralized*, formal politics in SSA. The real politics takes place where the populace's problems emerge, are defined and are solved, namely, at the community level. For this reason, the effects and effectiveness of non-formal politics are much more direct and palpable than those of the formal political discourse. Non-formal politics therefore tends to attract more participants than state-level politics, where and when it exists. But the actual reasons for its resurging poularity and effectiveness are, as we will soon see, more fundamental.

The recent proliferation of so-called grassroots 'non-governmental organizations' (NGOs) in Africa is not indicative of a liberalization of political activity in the same sense as the economic liberalization imposed from above. Indeed many of these organizations have been in some form of existence in one form or another for decades, sometimes even centuries. The recent attention being paid to them by analysts and policy makers alike reflects, rather, a belated acknowledgement and recognition of the power, effectiveness and delegitimating potential of non-formal politics. It may also indicate a tightening of the already-constricted political space that Africans chronically work within, for, as Chazan has argued, the extent of recorded participation in the two spheres of political activity may "[vacillate] according to circumstances, but in general...the aims, scope, intensity, and impact of non-formal participation are augmented as opportunities for legitimate (*sic*) political action decline."[49]

The new politics of the new culture of development we are advocating is in recognition of this fact of contemporary political life in sub-Saharan Africa, namely, that in immensely pluralistic countries where irredentist pressures are ever-present and are easily actuated, the centrality of voluntary, non-formal, community- or even ethnicity-based politics must be promoted to blunt the effects of the fissions in the body politic that have prevented any meaningful development from taking place at the macro- or national level. (We need a micro-level politics to achieve a macro-level economic development, as it were).

But, more importantly, such politics will successfully neutralize the site of the state as *the* prime economic prize to be captured at all costs, thereby thwarting also the felt necessity of resource distribution by holders of state power among clientelist networks to ensure their reproduction. As Diamond, Linz and Lipset have argued in a different but not unrelated context, an essential component of such democratizing politics is the active functionality of a broad spectrum of interests and interest-groups— groups founded on a variety of factors such as religion, region, ethnicity, class and occupation—*independently of the state*. Their most important democratizing role, especially in the context of a system of governance in which formal oppositional politics is either prohibited or is heavily circumscribed, is to push for the institutionalization of democratic procedures in the realm of formal politics. They do this through, for instance (1) the provision of fora for active pluralistic political participation; (2) the provision of political experience that helps groom future political leadership; and, (3) providing limits and checks, generally, on government power and prerogatives. "A pluralistic civil society featuring a network of vigorously organized groups, voluntary associations, and media independent of the state enhances the stability of a democracy."[50]

Structure and Practice in the New Politics

Participatory political practice, as we use it in this context, consists of all the purposive actions of individuals or groups to secure defined objectives, or facilitate the attainment of given goals, within the established political processes of a country or political entity. By this definition, contemporary *formal* politics in Africa is truly non-participatory, because single-party systems have, in the majority of countries, successfully usurped the entire political space, allowing little room within the formal structures extant for the advancement of particular, non-party interests.

But, by the same definition, political practice is alive and well in Africa, as the non-formal sector has been widely and successfully used to influence political outcomes at the centre, or to advance particularized interests of groups or individuals. Thus, the 'departicipation' in politics popularly observed is, as Chazan has observed, of a specific type: it refers to the absence of voluntary, formal participation in the structures of government extant, and to the absence of institutionalized channels for the upward-routing of popular opinion.[51] It does not, however, refer to voluntary political participation, in the broadest sense of the term, in *all* spheres of political endeavour.

The analytic myopia that leads students of African politics to regard non-formal political activity as not politics proper stems, in our view, from a number of cultural and intellectual biases. The first is that most Westerners still equate periodic elections and suffrage of any degree with political participation proper, if not democracy generally. Thus, in Africa, where the exercise of the franchise is wholly absent or irregular or uninstitutionalized, popular political participation is deemed non-existent or even impossible. We will, however, all do well to heed Valerie Bunce's caveat which, while noting the importance of competitive elections still asserts, in essence, that elections may be necessary but hardly sufficient for democracy. "Democratic elections", she writes, "are nice, but democratic *governance* is crucial."[52] (Emphasis added). Competitive elections, in other words, matter; but it is meaningful participation *as defined jointly by the government and citizenry* that counts.

Secondly, many analysts cannot see politics as taking place in any other sphere but the centre of the established polity, i.e. in the arena of the state. Thus community-level deliberations that appoint representative leadership, that adjudicates disputes, or that vests authority in traditional chieftaincy is seen as not properly political, or, as Chazan puts it in the quote above, as "legitimate political activity".

Thirdly, 'ethnic politics'—i.e. political processes not concerned primarily with the modern nation-state of which the particular ethnic group is a part, but rather with the narrow political interests of a group of people self-identified by some common criteria of language, culture or geographic origin—is deemed, often pejoratively, "tribal" and therefore sectarian, hence also not properly participatory. Yet, given the history and structure of cultural pluralism in these countries as expostulated in Chapter Two, a devolved mode of governance in which regional and ethnic groups have a fair degree of autonomy from the central state to further their particular interests becomes, in itself, a condition for, and a consolidation of, democracy in the nation. In the absence of democratic tendencies in the polity, particularized interest groups such as those based on ethnicity serve as a bulwark against the abuses of the central authority, and the training ground— often the only one available—for effective democratic leadership for some future date. "They are the first and best line of defence when the survival of democracy is threatened."[53]

It would seem, therefore, that an ethnocentricism of a most blinding sort underlies the Western bias towards that politics that takes place within the formal structures of the state; all others are, by inference, not 'legitimate' political practices worthy of note or serious analytical attention. Yet in SSA, non-formal participatory structures, in both urban and rural areas, have been the backbone of community interaction, politics and decision-making for centuries.

There are two identifiable types of political organization predating the colonial era which have survived, with modifications, to this day.[54] The first comprises voluntary organizations narrowly concerned with a particular set of parochial issues: crafts unions, market women's organizations, associations of traditional rulers, associations of herbalists and traditional healers, religious societies, revolving-credit organizations, youth organizations, etc. These are, in the main, 'interest-group' organizations whose members voluntarily bond together around their common interests, with open discussion of all issues, and a rotating leadership. They tend to be urban-based, though rural ones are not unknown, and have memberships cutting across ethnicity, age and class. Interest-group voluntary organizations of this sort are thus horizontally-structured, semi-formal or informal, democratic associations organized around well-defined interests or potential advantage.[55]

The second type of political association is an essentially ascriptive one. It consists of kinship organizations, ethnic organizations, 'home-town' associations, *'associations des origionnaires'* in Francophone West Africa, etc. These groups are normally distinguished by an ascriptive characteristic—ethnicity, kinship, geographical origin, and so on. They tend to be organized, more or less, along patterns of authority traditional to the members' customary practices, and coalesce mainly around a commonly-subscribed language, history, culture, or other such primordial ties. Participation and membership are still, nonetheless, voluntary, though there exists a greater degree of homogeneity than is found in the first type of voluntary association. Ascriptive associations also tend to be more vertically structured.

These structural differences notwithstanding, there are three areas of commonality between the two types of organization. First, involvement in either group is strictly voluntary and wholly participatory. Secondly, they both tend to be limited in their objectives; and thirdly, the unit of political activity always remains the group, never the individual. They both tend, in addition, to be geographically circumscribed in objective, politically circumscribed in activity, and quite insusceptible to the manipulations of central government. The unit, scope and dynamics of political activity differ, therefore, from those that obtain in the formal sector: the one is inherently and functionally participatory and democratic where the other is not. In this sense, non-formal, voluntary, political organizations are a simple outgrowth of the political culture of voluntarism and group action anchoring African social traditions and political practices, though their contemporary resurgence may have more to do with the effective proscription of meaningful political participation in the formal state sector than the staying power of traditional African politics as such.

These voluntary associations are, today, the only true outlets for mass-participatory, democratic politics on the African continent, the recent moves towards political liberalization and policy decentralization notwithstanding. In addition, they are very successful at providing for a substantial proportion of their constituencies' material and communal needs, especially in circumstances where governments and national political parties, despite the resources at their disposal, are unable or unwilling to provide them. For this reason of material gain alone, if for no other reason, it is not uncommon to find individuals belonging to one or more voluntary association of both types concurrently.[56]

We would argue that, in the new development climate being advocated here, given the sheer numbers and effectiveness of non-formal associations across the continent, central government should enable them—by providing the productive resources and the political space to, especially, those that are regionally-based—to facilitate community-specific, collectively-defined and -implemented developmental objectives and projects as dictated by their needs. This devolution of power, and the decentralization of policy-making that is concomitant with it, would ensure (1) that central government ceases to be the prime political prize, given its monopolization of resources, that groups and individuals vie for; (2) that the intended recipients of the development projects can define their own needs and capabilities, including technological limits; (3) that there is broad-based, uncoerced, mass participation in the making of decisions that affect the daily lives of the citizenry; and (4) that leadership can be more immediately held responsible for its actions, given its proximity to the community. Central government will, consequently, limit itself to providing broad oversight, support services, and institutional accountability for these organizations; to providing those public goods and services that only government can efficiently provide; and, in a general Hobbesian sense, to maintaining the democratically-defined rules by which the political game is played. This will reduce the necessity for favouritism, ethnicity-based allocational biases, and the skewing of developmental objectives along rural/urban or ethnicity/ regional lines.

But one reason why the devolution of the state's decision-making powers is particularly germane at this time is that, as Chazan observes, there has been a marked change, since the onset of the various African crises in the mid-1970s, in addition to the growth in their numbers and membership, in the functions and objectives of many voluntary associations. They have become more overtly political, struggling directly with central government for the material needs of their members. Thus, because they are concerned, for example, to provide scarce goods and welfare services for their membership, these associations have become adept fundraisers, and are now capable of providing rather extensive social services, food and, especially, basic health care to their members with a consistency and efficiency that government has not had. Indeed ability to deliver welfare services, and even large-scale development projects, has become a most attractive asset, and associations are growing in direct relationship to the resources they are able to command, control and distribute. Increasingly, therefore, and especially in West Africa, these associations are commanding a substantial proportion of non-governmental resources.[57]

The second rationale for shifting resources to them relates to their internal organizational participatory practices: they provide much-needed outlets for small-scale, unregulated, political discussion and meaningful political inclusion that are not available at the abstract level of the state. Thus they are real islands of democracy which should be nurtured and encouraged, not suppressed and undermined. Leadership in these associations, and changes in leadership, unlike at the national level, occur by popular acclamation. Constitutional guidelines and by-laws provide for orderly transitions in a manner rarely seen at the central state level; and, indeed, a regular turnover of leadership is the norm.[58] There is also a well-entrenched tradition of reciprocal relations and obligations between leadership and general membership, such that decision-making is, more often than not, consultative, discursive, and collective, and rarely capricious, personality-based or -driven, or by executive pronouncement. Thus non-formal structures not only allow for political participation on a broad scale, they also enable substantive interchange, the influencing of decisions by ordinary people (and hence the empowerment of nominally powerless citizens), and could easily have provided the institutional checks against those hegemonic forces in African society whose conduct deepened and extended the debt/development crises through the 1980s.

The most profound shift in their activities in the past decade-and-a-half, however, has been in the area of political action at the national level in furtherance of members' social objectives. Increasingly, they are more openly representing distinct constituents' demands on central government, and attempting to influence policy decisions that touch these demands.[59] Thus their activities appear to be shifting, however tentatively, away from narrow, interest-group politics towards broader policy issues at the centre, with more profound implications for society, governance and the democratizing process at large.

This shift has brought to the fore a novel character of these associations: they are becoming vigilant monitors of the activities and decisions of the political centre, an activity indispensable to the completion of their new mission of direct advocacy and oversight. They are thus increasingly becoming adept at using radio, audio-tapes and other communications media and techniques to forge informal networks for information-gathering and -dissemination to facilitate their new and emerging tasks.[60] This expansion of their area of poliitical activity has been accompanied by an increase in the intensity of all their activities: more direct 'lobbying' of individual policy makers, petitioning of government decisions, strikes and demonstrations, etc., are now all seen as equally viable tactics of political struggle in a way that they never were before. Even violence as a means of political participation, in the Fanonian sense, is no longer the sole province of student groups. A motley slew of interest-groups, from market women to trade unions to professionals' associations, engage in it when it suits their purposes.

These three new dimensions in which voluntary associations are being transformed—bold movement towards specific struggles at the centre, broadening the area of focus of their activites, and deepening the intensity of their engagements—are importantly interrelated. Clearly, the ability to satisfy members' basic needs and successfully represent their interests with government could lead to further expansion of membership rolls, and hence an improved position of political bargaining-power against government. Within the association, this may encourage even greater participation as expectations are raised with the first few real successful campaigns.

Thus what were once largely benign, narrow-interest organizations have been transformed, since the crisis of the late 1970s that openly politicized their activities, into formidable pressure groups on government. Mass participatory, non-formal politics is providing the decentralized opposition and systemic checks that are denied formally at the centre, and is growing in direct proportion as governments' willingness to disallow formal oppositional politics, or their inability to provide a thriving socio-economic environment. This would appear to bear out Cohen's prediction that "great contrasts in political and socioeconomic opportunities for individuals and groups amidst a general condition of scarcity may stimulate new forms of political action" in sub-Saharan Africa.[61] But Africans may well be gravitating towards these groups in greater numbers for reasons of familiarity, proven effectiveness, general political efficacy, and lack of options.

Whatever the reasons for this current resurgence and intensification of non-formal associational politics in Africa, its focus still remains primarily protest politics, and only secondarily does it focus on constructive, system-reconstitutive activity. Still, these organizations' effectiveness in making real gains cannot be discounted, as their activities, unlike those of formal political parties, tend to be more instrumental than symbolic, and therefore effective in delivering the narrowly-defined objective of each struggle. And, with a measure of active governmental promotion and encouragement, it would only be a matter of time before they concern themselves with reconstitutive political activity proper.

It is for these, and similar, reasons that we advocate decentralization of political activity as a key component of the new culture of development we have proposed as a solution for the debt/developent crises in Africa. The transfer of responsibility from the central state to independent or semi-autonomous entities in the various regions of a country, be they local governments, ethnic associations and other non-governmental organizations, or even production units such as state farms and private firms, will go a long way towards blunting some of the more substantive irrationalities of economics and politics that are seen in the centralized state, and that intermittently lead to developmental crises of all sorts. It will help contain the ethnicity-based irredentism that creates structural instability, and help curb the need for the clietelist development strategies that are deployed by incumbent governments to maintain a chimeral sense of the citizenry's meaningful participation in the political process or, indeed, to postpone the inevitable reforms that will produce systemic soundness and social stability. People who are allowed free political space are often less reluctant to occupy open economic space as well (although a more open economic climate would also, ineluctably, lead to demands for political opening as well, as rising expectations are activated). Whichever option Africa chooses to exercise first, it would be, at last, partially, though mercifully, on its way to finding some coherent solutions to its external debt and internal development crises.

Notes

1. See H. Brewster and C.Y. Thomas, Aspects of the Theory of Economic Integration, **Journal of Common Market Studies**, Vol. III, No. 2 (Dec. 1969), pp. 110-132.
2. See John Roemer, **Free To Lose: An Introduction to Marxist Economic Philosophy** (Cambridge, MA.: Harvard Univ. Press, 1988); and his **A General Theory of Exploitation and Class** (Cambridge, MA.: Harvard Univ. Press, 1982).
3. See, for instance, O'Cleireacain, op. cit., ch. 10; and Nafziger, op. cit., ch. 8 and 9.
4. See Joshua Greene, **The External Debt Problem of Sub-Saharan Africa** (Washington, D.C.: IMF Staff Working Paper WP/89/23, 1989), p. 3.
5. Congdon, op. cit., p. 157.
6. Ibid.
7. U.N., **Financing Africa's Recovery** (N.Y.: May, 1988).
8. W. Max Corden, **An International Debt Facility** (Washington, D.C.: IMF Working Paper WP/88/16, 1988).
9. See World Bank, **Developing Country Debt: Implementing the Concensus**, pp. xix-xx.
10. Nafziger, op. cit., p. 186.
11. **New York Times**, June 14, 1989.
12. **Akasanoma** (London: Dec. 18, 1989), p. 2.
13. Ibid., citing the *'Caisse Centrale de Cooperation Economique'*, the French foreign-aid agency.
14. Nafziger, op. cit., p. 186-7.
15. **West Africa** (London: Dec. 18-24, 1989), p. 2117.
16. See William Cline, **International Debt: Systemic Risk and Policy Response** (Cambridge, MA.: MIT Press, 1984), ch. 4; and Jeffery Sachs, Conditionality, Debt Relief, and the Developing Country Debt Crisis, in J. Sachs, ed., **Developing Country Debt and the World Economy** (Chicago: Univ. of Chicago Press, 1989), p. 279.
17. The eleven countries that had been servicing their loans were Botswana, Burundi, Djibouti, Ethiopia, Kenya, Lesotho, Mauritius, Rwanda, Seychelles, Swaziland and Zimbabwe.
18. Some of the more telling examples of repudiation or default include: Edward III's default in the fourteenth century that brought down the Bardi and Peruzzi banks of Florence; Edward IV's a century later, that ruined the de Medicis; Argentina's insolvency of 1890 that nearly bankrupted Baring's of London; Portugal's defaults in the same year; Turkey's bankruptcy of 1876; and default by Cuba and Ghana in the 1960s. For detailed discussion of these and similar repudiations or

defaults, see the following: J. Makin, op. cit., ch. 2; H. Feis, op. cit., pp. 18-20 and p. 244; C. Diaz-Alejandro, **Stories of the 1930s for the 1980s**, in P. Armella et.al., eds., op. cit., pp. 5-35; and A. Kaletsky, **The Costs of Default** (N.Y.: Priority Press, 1985), ch. 3-7.

19. Graham Bird, Debt Swapping in Developing Countries: A Preliminary Investigation, **Journal of Development Studies**, Vol. 24, No.3 (April 1988), p. 293 ff. For the mechanics of debt swapping, see World Bank, **World Development Report 1987** (Washington, D.C.: Feb. 1987), pp. xxxii-xxxiv.

20. See World Bank, **Developing Country Debt**, p. xxxiii.

21. Countries with larger commercial debts, proportionately, than the African average include Nigeria, Côte d'Ivoire, Zaire, Gabon and Cameroon.

22. **West Africa**, (London: Nov. 6-12, 1989), p. 1861.

23. This author's personal conversation with a high government official of the Ministry of Finance and Economic Planning, Accra, Ghana, Dec. 1989, who insisted on anonymity.

24. See Economic Commission for Africa, **African Alternative Framework**, ch. 5, pp. 38-46.

25. See Jacob Viner, **The Customs Union Issue** (N.Y.: Oxford Univ. Press, 1950); and R.G. Lipsey, The Theory of Customs Unions: A General Theory, **Economic Journal**, No. 70 (Sept. 1960), pp. 496-513.

26. Viner defines 'trade creation' as the shift in trade, due to the formation of an integrated regional economy, from a high-cost source outside the integrated region to a low-cost one inside it. 'Trade diversion' is the shift in supply sources from a low-cost one outside of the union to a high-cost one within it. If there is more trade diversion than creation within the union, the net effect of the regionalization of the economy on global welfare is negative.

27. See Viner, op. cit., and Lipsey, op. cit. See, also, W.A. Axline, Underdevelopment, Dependence and Integration: The Politics of Regionalism in the Third World, **International Organization**, Vol. 3 (Winter 1977), p. 1 ff.; and J. de Melo and A. Panagariya, **The New Regionalism in Trade Policy** (Washington, D.C.: World Bank, Centre for Economic Policy Research, 1992), pp. 12-24.

28. For informative discussions of Third World critiques of neo-classical integration (especially Customs Union) theory, see: I. Abdala, Economic Integration and Third World Collective Self-Reliance, **Third World Forum**, Occasional Paper No. 4 (1979), p. 10 ff.; J.W. Sloan, The Strategy of Developmental Regionalism: Benefits, Distribution, Obstacles and Capacities, **Journal of Common Market Studies**, Vol. 10, No. 2 (Dec. 1971), p. 142 ff.; S. Olofin, ECOWAS and the Lome Convention: An Experiment in Complementary or Conflicting CU Arrangements?, **Journal of Common Market Studies**, Vol. 16, No. 1 (Sept. 1977), pp.

53-72; H.M.A. Onitiri, Towards a West African Economic Community, **Nigerian Journal of Economic and Social Studies**, Vol. 5, No. 1 (March 1963), p. 23 ff.; H. Brewster and C.Y. Thomas, op. cit.; G.C. Abangwu, A Systems Approach to Regional Integration in West Africa, **Journal of Common Market Studies**, Vol. XIII, Nos. 1 and 2 (1975); S.K.B. Asante, **The Political Economy of Regionalism in Africa** (N.Y.: Praeger, 1986); and A.M. El-Agraa, **The Theory and Measurement of International Economic Integration** (N.Y.: St. Martin's Press, 1989).

29. In SSA alone, there have been no fewer than twelve such integrationist experiments since 1955, the most 'successful' ones to date being the Economic Community of West African States (ECOWAS), the East African Community, the *Union des Etats d'Afrique Centrale* (UDEAC), the Southern African Development Coordination Council (SADCC), the *Communauté des Etats de l'Afrique de l'Ouest* (CEAO), the Preferential Trade Area for Eastern and Southern Africa, and the *Union Monétaire Ouest Afrique* (UMOA). In South America the Andean Pact and the Latin American Free Trade Area (LAFTA) dominated economic development rhetoric in the 1960s and 1970s, in much the same way that the Central American Common Market dominated development aspirations in that region in the 1960s. The Caribbean Community and Common Market (CARICOM) is, today, an important aspect of Caribbean development strategy. And in Asia, the Association of East Asian Nations (ASEAN) has been in operation, with varying degrees of success, since 1967.

30. The term 'static effects' refers to the analytical results obtained by comparing two states of equilibria for their allocative efficiency, the one before, and the other after the formation of the regional economic system.

31. 'Dynamic effects' refer to all the factors that, collectively and in a sequentially interactive manner, influence the rate of growth of the economies of member-countries as a result of regional integration. See Olofin, op. cit., and El-Agraa, op. cit.

32. Abdala, op. cit., p. 15.

33. See Bela Balassa, **The Theory of Economic Integration** (London: Allen Unwin, 1962).

34. See J. Tinbergen, **International Economic Integration** (Amsterdam: Elsevier, 1965).

35. See Peter Robson, **The Economics of International Integration** (London: G. Allen and Unwin, 1980), 'Introduction'.

36. See Lipsey, op. cit., p. 500.

37. T. Hitiris, **European Community Economics** (N.Y.: St. Martin's Press, 1991), p. 3.

38. de Melo and Panagariya, op. cit., p. 14-24.
39. See, for instance, Hitiris, op. cit., pp. 22-25.
40. Compare, for instance, the analysis of ch. 7 of H.G. Grubel, **International Economics** (Ontario: Richard Irwin, 1977) with that of Ch. 27.
41. See El-Agraa, op. cit.
42. This argument has a long and distinguished, though often unheeded, pedigree. See, for instance, D. Young, **International Economics** (Scranton: Intext Publishers, 1970); C.A. Cooper and B.F. Massell, Towards a General Theory of Customs Unions for Developing Countries, **Journal of Political Economy**, Vol. LXXI, No. 1 (Oct. 1965), pp. 212-219; M.E. Kreinin, On the Dynamic Effects of Customs Unions, **Journal of Political Economy**, Vol. LXXII, No. 2 (April 1964), pp. 193-195; and A.M. El-Agraa, op. cit.
43 See El-Agraa, op. cit., pp. 26-27.
44. It is true that if $g_K, g_L = 0$, g_I will be zero. But this is not necessary to obtain low (or no) growth in industrial output. If market size (demand) does not increase, there is no incentive for entrepreneurs to increase investment, capacity use, or employment. Hence K and L will likely not grow.
45. We have assumed, for convenience, that $\theta(0)$, $\theta'(0) = 0$. The linearity of the relationships, of course, follows from the simple forms chosen. There is, however, no reason why they cannot be non-linear.
46. See, for instance, Nelson Kasfir, Departicipation and Political Development in Black African Politics, **Studies in Comparative International Development**, Vol. 9, No. 3 (Fall, 1984); and Chazan, N., Mortimer, R., Ravenhill, J., and Rothchild, D., **Policy and Society in Contemporary Africa** (Boulder: Lynne Rienner, 1992), especially ch. 5-8.
47. See, for instance, K.W.J. Post and M. Vickers, **Structure and Conflict in Nigeria 1960-1966** (London: Heinemann, 1973), ch. 2.
48. See, as examples, M. Bratton, Beyond the State: Civil Society and Associational Life in Africa, **World Politics**, Vol. XLI, No. 3 (1989), pp. 407-430; and L. Diamond, Class Formation in the Swollen African State, **Journal of Modern African Studies**, Vol. 25, No. 4 (1987), pp. 567-590.
49. See Naomi Chazan's The Politics of Participation in Tropical Africa, **Comparative Politics**, Vol. 14, No. 2 (Jan. 1982), pp. 170 ff., on which some of these arguments are based.
50. T. Resler and R. Kanet, Democratization: The National-Subnational Linkage, **In Depth**, Vol. 3, No. 1 (Winter 1993), p. 15.
51. Chazan, op. cit., p. 171.

52. V. Bunce, Prospects for a Democratic Transition: The Soviet Union, in **Rackham Reports 1990-91** (Ann Arbor: Rackham School of Graduate Studies, Univ. of Michigan, 1991), p. 69.

53. C. Gershman, The United States and the World Democratic Revolution, in B. Roberts, ed., **The New Democracies: Global Change and U.S. Policy** (Washington, D.C.: Washington Quarterly, 1990), p. 11.

54. We are following Naomi Chazan's taxonomy and analyses closely here. See Chazan, **The Politics of Participation....**

55. See K. Little, **West African Urbanization: A Study of Voluntary Associations in Social Change** (Cambridge: Cambridge Univ. Press, 1977).

56. Margaret Peil highlights this multiple membership issue in her **Nigerian Politics: The People's View** (London: Cassel, 1976).

57. For illustrations, see J.Barkan, M. McNulty and M. Ayeni, 'Hometown' Voluntary Associations, Local Development, and the Emergence of Civil Society in Western Nigeria, **Journal of Modern African Studies**, Vol. 29, No. 3 (1991), pp. 457-480; P. Kwame, The Future of Chiefs in Ghana, **West Africa** (June 26-July 3, 1987); Peil, **Nigerian Politics...**; and O. Ola, Traditional Political Systems in a Modernizing Africa, **Présence Africaine**, Vol. 96 (1985), pp. 641-692.

58. There is an extensive literature on, for instance, women's voluntary organizations that provide excellent case studies of the normal workings of these organizations. See, as examples, K. Little, **African Women in the Towns** (Cambridge: Cambridge Univ. Press, 1975); M. Bratton, **Beyond the State...**; and M. Peil, **Nigerian Politics...** .

59. See D. Rothchild, Comparative Public Demand and Expectation Patterns: The Ghana Experience, **African Studies Review**, Vol. 22, No. 1 (April 1989), pp. 127-148.

60. In Côte d'Ivoire, the 'code name' for these informal communications and information networks is 'Radio Treichville', Treichville being a small village in Senegal which was a hotbed of clandestine, anti-colonial political activity in the 1950s. In parts of Anglophone West Africa, they are called 'bush telegraph'.

61. M. Cohen, **Urban Policy and Political Conflict in Africa: A Study of the Ivory Coast** (Chicago: Univ. of Chicago Press, 1974), p. 3.

Conclusion

We were concerned, in this work, to show the multifariousness of Africa's external debt crisis of the 1980s, and to delineate those lines of analysis and policy that provide a more comprehensive framework for addressing the problem than has hitherto been the case. Along the way we sought, also, to show the theoretical and policy bankruptcy of the resurgent orthodoxy that was/is being popularly advocated as the solution of choice for the crisis. More specifically, we attempted to show that Africa's debt crisis was not a crisis in the narrow sense in which it has traditionally been understood, namely, a problem of transfer bottlenecks brought about by temporary illiquidity in economies which, by implication, are otherwise structurally sound and potentially productive. To the contrary, we argued that problems of illiquidity in SSA were only symptomatic of a much deeper problem ensconced in the very structures of economy and politics in these countries and, beyond these, in the structure and mode of interaction between these economies and the larger global political economy.

The crisis arose, as we see it, from two distinct, though functionally interdependent, developments: (1) the fact that Africa's debt obligations were growing faster than its income or export earnings in the period under question and, consequently, (2) the fact that it could not sustain debt service when there were equally compelling competing claims on its resources for domestic economic development. The policy dilemma for African governments, therefore, was how to optimally satisfy both claims on their income without compromising unduly their long-term developmental goals, especially as income growth over the period was practically non-existent. Thus Africa's debt crisis, coming as it did from the structural economic inadequacies that have made low-income performance the norm on the continent, is more appropriately seen as a joint crisis of debt-and-structural-underdevelopment, in which the one is analytically meaningless outside of the other.

The popular definition we adopted at the beginning as a working hypothesis—that debt crises occur when a country's rate of income or export-revenue growth lags behind that of its debt—is, seen in this light, very superficial indeed, as it would not lead to addressing the question of whether or not the poor income performance may indicate a built-in (i.e. structural) pathology in the economy, or merely the presence of temporary bottlenecks that are easily remedied by marginal adjustments in economic policy. The neo-orthodox view of the debt crisis, which is wholly predicated on this definition, is thus particularly acontextual and ahistorical, and therefore subject to the same analytical criticism as neo-classical economic theory in general. We therefore redefined the crisis to reflect the international and domestic structural contexts that give it meaning, and to show that it depends, very importantly, on the economy's solvency, i.e. on the country's ability *and* willingness to pay its obligations.

Using case studies and other empirical evidence, we showed that the neo-orthodox prescription and prognosis following from its definition and analysis of the crisis, actually exacerbated the crisis in the immediate- and medium-term; that, in the African context, the external orientation of economic production and the peculiarities of domestic politics served to shore up those forces that created and/or reproduced the debt-underdevelopment crisis couple; that, given the policy dilemma mentioned above, in the 1980s' global economic climate of worsening trade terms, low commodity prices, tight credit markets and unstable currency exchange-rates, African governments were forced to meet one obligation at the expense of the other, and that the preference for meeting the external obligation at the cost of domestic social welfare and economic development may be roundly attributed to these adjustment policies of the new orthodoxy.

We showed, further, that the projected positive effects of the adjustment did not materialize to any appreciable degree, and where and if they did, they did so at very substantial economic, human and social cost. The new orthodoxy also unfairly imposed the costs of adjustment on the debtor-nations alone, disclaiming, in effect, the creditors' equal culpability in the creation of the crisis. And, finally, it tended to skew the internal social and economic costs of adjustment in favour of the wealthier and least vulnerable strata of African society.

We argued further that, until six years or so ago, the neo-orthodox analysis had outrightly discounted arguably the most effective short-term remedy for the crisis—debt forgiveness or repudiation—not on the strength of their economic inadequacy, but on the political grounds of them being "too extreme", on arguments of moral hazard, and on their supposed precedential effect on international lending. It had settled, rather, on the ineffective middle ground of debt rescheduling and restructuring, on debt-for-equity exchanges, on some measure of adjustment financing, on "structural adjustment', and the like.

In the same vein did the resurgent orthodoxy argue that the long-run, internal structural causes of the crisis were particularly susceptible to stringent *laissez-faire* policies that properly belong to another era and global economic circumstance. We showed, however, that in the uniqueness of Africa's economic structures, *laissez-faire*, where applied (e.g. in agriculture and trade) achieved few of the objectives expected, or, in what functionally amounts to the same thing, achieved them at politically and socially unacceptable cost. The professed transformative character of the free market thus never quite materialized in SSA. Indeed, evidence was presented to show that, in the developing world, transformation occurs precisely where and when governments *do not* allow naked market forces free reign over economic outcomes. South Korea, Taiwan and Singapore are prime examples of this.

Even more worrisome in the African case was the short shrift given by the new orthodoxy to the long-observed disruptive social and economic effects of unbridled market allocation, and therefore the tendency to crisis that inheres in *laissez-faire*. Africa was thus caught in a web of ideological intrigue, in which a blind celebration of the market was being imposed on it from the outside as *the* remedy for its debt-underdevelopment crisis, regardless of the structural realities on the ground. That the domestic economic impact of these policies was largely negative, and that they actually deepened the crisis in both the short and medium terms, therefore, should hardly be surprising.

We proposed, on the contrary, a system of analysis and set of policies aimed at eliminating the disjuncture between Africa's production structure and consumption needs, and that between its production and resource base, that underlie many of the causes of the poor income performance driving the crisis. In other words, since we saw the debt crisis as stemming primarily from structural disarticulation in the African economy, we advocated, as a long-term solution, the integration of the structures of the domestic economy via a purposive programme of balanced investment, to be extended regionally over time, as arguably the best way to achieve and sustain that balanced growth necessary to transform the economy and to prevent, in future, low income performance and the need for massive external debt acquisition.

Our proposed solution also stemmed from the argument that, to the extent that the immediate precipitatory factors of Africa's debt crisis were external in origin, a structural delinkage of modest proportions from the current international economy, done simultaneously with the integration of the individual economies, internally and regionally, will best succeed in generating the requisite developmental forces that will sustain growth. That Africa's policy makers were, in the mid-1980s, considering a move in that direction under the 1980 'Lagos Plan of Action', and the budding regional economic systems in West and Southern Africa, bear out the political efficacy of this strategy, and the accepted need, by African governments, to seek structural integration of the African economy as a first step towards the continent's long-term economic viability.

We argued, however, that given the many centrifugal forces tugging at African nations, such developments on the economic front will only succeed if sub-national interests are directly and formally involved in national decision-making processes. In other words, there has to be a commensurate political opening for the participation of citizens in the development of their own communities. Thus a new structure of politics was also called for that would seek the decentralization of both economic and political decision making, and that would free government to do what it does best—provide public goods, provide general policy directions for the attainment of social objectives, regulate economic and political activity to conform to the stated social goals, collect and redistribute productive resources, and generally enforce and adjudicate the rules of the development game.

Our advocacy of decentralization was based on empirical, practical and philosophical grounds. In the first place, non-formal political/ social organizations already provide the primary avenue for mass political and economic participation in Africa. They are established organizations with long traditions of participatory democracy and service delivery, and are widely accesible and generally effective.

Secondly, our position stems from the proposition that the people's control over their own productive capacity and the fruits of their efforts, including the surplus, is the true meaning of "public ownership of the means of production", and that it affords the most effective way of, not only thwarting the emergence of hegemonic, non-democratic institutions in society, but also ensuring the people's control, by and large, over their own economic and social destiny. In this regard, we are in full accordance with Roemer's contention that class-based oppression need not occur, in the classical Marxian sense, only at the point of production. It may also occur, more pervasively and therefore more treacherously, in the unequal distribution of property in the means of production, *and in the unequal access to, and control of, related resources, including political resources*—all of which, in contemporary Africa, favour the state at the expense of the peasantry, urban workers, and ethnic groups not represented in the ruling power structure.

Thirdly, decentralization of decision-making in the polity necessarily means that the state ceases to be the sole repository of productive resources, from which all largesse flows to political and ethnic clients it deems vital to its survival. The state thus ceases to be the prime political and economic prize that it currently is—the jewel in a system of spoils—and the source of much of the instability in society, as various groups constantly struggle among themselves to capture it for their own parochial ends.

We argued, in sum, that these transformations in African economic and political thinking and development practice will go a long way towards defining a new culture of development on the continent which, if properly realized, should blunt the more debilitating forces in the global economy that precipitate Africa's periodic economic crises. Table 7 provides a ready summary of these arguments.

TABLE 7
A Problem-Solution Grid for Africa's Debt-and-Development Crisis

SECTOR AND PROBLEM	NEO-ORTHODOX SOLUTION	PROPOSED STRUCTURALIST ALTERNATIVE
LOW-LEVEL OR NURKSIAN EQUILIBRIUM	Market allocation; foreign capital inflows	Decentralized market production
NON-DEVELOPMENTAL STATE	1) Weaken state by funding civic organizations instead. 2) Eliminate state's hold over micro-economic policies by getting it out of economic activities. 3) Multi-party politics.	Community-based, decentralized, participatory governance.
PRIMARY EXTERNAL ECONOMIC RELATIONS	Free trade	Regional economic integration; therefore restricted trade liberalization
IDEOLOGY	Neo-classical ('*laissez-faire*')	New Culture of Development

We, at the same time, see these proposals not as fully developed intellectual constructs, but as mere indicators of the possible direction that new research on African political economy should take. For instance, the practical problems inherent in decentralizing economic and political activity, while simultaneously using the central authority of the state to ensure the attainment of sectoral complementarity and balanced investment in the economy, are bound to be formidable. Even on the theoretical front, it will require major new thinking on

(1) how the proposed minimalist state would be structured so as to make it neither a political hegemon nor an ineffectual entity; (2) what the parameters of its social role would be; (3) how to foster the emergence of a true civil society that will be a comparable partner with the state in the development process; and, especially, (4) the mode of interaction between such a state and such a civil society.

The issue of regionalism also requires further study, especially in view of the fact that existing integration experiments in Africa have focussed inordinately on the mere expansion of markets, with very little concurrent thought given to the active promotion and expansion of complementary *production* structures and activities across the integrated region. It is as though, in some vulgar Keynesian sense, production is supposed to expand automatically, and in the proper mix, in response to market widening. In the end, it is precisely this skewed approach to integration, and lack of understanding of the supply inelasticities in African economies, that will lead to regional economic *dis*integration.

Thirdly, the issue of balanced investment and growth, in the Nurksian sense, is particularly ripe for further research. Many African countries are today feeling the adverse impact of the unbalanced investment policies of the past, which is already pushing them to a new thinking on the distribution of public-investment outlays. For instance, one of the largest, cumulative public-expenditure items in the first ten or fifteen years of Ghana's independence was education. Heavy investments were made across the country, but especially in rural areas, in school buildings and related infrastructure, in instructional materials, and in teacher training. Primary school education was made compulsory and free. Secondary education was a little more restricted, but mainly due to highly selective entrance examinations rather than government policy; but it was still widely and affordably available. Tertiary education at the three national universities was also free, and higher, post-graduate training abroad, when available, was either financed or subsidized by government.

By the mid-1970s when, in the wake of the 1973 oil-price shock and subsequent downturn in world economic activity, the Ghanaian economy, in which a smaller proportion of government spending had gone to build a productive capital base, started its long trek backwards, there was not sufficient economic and job growth to absorb these well- and expensively-trained graduates. Thus a lop-sided public investment strategy had expanded the human-capital base, but not the productive, non-human capital that would create the necessary jobs to absorb them. Ghana, therefore, became a net exporter of university graduates and other highly educated professionals. The Persian Gulf, other African countries with better economic and employment opportunities, western Europe and North America were the main beneficiaries of Ghana's loss. It has been only since 1985 that these education policies have come under critical review in an attempt to resolve the glaring imbalance between economic/job growth and human-capital formation.

Other African countries, which obtained their independence much later than Ghana, have taken their supply-side policy cue from the Ghanaian experience. Zimbabwe, for one, earlier in its independence, cited that experience as the reason for its slower expansion of manpower resources, and its relatively faster expansion of productive, growth-inducing, economic activity. However, political pressures from below very quickly brought this measured and well-advised approach to a stop and, since 1990, Zimbabwe, like Ghana in the late 1970s and 1980s, has been experiencing an increasing 'brain-drain' problem. Botswana, also, has been using its diamond-driven economic bonanza to spread government investment into other sectors to create vertically-integrated production activities—aquaculture, animal husbandry, agro-industry, light processing, etc.—also with the objective of ensuring a faster job-growth rate than labour-force growth. It has been, in this manner, also highly successful in insulating its economy against much of the instability in commodity prices, and against many of the other external shocks of the 1970s and '80s, such that Botswana, today, has one of the most consistently high economic performances in the world.

The joint crisis of debt and development in Africa, therefore, in spite of the gloomy pall that it has cast on Africa's economic prospects for the past decade-and-a-half, has presented us with the opportunity to *strategically re-think* many of the development issues that have only been addressed in an *ad hoc* fashion, usually in response to one or another crisis, over the past forty years or so. Unfortunately, the response of policy makers and analysts to the crisis can only be interpreted as taking the path of least resistance: applying a purist's, and therefore facile, version of liberal economic theory to the crisis, accepting uncritically the received orthodoxy's claim to universal answers for local problems, and its tantalizing promises of glory at the end of some murkily defined long-run. Yet if there is one bright spot in the sea of analytical and policy bankruptcy that has gripped the continent, its internal and external advisors, its well-wishers and detractors alike, it is that some, admittedly swimming against a strong intellectual tide, are striving valiantly to expose the false prophet of the new liberalism for what it really is, and are looking beyond the new orthodoxy for less facile but more genuine solutions for Africa's economic problems.

Bibliography

Abangwu, A.C. A Systems Approach to Regional Integration in West Africa. **Journal of Common Market Studies**. Vol. XIII, Nos. 1 & 2, 1975.

Abdala, I. Economic Integration and Third World Collective Self-Reliance. **Third World Forum**. Occasional Paper No. 4, 1979.

Aboyade, O. **Integrated Economics: A Study of Developing Economies**. London: Addison-Wesley, 1983.

Adedeji, A. Foreign Debt and Prospects for Growth in Africa During the 1980s. **Journal of Modern African Studies**. Vol. 23, No. 1, 1985. Pp. 53-74.

el-Agraa, A.M. **The Theory and Measurement of International Economic Integration**. N.Y.: St. Martin's Press, 1989.

Amin, S. **Accumulation on a World Scale, Vols. 1 & 2**. N.Y.: Monthly Review Press, 1974.

Amin, S. **Unequal Development**. N.Y.: Monthly Review Press, 1976.

Anderson, P. Roberto Unger and the Politics of Empowerment. **New Left Review**. No. 173, Jan.-Feb. 1989. Pp. 93-107.

Aronson, J.D., ed. **Debt and the Less Developed Countries**. Boulder: Westview Press, 1979.

Arrighi, G. and Saul, J. **Essays on the Political Economy of Africa**. N.Y.: Monthly Review Press, 1973.

Asante, S.K.B. **The Political Economy of Regionalism in Africa**. N.Y.: Praeger, 1986.

Bairoch, P. **The Economic Development of the Third World since 1900**. Berkeley: Univ. of California Press, 1975.

Baker, S. **An Introduction to International Economics**. N.Y.: Harcourt Brace Jovanovich, 1990.

Baran, P. **The Political Economy of Growth**. N.Y.: Monthly Review Press, 1968.

Bartlett, B. The State and the Market in sub-Saharan Africa. **World Development**. Vol. 12, No. 3, Sept. 1989. Pp. 293-314.

Barbone, L. and Rivera-Batiz, F. Foreign Capital and the Contractionary Impact of Currency Devaluation, with an Application to Jamaica. **Journal of Development Economics**. Vol. 26, 1987. Pp. 1-15.

Barkan, J., McNulty, M. and Ayeni, M. 'Hometown' Voluntary Associations, Local Development and the Emergence of Civil Society in Western Nigeria. **Journal of Modern African Studies**. Vol. 29, No. 3, 1991. Pp.

Basu, K. **The Less Developed Economy: A Critique of Contemporary Theory**. Oxford: Basil Blackwell, 1984.

Berg, A. **The Nutritional Factor: Its Role in National Development**. Washington, D.C.: World Bank, 1983.

Berg A. and Sachs, J. **The Debt Crisis: Structural Explanations of Country Performance**. NBER Working Paper No. 2607, June 1988.

Bhagwati, J.N. **Import Competition and Response**. Chicago: Univ. of Chicago Press, 1982.

Bhagwati, J.N. **International Trade: Selected Readings**. Cambridge: MIT Press, 1981.

Bird, G. Debt Swapping in Developing Countries: A Preliminary Investigation. **Journal of Development Studies**. Vol. 24, No. 3, April 1988. Pp. 293-309.

Block, F. **The Origins of International Economic Disorder**. Berkeley: Univ. of California Press, 1983.

Bluestone, B. and Harrison, B. **The Deindustrialization of America**. N.Y.: Basic Books, 1982.

Bond, M.E. Agricultural Response to Prices in sub-Saharan African Countries. **IMF Staff Papers**. Vol. XXX, Nos. 3-4, 1983.

Boyd, D. Hanging Separately: U.S. Deficits and Third World Adjustment. **TransAfrica Forum**. Summer, 1988. Pp. 41-48.

Bratton, M. Beyond the State: Civil Society and Associational Life in Africa. **World Politics**. Vol. XLI, No. 3, 1989. Pp. 407-430.

Brewster, H. and Thomas C.Y. Aspects of the Theory of Economic Integration. **Journal of Common Market Studies**. Vol. VIII, No. 2, 1969. Pp. 110-132.

Browne, R.S. The Debt Crisis: The Need for Collective Action. **TransAfrica Forum**. Spring, 1986. Pp. 9-20.

Callaghy, T. Africa's Debt Crisis. **Journal of International Affairs**. Vol. 38, No. 4, 1984.

Callaghy, T. **The State-Society Struggle: Zaire in Comparative Perspective**. N.Y.: Columbia Univ. Press, 1984.

Callaghy, T. External Actors and the Relative Autonomy of the Aristocracy in Zaire. **Journal of Commonwealth and Comparative Politics**. Vol. 21, No. 3, 1983. Pp. 55-72.

Campbell, B. amd Loxley, J., eds. **Structural Adjustment in Africa**. N.Y.: St. Martin's Press, 1989.

Cardoso, F.H. Dependence and Development in Latin America. **New Left Review**. July-Aug. 1972. Pp. 83-95.

Caves, R. and Jones, R. **World Trade and Payments**. Boston: Little, Brown and Co., 1981.

Charney, C. Political Power in the Neo-Colonial African States. **Review of African Political Economy**. Vol. 38, April 1987. Pp. 50-72.

Chazan, N. The Politics of Participation in Tropical Africa. **Comparative Politics**. Vol. 14, No. 2, Jan. 1982. Pp. 169-189.

Chazan, N., Mortimer, R., Ravenhill, J. and Rothchild, D. **Politics and Society in Contemporary Africa**. Boulder: Lynne Rienner, 1992).

Chenery, H. and Syrquin, M. **Patterns of Development, 1950-1970**. Washington, D.C.: World Bank, 1975.

Chiang, A.C. **Fundamental Methods of Mathematical Economics**. N.Y.: McGraw-Hill, 1974.

Chuta, E. and Sethuraman, S.V. **Rural Small-Scale Industries and Employment in Africa and Asia**. Geneva: ILO, 1984.

Clandon, M.P., ed. **World Debt Crisis: International Lending on Trial**. Cambridge, MA.: Ballinger Publishing, 1986.

Clapham, C. **Private Patronage and Public Power**. London: Pinter Printers, 1982.

Clark, N. and Juma, C. **Long-Run Economics: An Evolutionary Approach to Economic Growth**. London: Pinter Printers, 1987.

Cline, W. **Policy Alternatives for a New International Economic Order**. N.Y.: Praeger, 1979.

Cline, W. **International Debt: Systemic Risk and Policy Response**. Washington, D.C.: Institute of International Economics, 1983.

Colman, D. and Nixson, F. **Economics of Change in Less Developed Countries**. N.Y.: John Wiley, 1978.

Commander, S., ed. **Structural Adjustment and Agriculture: Theory and Practice in Africa and Latin America**. London: Overseas Development Institute, 1989.

Congdon, T. **The Debt Threat: The Dangers of High Real Interest Rates for the World Economy**. Oxford: Basil Blackwell, 1988.

Cooper, C.A. and Massell, B.F. Towards a General Theory of Customs Unions for Developing Countries. **Journal of Political Economy**. Vol. LXXI, No. 1, October 1965.

Cooper, R.N. **Economic Policy in an Interdependent World: Essays in World Economics**. Cambridge, MA.: MIT Press, 1986.

Corbridge, S. The Assymetry of Interdependence: The U.S. and the Geopolitics of International Financial relations. **Studies in Comparative International Development**. Vol. XXII, No. 1, Spring 1988. Pp. 3-29.

Corden, W.M. **Protection, Growth and Trade**. Oxford: Basil Blackwell, 1985.

Corden, W.M. Macroeconomic Adjustment in Developing Countries. **World Bank Research Observer**. Vol. 4, No. 1, Jan. 1989. Pp. 52-64.

Cornia, G.A., Jolly, R. and Stewart, F., eds. **Adjustment with a Human Face: Protecting the Vulnerable and Promoting Growth, Vol. 1 and 2**. Oxford: Clarendon Press, 1987.

Damachi, U.G., Roth, G. and Ali Taha, A-R. **Development Paths in Africa and China**. Boulder: Westview Press, 1976.

Debreu, G. **Theory of Value**. N.Y.: John Wiley, 1959.

Delamaide, D. **Debt Shock: The Full Story of the World Debt Crisis**. N.Y.: Doubleday, 1984.

Diamond, L. Class Formation in the Swollen African State. **Journal of Modern African Studies**. Vol. 25, No. 4, 1987.

Diaz-Alejandro, C. Latin American Debt: I Don't Think We Are in Kansas Anymore. **Brookings Papers on Economic Activity**. Vol. 2, 1984. Pp. 335-403.

Dornbusch, R. Policy and Performance Links Between LDC Debtors and Industrial Nations. **Brookings Papers on Economic Activity**. Vol. 2, 1985. Pp. 303-368.

Dornbusch, R. **Open Economy Macroeconomics**. N.Y.: Basic Books, 1980.

Eaton, J. and Gersovitz, M. **Poor Country Borrowing in Private Financial Markets and the Repudiation Issue**. Princeton, N.J.: International Finance Section, Princeton Univ. 1983.

Economist Intelligence Unit. **Country Profile, 1986-87: Zaire, Rwanda and Burundi, Vol. 1**. London: The Economist, 1987.

Economist Intelligence Unit. **Quarterly Economic Review of Zaire, Rwanda and Burundi, Vol. 3**. London: The Economist, 1983.

Economist Intelligence Unit. **Quarterly Economic Review of Zaire, Rwanda and Burundi, Vol. 2**. London: The Economist, 1985.

Economist Intelligence Unit. **Zaire to the 1990s: Will Retrenchment Work?**. Special Report 227 by Gregory Kronsten. London: The Economist, July 1985.

Edwards, S. Exchange Rate Misallignment in Developing Countries: A Preliminary Investigation. **World Bank Research Observer**. Vol. 4, No. 1, Jan. 1989. Pp. 3-21.

Ekeh, P. Developoment Theory and the African Predicament. **Africa Development**. Vol. XI, No. 4, 1986. Pp. 1-17.

Fatton, R. **State and Civil Society in Africa**. Paper presented at the 32nd. Annual Meeting of the African Studies Association. Atlanta, GA., Nov. 1989.

Fearon, J. International Financial Institutions and Economic Policy Reform in Africa. **Journal of Modern African Studies**. Vol. 25, No. 3, 1987. Pp. 403-433.

Feinberg, R. and Kallab, V. **Adjustment Crisis in the Third World**. New Brunswick: Transaction Books, 1984.

Flemming, J.M. **External Economies and the Doctrine of Balanced Growth**. Economic Journal. Vol. 65, 1955.

Frank, A.G. **Dependent Accumulation and Underdevelopment**. N.Y.: Monthly Review Press, 1979.

Friedman, B. **Day of Reckoning: The Consequences of American Economic Policy Under Ronald Reagan**. N.Y.: Random House, 1988.

Fry, M.J. **Money, Interest and Banking in Economic Development**. Baltimore: The Johns Hopkins Univ. Press, 1988.

Gauher, A. **Regional Integration: The Latin American Experience**. London: Third World Foundation, 1985.

George, S. **A Fate Worse than Debt: The World Financial Crisis and the Poor**. N.Y.: Grove Press, 1988.

Gerschenkron, A. **Economic Backwardnes on Historical Perspective**. N.Y.: Praeger, 1965.

Good, K. Debt and the One-Party State in Zambia. **Journal of Modern African Studies**. Vol. 27, No. 2, 1989. Pp. 297-313.

Greene, J. **The External Debt Problem of Sub-Saharan Africa**. Washington, D.C.: IMF Staff Working Papers WP/89/23, 1989.

Grosse, R. Resolving Latin America's Transfer Problem. **World Economy**. Vol. 11, No. 3, Sept. 1988. Pp. 417-436.

Grubel, H. **The International Monetary System**. N.Y.: Penguin Press, 1984.

Grubel, H. **International Economics**. Homewood, Ill.: Richard D. Unwin, 1977.

Gutkind, P. and Wallerstein, I. **The Political Economy of Contemporary Africa**. Beverley Hills: Sage Publications, 1976.

Guttentag, J. and Herring, R. **The Lender-of-Last-Resort Function in An International Context**. Princeton, N.J.: International Finance Section, Princeton Univ., 1983.

Hafkin, N. and Bay, E. **Women in Africa: Studies in Social and Economic Change**. Palo Alto: Stanford Univ. Press, 1976.

Hassan, J. **Agricultural Development and Pricing Policy**. Unpublished M.A. Thesis. Lusaka: Univ. of Zambia, 1986.

ul-Haq, M. Beyond the Slogan of South-South Cooperation. **World Development**. Vol. 8, 1980. Pp. 743-751.

Hewitt, A. The Lome Convention: Entering A Second Decade. **Journal of Common Market Studies**. Vol. XXIII, No. 2, Dec. 1984. Pp. 95-115.

Hirschman, A.O. **Essays in Trespassing: Economics to Politics and Beyond**. N.Y.: Cambridge Univ. Press, 1981.

Hutchful, E. International Debt Renegotiation: Ghana's Experiences. **Africa Development**. Vol. IX, No. 2, 1984. Pp. 5-26.

International Development Research Council (IDRC). **The Zambian Economy: Problems and Prospects**. Ottawa, Canada: 1985.

Institute for International Economics. **Policy Analyses in International Economics, Vol. 14**. Wsahington, D.C.: 1987.

Jackson, R.H. and Rosberg, C.G. **Personal Rule in Black Africa: Prince, Aristocrat, Prophet, Tyrant**. Los Angeles: Univ. of California Press, 1982.

Johnson, H.G. **International Trade and Economic Growth**. London: Allen and Unwin, 1958.

Journal of Development Planning. No. 16, 1985. Special Issue on 'The Debt Problem: Acute and Chronic Aspects'.

Journal of Development Studies. Vol. 21, No. 3, April 1985. Special Issue on 'Industrialization in the Third World'.

Kahler, M. **The Politics of International Debt**. Ithaca: Cornell Univ. Press, 1986.

Kaldor, N. Devaluation and Adjustment in Developing Countries. **Finance and Development**. Washington, D.C.: June, 1983. Pp. 28-41.

Kaldor, N. Mrs. Robinson's Economics of Imperfect Competition. **Economica**. Vol. 1, 1934.

Kaletsky, A. **The Costs of Default**. N.Y.: Priority Press, 1985.

Kasfir, N. Departicipation and Political Development in Black African Politics. **Studies in Comparative International Development**. Vol. 9, No. 3, Fall 1984.

Kaufmann, H. **Interest Rates, the Markets and the New Financial World**. N.Y.: Times Books, 1986.

Keynes, J.M. **The General Theory of Employment, Interest and Money**. N.Y.: HBJ, 1964.

Keynes, J.M. The German Transfer Problem. **Economic Journal**. March 1929.

Keynes, J.M. **The Economic Consequences of the Peace**. London: Macmillan, 1919.

Kharas, H. and Levinsohn, J. LDC Savings Rates and Debt Crises. **World Development**. Vol. 16, No. 7, 1988. Pp. 779-786.

Kindleberger, C. **International Capital Movements**. Cambridge: Cambridge Univ. Press, 1987.

Kindleberger, C. **The World in Depression, 1929-1939**. Berkeley: Univ. of California Press, 1973.

Kindleberger, C. **Manias, Panics and Crashes**. N.Y.: Basic Books, 1978.

Kindleberger, C. and Laffargue, J.P., eds. **Financial Crisis: Theory, History and Policy**. Cambridge: Cambridge Univ. Press, 1982.

Korner, P., Maass, G., Siebold, T. and Tetzlaff, R. **The IMF and the Debt Crisis: A Guide to the Third World's Dilemmas**. London: Zed Books, 1986.

Krafona, K. **Peoplecracy: A New Vision of Democracy for the New Nations of Africa**. London: AfroWorld Publishing, 1985.

Kreinin, M.E. On the Dynamic Effects of Customs Unions. **Journal of Political Economy**. Vol. LXII, No. 2, April 1964.

Krugman, P. **Has the Adjusiment Process Worked?** Washington, D.C.: Institute of International Economics, 1991.

Krumm, K. **The External Debt of Sub-Saharan Africa**. World Bank Staff Working Paper No. 741. Washington, D.C.: World Bank, 1985.

Kwarteng, C. Difficulties in Regional Economic Integration: The Case of ECOWAS. **TransAfrica Forum**. Vol. 5, No. 2, Winter 1988. Pp. 17-25.

Landreth, H. **History of Economic Theory: Scope, Method and Content**. Boston: Houghton Mifflin, 1976.

Landsberg, M. Export-Led Industrialization in the Third World: Manufacturing Imperialism. **Review of Radical Political Economics**. Vol. 11, No. 4, Winter 1979. Pp. 50-63.

Leibenstein, H. **Economic Backwardness and Economic Growth**. N.Y.: John Wiley, 1957.

Leijonhufvud, A. **On Keynesian Economics and the Economics of Keynes**. N.Y.: Oxford Univ. Press, 1968.

Leo, C. **Land and Class in Kenya**. Toronto: Univ. of Toronto Press, 1984.

Lever, H. and Huhne, C. **Debt and Danger: The World Financial Crisis**. Hammondsworth: Penguin, 1985.

Lewis, W.A. **The Evolution of the International Economic Order**. Princeton: Princeton Univ. Press, 1978.

Leys, C. **Underdevelopment in Kenya**. Berkeley: Univ. of California Press, 1975.

Liepietz, A. **The Enchanted World: Inflation, Credit and the World Crisis**. London: Verso, 1985.

Lindert, P. and Morton, P. **How Sovereign Debt Has Worked**. UC-Davis Institute of Governmental Affairs Research Program in Applied Macroeconomics and Macro Policy. Working Paper No. 45. Aug. 1987.

Lipson, C. **Standing Guard: Protecting Foreign Capital in the Nineteenth and Twentieth Centuries**. Berkeley: Univ. of California Press, 1985.

Little, K. **West African Urbanization: A Study of Voluntary Associations in Social Change**. Cambridge: Cambridge Univ. Press, 1977.

Lizondo, J.S. Exchange Rate Differentials and Balance-of-Payments Under Dual Exchange Markets. **Journal of Development Economics**. Vol. 26, 1987. Pp. 37-53.

Lombardi, R. **The Debt Trap: Rethinking the Logic of Development**. N.Y.: Praeger, 1985.

Love, J. Export Instability: An Alternative Analysis of the Causes. **Journal of Development Studies**. Vol. 21, No. 2, Jan. 1985. Pp. 243-252.

Mabbs-Zeno, C. and Krissoff, B. **Tropical Beverages in the GATT**. U.S. Dept. of Agriculture, Economic Research Service. Dec. 1989.

Makgetla, N.S. Theoretical and Practical Implications of IMF Conditionality in Zambia. **Journal of Modern African Studies**. Vol. 24, No. 3, 1986. Pp. 395-422.

Makin, J. **The Global Debt Crisis**. N.Y.: Basic Books, 1984.

Massell, B. Export Instability and Economic Structure. **American Economic Review**, Vol. LX, No. 4, 1970. Pp. 618-630.

Mathur, A. Balanced vs. Unbalanced Growth: A Reconciliatory View. **Oxford Economic Papers**. Vol. 18, 1966.

Marsden, K. Why Asia Boomed and Africa Busted. **Wall Street Journal**. June 3, 1985.

Meier, G. **Leading Issues in Economic Development**. London: Oxford Univ. Press, 1970.

Meller, P. and Solimano, A. A Macro Model for a Small Open Economy Facing a Binding External Constraint (Chile). **Journal of Development Economics**. Vol. 26, 1987. Pp. 25-35.

de Melo, J. and Panagariya, A. **The New Regionalism in Trade Policy**. Washington, D.C.: World Bank, Center for Economic Policy Research, 1992.

Milliband, R. **The State in Capitalist Society**. N.Y.: Basic Books, 1969.

Minsky, H. **Can It Happen Again: Essays on Instability and Crisis**. Armonk, N.Y.: M.E. Sharpe, 1982.

Moffitt, M. **The World's Economy: International Banking from Bretton Woods to the Brink of Insolvency**. N.Y.: Simon and Schuster, 1983.

Monthly Review. Vol. 35, No. 8, Jan. 1984. Pp. 1-10. Review of the Month: 'The Two Faces of Third World Debt'.

Moore, W.E. **World Modernization: The Limits of Convergence**. N.Y.: Elsevier-Holland, 1979.

Morgan Guaranty. **World Financial Markets**. Feb. 1986, Sept. 1986 and June-July 1987 issues.

Mosley, P., Harrigan, J. and Toye, J. **Aid and Power: The World Bank and Policy-based Lending, Vol. 1**. London: Routledge, 1991.

Nafziger, E.W. **The Debt Crisis in Africa**. Baltimore: The Johns Hopkins Press, 1993.

Nelson, R.R. A Theory of the Low-Level Equilibrium Trap in Underdeveloped Economies. **American Economic Review**. Vol. 46, 1956. Pp. 412-422.

Nove, A. **The Economics of Feasible Socialism**. London: George Allen and Unwin, 1983.

Nunnenkamp, P. **The International Debt Crisis of the Third World: Causes and Consequences for the World Economy**. Sussex: Wheatsheaf Books, 1986.

Nurkse, R. **Problems of Capital Formation in Underdeveloped Countries**. N.Y.: Oxford Univ. Press, 1962.

Nyang'oro, J. The State of Politics in Africa: The Corporatist Factor. **Studies in Comparative International Development**. Vol. 24, No. 1, Spring 1989. Pp. 5-19.

Nyang'oro, J. and Shaw, T., eds. **Corporatism in Africa: Comparative Analytics and Practice.** Boulder: Westview Press, 1989.

Nzongola-Ntalaja. **The Crisis in Zaire: Myths and Realities.** N.J.: Africa World Press, 1986.

O'Cleareacain, S. **Third World Debt and International Public Policy.** N.Y.: Praeger, 1990.

OECD. **External Debt of Developing Countries: 1983 Survey.** Geneva: OECD, 1984.

Ofuatey-Kodjoe, W. U.S. Economic Policy Toward Africa: Impact and Implications. **TransAfrica Forum.** Vol. 5, No. 2, Winter 1988. Pp. 3-15.

Olofin, S. ECOWAS and the Lome Convention: An Experiment in Complementary or Conflicting CU Arrangements. **Journal of Common Market Studies.** Vol. 16, No. 1, 1977.

Onitiri, H. Towards a West African Economic Community. **Nigerian Journal of Economic and Social Studies.** Vol. 5, No. 1, March 1963.

Oxford International Associates. **External Debt Management in Zambia.** Oxford, 1988.

Parfitt, T. Lies, Damned Lies amd Statistics: The World Bank/ECA Structural Adjustment Controversy. **Review of African Political Economy.** No. 47, Spring 1990.

Parfitt, T. and Riley, S.P. Africa in the Debt Trap: Which Way Out?. **Journal of Modern African Studies.** Vol. 24, No. 3, 1986. Pp. 519-527.

Parfitt, T. and Riley, S.P. **The African Debt Crisis.** London: Routledge, 1989.

Parry, J.H. **The Establishment of the European Hegemony, 1415-1715.** N.Y.: Harper and Row, 1961.

Pasinetti, L. **Growth and Income Distribution.** Cambridge: Cambridge Univ. Press, 1974.

Petras, J. **Critical Perspectives on Imperialism and Social Class in the Third World.** N.Y.: Monthly Review Press, 1978.

Phillips, R. The Role of the IMF in the Post-Bretton Woods Era. **Review of Radical Political Economics.** Vol. XV, No. 2, Summer 1983.

de Piniès, J. Debt Sustainability and Overadjustment. **World Development.** Vol. 17, No. 2, 1989. Pp. 29-43.

Pippenger, J.E. **Fundamentals of International Finance.** Englewood Cliffs: Prentice-Hall, 1984.

Polanyi, K. **The Great Transformation.** Boston: Beacon Press, 1940.

Poulantzas, N. **State, Power, Socialism.** London: NLB and Verso, 1978.

Price, R.M. Neo-Colonialism and Ghana's Economic Decline: A Critical Assessment. **Canadian Journal of African Studies.** Vol. 18, No. 1, 1984. Pp. 160-176.

Ravenhill, J. Adjustment with Growth: The Fragile Concensus. **Journal of Modern African Studies**. Vol. 26, No. 2, 1988. Pp. 179-210.

Resler, T. and Kanet, R. Democratizaiion: The National-Subnational Linkage. **In Depth**. Vol. 3, No. 1, Winter 1993.

Ricardo, D. **Principles of Political Economy and Taxation**. London: John Murray, 1917.

Rist, C. **History of Monetary and Credit Theory**. N.Y.: Augustus M. Kelley Publishers, 1966.

Robson, P. **The Economics of International Integration**. London: George Allen and Unwin, 1980.

Rodney, W. **How Europe Underdeveloped Africa**. Washington, D.C.: Howard Univ. Press, 1974.

Roemer, J. **Analytical Foundations of Marxian Economic Theory**. Cambridge: Harvard Univ. Press, 1974.

Roemer, J. **Free To Lose: An Introduction to Marxian Economic Philosophy**. Cambridge: Harvard Univ. Press, 1988.

Rostow, W.W. **The Stages of Economic Growth: A Non-Communist Manifesto**. Cambridge: Cambridge Univ. Press, 1960.

Rothchild, D. Comparative Public Demand and Expectation Patterns: The Ghana Experience. **African Studies Review**. Vol. 22, No. 1, April 1989.

Rothchild, D. and Olorunsola, V. **State vs. Ethnic Claims: African Policy Dilemmas**. Boulder: Westview Press, 1983.

Rwegasira, D. Exchange Rates and the Management of the External Sector in Sub-Saharan Africa. **Journal of Modern African Studies**. Vol. 22, No. 3, 1984. Pp. 451-467.

Sachs, J., ed. **Developing Country Debt and the World Economy**. Chicago: Univ. of Chicago Press, 1989.

Sachs, J. The Debt Crisis at a Turning Point. **Challenge**. May-June, 1988. Pp. 17-26.

Sachs, J. External Debt and Macroeconomic Performance in Latin America and East Asia. **Brookings Papers on Economic Activity**. Vol. 2, 1985. Pp. 523-573.

Sachs, J. **Trade and Exchange Rate Policies in Growth-Oriented Adjustment Programs**. NBER Working Papper No. 2226. April, 1987.

Sandbrook, R. and Barker, J. **The Politics of Africa's Economic Crisis**. Cambridge: Cambridge Univ. Press, 1985.

Sampson, A. **The Money Lenders: Banks in a Dangerous World**. London: Hodder and Stoughton, 1981.

Saunders, P. and Dean, A. The International Debt Situation and Linkages Between the Developing Countries and the OECD. **OECD Economic Studies**. No. 7, Autumn 1986. Pp. 156-203.

Schatz, S. Laissez-faireism for Africa?. **Journal of Modern African Studies**. Vol. 25, No. 1, 1987. Pp. 129-138.

Schoenholtz, A. The IMF in Africa: Unnecessary and Undesirable Western Restraint on Development. **Journal of Modern African Studies**. Vol. 25, No. 3, 1987. Pp. 403-433.

Sewell, J. and Gambino, A. Is the International Community Keeping Its Promise to Africa?. **TransAfrica Forum**. Vol. 3, No. 5, Spring 1988. Pp. 3-15.

Singer, H. and Gray, P. Trade Policy and Growth of Developing Countries: Some New Data. **World Development**. Vol. 16, No. 3, 1988. Pp. 395-403.

Singh, A. The Present Crisis of the Tanzanian Economy: Notes on the Economics and Politics of Devaluation. **Africa Development**. Vol. IX, No. 2, 1984. Pp. 28-42.

Sklar, R. Beyond Socialism and Capitalism in Africa. **Journal of Modern African Studies**. Vol. 26, No. 1, 1988. Pp. 1-21.

Sloan, J.W. The Strategy of Developmental Regionalism: Benefits, Distribution, Obstacles and Capacities. **Journal of Common Market Studies**. Vol. 10, No. 2, Dec. 1971.

Smith, G. and Cuddington, J., eds. **International Debt and the Developing Countries**. Washington, D.C.: World Bank, 1985.

Steel, W. Recent Policy Reforms and Industrial Adjustment in Zambia and Ghana. **Journal of Modern African Studies**. Vol. 26, No. 1, 1988. Pp. 157-164.

Stewart, F. The International Debt Situation and North-South Relations. **World Development**. Vol. 13, No. 2, 1985. Pp. 191-204.

Stochel, A., Vincent, D., and Cuthbertson, S., eds. **Macroeconomic Consequences of Farm Support Policies**. Durham: Duke Univ. Press, 1989.

Szeftel, M. **Conflict, Spoils and Class Formation in Zambia**. Unpublished Ph.D. dissertation. Univ. of Manchester, 1978.

Taylor, D.R.F. and MacKenzie, F., eds. **Development From Within: Survival in Rural Africa**. London: Routledge, 1992.

Thomas, C.Y. **Dependence and Transformation**. N.Y.: Monthly Review Press, 1974.

Thomas, C.Y. **The Poor and the Powerless: Economic Policy and Change in the Caribbean**. N.Y.: Monthly Review Press, 1988.

Tore, R. **Crisis and Recovery in Sub-Saharan Africa**. Paris: OECD, 1985.

Toyo, E. Recovery from Economic Decline: Lessons for a Developing Economy. **Africa Development**. Vol. XII, No. 3, 1987. Pp. 5-50.

UNCTAD, **Trade and Development Report, 1991**. N.Y.: United Nations, 1991.

U.N. Economic Commission for Africa. **African Alternative Framework to Structural Adjustment Programmes for Socio-Economic Recovery and Transformation (AAP-SAP)**. E/ECA/CM.15/6/Rev. 3. Addis Ababa: ECA, April 10, 1989.

U.N. Economic Commission for Africa. **South African Destabilization: The Economic Cost of Frontline Resistance to Apartheid**. Addis Ababa: ECA, 1989.

Unger, R. **Social Theory: Its Situation and Its Task**. N.Y.: Cambridge Univ. Press, 1987.

Unger, R. **False Necessity: Anti-Necessitarian Social Theory in the Service of Radical Democracy**. N.Y.: Cambridge Univ. Press, 1987.

Viner, J. **The Customs Union Issue**. N.Y. Oxford Univ. Press, 1950.

Wallerstein, I. **The Capitalist World Economy**. Cambridge: Cambridge Univ. Press, 1979.

Wallerstein, I. **The Modern World-System I**. N.Y.: Academic Press, 1974.

Weber, M. **Economics and Society**. G. Roth and C. Wittich, tr. N.Y.: Bedminster, Press, 1968.

Weber, M. **The Theory of Social and Economic Organization**. A.M. Henderson and T. Parsons, tr. N.Y.: Oxford Univ. Press, 1947.

Weeks, J., ed. **Debt Disaster? Banks, Governments and Multilaterals Confront the Crisis**. N.Y.: New York Univ. Press, 1989.

Wood, A. and Lajo, M. **IMF Policies in the Third World: Case Studies of Turkey, Zaire and Peru**. London: Univ. of East Anglia, 1985.

World Bank. **Financing Adjustment with Growth in Sub-Saharan Africa, 1986-1990**. Washington, D.C.: World Bank, 1986.

World Bank. **Accelerated Development in Sub-Saharan Africa**. Washington, D.C.: World Bank, 1982.

World Bank. **Developing Country Debt: Implementing the Concensus**. Washington, D.C.: World Bank, Feb. 1987.

World Bank. **Sub-Saharan Africa: From Crisis to Sustainable Growth. A Long-Term Sustainable Perspective Study**. Washington, D.C.: World Bank, 1989.

World Bank. **Towards Sustained Development in Sub-Saharan Africa**. Washington, D.C.: World Bank, 1986.

World Bank. **Africa's Adjustment and Growth in the 1990s**. Washington, D.C.: World Bank, 1989.

World Bank. **Zambia: Country Economic Memorandum—Issues and Options for Diversification**. Washington, D.C.: World Bank, 1984.

World Bank. **Adjustment Lending: An Evaluation of Ten Years of Experience**. Washington, D.C.: World Bank, 1988.

Young, C. and Turner, T. **The Rise and Decline of the Zairean State**. Madison: Univ. of Wisconsin Press, 1985.

Yusuf, S. and Peters, K. **Capitalist Accumulatiuon and Economic Growth: the Korean Paradigm**. World Bank Staff Working Paper No. 712. Washington, D.C.: 1985.

Zambian Government. **Restructuring in the Midst of Crisis**. Lusaka: Government Printing Office, 1984.